Mark's Memory Resources and
the Controversy Stories (Mark 2:1–3:6)

Linguistic Biblical Studies

Series Editor

Stanley E. Porter

Professor of New Testament at McMaster Divinity College
Hamilton, Ontario

VOLUME 2

This series, Linguistic Biblical Studies, is dedicated to the
development and promotion of linguistically informed
study of the Bible in its original languages. Biblical studies
has greatly benefited from modern theoretical and applied
linguistics, but stands poised to benefit from further inte-
gration of the two fields of study. Most linguistics has
studied contemporary languages, and attempts to apply
linguistic methods to study of ancient languages requires
systematic re-assessment of their approaches. This series
is designed to address such challenges, by providing a
venue for linguistically based analysis of the languages of
the Bible. As a result, monograph-length studies and col-
lections of essays in the major areas of linguistics, such as
syntax, semantics, pragmatics, discourse analysis and text
linguistics, corpus linguistics, cognitive linguistics, comparative linguistics, and the like, will be encouraged, and
any theoretical linguistic approach will be considered,
both formal and functional. Primary consideration is given
to the Greek of the New and Old Testaments and of other
relevant ancient authors, but studies in Hebrew, Coptic, and
other related languages will be entertained as appropriate.

Mark's Memory Resources and the Controversy Stories (Mark 2:1–3:6)

An Application of the Frame Theory of Cognitive Science to the Markan Oral-Aural Narrative

By

Yoon-Man Park

BRILL

LEIDEN • BOSTON
2010

This book is printed on acid-free paper.

Library of Congress Cataloging-in-Publication Data

Park, Yoon-Man.
  Mark's memory resources and the controversy stories (Mark 2:1–3:6) : an application of the frame theory of cognitive science to the Markan oral-aural narrative / by Yoon-Man Park.
    p. cm. — (Linguistic biblical studies, ISSN 1877-7554 ; v. 2)
  Includes bibliographical references and index.
  ISBN 978-90-04-17962-2 (hardback : alk. paper) 1. Bible. N.T. Mark II, 1-III, 6—Language, style. 2. Bible. N.T. Mark II, 1-III, 6—Criticism, interpretation, etc. 3. Bible—Hermeneutics. I. Title. II. Series.

  BS2585.52.P35 2009
  226.3'0663—dc22

2009035702

ISSN 1877-7554
ISBN 978 90 04 17962 2

PRINTED IN THE NETHERLANDS

To
Yoon-Jung

CONTENTS

PART ONE

ORAL-AURAL COMMUNICATION AND FRAMES

PREFACE

A long time ago, A.T. Robertson proposed that "it is the task and the duty of the N.T. student to apply the results of linguistic research to the Greek of the N.T."[1] The progress made in the study of the New Testament language over the last decades is, in fact, a result of application of modern linguistic theories to the study of the Greek language. Yet the use of modern linguistic methods for the study of the New Testament language is only in the beginning stages; and also many biblical scholars do not seriously recognize the benefits of studying the New Testament from the insights of modern linguistics. This book aims to make at least some contribution to a better understanding of the ancient Greek text of the New Testament.

Scholars now are in a better position to understand the documentary nature of the Gospel of Mark. In particular, it has been proposed as a result of the interdisciplinary work between classic literature and biblical literature that the Gospel is a product of oral-aural communication cultures and it is written to help speakers and hearers to remember what they have been familiar with. Furthermore, modern linguistics has made considerable advances since Ferdinand de Saussure. This book makes an attempt to apply the frame theory from cognitive linguistics, a linguistic theory which the meaning of a word, phrase, clause, sentence, paragraph and a thematic unit can only be properly understood against the background of a particular body of knowledge and assumptions. The reason that the present study employs the frame theory as a methodology is because of the belief that the theory may lead us to a better position to see the ways in which such an ancient text as the Gospel of Mark may have been communicated.

This volume is a revision of my doctoral dissertation from the University of Toronto. As most research students discover, no man is an island. I am grateful to the many who have aided me to study on this work. I am especially thankful to Professor Stanley E. Porter who was not only the supervisor of my doctoral dissertation but also of my graduate thesis in England. Professor Porter is the one who

---

[1] A.T. Robertson, *A Grammar of the Greek New Testament in the Light of Historical Research* (Nashville: Broadman Press, 4th edn, 1934), p. 3.

had encouraged me to approach the New Testament in linguistic and grammatical terms; and has guided me to bring in modern cognitive linguistics as well as frame semantics for the study of Mark's ancient text. I also want to express my gratitude to Professor David Rhoads who was an external examiner of the dissertation. His comments and critical evaluation on my work, particularly in literary terms, were extremely helpful. I also owe much gratitude to Professor Terry Donaldson who was one of the readers of the dissertation. The insightful comments he provided me after a meticulous reading improved my work significantly. And also I want to give thanks to Professor Elizabeth Cowper from the linguistics department of the University of Toronto; as a linguist her comments on my work were invaluable.

My gratitude should also go to my parents; they have always and happily offered their unconditional support and prayer. I also want to acknowledge my gratefulness to the believers at the House of Somang. The care and attention they have shown to me and my family over the last nine years has been a lesson in Christian virtue. Many thanks must also go to the Holy Mountain Church in Toronto, the Yoellin Church in London, England, and the Pomo Church in Korea. Their gracious financial support has enabled me to complete my study abroad.

Finally, let me offer my most special thanks to my family, my precious sons, Sye Young and Sye Min, and my wise and considerate wife, Yoon Jung Hwang. Without their prayers, patience, love, care, laughter, and staying by me, I would not have been able to complete my work. I would like to dedicate this work to my wife who has showed me what a sacrificial love is.

Ἐμοὶ γὰρ τὸ ζῆν Χριστὸς καὶ τὸ ἀποθανεῖν κέρδος (Philippians 1.21)

Yoon-Man Park

ABBREVIATIONS

AB	Anchor Bible
AI	*Artificial Intelligence*
AS	*American Scholar*
ASTI	Annual of the Swedish Theological Institute
ATR	*Anglican Theological Review*
BDAG	Walter Bauer, Federick W. Danker, William F. Arndt, and F. Wilbur Gingrich, *A Greek English Lexicon of the New Testament and Other Early Christian Literature*, 3rd edn. *(Chicago: The University of Chicago Press, 2000)*
BBR	*Bulletin for Biblical Research*
B.C.E	"Before the common (or Christian) era"
BDF	F. Blass, A. Debrunner and Robert W. Funk, *A Greek Grammar of the New Testament and Other Early Christian Literature* (Chicago: The University of Chicago Press, 1961)
BETL	Bibliotheca ephemeridum theologicarum lovaniensium
BS	*Balkan Studies*
BTB	*Biblical Theology Bulletin*
BZ	*Biblische Zeitschrift*
CBQ	*Catholic Biblical Quarterly*
C.E.	"Common (or Christian) era"
CJ	*The Classical Journal*
CL	*Cognitive Linguistics*
CP	*Cognitive Psychology*
CQ	*Classical Quarterly*
CS	*Cognitive Science*
ExpTim	*Expository Times*
HSCP	Harvard Studies in Classical Philology
HSCL	Harvard Studies in Comparative Literature
HTR	*Harvard Theological Review*
HTKNT	Herders theologischer Kommentar zum Neuen Testament
HTS	*Hervormde Teologiese Studies*
ICC	International Critical Commentary
INT	*Interpretation*
JBL	*Journal of Biblical Literature*
JJS	*Journal of Jewish Studies*

JML	*Journal of Memory and Language*
JEP	*Journal of Experimental Psychology: Learning, Memory, and Cognition*
JSNT	*Journal for the Study of the New Testament*
JSNTSup	Journal for the Study of the New Testament—Supplement Series
JTS	*Journal of Theological Studies*
JVLVB	*Journal of Verbal Learning and Verbal Behavior*
LCL	Loeb Classical Library
LXX	Septuagint
NCBC	New Century Bible Commentary
NLH	*New Literary History*
RSV	Revised Standard Version
NovT	*Novum Testamentum*
NIBC	New International Biblical Commentary
NovTSup	Novum Testamentum, Supplements
NT	*Notes on Translation*
NTS	New Testament Studies
OT	*Oral Tradition*
PS	*Psychonomic Science*
PB	*Psychological Bulletin*
PR	*Psychological Review*
QS	*Quaderni di Semantica*
SBL	Society of Biblical Literature
SF	*Social Forces*
SNTSMS	Society for New Testament Studies Monograph Series
TPAPA	*Transactions and Proceedings of the American Philological Association*
TE	*Theologia Evangelica*
WBC	Word Biblical Commentary
WTJ	*Westminster Theological Journal*
WUNT	Wissenschaftliche Untersuchungen zum Neuen Testament

LIST OF ILLUSTRATIONS

FIGURES

TABLES

CHAPTER ONE

INTRODUCTION

The statement that the Gospel of Mark was written to be read out (thus oral narrative) and listened to (aural narrative), rather than read to oneself, is no longer new in current biblical scholarship.[1] What has received very little attention, however, is the fact that the Gospel of Mark was, though a written document, stored in and recalled from memory, rather than in a written form, on the part of the original audience. This fact is neglected partly because scholars' reading and analysis of the Gospel still proceed by means of the modern practice of individual silent readings of the printed texts.[2] Nor do we need to worry about losing information we get from reading because of the physical permanence of the book. Yet the situation of the first-century Mediterranean world was completely different from our modern one, as will be observed; never has the written document gained such status as in the twenty-first century. For the majority of people in oral-performance and aural-reception cultures such as those in the first century, the written document did not replace the essential role of human memory in the preservation and communication of information; rather an ancient text was a representation of what people were already familiar with (see below).

Indeed, the issue of memory has not been entirely ignored in biblical studies.[3] Modern biblical scholarship's concern about memory,

---

[1] For such a general assertion of the communication mode of the Markan narrative, see Joanna Dewey, "The Gospel of Mark as an Oral-Aural Event: Implications for Interpretation," in *The New Literary Criticism and the New Testament* (Valley Forge, Pennsylvania: Trinity Press International, 1994), pp. 145–63; Whitney Shiner, *Proclaiming the Gospel; First Century Performance of Mark* (Harrisburg: Trinity Press International, 2003).

[2] Thus W. Den Boer, *The Art of Memory and its Mnemotechnical Traditions* (Amsterdam: North Holland Publishing, 1986), p. 90, rightly says, "Since Western civilization began to regard the *written* source as the preserver of the past, memory—and along with it the oral tradition—has been employed less frequently: the result is an underestimation of the function of memory in the social structure."

[3] For example, Birger Gerhardsson, *Memory and Manuscript: Oral Tradition and Written Transmission in Rabbinic Judaism and Early Christianity with Tradition and Transmission in Early Christianity. Foreword by Jacob Neusner* (Grand Rapids,

however, has been focused primarily on its role in the pre-canonical synoptic transmission, failing to extend its effects into the communicative process of the canonical written Gospels.[4] This shortfall is due to historical critics' failure to recognize that the written transmissions of the Jesus traditions were not necessarily intended to bring about a radical shift away from oral to textual transmission on the part of their first audience. Most of the population who lived in the first-century Mediterranean world, as will be explored in the chapter that follows, was non-literate, and oral performance and aural reception, even after the production of the Gospels, was the only communicative means to acquire and transmit the tradition. It must be believed that human memory has played a crucial role in that particular environment. Since oral-aural communication has an evanescent property as opposed to writing, as Walter Ong points out, the non-literate audience must rely on memory for the preservation and transmission of tradition, whether it is oral or written.[5] If the listening audience cannot understand quickly and remember readily what is told, the information of oral-aural performance is lost. It is in no way, then, an exaggeration to say that the Markan oral-aural narrative was constructed in such a way as to facilitate the memory process of a listening audience. However, the question is just how the Markan narrative was organized in such a way as to enable the original listening audience to properly comprehend and recall from memory what they had heard. This is

---

Michigan: Eerdmans, 1998; *idem, The Reliability of the Gospel Tradition* (Peabody: Hendrickson, 2001); Werner H. Kelber, *The Oral and the Written Gospel: The Hermeneutics of Speaking and Writing in the Synoptic Tradition, Mark, Paul, and Q* (Philadelphia: Fortess 1983); *Semeia* 52 (2005) entitled *Memory, tradition, a text the Past in Early Christianity*; James D.G. Dunn, *Jesus Remembered* (Grand Rapids, Michigan: Eerdmans, 2003), pp. 238–54; see also the book edited by Richard Horsley et al., *Performing the Gospel: Orality, Memory, and Mark* (ed. Richard A. Horsley, Jonathan A. Draper, and John Miles Foley; Minneapolis: Fortress, 2006); Richard Bauckham, *Jesus and the Eyewitnesses: The Gospels as Eyewitness Testimony* (Grand Rapids, Michigan: Eerdmans, 2006), pp. 264–357.

[4] For the works focused on memory role for early synpotic memory processes, or in relation to the studies of historical Jesus, see Gerhardsson, *Memory and Manuscript*; Kelber, "The Case of the Gospels; Memory's Desire and the Limits of Historical Criticism," *OT* 17 (2002), pp. 55–86; Alan Kirk and Tom Thatcher, "Jesus tradition as Social Memory," *Semeia* 52 (2005), pp. 25–42; Barry Schwartz, "Christian Origins: Historical Truth and Social Memory," *Semeia* 52 (2005), pp. 43–56; Richard A. Horsley, "Prominent Patterns in the Social Memory of Jesus and Friends" *Semeia* 52 (2005), pp. 57–78, Bauckham, *Eyewitnesses*, esp. pp. 240–89.

[5] Walter Ong, *Orality and Literacy: The Technologizing of the Word* (New York: Methuen, 1982), pp. 31–32.

the question underpinning this study, a study in which I will consider how human memory would have operated in the understanding and remembering of the Markan oral-aural narrative.

A. Methodology

What type of memory model, then, can best explain memory processing in relation to the performance and reception of the Markan oral-aural narrative? Before answering this question, two things must be mentioned about the nature of human memory for the present study. First, we need to define what memory is. The term memory is generally used in everyday discourse in reference to a single unified capacity to remember information. But cognitive scientists (including cognitive psychologists and linguists) assert that memory includes a range of mental processes such as encoding, storing, and retrieval of information.[6] Following those cognitive psychologists, I will refer to memory as a cognitive system which processes, stores and remembers our general knowledge about the actual world and a story world. Despite recent biblical scholars' increasing concern about memory, unfortunately, they have rarely made any use of the idea that human memory is a cognitive system which includes comprehending, storing, and remembering. They have limited their focus predominantly to its role of remembering or memorizing (i.e., one stage only of memory processing) in the transmission of the Jesus traditions and the formation of the Gospels.[7] With the communicative dimension of the completed Gospel in view, however, I will explore how the Gospel of

---

[6] See, for example, Allan Baddley, *Human Memory: Theory and Practice* (Hove and London: Lawrence Erlbaum, 1990), pp. 4–8; and Kathleen M. Galotti, *Cognitive Psychology in and out of the Laboratory* (Pacific Grove, California: Brooks/Cole, 1999), pp. 126–28.

[7] In relation to scholars' various suggestions of memory as a mechanism for controlling Jesus traditions, for example, consider Gerhardsson (*Memory and Manuscript*, pp. 328, 332, 335 and *Reliability*, pp. 22–23, 41–65)'s hypothesis of almost verbatim memorization by Jesus' disciples; Kelber's stress (*Gospels*, pp. 14–34, 90–131) on the evangelists' creative remembering; Kenneth E. Bailey's ("Informal Controlled Oral Tradition and the Synoptic Gospels," *Themelios* 20 (1994), pp. 4–11) argument of "informal controlled oral tradition"; Dunn's idea (*Jesus*, pp. 130–32) of Jesus remembered by the earliest Christians. But Bauckham (*Eyewitnesses*, pp. 319–57) attempts to employ cognitive scientists' idea of memory for his argument that the transmission of the Jesus tradition was controlled by eyewitnesses (see below).

Mark is constructed to facilitate the audience's memory processes such
as comprehension, storing, and remembering.

Second, we must be cautious about attributing memory solely to
an individual operation. Memory, according to social memory theorists, is a social phenomenon.[8] Jeffrey Prager, a sociologist, argues
that "memories are not so much the product of an individual mind
as the result of an individual's relation both to self and to the outside
world."[9] Likewise, quoting J. Assmann, Alan Kirk states that memory
is "a social reality, as a function of the individual's membership in
various social groups."[10] To be sure, human memory operates through
individual minds. What is also to be kept in mind, nonetheless, is that
the individual's memory is "embedded in the social universe that helps
shape it."[11] Richard Bauckham is then right when he asserts that "[t]he

---

[8] The term "social memory" was used for the first time in Maurice Halbwach's
book, *The Collective Memory*, and widely reused in the social sciences and humanities.
See Maurice Halbwachs, *The Collective Memory* (trans. Francis J. Ditter Jr. and Vida
Yazdi Ditter; New York: Harper and Row, 1950). The idea of social memory or cultural memory is introduced into biblical study by Werner Kelber's "Memory's Desire,"
pp. 55–86. Kelber ("Memory's Desire," p. 56) states, in line with Maurice Halbwachs,
that memory is social and inseparably related to group identity, and that the evangelist
(or their memories) "selects and modifies subjects and figures of the past in order to
make them serviceable to the image the community wishes to cultivate of itself." The
implication is that the "social memory" or "cultural memory" model rightly draws
our attention to how oral memory, which may have influenced the formation and
composition of the Gospels, is closely related to social or cultural environments and
conditions. Despite such an important insight, however, the social memory model
does not yet provide a theoretical basis to investigate how the speaker and audience's
mental (or cognitive) processes operate in understanding and remembering words,
clauses, sentences and paragraphs or episodes in narrative discourse. This is, in my
judgment, mainly because for the social memory model the texts are cultural or social
phenomena, rather than linguistic or discourse units. For the social memory model,
symbolic forms such as images, gestures, dances, rites, festivals, customs are understood as "semantic units" that refer to communal memory that is preserved in the
life of the community. See Jan Assmann, "Form as a Mnemonic Device: Cultural
Texts and Cultural Memory," in *Performing the Gospel: Orality, Memory, and Mark*
(ed. Richard A. Horsley, Jonathan A. Draper, and John Miles Foley; Minneapolis:
Fortress, 2006), pp. 67–77, esp. 76; Jeffrey Prager, *Presenting the Past: Psychoanalysis
and the Sociology of Misremembering* (Cambridge: Harvard University Press, 1998),
p. 69; Barry Schwartz, "The Social Context of Commemoration: A Study in Collective
Memory," *SF* 61 (1982), pp. 374–97.
[9] Prager, *Presenting the Past*, pp. 59–60.
[10] Alan Kirk, "Social and Cultural Memory," *Semeia* 52 (2005), p. 2.
[11] Prager, *Presenting the Past*, p. 81. Indeed, such a stress on the social formation
of individual memory should not lead to the expense of individual memory itself. My
point is that memory is more than just a personal act in the sense that individuals are
always related to cultural forms and social context.

more we tell our memories, privately and socially, the more the scripts, the expectations, and the goals of our social contexts serve to interpret them."[12] This is more the case for ancient Mediterranean culture marked by community-oriented worldview than it is for a modern western world marked by individualism. In particular, it must also be noted that the reason that the early Christian church may have got together a community (or as ἐκκλασία) is because the Christian believers shared the communal memories of Jesus as the basis of its identity. This means that the Gospels produced by the interpersonal early church are ones that presuppose such collective memory (see Chapter Two and Three).[13]

Once the two points above are made, we are in a better position to investigate what type of memory or cognitive models operated in processing the Gospel of Mark. In fact, since the concern of this study is the Gospel of Mark in its *written* form, though intended for oral performance and aural reception, in order for us to explore its cognitive processes (e.g., encoding, understanding, and recalling), it is necessary to employ a cognitive model which can illuminate the relationship between memory and language production and use. I will draw on frame theory, which, regarding human memory or cognitive processing of story, has been developed and used in a wide range of fields, including linguistics, artificial intelligence, cognitive psychology, classics, and pedagogy since being introduced to psychology by Frederick C. Bartlett.[14]

1. A Brief History of Development of Frame Theory

1.1. Frame Theory, Cognitive Psychology and Artificial Intelligence

Frame theory was originally developed in the field of cognitive psychology, which is concerned with how people perceive, comprehend, and recall information in both the actual world and a story world.

---

[12] Bauckham, *Eyewitnesses*, p. 337.
[13] For a major discussion over a closely interacting relationship between the individual and shared memories of the eyewitnessed in the Gospels, see Bauckham, *Eyewitnesses*, pp. 310–18. Georgia Masters Keightley, "Early Christian Collective Memory and Paul's Knowledge of Jesus," *Semeia* 52 (2005), p. 136, thus, says, "the Christian church...is constituted by a body of shared memories."
[14] Frederic C. Bartlett, *Remembering; A Study in Experimental and Social Psychology* (Cambridge: Cambridge University Press, 1932).

Cognitive psychologists believe that memory is one of the most basic cognitive processes and that the way memory works in the real world and a story world relies on the operation of "world knowledge"[15] and frames.[16] Frames have been one of the major research fields of the cognitive psychologist in relation to human cognitive models. Artificial intelligence has been interested in developing computer programs capable of acquiring natural discourse and of understanding it.[17] Because computer scientists have investigated the issues common to those of cognitive psychology (e.g., the nature of cognition; how information is perceived, stored, and recalled), frame theory has been developed also in the field of artificial intelligence, and their ideas have been incorporated into the formation of a theory of human cognitive processing by virtue of frames. Both fields share a common assumption in that they view human memory processing as frame-based.[18] Because of this common ground, cognitive psychology and artificial intelligence (including cognitive linguistics, see below) have come to found an interdisciplinary field called cognitive science.[19]

1.1.1. Frederick Bartlett

In his highly influential book, *Remembering*, first published in 1932, Bartlett, a cognitive psychologist, mainly focused on how and what people remember. Bartlett proposed that individuals acquire and remember new material in terms of existing knowledge structures in the memory. Such memory systems were called by Bartlett "schemata" (or schemas; singular, schema). Bartlett defined a schema as an "active organization of past reactions, or of past experiences, which must always be supposed to be operating in any well-adapted organic response."[20] These schemata are opened when an individual tries to

---

[15] For the definition of 'world knowledge,' see glossary.

[16] For a general agreement regarding this idea, see Robert J. Sternberg, *Cognitive Psychology* (Forth Worth: Harcourt Brace College Publishers, 1996), pp. 198–201.

[17] On scholars' interests in this field, see Sternberg, *Cognitive Psychology*, pp. 468–69.

[18] W.G. Lehnert, "The Role of Scripts in Understanding," in *Frame Conceptions and Text Understanding* (ed. Dieter Metzing; Berlin/New York: de Gruyter, 1980), p. 85; and see also Marvin Minsky, "A Framework for Presenting Knowledge," in *The Psychology of Computer Vision* (ed. Parick Henry Winston; New York: McGraw-Hill, 1975), pp. 211–77; Roger C. Schank and Robert P. Abelson, *Scripts, Plans, Goals and Understanding: An Inquiry into Human Knowledge Structures* (Hillsdale, New Jersey: Erlbaum, 1977), pp. 67–68.

[19] Galotti, *Cognitive Psychology*, pp. 17–18.

[20] Bartlett, *Remembering*, p. 201.

comprehend a new story. Bartlett demonstrated the role of schemas in the story recall process by using the method of "serial reproduction," in which participants were asked to recall the story (i.e., "The War of the Ghosts") on more than one occasion, with varying retention intervals, ranging from fifteen minutes to six and a half years; as a result, he found that people tend to change aspects of the story unfitting with their knowledge of the world so that adapted it to their expectations of the world.[21] His conclusion is that the principle of memory is an active reorganization or reconstruction of events ("effort after meaning," to use his own term), not an exact reproduction, on the basis of schemata.[22] Bartlett's idea that the individual is making the story meaningful according to the cognitive models (or schemata) is important for the study of oral-aural narrative comprehension (see Chapters Two and Three).[23]

1.1.2. Marvin Minsky

Although a groundbreaking contribution to defining memory in terms of organized structures, schemata, or frames, Bartlett's study is insufficient to explain the fuller substance of memory, including how frames form, what type of knowledge frames comprise, how frames work, and their effect on comprehending and remembering a story. In 1975, Marvin Minsky, a researcher of artificial intelligence, in his article, "A Framework for Representing Knowledge," called knowledge structures in memory "frames."[24] Like schemata, frames were understood by him as theoretical data structures about stereotyped situations, which hold large chunks of interrelated information.[25] The typical characteristics of actions and events, in Minsky's theory, are extracted from repetitious acts in everyday life (e.g., being in a certain kind of living room, or going to a child's birthday party) and stored as the default value of the frame.[26] Minsky, for instance, proposed that

---

[21] Bartlett, *Remembering*, pp. 62–196.
[22] Bartlett, *Remembering*, pp. 205–208. Indeed there is an important difference between Bartlett's material and the oral-aural Gospels traditions. In Bartlett's experiment, the story was transmitted only by relying on the individual's memory, whereas the Gospel of Mark was orally performed before a public audience, probably quite regularly in a worship situation.
[23] For the phrase, see Bartlett, *Remembering*, p. 44.
[24] Minsky, "Framework," pp. 211–77.
[25] Minsky, "Framework," pp. 211–13.
[26] Minsky, "Framework," p. 212.

the BIRTHDAY PARTY frame[27] consists of hierarchical data structures. At the top of the structure there is fixed information (going to a birthday party) and on the lower level variable information (e.g., presents, cake, games).[28] The fixed information is the content that must occur to represent the frame, and the variables are the ones that may change with the situation.[29] Frames have "slots" filled with default values and the slots may be filled by specific instances and data as the situation changes, but if there is a lack of matching data, the default value serves to fill in the slots.[30] Minsky also proposes that there are varying frames beyond a verb frame: He arranges different kinds of frames hierarchically, such as surface syntactic frames (mainly verb cases), surface semantic frames (deep syntactic frames), thematic frames (topics, activities and so on), and narrative frames (stories, explanations, and arguments).[31] One of Minsky's key contributions to current frame theory is that the components of frames can be used to guide how to take action, what to expect to happen next, and what to do if these expectations fail.[32] These features of frames are informative in exploring how frames aided Mark's original audience to understand readily and quickly the narrative during oral performance.

1.1.3. *Roger C. Schank and Robert P. Abelson*

Roger Schank and Robert Abelson in their book, *Scripts, Plans, Goals and Understanding,* claim that human memory is organized around personal experiences called script or episodic memory; and hence scripts include the ability to recognize repeated and similar sequences of events. They used the term script in a more particular sense to refer to a specific sequence of events and actions on a specific occasion rather than to general knowledge structures.[33] Schank and Abelson suggest

---

[27] I will use capitals in this study to represent the concept and thus frame underlying the word meaning.

[28] Minsky, "Framework," p. 212.

[29] Minsky, "Framework," pp. 212–13.

[30] Minsky, "Framework," pp. 212–13.

[31] Minsky, "Framework," p. 245.

[32] Minsky, "Framework," p. 212.

[33] Schank and Abelson, *Scripts,* pp. 36–68. Schank has continued in developing his theory. But his earlier work is here referred to because it contains his essential idea. For Schank's later study of the workings of memory, see Roger C. Schank and Robert P. Abelson, "Knowledge and Memory: The Real Story," in *Knowledge and Memory: The Real Story* (Hillsdale, New Jersey: Lawrence Erlbaum, 1995), pp. 1–85.

that people's knowledge of what is happening when going to certain locations is commonly shared and framed in very similar ways.[34]

The best known example of a script is that of a restaurant. Think about what makes up your knowledge about going to a restaurant. It typically consists of a sequence of goal-directed actions, such as entering, ordering, eating, paying the bill, and leaving.[35] That sequence is causally and temporally ordered and includes the actors, objects, and locations corresponding to it. The speaker (or the text) can communicate with the hearer by using this scripted (or framed) knowledge. It is not necessary for the text to spell out all the details of every action performed in the course of events since both parties already have a shared knowledge. What the text needs to mention is one key action from this scripted sequence; it activates all the other events.[36] Importantly, Schank and Abelson argue that language production and use (semantic memory) can be explained by scripts (or frames).[37] For example, the RESTAURANT frame, which is stored in terms of the repetitive experience of going to a restaurant, serves to associate with it a number of concepts such as customer, waiter, ordering, eating, and the bill. In this case a script-like frame or event frame can be used as an organizer of varying concepts when an individual produces language and narrates an event.

1.1.4. *David Rumelhart*
As a scholar in the fields of cognitive psychology and artificial intelligence, Rumelhart explores more thoroughly the nature of frames, and his works contribute to understanding the operations of frames in story comprehension, remembering, and solving problems. Rumelhart and Andrew Ortony, in their article "The Representation of Knowledge in Memory," lay out in particular the following points about frames, which they call "schemas":

(1) Schemas are data structures that represent generic concepts stored in memory.
(2) Schemas exist for generalized concepts that underlie objects, situations, events, actions, and sequences of actions.

---

[34] Schank and Abelson, *Scripts*, pp. 44–45.
[35] Schank and Abelson, *Scripts*, pp. 42–46.
[36] Schank and Abelson, *Scripts*, pp. 46–50. They call such a key action "script pointer." I will deal with it in due course.
[37] Schank and Abelson, *Scripts*, p. 18.

(3) Schemas are not atomic. Each contains, as part of its specification, the network of interrelations that is believed to generally hold the constituents of the concept in question.

(4) Schemas in some sense represent concept stereotypes.[38]

Rumelhart holds that frames ("schemas," to use Rumelhart's term) ultimately make discourse comprehensive and remembering possible. Comprehension, according to Rumelhart, is a process of finding frames which best explain the whole of the incoming information.[39] The failure to understand a story, thus, means a failure to identify the appropriate frames that enable an understanding of the input. Since people can remember only what they comprehend, frames play the same crucial role in remembering a story: Frames are the devices whereby the initial comprehension takes place and as such they determine what is remembered.[40]

1.2. *Frame Theory and Cognitive Linguistics*

In the field of linguistics frame theory has been developed primarily in the field of cognitive linguistics as part of research into what determines the meaning of linguistic forms (i.e., semantics). Approaching language from a cognitive perspective, cognitive linguists' fundamental assertion is that linguistic forms are "related to and motivated by human conceptual knowledge, bodily experience, and the communicative functions of discourse."[41] This way of understanding the meaning of linguistic forms, however, had not been taken seriously among linguists such as structural linguists and transformational generative theorists, until the rise of cognitive linguistics.[42] Structural linguistics'

---

[38] David E. Rumelhart and Andrew Ortony, "The Representation of Knowledge in Memory," in *Schooling and the Acquisition of Knowledge* (ed. Richard C. Anderson, Rand J. Spiro and William E. Montague; New York: Lawrence Erlbaum, 1977), p. 101.

[39] Rumelhart and Ortony, "Memory," pp. 111–14; David E. Rumelhart, "Schemata: The Building Blocks of Cognition," in *Theoretical Issues in Reading Comprehension* (ed. R.J. Spiro, B.C. Bruce and W.F. Brewer; Hillsdale, New Jersey: Erlbaum, 1980), pp. 47–52.

[40] Rumelhart, "Schemata," pp. 49–51.

[41] Raymond W. Gibbs, "What's cognitive about cognitive linguistics?," in *Cognitive Linguistics in the Redwoods: The Expansion of a New Paradigm in Linguistics* (ed. Eugene H. Casad; Berlin / New York: Mouton de Gruyter, 1996), p. 27.

[42] John Taylor, *Linguistic Categorization: Prototypes in Linguistic Theory* (Oxford: Clarendon, 2nd edn, 1995), pp. 16–20. But Robert Müller,"Wortfeldtheorie und Kognitive Psychologie," in *Studies in Lexical Field Theory* (ed. P.R. Lutzeier; Tübingen: Max Niemeyer Verlag, 1993), p. 215, states, "Saussure already claimed that everything

key argument is that "the meaning of a linguistic form is determined by the language system itself."[43] For structural linguists language is then "a self-contained system, with its own structure, its own constitutive principles, its own dynamics."[44] Human beings play no role at all in this account of language and its meaning. Noam Chomsky's generative-transformational theory, therefore, appears to overcome the weakness of structural linguistics; according to Chomsky, language is a "system of knowledge" in a person's brain and it is the internalized language faculty that determines a person's grammatical competence and language use.[45]

Despite the alternative advent of the generative-transformational paradigm for structural linguistics, the former theory also may be called "autonomous linguistics" in that, as George Lakoff rightly notes, Chomsky's theory of language rests on the fundamental assumption that "language is a separate 'modular' system independent of the rest of cognition" or extra-linguistic knowledge.[46] On the contrary, cognitive linguistics believes:

> Language is not an autonomous cognitive faculty. The basic corollaries of this hypothesis are that the represenatation of linguistic knowledge is essentially the same as the representation of other conceptual structures, and that processes in which that knowledge is used are not

---

in language has a psychological aspect. Nevertheless he and his followers' endeavours were directed at separating linguistics from neighbouring sciences. The time has come for linguistics to pay more attention to the results of the research of cognitive psychologists." Furthermore, humans' use of knowledge structure stored in the mind is implied in the concept of 'langue' which was suggested by Ferdinand de Saussure, the founder of modern linguistics. Saussure, *Course in General Linguistics* (New York: McGraw-Hill, 1959), pp. 9, 13–14, made the distinction between "langue" or "language" and "parole" or "speaking": "langue" is "both a social product of the faculty of speech and a collection of necessary conventions that have been adopted by a social body to permit individuals to exercise that faculty; and it is *the sum of word images stored in the minds of all individuals... a storehouse filled by the members of a given community*"; by contrast, "parole" is "the executive side of speaking... an individual act" [my italics]. This shows that mental frame and "langue" can be understood as quite similar concepts in that both of them refer to a set of concepts stored in mind, and views our actual speech in a specific domain is an expression of our mental frame or "langue" of it.

[43] Taylor, *Linguistic Categorization*, p. 16.
[44] Taylor, *Linguistic Categorization*, p. 16.
[45] Noam Chomsky, *Knowledge of Language: Its Nature, Origin, and Use* (New York: Praeger, 1986), p. 24.
[46] George Lakoff, *Women, Fire, and Dangerous Things: What Categories Reveal about the Mind* (Chicago and London: The University of Chicago Press, 1987), p. 58.

fundamentally different from cognitive abilities that human beings use outsi-de the domains of language.[47]

Such a belief of the representation of linguistic knowledge leads cognitive linguists to be concerned with how "perception, memory, attention, social interaction, personality and other aspects of experience" are crucially implicated in the structure and functioning of language.[48] And it is out of this concern about how people represent their linguistic knowledge that many cognitive linguists start drawing attention to cognitive models such as frames as a means of language comprehension.[49]

1.2.1. *Charles Fillmore*

Frames, according to cognitive psychology mentioned above, are mental knowledge structures accumulated through recurrent cultural experiences. Sharing the insights of the knowledge structure, cognitive linguistics is particularly interested in the role of frames as cognitive models for language production and comprehension.

In his early work, Charles Fillmore, proposes "case frames," whose fundamental point is that in order to understand a verb ("event"), its semantic role must be parsed into certain meaning structures in a sentence.[50] He claims that the semantic role of the sentence (i.e., nominals in it) can be defined in relation to the verb

---

[47] William Croft and D. Alan Cruse, *Cognitive Linguistics* (Cambridge: Cambridge University Press, 2004), p. 2.

[48] For example, see George Lakoff, "Some Remarks on AI and linguistics," *CS* 2 (1978), pp. 267–75 (the quotation from p. 274). Such a cognitive approach to linguistic form has been increasingly used by modern discourse analysts. See, for example, Gillian Brown and George Yule, *Discourse Analysis* (Cambridge: Cambridge University Press, 1983), pp. 24–25. In fact, this tenet of cognitive linguistics has already been recognized by some New Testament Greek grammarians and applied to Greek verbal aspect theory. For example, with respect to the Greek tenses which have traditionally been argued as referring to objective time-related categories, Stanley E. Porter, *Verbal Aspect in the Greek of the NT, With Reference to Tense and Mood* (New York: Peter Lang, 1989), p. 86 says, "Rather than reflecting a temporal distinction or a differing objective characterization of the kind of action, each choice of verb tense reflects an attempt by the speaker to grammaticalize his conception of the process." And see also *idem, Idioms of the Greek New Testament* (Sheffield: Sheffield Academic Press, 2nd edn, 1994), pp. 20–49; K.L. McKay, *Greek Grammar for Students: A Concise Grammar of Classical Attic with Special Reference to Aspect in the Verb* (Canberra: Australian National University, 1974) and Buist M. Fanning, *Verbal Aspect in NT Greek* (Oxford: Clarendon Press, 1990).

[49] B. Rudzka-Ostyn, *Conceptualizations and Mental Processing in Language* (Berlin: Mouton de Gruyter, 1993), pp. 1–2.

[50] Charles Fillmore, "The Case for Case," in *Universals of Linguistic Theory* (ed. E. Bach and R.T. Harm; New York: Holt, Rinehart and Winston, 1968), pp. 1–90.

by such case concepts as Agentive, Instrumental, Objective, Facti-
tive, Locative, Benefactive and so on.[51] Yet in his later works Fillmore
extends his theory of "case frame" to "frame semantics," in which
larger cognitive structures are suggested "as a new layer of semantic
role notions in terms of which whole domains of vocabulary could be
semantically characterized."[52] As regards the understanding of words,
Fillmore proposes that words "represent categorizations of experience,
and each of these categories is underlain by a motivating situation
occurring against a background of knowledge and experience"; hence,
lexical items evoke frames, and the hearer invokes the frames upon
hearing an utterance in order to understand it.[53] For Fillmore "nobody
can really understand the meanings of the words in that domain who
does not understand the social institutions or the structures of experience [frames of lexical items] which they presuppose."[54] Fillmore, for
instance, says that the meaning of WEEKEND can only be explained
in the context of conventional knowledge that a week consists of a
seven-day cycle within which "a relatively larger continuous block of
days" is assigned "to public work and two continuous days to one's
private life."[55] If the language user is unfamiliar with such background
concepts of the word, he or she has no basis for an understanding of
WEEKEND.

Besides, for Fillmore a frame is "a system of categories structured in
accordance with some contexts which are some body of understand-
ings, some pattern of practices, or some history of social institutions."[56]
The interpreter who shares this kind of contextual knowledge can use
that frame to infer the concept of a word. Fillmore provides another
example: "We never open our presents until the morning."[57] Though
no explicit mention of Christmas is made in the sentence, Western

---

[51] Fillmore, "Case," pp. 31–32; cf. Minsky, "A Framework," p. 235.
[52] Charles Fillmore, "Frame Semantics," in *Linguistics in the Morning Calm* (ed.
The Linguistics Society of Korea; Seoul: Hansin, 1982), p. 115. For Fillmore's initial
book about frames, see "An Alternative to Checklist Theories of Meaning," in *Proceedings of the First Annual Meeting of the Berkeley Linguistics Society* (ed. Cathy Cogen
et al.; Berkeley: Berkeley Linguistics Society, 1975), pp. 123–31; and for reference to
the semantics of understanding, see "Frames and the Semantics of Understanding,"
QS 6 (1985), pp. 222–54.
[53] Fillmore, "Frame Semantics," pp. 111–12.
[54] Fillmore, "Frame Semantics," p. 116.
[55] Fillmore, "Frame Semantics," p. 119.
[56] Fillmore, "Frame Semantics," p. 119.
[57] Fillmore, "Semantics of Understanding," p. 234.

readers have no difficulty interpreting the noun "presents" as a Christimas present because of the CHRISTMAS frame strongly implied in this sentence. Therefore, "the process of understanding a text involves retrieving or perceiving the frames evoked by the text's lexical content and assembling this kind of schematic knowledge... into some sort of 'envisionment' of the 'world' of the text."[58]

1.2.2. A.J. Sanford and S.C. Garrod

Sanford and Garrod, linguists in the field of discourse analysis, draw their attention to demonstrating that much human understanding of discourse (from single sentence to fuller discourse) depends upon not just "the semantics of words" but rather "pragmatic knowledge, or knowledge of how things normally work."[59] They assert that discourse is a "contract" between a speaker/writer and a hearer/reader:

> A writer wishes to convey an idea to his readers. In essence, this means that he must establish in the mind of his reader a situational model [a frame] which is the same as (or closely similar to) the one in his own mind. He can then refer to this model as his discourse unfolds and be reasonably certain that what he says will be intelligible. In the absence of such a common model, a discourse will be unintelligible, even if every sentence in it is coherent and grammatical.[60]

When hearing information, a hearer/reader calls up background knowledge (or frames) in an attempt to find recognizable data corresponding to what the input is about. And then the opening frame serves him or her to process the subsequent text as much as possible. In general, the idea of discourse as a "contract" between a speaker/writer and a hearer/reader, as will be discussed, is exactly the case for oral-aural narrative whose performance and transmission is based on the interaction between speakers and listeners.

Regarding the basic principles of textual comprehension, Sanford and Garrod are in line with many other scholars in the field of artificial

---

[58] Fillmore, "Frame Semantics," p. 122.

[59] A.J. Sanford and S.C. Garrod, *Understanding Written Language: Explorations of Comprehension Beyond the Sentence* (Chichester: John Wiley and Sons, 1981), p. 53.

[60] Sanford and Garrod, *Understanding*, pp. 8–9. Likewise, see Susan E. Haviland and Herbert H. Clark, "What's New? Acquiring New Information as a Process in Comprehension," *JVLVB* 14 (1974), p. 513: "The speakers's purpose is to provide new information to his audience, and the listener's is to extract the new information and integrate it with old information already in memory, Indeed, *communication is a cooperative effort between the speaker and listener.*" [italics are mine]

intelligence, and they say that mental frames allow the hearer/reader
to interpret references to a predictable sequence of behaviour. An
example is provided:

> (15) John was in court since Mary had filed a divorce petition.
> (15') He was worried about the alimony she might get.
> In order to integrate these two sentences, it is necessary to invoke a rep-
> resentation of the sequence of events in a divorce case. Only by relating
> (15') to such a representation is it possible to interpret the appearance
> of alimony and to interpret why he should be worried.[61]

Each frame contains in long-term memory the "slots" and roles to be
filled in by its participants (thus in the DIVORCE frame above John and
Mary fill in the slots of husband and wife respectively). The prototypical properties in the frame offer a guideline for expecting, understanding, and remembering the input correctly.[62]

1.2.3. George Lakoff

Lakoff's basic concern centres around "how linguistic expressions
and the concepts they express can be meaningful."[63] He suggests that
the problem of the objectivist (or Saussurean) approach to meaning
is that it does not take seriously the existence and activity of human
beings: "Linguistic expressions and the concepts they express are symbolic structures, meaningless in themselves, that get their meaning
via direct, unmediated correlation with things and categories in the
actual world (or possible worlds)."[64] In contrast, the cognitive linguist
approaches meaning in terms of human knowledge structures stored
through cultural experiences and "the nature and experience of the
organisms doing the thinking."[65] Lakoff calls in his book, *Women, Fire,
and Dangerous Things*, knowledge structures as "Idealized Cognitive
Models (ICMs)," or frames, schemata, and scripts, and proposes them
to be the central organizers of our knowledge and linguistic expressions and the concepts.[66] Each ICM, according to Lakoff, is structured
in such a way as to allow us to acquire, understand, and communicate knowledge; and its structuring principles are divided into four:

---

[61] Sanford and Garrod, *Understanding*, pp. 53–58.
[62] Sanford and Garrod, *Understanding*, pp. 111–18.
[63] Lakoff, *Women*, p. 266.
[64] Lakoff, *Women*, p. 266.
[65] Lakoff, *Women*, p. 266.
[66] Lakoff, *Women*, p. 68.

(1) prepositional structure, (2) image-schematic structure, (3) metaphoric mapping, and (4) metonymic mappings.[67] And an important
insight of this book and another, *Metaphors We Live By*, is that structures of the image-schematic model mapped in terms of human bodily
experience provide basic principles to determine the structural pattern
of the rest of the ICMs.[68] I agree basically with Lakoff's idea of the
structures of frames, and in what to follow will be using it as a theoretical basis for analyzing the ways in which Mark and his audience
would have structured the elements of frames as evoked in the Markan
Controversy Stories.

1.3. *Frame Theory in Biblical Studies and Bible Translation*

We have already stated that memory has been of increasing concern in
recent biblical scholarship. Only very few scholars, nonetheless, have
made an attempt to relate specific memory resources to New Testament studies. Biblical scholars' use of frame theory has been made in
three different areas: The transmission and preservation of the pre-
Gospel traditions, the semantics of New Testament texts, and Bible
translation. First, Richard Bauckham, a major New Testament scholar,
has recently made use of frame theory in an attempt to account for
the eyewitnesses's memory models behind the Gospels.[69] Stressing the
cognitive and communicative dimension of the forms in which the
Gospel traditions are cast, Bauckham asserts that "[m]emories must
be told in forms corresponding to socially available schemata if those
who tell their memories are to be successful in communicating with
others."[70] Bauckham's primary concern is then to suggest frames or to
"recollective memories" (to use his term), which he uses to include "the
schemata for events and stories, frames for knowledge about objects
and places,"[71] as memory resources that enabled the eyewitnesses of
the history of Jesus to preserve and communicate the Gospel traditions
reliably.[72] One of the most important arguments of Bauckham, which,

---

[67] Lakoff, *Women*, pp. 68, 267–88.
[68] Lakoff, *Women*, pp. 282–84 and George Lakoff and Mark Johnson, *Metaphors We Live By* (Chicago: The University of Chicago Press, 1980).
[69] Bauckham, *Eyewitnesses*, pp. 319–57.
[70] Bauckham, *Eyewitnesses*, pp. 346–47.
[71] Bauckham, *Eyewitnesses*, pp. 326, 335.
[72] Bauckham, *Eyewitnesses*, pp. 324–57, esp. 330–52. For this purpose, he suggests ten factors in relation to the events of the history of Jesus which may have been
remembered and transmitted reliably by the eyewitnessess's frame memory: (1) unique

in my judgment, New Testament scholars must take seriously, is that the eyewitnessess's frame memory behind the Gospels makes it unnecessary for us to postulate a long process of community development of the traditions or narrative forms (i.e., the form-critical paradigm) since it is a universal phenomenon of human memory to employ stereotyped forms of utterances (see below).[73] Despite his innovative employment of cognitive models into the account of the eyewitness memories behind the Gospels, however, Bauckham's concern does not go beyond proving the trustworthiness of the Gospel traditions. In this book, I will expand the role of frame to the understanding and communication of the completed Gospel.[74]

Second, several scholars such as Eugene A. Nida and J.P. Louw, and Paul Danove, have made use of semantic theory[75] and Fillmore's case frame[76] to explore the semantic meaning of New Testament texts. In

---

or unusual event; (2) salient or consequential event; (3) an event in which a person is emotionally involved; (4) vivid imagery; (5) irrelevant detail; (6) point of view; (7) dating; (8) gist and details; (9) frequent rehearsal; (10) story script.

[73] Bauckham, *Eyewitnesses*, pp. 349–51. A similar argument was made by Francis Glasson, "The Place of the Anecdote: A Note on Form Criticism," *JTS* 32 (1981), pp. 142–50, although he did not make use of a cognitive model in his argument against form criticism. Glasson ("Anecdote," p. 147) states, "if…we cannot speak or write without falling into some utterance which can be classified and identified as a particular Form, how fallacious it is to argue that, because the Gospel material can be classified into various Forms, this is an infallible sign of community transmission."

[74] Likewise, what merits mentioning here is N.T. Wright's understanding and use of concept "story" or "worldview" in his three-volume research of Christian origins and the question of God. Although not using the term frame, Wright is closer to the concept of the frame when seeing "knowledge of particular as taking place within the larger framework of the story of worldview which forms the basis of the observer's way of being in relation to the world"; so "all worldviews [e.g., in the case of the early Christians monotheism, election, (new) covenant and Jesus as the eschatological messiah of God] are at the deepest level shorthand formulae to express stories [e.g., early Christian stories of Jesus and Paul's writings]." Thus, Wright's task throughout the project involves the discernment and analysis of first-century Jewish and Christians worldviews and stories and their implications. For the quotation above, see N.T. Wright, *The New Testament and the People of God* (Minneapolis: Fortress, 1992), pp. 37, 78–79; and for Wright's other volumes, see *Jesus and the Victory of God* (Minneapolis: Fortress, 1996); *The Resurrection of the Son of God* (Minneapolis: Fortress, 2003).

[75] See Eugene A. Nida and J.P. Louw, *Lexical Semantics of the Greek New Testament* (Atlanta, Georgia: Scholars Press, 1992); for a dictionary based on semantic domains, see *idem*, *Greek-English Lexicon of the New Testament: Based on Semantic Domains* (2 vols.; New York: United Bible Societies, 1988).

[76] Paul Danove, *The End of Mark's Story: A Methodological Study* (Leiden: Brill, 1993); *idem*, *Linguistics and Exegesis in the Gospel of Mark: Applications of a Case Frame Analysis* (Sheffield: Sheffield Academic Press, 2001).

particular, Nida and Louw endeavor to classify the lexical items of New Testament in terms of "the number and type of shared semantic features."[77] Stanley Porter also stresses the need of semantic domain theory in New Testament linguistic studies, by pointing out that "language users use words to divide the world, experience, feelings, in fact all that they talk about, into various realms delimited by words. Thus the words of a language are not simply found in alphabetical lists but they are found grouped in users' minds according to the [semantic] fields they occupy."[78]

Third, as Croft and Cruse rightly point out, "Sometimes linguistic differences across languages represent differences in how much information is specified in the frame, rather than something about the inherent structure of the profiled concept."[79] The implication is that on the part of a translator, frame recognition is necessary in understanding "the nature of semantic differences between words and their apparent translation equivalents in different languages."[80] Thus, several attempts to apply the notion of cognitive frames to Bible translation have been made in recent biblical scholarship.[81] In particular, Richard Hoyle, a Bible translator, in his doctoral dissertation, "Scenarios, Discourse and Translation," adapts scenario theory to the translation theory of New Testament Greek and modern Parkari text as well as to discourse analysis.[82] Hoyle is the first person who, for New Testament discourse analysis and translation theory, makes use of scenario or frame theory, which is concerned with lexical semantics based on the original speaker and audience's real-life or culture. In his research Hoyle attempts to overcome the weakness of the semantic domain theory of Nida and Louw which arises because their classification of

---

[77] Nida and Louw, *Lexical Semantics*, p. 110. On Hoyle's criticism of Nida and Louw's semantic domain, see Hoyle, "Scenarios," Chapter Five.

[78] Stanley E. Porter, *Studies in the Greek New Testament* (New York: Peter Lang, 1996), p. 70.

[79] Croft, and Cruse, *Cognitive Linguistics*, p. 20.

[80] Croft, and Cruse, *Cognitive Linguistics*, p. 19.

[81] Timothy Wilt, "Translation and Communication," in *Bible Translation: Frames of Reference* (ed. Timothy Wilt; Manchester: St. Jerome Publishing, 2003), pp. 27–80, esp. 43–59; Robert Bascom, "The Role of Culture in Translation," in *Bible Translation: Frames of Reference* (ed. Timothy Wilt; Manchester: St. Jerome Publishing, 2003), pp. 81–111, esp. 99–110.

[82] Richard A. Hoyle, "Scenarios, discourse and translation: the scenario theory of cognitive linguistics, its relevance for analysing New Testament Greek and modern Parkari texts," Ph.D. diss. The University of Surrey Roehampton, 2001.

lexical items is primarily based on the number and type of shared semantic features rather than on cultural experiences. Hoyle's main concern is to show that scenario theory may shed light on solving translation difficulties arising primarily because of the cultural divide between the original speaker and audience and the modern speaker/reader. Hoyle, thus, says:

> Sometimes we are given clues to understand why characters act the way they do, but do not spot them. Instead, we infer our own reasons, from our own viewpoint, e.g., in Luke 10.25–37, the parable of the good Samaritan, why did the priest and the Levite pass by on the other side? Most English readers conclude they were uncaring people, who did not not love their neighbour, unlike the Samaritan, who cared. But the text does not say! Is it important to know why characters act as they do? What clues are in the text? If we know why they acted in this way, why should we 'add' it to the text in a translation? Is there an applicable theory?[83]

He proposes that scenario theory provides a theoretical basis for solving these problems in the sense that it can aid translators to identify the original speaker and audience's scenarios and understandably translate them in accordance with that of the target audience/reader.

Hoyle strives hard to integrate the insights from cognitive psychologists and from linguists regarding frame theory, and to adjust them to aid the analysis of the lexical and grammatical items of the New Testament writings. In investigating the cognitive processings of linguistic items in the Gospel of Mark, I will make frequent references to his book.

1.4. *Frame Theory and Homeric Studies: David Rubin and Elizabeth Minchin*

Scholars in the field of the oral epic, Rubin and Minchin respectively published books related to the issue of the relation of oral tradition and frames.[84] Rubin in his book, *Memory of Oral Tradition*, provides script-like frames as a model of memory for the transmission and

---

[83] Hoyle, "Scenarios," p. 6.

[84] David Rubin, *Memory in Oral Traditions: The Cognitive Psychology of Epic, Ballads, and Counting-out Rhymes* (Oxford: Oxford University Press, 1995), pp. 15–38, 210–20. Elizabeth Minchin, *Homer and the Resources of Memory: Some Applications of Cognitive Theory to the Iliad and the Odyssey* (Oxford: Oxford University Press, 2001), pp. 1–72.

preservation of oral tradition, which to survive must be stored in one person's memory and be passed to another person. Rubin says:

> In oral traditions...the immediate local context of cues is more important than the overall global structure of the whole piece...This may be one reason why scripts, which are action sequences that occur in a set order, and causal chains, in which sequential ideas are logically related, are easy to apply. Common scripts in the traditions discussed here include the sequence of concrete actions taken in arming a hero or the hero's horse, assembling an army, joining battle, and wrecking a train. The scripts are at least as well formed and strict as an undergraduate's knowledge of the undergraduate's knowledge of the sequence of events that occurs in going to the dentist's office or a fast-food restaurant (Bower, Black, & Turner, 1979). As most oral traditions are collections of concrete actions, scripts are well suited for their description.[85]

There are various scripted or framed data in oral tradition such as descriptions of routine actions, which in modern stories seems mundane, often with implied background information. But in oral tradition they are important devices for the speaker and the audience to process and remember a story readily.[86]

Elizabeth Minchin defines oral remembering (and the structure of oral narrative) as "typical scenes," or "themes" in accordance with A.B. Lord.[87] And basing her methodology on Schank and Abelson's script theory, she identifies "typical scenes," or "themes" with scripts, and proposes oral narrative as "scripted story."[88] Minchin defines, for example, Homer's contest scene as the "contest" script and analyses it as follows:

> The prizes are set up
> A challenge is announced
> Competitors come forward
> Preparations for the competition are made by:
>   drawing of lots
>   taking one's mark
>   judge/witness appointed
> The Contest takes place:
>   engagement
>   performance

---

[85] Rubin, *Oral Tradition*, p. 11.
[86] Rubin, *Oral Tradition*, p. 210.
[87] A.B. Lord, *The Singer of Tales* (Cambridge, Massachusetts: Harvard University Press, 1960).
[88] Minchin, *Memory*, pp. 32–43.

> reaction of spectators
> the end of the contest
> identification of victor
> Collection of prizes.[89]

The contest script contains major events and their details. Minchin suggests that since the sequence of the event was stored as a cluster of ideas in the minds of the oral performer and the audience, it may serve as an efficient memory device for the oral perfomer to tell a story with convenience and for the audience to understand and remember the story.[90] The speaker, moreover, uses such sequences to create a "semblance of reality, for scripted details are reassuringly familiar and in this respect persuasive."[91]

Basically I agree with Rubin and Minchin's idea about frames as memory devices for an oral-aural narrative, and follow the analysis of the sequence of actions in terms of frames. But since there are not only frames for events but also for persons and things, including their roles in the lexical and semantic structure of an episode, I will demonstrate the impact of frames at the word, sentence, and paragraph levels.

In brief, we have surveyed the mental knowledge structures or cognitive models developed and applied in the fields of cognitive psychology, artificial intelligence, cognitive linguistics, and applied to Bible translation, discourse analysis and Homeric narrative. The scholars in artificial intelligence and cognitive psychology have been concerned with the roles which frames play for story comprehension and recall. For linguists, the mental frame is of importance because of their belief that the production and use of a word or a lexical item and grammatical categories are inseparably connected to the activities of human cognition. In particular, frame theory has been used by discourse analysists to spell out the impact of frames on a hearer/reader's cognitive processing (expectation, inference, and coherent understanding) of discourse units, including at the sentence and paragraph levels. Likewise, in biblical studies frames have been discussed by a few scholars with three different areas (eyewitness memory, semantic meaning of New Testament language and bible translation) of concern, but no

---

[89] Minchin, *Memory*, pp. 43–44 (the original is italicized).
[90] Minchin, *Memory*, pp. 39–42, 70–71.
[91] Minchin, *Memory*, p. 71.

attention has been paid to analyzing the narrative discourse as a whole in terms of frames. Recognizing the vital role of human memory for the communication of oral-aural narrative, Rubin and Minchin have also developed frame theory to explain the "themes" of oral-aural narrative which consist of the typically recurrent sequence of actions (to use Minchin's word "typical scenes") of the script-like frame. Although different terms have been used in different fields, it is obvious that using cognitive models like frames (or scripts, scenarios, and schemata) is a distinctive feature of cognitive or human memory processing for the comprehension of world knowledge, everyday experience, language and narrative. Accordingly, I believe that frame theory may also shed light on illuminating the cognitive aspects of the Markan oral-aural narrative processing.[92]

---

[92] The word schema, a counterpart of frame, comes from the Greek word σχῆμα, "form, shape, person, way of a thing, constitution of a thing." See H.G. Liddell and R. Scott, *Greek-English Lexicon with a Supplement* (Oxford: Clarendon, 1968), σχῆμα. In fact, the notion that it is through existing knowledge structure, frames, that we understand the incoming information is not just modern construct, but dates back to the ancient Greek philosophers, such as Plato and Aristotle, as well as Kant. Marshall, *Schemas*, pp. 4–7, rightly traces the meaning of the word schema back to Plato and Aristotle. Marshall, *Schemas*, p. 7, says that Plato and Aristotle thought that a schema was an aspect of memory that contains characteristics about objects and concepts. Marshall, *Schemas*, p. 7, goes on to say that these characteristics were organized in memory to form a framework so that "other instances that have the same or similar structure" could be recognized in the future. According to Aristotle, the importance of *schemata* or *categories* is that they allow recognition and understanding of basic properties [e.g., as cited by Marshall, Aristotle, *Metaphysics*, 999A, 1017A, 1002A, 1026B, 1035B, 1032B, 1054B; *The Categories of Interpretation*, 1b: 4.25–30]. From Plato, we have *schema* in the sense of a general framework or basic outline, so that we can talk about a schema of a king or a schema of a good man [e.g., Plato, *Theaetetus*, 163B; *The Laws*, 4.718B; *Timaeus*, 22c; *The Meno*, 74D; *The Laws*, 2. 655A–B]." The idea of frame or schemats is also dealt with by Kant. According to Marshall, *Schemas*, pp. 7–8, "Essentially, Kant [in his *Critique of Pure Reason* (trans. Norman Kemp Smith; New York: St. Martin's Press, 1968)] believed that there are pure concepts or categories of understanding that exist a priori in the mind. The difficulty is to apply these abstract categories to perceived real-world objects, thus linking the concepts (the innate understanding) and the percept (the perceived phenomenon). For Kant, the schema was that link. He postulated the existence of three things: the a priori categories, or pure concepts of understanding, the empirical information derived through sensory perception, and the schema, which links sensibility and understanding (1787/1968, pp. B176–180)."

B. Frame and Mark

1. *What is a Frame?*

As observed above, a frame (or its counterparts, script, schema, scenario, cognitive model, experiential gestalt, base, scene), though having no fixed definition, is most often used to refer to an organized mental structure of knowledge that holds large chunks of related information in a particular domain. Broadly speaking, frame theory, according to David E. Rumelhart, is "about how [such] knowledge is represented and about how that representation facilitates the *use* of the knowledge in particular ways."[93] Regarding the formation of such knowledge, frame theory proposes that the typical characteristics of an action, person, and thing are abstracted from any recurring routine experiences and stored as the default values of the frame. All knowledge is bunched into a frame in an ordered and predictable pattern, and retrieved as needed. The cumulative evidence from cognitive linguistics and psychology, as discussed above, substantiates the hypothesis that it is in terms of an existing mental knowledge framework that people acquire incoming knowledge, experience, and events in stories, and are thus able to retrieve them from memory. Framed knowledge aids people to readily process what is happening in the real or story world by allowing them to make predictions as to what will take place and by allowing them to make inferences. Such culture-based, conventionalized knowledge includes information about our physical environment (e.g., the DOWNTOWN frame includes information concerning many buildings and roads with traffic lights), what typifies certain individual characters, and how the parts of the human body are organized. All this information is 'prototypically'[94] stored in our frame and evoked to process the information belonging in that frame. So, it can determine not only how people behave in all kinds of social contexts (e.g., in a restaurant, in a church service, or when buying goods at a shop and so on) but also the meaning of linguistic items.[95]

---

[93] Rumelhart, "Schemata," p. 33.

[94] See glossary on the concept prototype.

[95] On the idea of frame theory that the meaning of a linguistic form is not independent of our understanding of real-world contingency, see Taylor, *Linguistic Categorization*, pp. 89–90; and see also Roger Schank, Lawrence Birnbaum, Jacob Mey, "Integrating Semantics and Pragmatics," QS 6 (1985), p. 315 and Croft and Cruse, *Cognitive Linguistics*, p. 98.

Frame theory holds that the frame is directly employed in such processes as structuring, comprehending, and recalling events in narrative texts. Frames, first of all, determine a way of structuring narrative discourse. Frames have stereotyped and culture-specific knowledge about routine activities; they make it possible for the actions and events of a story world to be organized in term of set expectations, or in deviation of such expectations. And frames are also language specific. A frame, according to cognitive linguists, is made up of a set of concepts associated in ordinary human experience, and the concepts are denoted by words;[96] hence the frame determines the narrative discourse to be structured in a coherent way; and frames enable the hearer/reader to process it as semantically and syntactically related (or meaningful).

Next, a listener/reader, as Bartlett suggests, does not hear/read an utterance in isolation but rather in relation to "a whole active mass of organized past reactions or experience," namely, a frame.[97] Consider an example provided by J.M. Bransford and M.K. Johnson:

> The procedure is actually quite simple. First you arrange items into different groups. Of course one pile may be sufficient depending on how much there is to do. If you have to go somewhere else due to lack of facilities that is the next step; otherwise, you are pretty well set. It is important not to overdo things. That is, it is better to do too few things at once than too many. In the short run this may not seem important but complications can easily arise. A mistake can be expensive as well. At first, the whole procedure will seem complicated. Soon, however, it will become just another facet of life. It is difficult to foresee any end to the necessity for this task in the immediate future, but then, one never can tell. After the procedure is completed one arranges the materials into different groups agains. Then they can be put into their appropriate places. Eventually they will be used once more and the whole cycle will then have to be repeated. However, that is part of life.[98]

---

[96] Timothy C. Clausner and William Croft, "Domains and Image Schemas," *CL* 10-1 (1999), p. 2 and Croft and Cruse, *Cognitive Linguistics*, pp. 14–16.

[97] Bartlett, *Remembering*, p. 213; cf. John M. Foley, *Immanent Art: From Structure to Meaning in Traditional Oral Epic* (Bloomington and Indianapolis: Indiana University Press, 1991); *idem, Singer*. One of Foley's main arguments in those books is that people's understanding of what is orally performed is not based on oral performance alone, but on their familiar knowledge of oral tradition that oral performance draws on. In this respect, it can be said that the communication of oral-aural narrative is very close to frame-based information processing. We will deal with this in detail in Chapter Two.

[98] J.D. Bransford and M.K. Johnson, "Contextual Prerequisites for Understanding: Some Investigations of Comprehension and Recall," *JVLVB* 11 (1972), p. 722.

For most individuals this passage would make little sense and when asked to recall it they would only be able to provide a few details. However, we can have much greater understanding and recall, if we are given the title 'washing clothes' before reading it, and the reason we can understand the passage is because we have our own frame for WASHING CLOTHES. To understand something means to open an adequate frame that offers a likely account of it, and to integrate it into something that is a part of the listener's knowledge of the frame. In such a process, the words and grammatical categories serve to activate mental frames for the understanding of a story. For this reason sentences and paragraphs, though perfectly grammatical, make little sense if a frame that allows a plausible account for them is not opened.

In addition to the important role of frames in comprehension, frame theory holds that frames guide the listener/reader in remembering a story. At recall frames enable people to determine what information they will retrieve. Frames provide background knowledge by which one understands incoming information; so people remember information in accordance with what they have understood about an event or story rather than the event or story as such. In this process of remembering frames usually affect the audience/reader's memory for the main theme or gist of a story.

2. To What Extent is the Application of Modern Frame Theory to Mark's Gospel Valid?

Given that the Gospel of Mark is an oral-aural narrative which is highly dependent on human memory for communication, there is no doubt that, in comprehending and recalling it, the original speaker and audience used cognitive models particularly relevant to such a communicative environment. I believe that a frame is a cognitive model which can illuminate memory processing of the Markan oral-aural narrative on the part of the original speaker and audience. Although there may be a question regarding the relevance of a modern cognitive model for understanding of Mark's Gospel, the application of frame theory to Mark's Gospel in this study is based on the assumption of cognitive theoreticians that the frame is a cognitive model based on the hardwiring of the brain, though its contents are culture specific.[99] Yet this

---

[99] Lakoff, *Women*, pp. 58–76, 121–25, 266–68, 282–83; Peter Stockwell, *Cognitive Poetics: An Introduction* (London and New York: Routledge, 2002), pp. 1–12; Croft and Cruse, *Cognitive Linguistics*, pp. 1–4.

idea has been rarely recognized until the development of cognitive science. With respect to human use of language, linguists prior to cognitive linguistics assumed, as discussed above, that language is a self-sufficient module separated from non-linguistic cognitive abilities.[100] But this assumption has been rightly criticized by many cognitive theoreticians (see above).[101] Instead, cognitive scientists' fundamental tenet is that comprehension and remembering incoming information, whether linguistic or real events, in terms of a cognitive model of frame is a fundamental process common to all human beings, regardless of culture and time.[102] It is on this hypothesis of cognitive linguistics that I will argue Mark's Gospel as a frame-based story with frame theory enhancing the understanding of the Gospel.

It must, however, not be ignored that, despite an understanding of frame-based story comprehension as universal, individual frames have 'local expressions' in terms of culture and language.[103] It is this assumption that I will keep in mind throughout this study. When it comes to culture, as will be observed, a memory frame, as an active cognitive device, is a structured cluster of knowledge that forms through recurrent human cultural and social experiences of real events or story. This is the reason why frame theory must be aided by social and cultural studies in order to understand the text produced in different cultural situations (see below). Besides, in order to investigate the frames and their role in understanding Mark's Gospel, since frames are not only culture specific but also language specific, it is necessary to explain how frames operate in specific linguistic expressions used in representing oral thoughts and features.

Likewise there is an issue to be addressed in association with the present argument. Concerning frame theory, in fact, modern cognitive linguists have been attempted to explain just how the reader comes

---

[100] Croft and Cruse, *Cognitive Linguistics*, p. 1.

[101] For example, Schank and Abelson, *Script*, pp. 1–11; Fillmore, "Semantics of Understanding," pp. 222–54 and Lakoff, *Women*, pp. xi–xvii, 5–11.

[102] Lakoff, *Women*, pp. 266–68, 282–83; Sandra P. Marshall, *Schemas in Problem Solving* (Cambridge: Cambridge University Press, 1995), pp. vi–ix, 3; Kathleen Callow, *Man and Message* (Lanham: University Press of America, 1998), pp. 32–33.

[103] Fillmore, "Frame Semantics," pp. 111–12, esp. 117–18; see also Lakoff, *Women*, pp. 266–68 and Dan Sperber and Deirdre Wilson, *Relevance: Communication and Cognition* (Oxford: Blackwell, 2nd edn, 1986), pp. 38–46. And a further explanation of the relation of universalism and relativism of human linguistic processing, see Bernd Heine, *Cognitive Foundations of Grammar* (Oxford: Oxford University Press, 1997), pp. 10–14.

to an understanding of the written document in terms of frame. So it may seem that frame theory may be applicable only to the analysis of the written text. But my whole study, particularly Chapter Three, is, in fact, organized in support of the argument that frame theory can also be used as an appropriate tool for analyzing an oral-aural narrative such as Mark's Gospel. It is, nonetheless, important to explain at this point two primary reasons why I believe that frame theory as developed in this study may enhance our understanding of the distinctive experience of the hearer as opposed to the reader.[104] First, it has been known that a "homeostatic" and conservative way of thinking is one of the features of oral cultures and communication, and the efficient communication of the oral text is based on this familiarity.[105] It is obvious that information explicitly and implicitly communicated by means of oral-aural narrative is what may already be stored in the original audience's long-term memory.[106] A frame, as will be observed, consists of stereotyped knowledge which is stored through cultural and social experience. Hence this feature of oral memory strongly enables us to believe that frame-based story processing was an essential way in which the Markan oral-aural narrative was communicated.[107] Second, once this first point is accepted, it leads us to another argument for the relevance of frame theory to the interpretation of the oral-aural narrative. A frame-related piece of information, as proved by Sanford and Garrod's experiments, can be processed and understood more quickly and straightforwardly than a frame-irrelevant one.[108] The argument is that frame-based story processing is a distinctive cognitive model that is capable of leading us to get at the original audience's hearing experience of the oral narrative whose property is evanescent[109] and

---

[104] For a good few scholars of Classics and of the New Testament who have already used frame theory to explain the communication and transmission of an oral narrative, see section 1.1.1.

[105] With regard to the homeostatic organization of oral cultures, see Jack Goody and Ian Watt, "The Consequences of Literacy," in *Literacy in Traditional Societies* (ed. Jack Goody; Cambridge: Cambridge University Press, 1968), pp. 30–31. For the definition of homeostatic, see glossary; and see Chapter Three on the features of oral cultures and communication.

[106] Eric A. Havelock, *Preface to Plato* (Cambridge, Massachusetts: Belknap, 1963), pp. 87–89; John Miles Foley, "The Traditional Oral Audience," *BS* 18 (1977), p. 148.

[107] On the relation between frame and socially shared knowledge, see Croft and Cruse, *Cognitive Linguistics*, p. 18.

[108] Sanford and Garrod, *Understanding*, pp. 111–18. For a further discussion, see Chapter Three.

[109] On the evanescent nature of oral communication, see above and Chapter Three.

thus is in need of quick understanding. Additionally, I will demonstrate in Chapter Three that the principles known as oral narrative's characteristics (thematic composition, episodic structure, gist memory, conservative repetition, and event-oriented flow) are not very different from the features of frame-based story.

3. *How Do We Identify Frames in Mark's Gospel?*

It is a universal phenomenon, as discussed below, that people use specific domain-related knowledge to process and understand incoming information. But when it comes to the application of frames to Mark's Gospel, another question arises: How do we know that there are certain frames operating in a given passage, and that they are ones which may have operated in the original audience's cognitive frames? Answering these questions is especially important when we draw on frame theory for understanding texts that come from different cognitive environments than those of modern interpreters. Before proceeding to further argument for various criteria to identify frames, we need to keep in mind what sort of text the Gospel of Mark is. Eric Havelock, a scholar of Classics, claimed that an ancient narrative reflects exactly the "nomos" and "ethos" of oral cultures and the audience.[110] This argument may be strengthened when we remember the homeostatic and conservative features of oral cultures or communication pointed out above. The implication is that as an oral-aural narrative Mark's Gospel itself is a direct indication of what sort of knowledge Mark's original audience was familiar with. This study will show that the understanding of the Gospel works best when based on that assumption.

In order to identify frames in certain passages, I will employ primarily two textual criteria from within Mark's Gospel material itself, such as linguistic expression and grammatical indicators, and three more criteria from outside the Gospel material itself, such as parallels from other New Testament literature and extra-biblical material, world knowledge, and socio-cultural knowledge. The first textual criterion is linguistic expression. Words are labels of concepts and frames consisting of a set of concepts (see Chapter Three), so they are capable of opening conceptual knowledge structures.[111] In this cognitive processing, the words symbolizing (denoting) such types of information

---

[110] Havelock, *Plato*, p. 87. For a further discussion, see Chapter Three.
[111] Croft and Cruse, *Cognitive Linguistics*, pp. 14–16.

as things, persons, and places are identified as indicators of the frames
or conceptual knowledge structures for the information referred to.
Understanding the meaning of the words, thus, implies that we are
capable of activating the frames related to the words. In particular,
since frames are conventional knowledge structures stored in the mind,
if and when the content and form of a story are expressed by means of
linguistic and thematic repetitions (i.e., parallel patterns), we can take
the repetitive patterns as strong evidence to show that certain frame
knowledge operates on the relevant passages. The second textual criterion is grammatical indicators. Frame theory postulates that grammar is a representation of human cognitive processing; so I will claim
that cognitive frames determine the language user's use of grammar.[112]
And for the identification of frames I will draw on Greek grammatical
and lexical indicators, such as the Greek article, adversative particles,
predicative participles, participial noun phrases, rhetorical questions,
evaluative language, and subjectless verbs.[113]

Once the textual criteria are acknowledged, three more resources
from without the Gospel material may be used to aid the recognition
of frames and their properties. The first is parallels from other New
Testament writings and extra-biblical materials. This is because it is
beyond doubt that certain kinds of knowledge (e.g., the SABBATH and
the SYNAGOGUE) were commonly shared, and expressed linguistically

---

[112] Charles Fillmore, "Scenes-and frames-semantics," in *Linguistic Structures Processing* (ed. A. Zampolli; Amsterdam: North-Holland, 1977), pp. 55–82; Lakoff,
Women, pp. 68–90, 260–303.

[113] Identification of frames and their contents in terms of Mark's textual evidence
itself, however, may seem a less objective methodology. But this doubt is groundless
when we remember three things mentioned above. The first is related to the nature
of Mark's oral-aural text that embodies the nomos and ethos of oral cultures and the
audience; the second is cognitive linguists' understanding of words and grammars
in terms of frames. The third is Sanford and Garrod's idea of how a text may be
communicated: Discourse is "a contract" between the speaker and the audience (see
above), a contract through which the speaker uses sentences and discourse to tell the
audience how to utilize the knowledge he or she already has. In fact, the belief that
frames and their components can sometimes simply be read off from the text material itself is not new in biblical scholarship. Some form critics have attempted to find
"forms," which the Gospel traditions have been cast into and transmitted through,
simply on the basis of the synoptic material itself. See Rudolf Bultmann, *The History
of the Synoptic Tradition* (trans. John Marsh; New York and Evanston: Harper and
Row, 1963) and Martin Dibelius, *From Tradition to Gospel* (trans. Bertram Lee Woolf;
New York: Charles Scribner's Sons, 1934). To the contrary, Detlev Drmeyer, *The New
Testament among the Writings of Antiquity* (trans. Rosemarie Kossov; Sheffield: Sheffield Academic Press, 1998), pp. 17–82, proposes that one should look to Hellenistic
or Greco-Roman literary conventions as parallel forms in the Gospels.

in documents not only among the early churches but also by closely related religious groups such as ancient Judaism and the early church. The second is world knowledge[114] (e.g., the PARALYTIC frame and its default components regarding the sick person's hands and legs unable to move properly; and the HOUSE frame and its default knowledge that a house has a door or doors and a flat roof). This kind of knowledge usually belongs in the listener's long-term memory; as a result, it is sometimes presupposed or omitted in the text. The recognition of world knowledge, thus, allows us to discover what sort of frames operate in the passage in question. The third piece of evidence from outside the Gospel to strengthen the identification of frames which is somewhat related to the first, comes from socio-cultural knowledge of the first-century Mediterranean world (e.g., Caesar as the title for Roman emperors). Frame theory assumes that frames are culture specific. Hence, in order to see whether some linguistic expressions have information ready for opening relevant frames, it would be instructive to survey the socio-cultural setting (i.e., cognitive environment) in which the text was produced and which may influence the structure and content of the audience's frame knowledge. If we can provide the socio-cultural knowledge associated with frames that is about to be opened by certain linguistic expressions, we find ourselves in a better position to identify the frames operative on a given passage.

4. *The Biblical Implications of the Application of Frame Theory to the Gospel of Mark*

First, frame theory enriches our reading of New Testament literature because it lays a theoretical foundation to bring in interdisciplinary work for the study of the text. For proper reading of New Testament writings, the past two decades have produced extensive literature dealing with various aspects of the Gospels in biblical scholarship.[115]

---

[114] For the definition of world knowledge, see glossary.

[115] One may refer to a historical aspect of the Gospels, focusing on its historical development stages; see, for example, Ethienne Trocme, *The Formation of the Gospel According to Mark* (trans. Pamela Gaughan; Philadelphia: The Westminster Press, 1975). Some of these studies focus on the socio-scientific perspectives of the Gospels; see, for example, Howard Clark Kee, *Community of the New Age* (Philadelphia: The Westminster Press, 1977); Stephen C. Barton, *Discipleship and Family Ties in Mark and Matthew* (Cambridge: Cambridge University Press, 1994). Other focus on literary approach to them, along with their rhetorical aspects; see Joanna Dewey, *Markan Public Debate: Literary Technique, Concentric Structure, and Theology in Mark*

All methodologies are legitimate in their own right. However, what we should not forget is that the New Testament text consists of language and grammar, thus linguistic knowledge must be an essential foundation to the study of the text. Accordingly, reading the text, as J.P. Louw claims, must include extra-linguistic features (e.g., medium of presentation and background and history of a text), para-linguistic features (discourse units, genre) and linguistic features (semantics, syntax, and grammar).[116] The implication is that finding the meaning of the text is a work that requires a methodology to incorporate its linguistic, extra-linguistic and para-linguistic features. I believe that cognitive linguistics and its frame theory has a theoretical basis to do so because it proposes that human linguistic capability is not different from human general cognitive capability (see above). Of course, it is true that frame theory takes primarily a linguistic approach to the text, but its concern is not just limited to its linguistic features. Rather the theory goes on to explain how the audience/reader processes in terms of cognitive frame language and textual comprehension by putting together linguistic and grammatical information, social and cultural knowledge, and literary idea. Hence I believe that frame theory is a linguistic methodology that may enrich the reading of the Gospels more comprehensively than any other methodologies do. Stanley Porter rightly points out that modern linguistics has been denigrated as an enterprise of relevance in the discipline of New Testament studies.[117] But this book will contribute to New Testament studies by providing cognitive linguistic theory, and in particular, the semantic field theory as a means of analyzing Mark 2.1–3.6.[118]

2:1–3.6 (SBLDS 48; Chico, California: Scholars, 1980); David Rhoads, Joanna Dewey, and Donald Michie, *Mark as Story: An Introduction to the Narrative of a Gospel* (Philadelphia: Fortress, 2nd edn, 1982); Mary A. Tolbert, *Sowing the Gospel: Mark's World in Literary-Historical Perspective* (Minneapolis: Fortress Press, 1989); Vernon K. Robbins, *Jesus The Teacher: A Socio-Rhetorical Interpretation of Mark* (Philadelphia: Fortress, 1992).

[116] J.P. Louw, "Reading a Text as Discourse," in *Linguistics and New Testament Interpretation. Essays on Discourse Analysis* (ed. David Allan Black, Katharine Barnwell and Stephen Levinsohn; Nashville, Tennessee: Broadman Press, 1992), p. 18.

[117] Porter, *Greek New Testament*, p. 51.

[118] There have been many important developments in relation to linguistic principles and paradigms in the field of modern linguistics, including cognitive linguistics. Some New Testament scholars have attempted to apply those principles to New Testament studies. For a brief but well-informed explanation of those attempts, see Stanley E. Porter, "Greek Grammar and Syntax," in *the Face of New Testament Studies: A Survey of Recent Research* (ed. Scot McKnight and Grant R. Osborne; Grand Rapids,

Second, this study may lead interpreters to an understanding of what cognitive models are available to the comprehension of Mark's Gospel, and of how frames would have efficiently helped the original audience to comprehend and recall the Gospel. To be sure, frame theory does not simply inform ways in which frames helped the original audience's comprehension and recall of the Gospel, but it also provides a modern interpreter with an excellent theoretical foundation for solving exegetical problems in interpreting the text. The communication between Mark and his historical audience was based on a shared body of knowledge.[119] While it is well structured grammatically and lexically, a story may lead to a lack of comprehension in the absence of such shared or background knowledge. (In Chapter Three, I will argue in favour of the assumption that Mark's original Christian audiences were capable of opening frames appropriate for understanding the Gospel of Mark.) This means that the main barrier to our appreciation as modern audiences/readers of the Markan oral-aural narrative is our ignorance of the background knowledge or frames on which the text is based.[120] The original texts not infrequently develop a story without providing enough of the kind of information which the modern reader needs to follow. As an example, Mark 3.6 says, ἐξελθόντες οἱ Φαρισαῖοι εὐθὺς μετὰ τῶν Ἡρῳδιανῶν συμβούλιον ἐδίδουν κατ' αὐτοῦ ὅπως αὐτὸν ἀπολέσωσιν. Surprisingly, we are told that they "went out [of the synagogue]" to destroy Jesus, though the presence of the Pharisees is never mentioned anywhere in the preceding passages of Mark 3.1–6. The text

Michigan: Baker Academic, 2004), pp. 76–103. And on works which adapt some principles of cognitive linguistics to Gospels studies, see Robert E. Longacre, "A Top-Down, Template-Driven Narrative Analysis, Illustrated by Application to Mark's Gospel," in *Discourse Analysis and the New Testament: Approaches and Results* (ed. Stanley E. Porter and Jeffrey T. Reed; JSNTSup 170; Sheffield: Sheffield Academic Press, 1999), pp. 140–68; *idem*, "Mark 5:1–43: Generating the Complexity of a Narrative from Its Most Basic Elements," in *Discourse Analysis and the New Testament: Approaches and Results* (ed. Stanley E. Porter and Jeffrey T. Reed; JSNTSup 170; Sheffield: Sheffield Academic Press, 1999), pp. 169–96; Hoyle, "Scenarios."

[119] On shared knowledge as a basic condition of communication, see Fillmore, "Frame Semantics," pp. 111–124 and Callow, *Man*, pp. 35–42.

[120] The high value of shared knowledge in understanding a text is also emphasised by social-scientific criticism of the New Testament. John E. Elliot, *What is Social-Scientific Criticism?* (Philadelphia: Fortress, 1993), pp. 11–12, states, "the New Testament…consists of documents written in what anthropologists call a 'high context' society where the communicators presume a broadly shared acquaintance with and knowledge of the social situation of matters referred to in conversation or writing. Accordingly, it is presumed in such societies that contemporary readers will be able to 'fill in the gaps' and 'read between the lines.'"

assumes the Pharisees existing in the synagogue as given information. On what theoretical foundation should we think of the presence of the Pharisees in the synagogue as default information? And the word οἱ Φαρισαῖοι begins with the Greek article οἱ, despite the fact that the word first occurs in that episode. This implies that the referent of the noun introduced by the article was already part of the audience's knowledge. What theoretical basis justifies the use of the article in that case? But frame theory proposes that "a frame organizes knowledge about certain properties of objects, courses of event and action which TYPICALLY belong together," giving a theoretical base to the modern interpreter for solving these.[121]

Third, since the frame can shed some light on the knowledge structures shared between the original speaker and audience, along with the underlying structure of the narrative, it will put us in a better position to discover the original meaning of the Gospel of Mark. I believe the quest for discovering such a meaning of the Gospel can be aided by bringing to the fore the cognitive processing which Mark and his original audience shared. Thus, frame theory will provide a modern reader/audience of the Gospel with a theoretical basis to account for the cognitive aspect of the interpretation, or meaning, of Mark's Gospel.

Finally, frame theory will contribute to discourse analytic studies of the New Testament. Issues of "prominence," "boundary markers," and "cohesion" have been of central concern to modern discourse analysts, not least to New Testament discourse analysts.[122] By highlighting the cognitive aspect of textual processing, frame theory helps interpreters determine prominence, episodic boundary markers, and semantic and lexical cohesion in discourse. For example, "Cohesion refers to the grammatical, semantic and contextual factors which hold a discourse together."[123] Thus, discourse analysts have developed the theme of cohesion, attempting to answer the questions around just how they (the speakers) combine unrelated words and sentences into

---

[121] Teun A. van Dijk, *Text and Context: Explorations in the Semantics and Pragmatics of Discourse* (London: Longman, 1977), p. 159.

[122] Porter, *Idioms*, pp. 304–307 and Jeffrey T. Reed, "The Cohesiveness of Discourse: Towards a Model of Linguistic Criteria For Analyzing New Testament Discourse," in *Discourse Analysis and the New Testament: Approaches and Results* (ed. Stanley E. Porter and Jeffrey T. Reed; JSNTSup 170; Sheffield: Sheffield Academic Press, 1999), p. 28.

[123] Porter, *Idioms*, p. 304. For the issues of episode or paragraph boundary markers and prominence, see chapters five and six.

a meaningful whole, and why some texts are considered to be semantically more coherent than others.[124] On the one hand, since a mental
frame has a set of interrelated concepts labelled by words, it makes
lexical cohesiveness possible within an episode, and since a frame, on
the other hand, has prototypical elements semantically interconnected
through human cultural experience within it, it enables an episode to
be semantically cohesive within its boundary (for details, see Chapters
Five and Six).[125] In Mark 3.3 and 3.5, for example, Jesus asks the man
with a withered hand to, "Get up to the middle (ἔγειρε εἰς τὸ μέσον)"
and "Stretch out your hand (ἔκτεινον τὴν χεῖρα)." The audience makes
the two sentences cohere by assuming that because the goal Jesus had
in asking the man to get up is achieved (i.e., the man really got up
and walked to the middle). Jesus is in a position to tell him to stretch
out his hand for healing. Frame theory allowed the original audience
to think of the two sentences as coherent, even though the text never
says that, in obedience to Jesus, the man actually got up and walked to
the middle. Because a script-type frame has as its elements sequenced
types of events, to hear one course of action in a script-type frame is
to bring to consciousness the other actions that are a part of the frame
as well.

5. The Relation of Frame Theory to Form Criticism: Similarities and Differences

Similarities: "Form," which has been mentioned since the rise of form
criticism in biblical studies, is an indication that the Synoptic Gospels
are based on framed knowledge. Having postulated the Jesus tradition as a creation being entirely post-Easter, form criticism argues that
each "form," or "genre," of the tradition grew out of specific activities
of the first churches.[126] Thus, each form has its own *Sitz im Leben*, or
life-setting, of the earliest churches.[127] For example, the "Controversy

---

[124] Reed, "The Cohesiveness of Discourse," p. 28.

[125] On the relation of a concept and a word, see Robert W. Howard, *Concepts and Schemata: An Introduction* (London: Cassell, 1987), pp. 17–19.

[126] Bultmann, *Synoptic Tradition*, p. 4, seems to use the word "genre" in both a sociological and an aesthetic term: "the literary 'category', or 'form' through which a particular item is classified is a sociological concept and not an aesthetic one, however much it may be possible by its subsequent development to use such forms as aesthetic media in some particular literary product."

[127] But Bultmann, *Synoptic Tradition*, p. 4, says, "The *Sitz im Leben* is not, however, an individual historical event, but a typical situation or occupation in the life of a community."

Stories" reflect a situation in which the earliest churches debated with the Jews about the necessity of observing the Jewish laws. It is certainly an exaggeration to say that the Synoptic tradition must be ascribed entirely to the creation of Easter faith.[128] Nonetheless, form criticism is right in saying that a form reflects a way in which the first Christian community understood and used the tradition. And each form, according to form criticism, was used to serve diverse needs that arose among the church's life (e.g., mission, sermon, defence, teaching). In that frames are information structures which form through repetitious social experience, hence allowing people to easily recognize and process other similar experience and events, it is possible to say that a form is a concept close to a frame, and that the early Christians organized and communicated in terms of frames the pre-Gospel traditions.[129]

Differences: There are significant differences between the two concepts of form criticism and frame theory, and the ways in which each theory is used for the analysis of the Gospel of Mark. First, each form

---

[128] In contrast to form criticism's argument that for the early Christians there was no disticiion between pre-Easter and post-Easter traditions of Jesus, many important books have proved that the Gospel writers distinguished Jesus' past history from their own present. See, for examples, C.F.D. Moule, *Essays in New Testament Interpretation* (Cambridge: Cambridge University Press, 1982), pp. 37–49; Eugene L. Lemcio, *The Past of Jesus in the Gospels* (SNTSMS 68; Cambridge: Cambridge University Press, 1991); Bauckham, *Eyewitnesses*, pp. 264–89; Gerd Theissen and Annette Merz, *The Historical Jesus* (trans. John Bowden; London: SCM, 1998). And see also Gehard Theissen, *The First Followers of Jesus: A Sociological Analysis of the Earliest Christianity* (London: SCM, 1978), p. 121 and Bailey, "Oral Tradition," pp. 5–10. Dunn, *Jesus*, p. 130, rightly argues that the data in the Synoptic Gospels are essentially touched by faith from the outset rather than by Easter faith: "The Synoptic tradition provides evidence not so much for what Jesus did or said in itself, but for what Jesus was *remembered* as doing or saying by his first disciples, or as we might say, for the *impact* of what he did and said on his first disciples."

[129] Bauckham, *Eyewitnesses*, pp. 346–51. Charles Fillmore, "Ideal Readers and Real Readers," in *Analyzing Discourse: Text and Talk* (ed. Deborah Tannen; Washington, D.C.: Georgetown University Press, 1982), p. 262, states, using the term "genre frame," "[g]enre frames arises from structured expectations created by familiarity with particular genres." He also says in "Frame Semantics," p. 117, "knowing that a text is, say, an obituary, a proposal of marriage, a business contract, or a folktale, provides knowledge about how to interpret particular passages in it, how to expect the text to develop, and how to know when it is finished. It is frequently the case that such expectations combine with the actual material of the text to lead to the text's correct interpretation....this is accomplished by having in mind an abstract structure of expectations which brings with it roles, purposes, natural or conventionalized sequences of event types, and all the rest of the apparatus that we wish to associate with the notion of 'frame'."

has been used by form critics as an objective textual device, but a frame is a mental or cognitive knowledge structure. With respect to textual processing frame theory is primarily concerned with *human cognitive activities or abilities* available for the production, processing, and comprehension of linguistic information. But form critics' concern with form is limited to exploring *early Christian communities' activities* related to the structure and uses of material, that is, pre-Gospel traditions, expressed by each form. Paying great attention to the unanonymous communities' development and use of the materials, as a result, they not only failed to take seriously the fact that human memory is involved in the formation of narrative forms and the Gospel traditions; but also they overlooked how they would be communicated to individuals in terms of cognitive processing.[130] Such a serious problem of form criticism has been clearly pointed out by Bauckham in favour of frame theory:

> The form critics never really addressed the question of where the forms came from....The psychological notion of schemata should enable research into the extent to which gospel narratives use cross-cultural story scripts that recur wherever people tell stories, being more or less inherent in the nature of telling a story, or conform to more culturally specific story scripts. Studies of the forms that stories take in the work of known ancient authors recounting their own experiences are also needed to substantiate the point that the relatively stereotyped forms of the Gospel traditions could be those given them by their earliest, eyewitness tellers.[131]

Second, in search of the meaning of the text expressed and structured by a specific form, form critics are interested in the pre-Gospel stages of each episode in the life of the early church as separate from the present narrative framework. On the contrary, for the same task frame theory is concerned with the completed text.

Third, frame theory assumes that meaning can be discovered by calling attention to the cognitive characteristics underlying the text and the audience/reader's cognitive processing of it. However, biblical scholars in the field of historical criticism have overlooked such a basic yet crucial aspect in interpreting the New Testament writings, assuming that the semantics or meaning of linguistic expressions in the

---

[130] For an excellent critique of form criticism from the perspective of frame theory, see Bauckham, *Eyewitnesses*, pp. 346–51.

[131] Bauckham, *Eyewitnesses*, p. 351.

Gospels lies in finding the correlation between the expressions and the actual world, which is called by Lakoff an "objective approach to the problem of meaning."[132] Indeed, that approach itself is not a problem at all. What is problematic is that in accounting for meaning they entirely ignore human beings. Historical critics have not taken seriously the fact that human cognitive processing is necessarily engaged in composing and comprehending linguistics expression made by the evangelists. Frame theory postulates that the reason the events in the Gospel of Mark and the concepts they express are comprehensible or meaningful is because they can be structured and processed in terms of a cognitive model or frame.

Finally, frame theory pays attention to the fact that a frame processes information on the basis of social stereotypes; accordingly, it may seem that it shares another common ground with form criticism, which is also dominated by historical concerns with the life situation of the early church. However, it must be noted that the historical interest of frame theory is motivated by a different reason than that of form criticism. Form criticism or the historical-critical method has focused its historical inquiry on the environment of the early church with the purpose of studying the formative processes of the Gospels, whereas frame theory as used in this study is concerned with the role of social and cultural knowledge in the production and the reception of Mark's completed text. Frame theory also holds that people understand a story world in terms of a frame which is culture specific, hence the present study is interested in exploring ways in which the original audience may understand the completed text in reference to frame knowledge.

C. The Scope and Procedure of Study

Mark's Controversy Stories (2.1–3.6) will be the passages on which this study will be focused. There are three cogent reasons to choose Mark 2.1–3.6 for analysis. First, the five stories of conflict in this section have long been known since the rise of form criticism as one of the most apparent examples of a collection being made through lengthy oral development within the early Christian communities due

---

[132] Lakoff, *Women*, pp. 265–67.

to the ecclesiastical need for debate with Jews or Jewish Christians.[133] But form criticism's account of existence of the material in 2.1–3.6 nowhere mentions human beings; it does not depend in any way on the nature of the human way of thinking, or on the cognitive nature of human beings. I take this to be the central problem with form critics' approach to the stories in 2.1–3.6. Instead, focusing on human beings' cognitive processing of the unit which has the stereotyped pattern of stories, I will show that frame theory has no need necessarily to postulate a long development of community tradition in relation to 2.1–3.6.

Second, 2.1–3.6 is a good place to examine how an oral-aural narrative discourse holds together in a coherent way. The unity of this section has been widely recognized. Some form critics have based their argument for unity on the repetitive pattern of sayings (e.g., pronouncements of Jesus) occurring in the five controversy stories,[134] and Joanna Dewey uses divergent rhetorical devices to argue for the section's tight structure—a structure that gives it a meaningful overall effect.[135] But it is a mistake to think that we can base the cohesion of some stories or linguistic expressions only on the syntactic structure and lexial items used in them. Rather we must take into consideration the hearer's cognitive effort to interpret in a coherent way what is heard.[136] Unbalanced claims by scholars in relation to the coherent connection of five stories in 2.1–3.6 should consequently be supplemented. The argument is that it is, along with the use of overt linguistic connections, by the hearer's cognitive frame that the coherent interpretation of the meaning intended in 2.1–3.6 is made possible.

Third and most importantly, one of the aims of this study is to show frames' role in organizing oral-aural narrative units such as an episodic structure and a larger thematic section (see below). In fact, Mark 2.1–3.6 as a whole betrays the "cognitive processes of oral operations" in the sense that its cluster of similar material (i.e., five contro-

---

[133] Edgar V. McKnight, *What is Form Criticism* (Philadelphia: Fortress Press, 1969), pp. 21–22, 25–28; E.P. Sanders and Margaret Davies, *Studying the Synoptic Gospels* (London: SCM; Philadelphia: Trinity Press International, 1989), pp. 148–62.

[134] See, for example, Vincent Taylor, *The Gospel According to St. Mark* (London: Macmillan, 1966), pp. 91–92; Robert Tannehill, "The Pronouncements Story," *Semeia* 20 (1981), pp. 1–13.

[135] Dewey, *Markan Public Debate*.

[136] Gillian Brown and George Yule, *Discourse Analysis* (Cambridge: Cambridge University Press, 1983), pp. 223–25.

versy stories) corresponds to the oral mind of associative thinking.[137]
The argument is that the larger thematic unit and the five episodic
structures within it are not very different from the characteristics of
frame-based story processing. Accordingly, I believe that 2.1–3.6 may
provide us with an instructive test case as to how hearers process not
only each episode but also a thematic cluster of similar episodes in an
oral-aural narrative in terms of frames.

This study is concerned generally with showing ways in which the
hearer recognizes frames and draws on them in the process of coming
to an understanding of what is heard. In doing so, the focal point of
this study falls on demonstrating two things: First, frames enable the
hearer to process the organizational structures that are present in the
oral-aural narrative (i.e., how the text says what it says); second, frames
serve the hearer's comprehension of information which the structures
represent (i.e., what the text says). Though the presence of the speaker
is implicit in the assumption that the Gospel of Mark is organized by
way of facilitating frames, the role of the speaker is outside the scope
of this study for the most part.

Our approach is cognitive in its analysis of those processes by which
Mark's oral-aural narrative comes to be understood by the audience.
This study is divided into two parts. The chief purpose of the chapters
in Part One of this study is to explore the notion that, as an oral-aural
narrative, Mark's Gospel is a frame-based story and has the specific
properties of frames. Thus, Chapter Two will survey the communication environments of the Gospel of Mark, and in particular in their
relation to the status of the written text, and will test a basic statement of this study that, though being written, the Gospel of Mark
is an oral-aural narrative intended to be stored in and remembered
from memory, not simply to be read from the written document.
And then Chapter Three will show that a frame, as a human memory
or cognitive system, plays a crucial role in the processing of the Markan oral-aural narrative. To support this argument it will be demonstrated that many of the features of orality underlying the Gospel (oral
memory and "oral expressions and thoughts," to use Ong's words)
share some common ground with the properties of frames characterized by cognitive linguistics and psychology. Chapter Four will introduce the structuring principles of frames, several types of frames, and

---

[137] Kelber, *Gospel*, p. 78.

the properties of frame-based information processing, which are all relevant to understanding the cognitive aspects of the structure, comprehension, and remembering of the Markan oral-aural narrative.

Part Two of this study is concerned with the specific application of frame theory to the investigation of Mark's Controversy Stories (2.1–3.6) on the theoretical grounds laid down in Part One. Chapter Five will focus on demonstrating the argument that frames help the audience identify such discourse units as a thematic unit, paragraphs or episodes, and sentences in Mark 2.1–3.6, arguing that frames may facilitate the organization of narrative into conceptually (or semantically) consistent chunks. Chapter Six will concentrate on exploring the specific ways in which the audience recognizes frames and makes use of them in the process of coming to an understanding of stories in Mark 2.1–3.6. In doing so, my concern is to show that Mark 2.1–3.6 is background knowledge or frame-based story and that frames were the cognitive models used to readily and quickly process and understand the Gospel in an oral and aural communicative situation. In Chapter Seven, this study will be concluded.

PART ONE

ORAL-AURAL COMMUNICATION AND FRAMES

CHAPTER TWO

MARK'S WRITTEN GOSPEL, ORALITY-AURALITY, AND MEMORY

The present chapter will test the statement that the Gospel of Mark is an oral-aural narrative intended to be stored in and remembered from memory. We will begin by surveying the communicative environments of Mark's written Gospel, clarifying the relationship of the writtenness and orality-aurality of Mark's Gospel. Then we will survey how human memory played a vital role in that environment.

A. Mark's Written Text in Ancient Orality-Aurality

Since the Gospel of Mark is in the form of a written document, in order to know the communicative nature of the Gospel, a closer examination is necessary of the relationship of orality and literacy and the use of written documents in antiquity. The four canonical Gospels were committed into writing between around 35–70 years after the crucifixion and resurrection of Jesus. It has been commonly believed that the traditions of the synoptic Gospels underwent a period of oral tradition or transmission before being written down.[1] If so, does the conversion of the oral tradition into written texts mean a transition from the orality[2] of the Gospels to its literacy?[3] Were orality and literacy incompatible in the first century world? The position of incompatibility of orality and literacy is advocated by Werner Kelber[4] and Barry

---

[1] Werner G. Kümmel, *Introduction to the New Testament* (trans. Howard C. Kee; Nashville: Abingdon, 1973), p. 47; Sanders and Davies, *Synoptic Gospels*, p. 141.

[2] In the present study orality is used as the term for representing spoken words.

[3] Likewise, this issue is related to the nature of the pre-Gospel tradition. Whether the pre-Gospel tradition is oral or literary has been a subject of debate among New Testament scholars. Thus, G. Widengren, "Tradition and Literature in Early Judaism and in the Early Church," *Numen* 10 (1963), pp. 42–83, argues against form criticism's assumption of oral transmission and Gerhardsson's one of textual transmission, saying that we do not know whether Jewish or Christian tradition was passed on orally or in writing. However, this issue may be resolved when we, as will be discussed below, keep in mind that ancient written texts were subject to oral communication.

[4] Kelber, *Gospel,* pp. 44–80, 90–93.

Henaut.[5] Henaut, though arguing in favour of the interplay of the oral and the written in pre-Gospel sources, makes a claim that the orality of the present Gospel is lost in the "language of textuality" made by the evangelist's redaction.[6] In particular, Kelber, in his book, *The Oral and Written Gospel*, discusses oral tradition and its relationship to Mark's written Gospel. Kelber discards both Bultmann's "evolutionary progression" and Gerhardsson's "passive transmission" as a model for the transmission of synoptic oral traditions[7] Instead, he argues for a model of radical disruption: Being written down, Mark's writing project has brought about "[the] disruption of the oral lifeworld, [and] the textually induced eclipse of voices and sound."[8] For Kelber, thus, it is misleading to think that Mark's Gospel is an oral-aural narrative, but rather the Gospel should be understood as evidence of a new textuality arising "out of the debris of deconstructed orality."[9] Such a view of Mark's written Gospel is fundamentally based on an assumption

---

[5] Barry W. Henaut, *Oral Tradition and the Gospels: The Problem of Mark 4* (JSNT-Sup 82; Sheffield: JSOT Press, 1993).

[6] Henaut, *Oral Tradition*, pp. 14, 115–16.

[7] Kelber, *Gospel*, pp. 1–43.

[8] Kelber, *Gospel*, p. 91. He goes on to argue that Mark's textualizing of the traditions is directed "against the prevailing authorities of oral transmission" (p. 130). Kelber's view is constantly criticised by many scholars for good reasons. For example, see, Anthony C. Thiselton, *New Horizons in Hermeneutics: The Theory and Practice of Transforming Biblical Reading* (Grand Rapids, Michigan: Zondervan, 1992), pp. 70–75 and Dunn, *Jesus*, pp. 199–204.

[9] Kelber, *Gospel*, p. 96. Kelber, "Jesus and Tradition: Words in Time, Words in Space," *Semeia* 65 (1995), pp. 139–67, seems to refer to the Gospel of Mark's use of oral performance in terms of "secondary orality," though only very briefly. For Kelber, *Gospel*, pp. 217–18, "primary orality" is oral forms in the pre-literary gospels which are diluted by the textuality of Mark's Gospel, so faintly left in it; and "secondary orality" functioned when the Gospel of Mark was read and heard by the audiences in the performance situation. But the problem with Kelber's such a distinction between "primary orality" and "secondary orality" is that, as Tolbert, *Sowing the Gospel*, p. 45 note 36, rightly notes, Mark's "oral legacy," that is, "primary orality," is in fact in accordance with a number of the rules of oral communication in rhetorical handbooks, that is, "secondary orality." For example, repetition with many variations that Kelber cites (*Gospel*, pp. 45–46, 67–68) occurs in *Ad Herennium* 4.42.54. This makes it impossible to divide the orality of Mark's Gospel into such categories as "primary" and "secondary." Above all, by admitting that ancient texts underwent "secondary orality", Kelber weakens his thesis somewhat regarding a radical disruption between oral and written. Other than his brief reference to oral performance, Kelber fails to seriously take into account the impact oral performance may have had on the composition of the Gospel of Mark. Consequently, given the performance situation of the first-century Mediterranean world, Kelber's argument (*Gospel*, p. 44) that by the writing act of Mark "the objectifying, controlling power of the written medium...can freeze oral forms and preserve them in fossilized profiles" is hardly possible.

of a great divide between orality and writtenness in first-century culture. But, in contrast to that assumption, the observations to follow will demonstrate that in the first century Mediterranean world, orality and literacy were never mutually exclusive but rather inseparably interconnected.

1. *The Communicative Environment of Mark's Written Gospel: Rhetorical Culture*

When we study a model of the communicative nature of the Gospel of Mark, serious consideration must be given to the first-century rhetorical culture in which Mark's written Gospel was born. Kelber sees that the first-century Mediterranean world was in a transitional culture from oral to manuscript or literate culture. It must be pointed out, first of all, that Kelber's view of the manuscript culture of the first century, which leads him to be in favour of "Markan textuality" as a radical departure from "Markan orality,"[10] is affected by that of a modern western print culture. Quintilian, a rhetorician of the first century, says, "It is one and the same thing to speak well and to write well: and a written speech is merely the record of a delivered speech."[11] Quintilian's point is that it is not possible to differentiate written speech from delivered speech, provided writing is entirely at the service of speaking in oral performance.[12] Besides, Vernon Robbins rightly rejects a theory of a direct shift from oral to manuscript culture, pointing out the fact that there was a rhetorical culture between the oral culture and scribal culture.[13] Identifying four different types of communicative cultures, that is, oral culture, rhetorical culture, scribal culture and print culture, Robbins says:

> The phrase 'oral culture' should be used for those environments where written literature is not in view. The phrase 'rhetorical culture', in contrast, should refer to environments where oral and written speech interact closely with one another. It would be best to limit 'scribal culture'

---

[10] Kelber, *Gospel*, pp. 17, 90–91.

[11] Quintilian, *Institutio oratoria* 12.10.51 (LCL; trans. Donald A. Russell; Cambridge, Massachusetts: Harvard University Press, 1921).

[12] See also Quintilian, *Institutio oratoria* 10.7.29: "writing will give us greater precision of speech, while speaking will make us write with greater facility."

[13] Vernon K. Robbins, "Writing as a Rhetorical Act in Plutarch and the Gospels," in *Persuasive Artistry. Studies in New Testament Rhetoric in Honor of George A. Kennedy* (ed. D.F. Watson; JSNTSup 50; Sheffield: JSOT Press, 1991), p. 145.

to those environments where a primary goal is to 'copy' either oralstate-
ments or written texts.[14]

The world in which the Gospels were written, according to Robbins,
was a rhetorical culture in which "writing...imitates both speech and
writing, and speech...imitates both speech and writing."[15] Robbins
provides a brilliant explanation about how such a close interaction of
orality and textuality took place in practice. For Robbins the hand copying or writing of the first-century Mediterranean world, which may be
related to the evangelist's redactional activities, can be best explained
in *progymnastic* composition (Elementary Exercises) in rhetoric. One
of the most important features of Hellenistic progymnastic practice
is recitation composition based on oral culture;[16] a teacher recited a
fable, anecdote, event, or saying in his own words to students and then
the students wrote brief units in their own words, and in recitation
composition the students recast the material by adding to it, subtract-
ing from it, rearranging it, and rewording it.[17] This recitation exercise
made it possible for the copying act to go beyond verbatim reproduction to rhetorical writings with many variations.[18]

Such a rhetorical culture and progymnastic composition, consequently, can lead us to make the arguments that such a radical gulf
between writing and speaking had never occurred in the first-century
Mediterranean world and that, contrary to Henaut's argument, the
evangelist's editorial work also reflected spoken words.

2. Production and Circulation of Ancient Written Texts and Mark's Gospel

Dictation was the normal mode used by the ancients to compose any
text.[19] In ancient Rome the elites usually dictated their official notes,
memoirs, reports and letters: Cicero, who usually had the assistance
of Tiro his secretary when he wrote letters, says in a letter to Atticus

---

[14] Robbins, "Writing as a Rhetorical Act," p. 145 and see also *idem*, "Oral, Rhetorical, and Literary Cultures: A Response," *Semeia* 65 (1995), pp. 77–82.

[15] Robbins, "Literary Cultures," p. 80 and see also Ong, "Text," pp. 16–25.

[16] Duane F. Watson and Alan J. Hauser, *Rhetorical Criticism of The Bible: A Comprehensive Bibliography with Notes on History and Method* (Leiden: E.J. Brill, 1994),
pp. 117–18.

[17] Robbins, "Writing as a Rhetorical Act," pp. 147–48.

[18] Robbins, "Writing as a Rhetorical Act," pp. 146–47.

[19] William Harris, *Ancient Literacy* (Cambridge, Massachusetts; London: Harvard
University Press, 1989), p. 36; Rosaland Thomas, *Literacy and Orality in Ancient
Greece* (Cambridge: Cambridge University Press, 1992), p. 91.

that he dictated two letters to him and sent one in his own hand the day before.[20] Pliny states that Julius Caesar used to dictate to his secretaries four letters at once on important matters, or seven letters simultaneously,[21] and Pliny mentions that he also composed his text mentally, memorized it overnight, and then dictated it the following morning.[22] Dictation was preferred by Dio Chrysostom to writing in his own hand.[23] In addition to the works of such literary men, dictation was frequently employed among the general public as well. In their research on a great number of non-literary Greek papyri dating principally from the Ptolemaic and Roman periods of Egyptian history, Adolf Deissmann, Gordon Bahr, and Richard Longenecker demonstrate that use of an amanuensis (i.e., use of dictation) was the common pattern of writing in the years before, during, and after the first Christian century.[24] The evidence is abundant.[25] Here is one example suggested by Deissmann, which is a letter from Thebes in the Ptolemaic period: This letter concludes with the words, "Written for him hath Eumelus the son of Herma…being desired so to do for that he writes somewhat slowly."[26] The concluding words clearly indicate that his letters were written to order by an amanuensis. Reasons for such a dictation of papyrus letters are the sender's illiteracy, slow or poor handwriting, physical disabilities, or the difficulty of obtaining the necessary materials for writing.[27]

---

[20] Cicero, *Epistulae ad Atticumi*, 10.3a.1 (LCL; trans, E.O. Winstedt; Cambridge: Harvard University Press, 1919). And on Cicero's employment of his secretary, Tiro, see also Gordon J. Bahr, "Paul and Letter Writing in the First Century," *CBQ* 28 (1966), pp. 469–70.

[21] Pliny, *Natural History* 7.25.91b (LCL; trans. H. Rackham; Cambridge, Massachusetts: Harvard University Press). And also Plutarch, *Caesar* 17.3b (LCL; trans. Bernadotte Perrin; Cambridge, Massachusetts: Harvard University Press, 1919).

[22] Henri-Jean Martin, *The History and Power of Writing* (trans. Lydia G. Cochrane; Chicago and London: The University of Chicago Press, 1994), p. 70.

[23] Dio Chrysostom, *Orations* 18.18 (LCL; trans. J.W. Cohoon; London: Heinemann, 1932).

[24] Adolf Deissmann, *Light from the Ancient East* (London: Hodder and Stoughton, 1927), pp. 166, 170–71, 172 note 2, 236–42; Bahr, "Paul," pp. 465–77; *idem*, "The Subscriptions in the Pauline Letters," *JBL* 87 (1968), pp. 27–41; Richard. N. Longenecker, "Ancient Amanuenses and the Pauline Epistles," in *New Dimensions in New Testament Study* (ed. R.N. Longenecker and M.C. Tenney; Grand Rapids, Michigan: Zondervan, 1974), pp. 281–97.

[25] In particular, on valuable and specific materials, see Longenecker, "Ancient Amanuenses," pp. 281–88.

[26] Deissmann, *Light*, pp. 166–67. The translation is from Deissmann.

[27] Longenecker, "Ancient Amanuenses," pp. 287–88; Bahr, "Paul," p. 469.

This habit of dictation, therefore, provides additional evidence that ancient writing reflected spoken words.[28] Of course, this is not to say that there was no writing in one's own hand.[29] But this does not bring any light to our present argument because the words were generally spoken as they were being written whether by authors themselves or by scribes.[30] In other words, since it was ancient authors's basic assumption that what they were writing would be read aloud,[31] a certain mode of writing must have been utilized to accommodate the ear

---

[28] Nonetheless, Kelber, "Orality, Rhetoric, and Scribality," *Semeia* 65 (1994), p. 207, asserts, "Dictation…was bound to slow down speech and to affect thought processes… [thus] was…discourse adjusted to the writing process." But two things must be mentioned against Kelber's assertion. One is that the use of Greek shorthand probably can compensate for the slowness of taking dictation. While systems of Latin shorthand have evidence for showing its first-century invention by Cicero, it is difficult to say with certainty the birth of Greek shorthand. But Bahr, "Paul," pp. 473–74, suggests that, though the oldest certain proof for the existence of Greek shorthand is P. Oxy. VI 724, "the existence of a workable system of Greek shorthand presupposes a period of development prior to the date of earliest document," that is, "probable to the first century;" what is more, evidence shows that "some kind of Greek shorthand has its origin in the fourth century B.C.E. On evidence, see Bahr, "Paul," p. 474. More importantly, the other is that it is possible to say that dictation, due to the general habit of slow note-taking, reflects the writing process; nonetheless, the fact, as mentioned above, that any ancient text was a product of an author's self-conscious composition of his or her work for the purpose of reading aloud before the listening audience, not the reading reader, leads to the argument that such an oral-aural environment played a decisive role in forming the stylistic features of writing the text and Mark's Gospel.

[29] Quintilian, *Institutio oratoria* 10.3.31, declared himself opposed to dictation. And Cicero, *Epistulae ad Atticum* 15.20.4, tells us that he thought he should write the particular letter discussing personal matters and making comment on the emperor in his own hand. And the Greek papyri discovered in Egypt also quite clearly indicate that not all letters were written by an amanuensis—particularly when sent among family members and where the contents were of more private or informal nature. For the latter, see Longenecker, "Ancient Amanuenses," p. 287.

[30] Gerhardsson, *Memory and Manuscript*, p. 47; Paul J. Achtemeier, "*Omne Verbum Sonat*: The New Testament and the Oral Environment of Late Western Antiquity," *JBL* 109 (1990), p. 15. In his book, *Books and Readers in the Early Church: A History of Early Christian Texts* (New Haven and London: Yale University Press, 1995), pp. 203–204, Harry Y. Gamble is quite right when he attempts to find the reason for reading aloud when dictating or writing in one's own hand in the character, "continuous script," of ancient texts—no division between words, sentences, or paragraphs, and no punctuation: "The relentless march of characters across the lines and down the columns required the reader to deconstruct the text into its discrete verbal and syntactical components. The best way to decipher a text written in this way was phonetic: sounding the syllables as they were seen and organizing them as much by hearing as by sight into a pattern of meaning."

[31] On silent reading in antiquity, see Frank D. Gilliard, "More Silent Reading in Antiquity: *Non omne verbum sonat*," *JBL* 112 (1993), pp. 689–96; A.K. Gavrilov, "Techniques of Reading in Classical Antiquity," *CQ* 47 (1997), pp. 56–73.

of the listening audience.[32] William Stanford, who has written a mono-graph on Greek euphony, says that "an ancient Greek or Roman had to pronounce each syllable before he could understand a written word. The written letters informed his voice; then his voice informed his ear; and finally his ear, together with the muscular movements of his vocal organs, conveyed the message to his brain."[33] It is by no means an exaggeration to say, therefore, that "the oral environment was so pervasive that no writing occurred that was not vocalized."[34]

How was Mark's Gospel then produced and circulated? It hardly seems easy to definitely answer this question, given the lack of evidence for the early Christian life of the first century. However, several frag-mentary materials from the early church provide a clue to the produc-tion of Mark's Gospel. The earliest piece of evidence much disputed by modern scholars that needs to be considered for the oral origin of the Gospel of Mark is the testimony from Papias (ca. 60–130), the Bishop of Hierapolis in Asia Minor. A passage from his lost book, *Interpre-tation of the Lord's Oracles*, dating about 101–108 C.E. is quoted by Eusebius in the fourth century:

> And the Presbyter used to say this, 'Mark became Peter's interpreter and wrote accurately all that he remembered, not, indeed, in order, of the things said or done by the Lord. For he had not heard the Lord, nor had he followed him, but later on, as I said, followed Peter, who used to give teaching as necessity demanded but not making, as it were, an arrangement of the Lord's oracles, so that Mark did nothing wrong in thus writing down single points as he remembered them. For to one thing he gave attention, to leave out nothing of what he had heard and to make no false statements in them.'[35]

---

[32] Gamble, *Books*, p. 204.

[33] W.B. Stanford, *The Sound of Greek: Studies in the Greek Theory and Practice of Euphony* (Berkeley and Los Angeles: University of California Press, 1967), p. 1.

[34] Achtemeier, "*Omne* Verbum Sonat," p. 15. It is on this basis that Kelber's asser-tion of "the textually induced eclipse of voices and sound" caused by "Mark's writing project" must be criticized. On those terms, see Kelber, *Gospel*, p. 91. In presuming the modern and Western readers' experience of silent reading, Kelber fails to take seriously the situation of oral performance of the ancient texts in which sound and voice were invariably present. This is one of the criticisms Tolbert levels against Kel-ber in *Sowing*, p. 45 note 36, and see also Achtemeier, "*Omne Verbum sonat*," p. 15 note 87.

[35] Eusebius, *Ecclesiastical History* 3.39.15 (LCL; trans, Kirsopp Lake; Cambridge, Massachusetts: Harvard University Press, 1965).

Before using this source as evidence it is necessary to discuss the much debated issue of the reliability of Papias's testimony. Many modern scholars have dismissed the reliability of the tradition from Papias primarily because they believe it was formulated to vindicate the apostolicity of Mark's Gospel.[36] Yet what is to be noted is that Papias's claim to apostolicity for the second Gospel is indirectly made through Peter rather than directly through Mark himself. The question is that if Papias wished to defend the apostolicity of Mark's Gospel, why did he not directly appeal to apostolic authorship just as the *Gospel of Thomas* and *Gospel of Peter* did, instead of fabricating the relationship between Mark and Peter?[37]

Besides, what must be considered is the status of Mark in the Gospels and in the early church. The Gospels make no reference to Mark at all and other New Testament writings also do not include "credentials to commend the name of Mark to the early church"; he was not an apostle and eyewitness to Jesus' ministry (Acts 12.12, 25; 13.5, 13; 15.37, 39; Colossians 4.10).[38] Unless such a Peter-Mark connection as described by Papias did reflect the general agreement accepted by the early church, accordingly, it hardly makes sense that Papias would choose that route as an apologetic defence of the Gospel. Of course, a question about the identification of Mark can be raised. Given that Mark was an extremely common name in the first century, no one can say with certainty who it is that Papias is referring to. A possible explanation for this, instead, is that Papias and many other Fathers directly identify Mark in 1 Peter 5.13 as the author of Mark's Gospel.[39]

---

[36] Piether J.J. Botha, "The Historical Setting of Mark's Gospel: Problems and Possibilities," *JSNT* 51 (1993), pp. 36–37; Joel Marcus, *Mark 1–8* (AB 27; Doubleday: New York, 1999), pp. 22–24; cf. Kümmel, *New Testament*, pp. 96–98.

[37] Lee Martin McDonald and Stanley E. Porter, *Early Christianity and Its Sacred Literature* (Peabody, Massachusetts: Hendrickson, 2000), p. 287.

[38] McDonald and Porter, *Early Christianity*, p. 287. Mark's relation to an apostle, Paul, was broken off as he decided to leave the missionary group (Acts 13.5, 13; 15.39). But later Mark was restored to Paul's favour (Colossians 4.10), but some wording from Paul was needed for him to be received, "if he comes to you, receive him." This means, "Mark was perhaps only slowly winning back his reputation in the Pauline churches," though he is finally commended as "very useful in serving me" (2 Timothy 4.11). For the picture of Mark in the early church, see Ralph Martin, *Mark. Evangelist and Theologian* (Grand Rapids, Michigan: Zondervan, 1973), pp. 53–54, esp. 53; *idem*, "Mark, John," in *The International Standard Bible Encyclopedia*. Vol. 3 (ed. Geoffrey W. Bromiley: Grand Rapids, Michigan: Eerdmans, 1986), pp. 259–60.

[39] Eusebius, *Ecclesiastical History* 2.15.1–2; 3.39.15; 6.25.5. And also, see Justin Martyr, *Dialogue with Trypho* 106.3; Clement of Alexandria, *Adumbrationes ad I Petr.* 5.13; Origen, *Commentary on Matthew* 1.

And, as Ralph Martin argues, the picture of Mark in New Testament writings (Acts 12.12, 25; 13.5, 13; 15.37, 39; Colossians 4.10; 2 Timothy 4.11; Philemon 24; 1 Peter 5.13) is a very consistent one, so it is not unreasonable to believe that they all refer to the same person.[40] What Papias primarily attempts to argue here, in fact, is not the apostolicity of Mark's Gospel itself, but the Gospel's lack of "order." He explains it on the basis of the sort of material available to Mark, which originated in Peter's oral preaching and teaching adapted to the needs of the hearers.[41] Peter in Papias's testimony is described as the reason for the lack of a sophisticated literary structure in Mark's Gospel. Hence it is hard to think that Papias fabricates the Petrine origin of Mark for such a disgraceful reason, particularly given the fact that Peter was a highly respected apostle in the early church. Not to mention, admitting that Papias has an apologetic tone cannot directly mean that he is lying.

Joel Marcus turns his attention to the intrinsic traits of Mark's Gospel to disprove its Petrine origin.[42] Marcus says, "Mark does not give the impression of being any closer to the events he describes than are Matthew and Luke, the later evangelists who appropriated his work," and thus it cannot be from eyewitness testimony.[43] A similar assumption was already made by Dennis Nineham more than a decade earlier to the effect that "if the organization of the material and the connexions between the incidents in Mark are theological in basis and intention, then they do not need the activity of eye-witnesses to explain them."[44] Certainly it is too simple to say that the Gospel of Mark consists of

---

[40] Ralph P. Martin, *Mark. Evangelist and Theologian* (Grand Rapid, Michigan: Zondervan, 1973), pp. 53–54. The argument that Mark in 1 Peter and in Acts is the same person can be also made by the fact that just as 1 Peter 5.12–13 links Mark with Silvanus in Rome, so Acts 15.22–40 describes Mark as a companion of Silvanus. See John H. Elliott, *1 Peter* (AB 37b; New York: Doubleday, 2001), pp. 887–88. We can infer that Mark apparently had joined Paul later, when he was in prison, possibly in Rome (Colossians 4.10; Philemon 24; 2 Timothy 4.11). And Mark's activity in Rome, as implied in 1 Peter 5.13, may have allowed him to have an opportunity to contact Peter toward the ending period of the apostle's life.

[41] Benjamin W. Bacon, *The Gospel of Mark: Its Composition and Date* (New Haven: Yale University Press, 1925), pp. 28–29; R.T. France, *The Gospel of Mark: A Commentary on the Greek Text* (Grand Rapids, Michigan: Eerdmans, 2002), p. 8; Martin Hengel, *Studies in the Gospel of Mark* (London: SCM, 1984), p. 49.

[42] Marcus, *Mark 1–8*, pp. 23–24; and see also Hugh Anderson, *The Gospel of Mark* (NCBC; Oliphants: London, 1976), pp. 16–18.

[43] Marcus, *Mark 1–8*, pp. 23–24.

[44] Dennis Nineham, "Eye-Witness Testimony and the Gospel Tradition," *JTS* 9 (1958), p. 24.

only Peter's living oral teaching, excluding the possibility that Mark also knew other traditions, whether oral or written, and would have composed his Gospel using them. The second Gospel, in fact, has not only many stories where Peter and the other disciples are not present (e.g., Mark 1.16–20 before their call; 14.43–52 after Jesus' arrest) but also "the rounded, stereotyped form of the Markan stories" which indicate Mark's own redaction.[45] We must, first of all, guard against assuming too easily that Peter had to preach only what he witnessed; rather it is not unreasonable to believe that his preaching could have included divergent stories he had heard from other witnesses or people. Next, Marcus and Nineham misunderstand the ancient historians' use of eyewitness testimony. For them eyewitness testimony means a report of objective fact or of events which have occurred in the past. However, this is not based on the ancients' view of eyewitness testimony. The ancient historians, as Samuel Byrskog argues, regarded "the oral history of an eyewitness" as consisting of "the complex interplay between historical truth and interpreted truth on all levels of tradition and transmission, from the eyewitness's involvement in the event to the final story."[46]

Since there is no compelling cause for doubting Papias's information, we need to take seriously his testimony about the Peter-Mark connection. Although many issues are connected with the Papian testimony, the primary concern of the present study is about the oral origin of Mark's Gospel stemming from the relationship of Peter and Mark. Papias, as pointed out, is here apologizing for the (chronological) disarrangement (οὐ μέντοι τάξει) of Mark's Gospel, and he believes that Mark's relationship with Peter will account for the defect. He therefore proceeds to say that Mark "followed" (παρηκολούθησεν) Peter as his "interpreter" (ἑρμηνευτὴς) who adapted his oral teaching to the needs of the hearer. Papias further stresses that Mark had heard Peter giving oral teachings and hence was capable of writing his Gospel "remembering" (ἀπεμνημόνευσεν) "accurately" the teachings. An important point can be made here on the basis of the tradition from Papias: The production of the Gospel of Mark is based on Mark's "memoirs" or

---

[45] Marcus, *Mark 1–8*, p. 23.
[46] Samuel Byrskog, *Story as History-History as Story: The Gospel Tradition in the Context of Ancient Oral History* (Boston: Brill, 2002), pp. 274–75; and also see Bauckham, *Eyewitnesses*, pp. 12–38, 319–58.

"notes" of Peter's oral preaching.[47] Such notes, as Barton points out, were used in antiquity as an "*aide-mémoire*: The substance of them is meant to be transmitted by word of mouth and memorized."[48] A view of the Gospel as memoirs or notes was consistently shared by some Fathers of the second century.[49] Explaining the common practice of his contemporary church worship, for example, Justin says that at the beginning of the service memoirs (ἀπομνημονεύματα) of the apostles, or the writings of the prophets were read.[50] No doubt by "memoirs" Justin apparently had the Gospels in mind (see below).

Importantly, there are a few ancient parallels for the production of the Gospel of Mark based on Mark's memoranda or notes of oral teaching.[51] One parallel can be taken from Quintilian, who shows how oral teachings or lectures in antiquity became a significant source of book production, both with and without their authors' consent. Quintilian says:

> Two books on the Art of Rhetoric are already circulating in my name, though they were never published by me nor prepared for this purpose. One is a two days' lecture course which was taken down by the slaves to whom the responsibility was given. The other lecture course, which spread over several days, was taken down by shorthand (as best they

---

[47] David Aune, *The New Testament in Its Literary Environment* (Philadelphia: Westminster Press, 1987), pp. 66–67, states that, the term ἀπομνημονεύματα is not only a reference to informal records of a philosopher, such as expanded *chreiai*, but also roughly synonymous with ὑπομνήματα, "notes." For the example of the use of "note-books" and "memoranda" as an aid to oral presentation, see Quintilian, *Institutio oratoria* 10.7.30–31.

[48] John Barton, *Holy Writings Sacred Text: The Canon in Early Christianity* (Louisville, Kentucky, WJK, 1997), p. 85.

[49] In addition to Justin Martyr to follow, for other examples, see Clement of Alexandria, *To Theodore* 1.20. Clement says that Mark composed his Gospel on the basis of his ὑπομνήματα (= ἀπομνημονεύματα), "notes." Cf. Eusebius, *Ecclesiastical History* 2.15, who understood the Gospel of Mark itself as ὑπομνήματα.

[50] Justin Martyr, *Apology* 1.67 (The Father of Church; trans. Thomas B. Falls; New York: Christian Heritage, 1948). For Justin's use of ἀπομνημονεύματα for the Gospels, see also *idem*, *Dialogue with Trypho*, 100.4; 101.3; 103.6, 8; 104.1; 105.1, 5, 6; 106.1, 4; 107.1 (trans. Williams A. Lukyn; London: Society for Promoting Christian Knowledge; New York: Macmillan, 1930).

[51] On the divergent ways for the book of the Greco-Roman world to be released or made public, see Raymond J. Starr, "Circulation of Literary Texts," *CQ* 37 (1987), pp. 213–16, who asserts five channels of book production and circulation: first, an author gives a gift copy to a friend; second, authors "recite the work to friends and allow them to have copies made"; third, he could deposit a copy in a public library, so that anyone in the public could copy it freely; fourth, an author asks his friend to make the book known; fifth, an author could send a copy to a bookdealer.

could) by some excellent young men who were nevertheless too fond of me, and therefore rashly honoured it with with publication and wide circulation. In the present work, therefore, there will be some things the same, many things changed, and very many things added, and the whole will be better written and worked up to the best of my ability.[52]

Quintilian tells that two similar versions to the present book were already circulating in his name among the people. He makes it clear that they were never published by him but by the auditors who took down his lectures. Furthermore, he indicates that the versions were more or less altered by them, and thus his present book is distinguished from them in that he has brought in additions and changes anew. Here is another example from the learned physician Galen, an approximate contemporary of Papias:

> As for the reason why many read my books as their own, this you know yourself, most excellent Bassus; for they were given to friends or pupils without an inscription (*choris epigraphes*), simply because they were not for publication but were done for those very people as they requested memoranda of what they had heard. Then when some died, anyone who got hold of the books and liked them took to reading them as their own..., [lacuna]..., [while others shared them with friends, who then] went home to their own country and after some delay, one in one place, one in another, started to perform their own demonstration [or: lectures] from them. In time they were all detected and a number of people inscribed my name on the texts which had once again been recovered; but when they discovered that they were different from the texts held by others they brought them to me and begged me to correct them.
>
> Now since, as I said, they had not been written for publication but according to the particular state and need of those who had requested them, it was only to be expected that some would have been expanded and others shortened, and that the explanation and the very teaching of the theorems would be complete in some cases and deficient in others. Particularly in the case of those that were written down from oral teaching, it was obvious that they would not have the instruction in a complete or accurate form, given that they neither wanted nor were able to leave everything learn everything accurately, before acquiring some practice in the essentials. Some of my predecessors called this type of book 'outlines,' just as some call them 'sketches' or 'introductions' or 'synopses' or 'guides.' I just used to give them to my students without

---

[52] Quintilian, *Quintilian* 1. preface 7–8 and also cited by Loveday Alexander, "Ancient Book Production and the Circulation of the Gospels," *The Gospels for All Christians: Rethinking the Gospel Audiences* (ed. Richard Bauckham; Grand Rapids, Michigan: Eerdmans, 1998), pp. 94–95.

any inscription (*choris epigraphes*), and thus later as they came into the hands of others, one gave them one title, one another.[53]

As Galen explains, it was the books given to his friends and pupils without his inscription that were often subject to mistreatments such as addition, omission, and expansion. Galen says those books were not for publication but were memoranda or notes written down from his oral teachings. Once the notes came into his auditors' hands, as Galen puts it, they started being freely performed in their name and widely circulated with many changes. Thus, it is apparent from the cases of Quintilian and Galen that Mark's use of notes or memoranda of oral presentation, such as noted by Papias, reflects one important model of book production and circulation in the ancient world.[54] If so, it is not unreasonable to believe that the Gospel of Mark, as Papias says, is the one that Mark committed to writing for oral teachings, and it that would have been adapted to the needs of his oral performance and particular context.

3. *The Use of Ancient Written Texts and Mark's Gospel*

Though it is not true that silent reading did not exist, it is undeniable that reading aloud was the most commonly practised approach to literary works.[55] For example, the author of *On the Sublime* keeps

---

[53] Galen, *De libris propriis* proem (Kühn XIV. 8–11 = *Scripta Minora* II. 91–93), cited and translated by Alexander, "Ancient Book," pp. 96–97.

[54] Loveday Alexander, "The Living Voice: Scepticism towards the Written Word in Early Christian and in Graeco-Roman Texts," in *The Bible in Three Dimensions. Essays in Celebration of Forty Years of Biblical Studies in the University of Sheffield* (ed. David J.A. Clines, Stephen E. Fowl and Stanley E. Porter; JSOTSup, 87; Sheffield: JSOT Press, 1990), pp. 94–97.

[55] In fact, in classical and medieval studies the recognition of public reading as the delivery medium of the relevant literature in the classical and medieval period becomes virtually commonplace. Note medieval literature is much later than biblical literature. For the classicists' arguments regarding this, see George L. Hendrickson, "Ancient Reading," *CJ* 25 (1929–30), pp. 182–96; Eugene S. McCartney, "Notes on Reading and Praying Audibly," *CLAP* 43 (1948), pp. 184–87; H. Van Dyke Parunak, "Oral Typesetting: Some Uses of Biblical Structure," *Biblica* 62 (1981), pp. 153–68; Walter Ong, *The Presence of the Word: Some Prolegomena for Cultural and Religious History* (New Haven and London: Yale University Press, 1967), pp. 17–58; idem, "Text as Interpretation: Mark and after," *Semeia* 39 (1987), pp. 7–26, esp. 18–19; William A. Graham, *Beyond the Written Word. Oral Aspects of Scripture in the History of Religion* (Cambridge: Cambridge University Press, 1987), pp. 33–35. And also for the arguments of the scholars of medieval literature, see Brian Stock, *Listening for the Text: On the Uses of the Past* (Baltimore: Johns Hopkins University Press, 1990); Nicholas Howe, "The Cultural Construction of Reading in Anglo-Saxon England," in

referring to the addressees of ancient literature as "hearers."[56] Quoting
the passages from Homer, Aratus, and Herodotus, Longinus explains
how to get the listener to be involved in the work: "You will make your
hearer more excited and more attentive, and full of active participation, if you keep him on the alert by words addressed to himself."[57]
Public reading was used as a dominant mode for the circulation of
books in the Greco-Roman world.[58] Tony Lentz states that the later
Greeks went through three stages for the production of their works:
Oral composition, written preservation and public reading from the
written text as a way of "publication."[59] There is also abundant evidence that public reading not only involved poetic and philosophical works but also historical works.[60] Suetonius, a Roman historian,
left a record of Augustus' enthusiasm for public reading: Augustus
would like to listen "with courtesy and patience to their readings, not
only of poetry and history, but of speeches and dialogues as well."[61]
Seneca tells that the historian Timagenes used to read his *Histories
of Augustus* aloud before the public;[62] and the historian of the early
second century B.C.E., Mnesiptolemus, according to Athenaeus, read
his *Histories* aloud as well.[63] The public reading of Christian books was
an apparent practice in Christian assemblies of the first and second

---

The Ethnography of Reading (ed. Jonathan Boyarin; Berkeley: University of California
Press, 1992), pp. 58–79; Ong, *Presence*, pp. 58–65.

[56] Longinus, *On the Sublime* 26.1–3; 15.2; 30.1 (trans. D.A. Russell; Oxford: Clarendon, 1965).

[57] Longinus, *On the Sublime* 26.3.

[58] Moses Hadas, *Ancilla to Classical Reading* (New York: Columbia University
Press, 1961), pp. 51, 60–64. And see also Harris, *Ancient Literacy*, pp. 220–29.

[59] Tony M. Lentz, *Orality and Literacy in Hellenic Greece* (Carbondale: Southern
Illinois University Press, 1989), pp. 93, 100–107.

[60] For the examples of public reading of the historical works, see Arnaldo Momigliano, "The Historians of the Classical World and Their Audiences," *AS* 47 (1977–78),
pp. 195–56.

[61] Suetonius, *The Deified Augustus* 89.3 (LCL; trans. J.C. Rolfee; London: William
Heinemann, 1913).

[62] Seneca, *On Wrath* 3.23.6 (LCL; trans. John W. Basore; Cambridge, Massachusetts: Harvard University Press, 1928): Seneca says, "He [Timagenes] gave readings
of the history which he had written...and the books which contained the doings of
Augustus Caesar he put in the fire and burned."

[63] Athenaeus, *The Deipnosophists* 10.432 B (LCL; trans. Charles B. Gulick; Cambridge, Massachusetts: Harvard University Press, 1930): Athenaeus tells, "Mnesiptolemus, at any rate, once gave a reading (ἀνάγνωσις) of his Histories, in which it was
recorded that Seleucus sprinkled barley-meal on wine."

century.[64] This is evident in Pauline literature. In 1 Thessalonians 5.27 Paul says: "I adjure you by the Lord that this letter be read to all the brethren"; and in Colossians 4.16 "…when this letter has been read among you, have it read also in the church of the Laodiceans" (RSV). These two passages show that the Pauline letters were being circulated for oral performance among early churches, and that the practice of public reading permeated the life of the early church. As Dewey points out, "Paul and his congregations lived in a largely oral media world, with minimal use of written texts or appeal to manuscript authority."[65] Paul's churches were not unique in their reliance on orality, but there is much evidence that public reading took place in the early church. Late in the first century, the author of Revelation anticipates his work to be performed orally: "Blessed is he who reads aloud (ὁ ἀναγινώσκων) the words of the prophecy, and blessed are those who hear (οἱ ἀκούοντες)" (1.3). The argument may be strengthened by evidence from the second sentury. Public or liturgical reading was so central for the writer of the Muratorian Canon (ca. 200 C.E.)[66] that it seems to have been a key test for the scripturality or apostolicity of Christians writings.[67]

---

[64] For excellent discussions of the issue, see Gamble, *Books*, pp. 82–143. It seems possible to think that this preference for an oral delivery over a written text may be explained on the basis of the idea that since the Gospel was originally communicated by Jesus Christ in a real situation, it must continue to be communicated orally rather than by written words, and this may be the case for the Gospels which, though written, must have been passed on in the "living voice" in the early church. However, though that may be the case, the oral performance of the Gospels, as observed above, must be understood primarily from the perspective of the literary form of ancient literature. See Barton, *Holy Writings*, p. 99 note 75.

[65] Joanna Dewey, "Textuality in an Oral Culture: a Survey of the Pauline Tradition," *Semeia* 69 (1995), p. 53.

[66] The Muratorian Canon has usually been dated to the late second or early third century. However Albert Sundberg and Geoffrey Hahneman have challenged in favour of a fourth-century date. See Albert C. Sundbert, "Canon Muratori: A Fourth-Century List," *HTR* 66 (1973), pp. 1–41; Geoffrey M. Hahneman, *The Muratorian Fragment and the Development of the Canon* (Oxford: Oxford University Press, 1992). But the subsequent scholarly discussions of its dating show that the earlier date must be vindicated. For the supporters of the earlier date, see Everett Ferguson, "Review of Geoffrey Mark Hahneman, The Muratorian Fragment and the Development of the Canon," *JTS* 44 (1994), pp. 691–976; Bruce M. Metzger, *The Canon of the New Testament: Its Origins, Development, and Significance* (Oxford; Clarendon, 1987), pp. 193–94; William Horbury, "The Wisdom of Solomon in the Muratorian Fragment, *JTS* 45 (1994), pp. 149–59; Charles E. Hill, "The Debate over the Muratorian Fragment and the Development of the Canon," *WTJ* 57 (1995), pp. 437–52.

[67] After explaining that the reason *Shepherd of Hermas* should be excluded by the writer of the "canon" from the list of scriptural books is because its authorship is relatively recent, the writer notes, "Therefore it must indeed be read, but cannot be

Of more importance for our present study is evidence from the Gospel of Mark itself. Is there any direct evidence that Mark's Gospel was intended and actually used to read aloud as well? In 13.14 Mark seems to leave an explicit indication that the Gospel was written to be read aloud before the listening audience: "But when you see the desolating sacrilege set up where it ought not to be (let the reader understand), then let those who are in Judea flee to the mountains" (RSV). For the present purpose it is crucial to clarify whose statement the parenthetical clause is, Jesus'or Mark's and what Mark has in mind by "the reader" (ὁ ἀναγινώσκων). First, apparently Mark 13.14 is in the middle of Jesus' apocalyptic discourse on the destruction of the temple, and thus the parenthetical clause seems part of Jesus' statement. No doubt characters within the story do not talk to "the reader" outside the story, and because in the story 13.14 echoes the same words in Daniel 11.31; 12.11. If so, it is to be seen that Jesus commands the reader of Daniel to understand the expressions in terms of his teaching. But there is a problem with this explanation. Whereas Jesus is speaking to his disciples using the second person plural, "the reader" is referred to in the third person singular imperative. And the fact that there is no reference to the written text of Daniel in Mark 13.14 (unlike Matthew 24.15) leads us to believe that "the reader" in Mark's version could not refer to the reader of Daniel. The clause could therefore not be an aside by Jesus. Rather this parenthetical comment must be Markan, just with as his other insertions in 2.10; 3.30; 7.11, 19. And the fact that the clause is referred to in the third person supports the assumption that "the reader" is Mark's insertion.

What then does Mark have in mind by the reader? At first glance, we are reminded of a private and individual reader who silently reads a book. But this is misleading. The word ἀνάγνωσις, "reading," in the ancient world, as we saw earlier, usually meant public reading or reading aloud.[68] If so, it is possible that by "reader" in the third person singular Mark refers to someone reading the Gospel aloud before an

---

publicly recited to the people in church—neither among the prophets, whose number is filled, nor among the apostles, who taught at the end of the times," cited from Hans von Campenhausen, *The Formation of the Christian Bible* (trans. J.A. Baker; Philadelphia: Fortress, 1972), p. 257. And for the relationship of canon and public reading in early church, see also Gamble, *New Testament Canon*, pp. 15–18, esp. 17.

[68] See Liddell and Scott, *Greek-English Lexicon*, αναγνωσις; ἀνάγνωσις. And this is also true of the early Fathers; see *A Patristic Greek Lexicon* (ed. G.W.H. Lampe; Oxford: Clarendon Press, 1961), ἀνάγνωσις and ἀνάγνωστης.

assembled audience.[69] Nonetheless this gives rise to a problem. Given that it is undoubtedly to the audience that Mark is focused on when communicating his whole discourse and Jesus' teaching, Mark 13 also has a specific audience in mind in his story (Peter, James, John, and Andrew, 13.3). What seems unusual is that Mark suddenly interrupts his discourse to point out how Jesus' teaching in 13.14 is extremely significant to the reader reading aloud the text before the audience rather than to the listening audience.[70] A solution can be found when we remember that a reader in antiquity often referred to "those listening to someone else performing a work of literature."[71] For example, Apuleius says at the beginning of his story, "Pay attention, reader [lector], and you will find delight."[72] When Apuleius addresses the "reader," he does not mean a private reader silently reading his novel or a public reader, but rather the one who is hearing the novel being read. This is why Apuleius can say in his prologue, "I would like...to caress your ears into approval with a pretty whisper."[73] Thus, it is in all probability that by the reader Mark denotes the audience listening to the speaker reading the Gospel aloud. Accordingly, Mark 13.14 must be used as direct evidence that Mark intended his Gospel to be read aloud before an audience,[74] and thus a transcription of an oral performance.[75]

---

[69] Tolber, *Sowing*, pp. 72–73 note 85; Fowler, *Reader*, p. 84.

[70] Many commentators ignore this problem by understanding "the reader" in Mark 13.14 in terms of the concept of a modern reader or by using interchangeably "the reader" and the listener without any explanation. For the former, see France, *Mark*, pp. 523–24 and Craig A. Evans, *Mark 8:27–16:20* (WBC 34B; Nashville: Thomas Nelson, 2001), p. 320; and for the latter, see Bas van Iersel, *Reading Mark* (trans. W.H. Bisscheroux; Collegeville, Minnesota: Liturgical Press, 1988), p. 158.

[71] Shiner, *Proclaiming the Gospel*, pp. 176–77.

[72] Apuleius, *Metamorphoses*, 1.1 (LCL; trans. J. Arthur Hanson; Cambridge, Massachusetts: Harvard University Press, 1989).

[73] Apuleius, *Metamorphoses*, 1.1.

[74] The vital role of hearing is stressed by constant repetition throughout the parables: "to hear" appears thirteen times in Mark 4.1–34. "Listen" at the beginning of Jesus' teaching in parables (4.3); "if any man (the one who) has ears to hear, let him hear" (4.9, 23) at the end of the parable of the sower and in the midst of the parable of a light under a bushel. Mark's Jesus explains what happens to four types of persons when λόγος is "heard" (4.15, 16, 18, 20). And the hearer of the parable is compelled to pay attention to what he or she "heard" (4.24). In Mark's Gospel how each group can hear the "word" plays a decisive role in dividing insiders and outsiders (4.12; 8.18). Such an emphasis on "hearing" in Mark makes perfect sense in light of the use of public reading of Mark's Gospel.

[75] Thus Walter Ong, *Rhetoric, Romance, and Technology: Studies in the Interaction of Expression and Culture* (Ithaca and London: Cornell University Press, 1971), p. 3, says, "Early written prose is more or less like a transcribed oration."

It is important to show that the Gospel of Mark was actually used for public reading in the early church. Several writings of the Fathers in the second century, which consider the present written four Gospels as authoritative Christian writings, support the idea that such a use of the Gospels was normal in the early church.[76] Justin Martyr is, apart from Papias in Eusebius's work, the first witness to acknowledge the public reading of several Gospels in the early church. Accounting for the regular Christian worship service at the time, he mentions the practice of reading the Gospels aloud: "On the day which is called Sunday we have a common assembly of all who live in the cities or in the outlying districts, and the memoirs of the Apostles or the writings of the Prophets are read, as long as there is time."[77] The "memoirs" in the *Apology*, as Abramowski notes, are used to mean the Gospels.[78] This is apparent in Justin's statement: "The Apostles in their memoirs, which are called Gospels, have handed down what Jesus ordered them to do."[79] The word "memoirs" is used here to refer to the Gospels. And what can be said with certainty is that Justin was acquainted with Mark's Gospel because he refers to a statement found only in Mark 3.16–17 and ascribes it to the memoirs of Peter. Consequently, it is evident that Mark's Gospel was read aloud in the worship service of the church early in the second century.[80]

4. *The Addressees of Early Christian Works: Aural Reception*

The very low literacy rates of first-century Mediterranean people also necessitated the orality of ancient texts and their oral performance. William Harris has sought to discover the extent of literacy in the ancient world on the basis of the definition of literacy as the ability to read or write at any level. He suggests that in the first century only 20–30 percent of males in Rome and Italy could read, and female literacy was less than 10 percent, with rates being much lower in rural than

---

[76] Barton, *Holy Writings*, pp. 104–105.
[77] Justin, *Apology*, 1.66.
[78] Luise Abramowski, "The 'Memoirs of the Apostle' in Justin," in *The Gospel and the Gospels* (ed. Peter Stuhlmacher; Grand Rapids, Michigan: Eermdmans, 1991), pp. 323–35.
[79] Justin Martyr, *Apology*, 1.67.
[80] Justin Martyr, *Dialogue with Trypho*, 106, quotes from the "memoirs of Peter" the name of the sons of Zebedee, "Boanerges" or "Sons of Thunders" which is only mentioned in Mark's Gospel.

in urban areas,[81] and in the western provinces of the Roman Empire only 5–10 percent of adult males were literate.[82] Thus Harris reaches the conclusion that the overall literacy of the population of the Roman Empire probably was below 10 percent and never exceeded 15 to 20 percent.[83] The implication is that the opportunities for the ancients to access any literature were extremely limited except through public performance, given that most people in the Greco-Roman world were illiterate.[84]

Is that rate of literacy true of early Christianity which, without doubt, showed a deep interest in religious texts? H.I. Marrou affirms that early Christianity was "a religion of the Book."[85] Given the custom of public reading in antiquity, however, it is anachronistic to assume that the familiarity with the written texts necessarily required early Christians to be capable of reading and writing them. Pointing out that there are a relatively small number of papyrus fragments of books of the New Testament dating from earlier than 200 C.E., Harris asserts then that an "illusion that Christianity was spread mainly by means of the written word [in the first three centuries] is possible only for those who exaggerate the literacy of the high Empire."[86] More importantly, what recent biblical studies of the social constituency of the early church have shown is that the early church attracted a socially diverse membership.[87] The social status of the early Christians were usually free craftspeople, artisans, and small traders some of whom had slaves and houses.[88] This means that early Christianity does not have any reason to have a literacy rate that was any higher or lower than that

---

[81] Harris, *Ancient Literacy*, pp. 266–67.

[82] Harris, *Ancient Literacy*, pp. 267–72.

[83] Harris, *Ancient Literacy*, p. 22.

[84] Indeed, it is true that such a low literacy rate is not the primary reason for oral performance practice because, as Hadas, *Ancilla*, pp. 60–64, rightly shows, the Roman "recitations" were a common practice among literate poets and philosophers. My argument is that most people in the first century had no other way to access a "book" but by public reading.

[85] Henri. I. Marrou, *A History of Education in Antiquity* (trans. George Lamb; New York: Sheed and Ward, 1956), pp. 315–16.

[86] Harris, *Ancient Literacy*, p. 299.

[87] For example, see E.A. Judge, *The Social Pattern of Christian Groups in the First Century* (London: Tyndale, 1960); Gerd Theissen, *The Social Setting of Pauline Christianity: Essays on Corinth* (trans. John H. Schutz; Philadelphia: Fortress Press, 1983); Wayne A. Meeks, *The First Urban Christians: The Social World of the Apostle Paul* (New Haven and London: Yale University Press, 1983), pp. 72–73.

[88] Meeks, *Urban Christians*, pp. 72–74.

of the general Roman society. It is warranted to say that for the early church the ability to read and write belonged to a small number of Christians. Accordingly, we must believe that for the majority of early Christians aural reception was the only mode of accessing Christian literature, and ancient authors and evangelists wrote their texts for the ear rather than for the eye.[89]

B. MEMORY IN THE ENVIRONMENT OF ORAL PERFORMANCE AND AURAL RECEPTION

What we have examined in the previous section is that, though recorded in the form of a written document, the Gospel of Mark is oral for early Christians in the sense that it is intended to be orally performed and aurally received. Such conclusion leads us to assume that the Markan oral-aural narrative relied on human memory for its preservation and communication. The present section discusses divergent milieus which may demonstrate the assumption above.

Unlike the modern Westerner who living in a print culture, for the ancients who were, as discussed above, in such a low literacy rate human memory played an essential role in preserving and communicating incoming information. Plutarch, for example, tells us that the Athenians who were caught in the hands of the Syracusans were set free for reciting the works of Euripides.[90] There were memorization competitions not only for school children but also for the educated elite.[91] And the training of memory, as Marrou notes, was considered

---

[89] Gamble, *Books*, p. 204. In a recent article Kelber also points out oral performance as the way of communicating a written text in the ancient world, but he never corrects his position that "writing, no matter how closely allied with oral sensibilities and practices, did make a difference." See Kelber, "Jesus and Tradition," pp. 153–160, esp. 153, 160. But what Kelber keeps failing to take into consideration is the presence of the listening audience when he thinks of the practice of writing. Given that, as mentioned so far, most people were illiterate who were expected to hear the text being read aloud, we must assume that the ancient author would write something after the pattern of speaking.

[90] Plutarch, *Nicias* 29 (LCL; trans. Bernadotte Perrin; London: William Heinemann, 1914).

[91] For the former Marrou, *History of Education*, p. 231 and for the latter Lucian, *the Mistaken Critic* 6 (LCL; trans. A.M. Harmon; Cambridge, Massachusetts: Harvard University Press, 1919).

the main aim of early education in the Greco-Roman world.[92] Seneca boasts that the ability of his memory, when he was young, was so powerful that he was able to recite repeatedly two thousand names in the same order, and he used to memorize more than two hundred lines of poetry in reverse.[93] Seneca goes on to introduce Latro who, having a remarkable memory, "could recall all the declamations he had ever spoken. He had thus made books superfluous—he used to say he wrote in his mind."[94] For the ancient, oral performance was a context where tradition or a story was transmitted from the memory of one individual to that of another, thus making it possible for a society to be constantly preserved.[95]

1. *The Speaker's Memory*

Ancient rhetoric has "memory" as one of its five divisions.[96] Quintilian says that "it is memory which has brought oratory to its present position of glory."[97] Indeed most ancient rhetoricians laid heavy stress on training the orator's memory in preparation for oral speech.[98] Part of the reason that it was suggested for the orator to memorize what he had to speak is related to the features of ancient texts. Entire texts were written by hand in capital letters, with no punctuation and no word divisions; thus it was hardly readable, unless the speaker was

---

[92] Marrou, *History of Education*, pp. 165–66, 230, 526–27, 375 and 559; Frances A. Yates, *The Art of Memory* (London: Routledge and Kegan Paul, 1966), pp. 1–49.

[93] Seneca, *Declamations* preface 2 (LCL; trans. M. Winterbottom; Cambridge, Massachusetts: Harvard University Press, 1974).

[94] Seneca, *Declamations* preface 18.

[95] On the function of ancient oral performance in preserving social tradition, see Bailey, "Oral Tradition," pp. 4–11, who argues that in the ancient and modern Mediterranean world the gathering of villagers, that is, the oral performance, played a role in the preservation of "informal controlled tradition."

[96] *Ad Hernnium* 1.3 says, "The Speaker, then, should possess the faculties of Invention, Arrangement, Style, Memory, and Delivery" and it explains memory as "the firm retention of the mind of the matter, words, and arrangement."

[97] Quintilian, *Institutio oratoria* 11.2.7.

[98] *Ad Herennium* 3.16.28–3.24.40; Cicero, *De oratore* 2.85.350–88 (LCL; trans. E.W. Sutton; Cambridge, Massachusetts: Harvard University Press, 1942); Quintilian, *Institutio oratoria* 11.2.1–51. For divergent examples about the ancient speaker's recitation from memory, see Yates, *Memory*, pp. 1–49; Marrou, *History of Education*, pp. 165–66, 230, 526–27, 375 and 559; Thomas H. Olbricht, "Delivery and Memory," in *Handbook of Classical Rhetoric in the Hellenistic Period 330 B.C.–A.D. 400* (ed. Stanley E. Porter; Leiden: Brill, 1997), pp. 159–67; Shiner, *Proclaiming the Gospel*, pp. 104–109; Lentz, *Orality*, pp. 90–108.

familiar with it prior to public reading.[99] And because the first- century texts were usually in the form of a scroll, with which the speaker could have experienced great difficulty in performing dramatically, when compared to the codex, it must have been considered by most performers very unwise to entirely rely on the written text without memorizing it.[100] Of course, as will be observed, it was not necessary that the speaker remember verbatim in a recitation: "[R]ecall of the general meaning and form is sufficient."[101]

2. The Hearer's Memory

For the majority of audiences, hearing, not reading, was the only medium through which to obtain and preserve the contents of the written texts for varying reasons such as low literacy, paucity of manuscripts, and mode of publication. Hence information stored in the written document, however well it may have been organized, remained useless if the audience could not, at the moment of oral presentation, store and understand it in their minds to later recall it effectively.[102] For this reason the memory of the hearer is what ancient rhetoric regarded vital in making an efficient arrangement of the argument. Thus, in *Ad Herrenium* we read that "since what has been said last is easily committed to memory, it is useful, when ceasing to speak, to leave some very strong argument fresh in the hearer's mind;"[103] "The Summing Up gathers together and recalls the points we have made—briefly...so that the hearer, if he has committed them to memory, is brought back to what he remembers."[104] As for Tacitus, he believed that the recollection of what was performed orally was also the responsibility of the hearer. He writes that "...our young men...hang round our public speakers in order to improve themselves...eager not only

---

[99] Marrou, *Education*, pp. 165–66, 230, 526–27 note 13 and 375, 559 note 30; Ong, *Orality*, p. 119; see also Thomas E. Boomershine, *Story Journey: An Invitation to the Gospel as Story telling* (Nashville: Abingdon Press, 1988), pp. 42–43 and Shiner, *Proclaiming the Gospel*, pp. 12–13. Thus, Harris, *Ancient Literacy*, p. 32, argues, "It is likely that during most of antiquity one was considered to know a text by heart even if, by modern standards, one's memory of it was inexact."

[100] Shiner, *Proclaiming the Gospel*, p. 103.

[101] Rubin, *Memory*, p. 6.

[102] On the discussion of oral culture or performance and human memory, see Ong, *Orality*, pp. 31–77, esp 31–33; and Rubin, *Memory*, pp. 9–10.

[103] *Ad Herennium* 3.10.18.

[104] *Ad Herennium* 2.30.47.

to hear but also to take home with them some striking and memorable utterance; they pass it on from mouth to mouth, and often quote it in their home correspondence with country and provinces."[105] For the hearer's memory practice, Lucian's work, *The Wisdom of Nigrinus*, is also illuminating. Lucian says that the principal speaker of the work, after having listened to the philosopher, was keen on calling his words into mind and repeating them to himself two or three times a day.[106]

3. *Memory and Writing*

William Harris claims that the Mediterranean world of the first century B.C.E. and C.E. was a flourishing period of literacy. It is worth considering, thus, the relationship of writing and memory.[107] Did the relatively high literacy rate lead to the evaporation of the emphasis on memory in Greco-Roman culture?

It is appropriate to begin with the ancients' view of writing. In modern western culture, writing and literacy are "essential human competencies (like the ability to add)" and thus determine human "ways of thinking about things" and events.[108] But the ancients had a completely different approach to writing from the moderns. Mary Carruthers, in her book, *The Book of Memory*, says that for the ancients "writing something down cannot change in any significant way…[their] mental representation of it, for it is the mental representation that gives birth to the written form, not vice versa."[109] Socrates in Plato's *Phaedrus* says that writing or written words are to remind one of what one already knows.[110] For the ancients, then, writing was not a supplanter of memory but rather at the service of memory.

Ancient rhetoric shows another example of how the ancients used the written texts in live performance. Ancient rhetoric was essentially the art of speaking, but there is no general ban against the use

---

[105] Tacitus, *Dialogue on Oratory* 20 (LCL; trans. William Peterson; Cambridge, Massachusetts: Harvard University Press, 1914).

[106] Lucian, *The Works of Lucian* 6 (LCL; trans. A.M. Harmon; London: William Heinemann, 1919).

[107] Harris, *Ancient Literacy*, pp. 222–29; Thomas, *Literacy and Orality*, pp. 158–70.

[108] Mary Carruthers, *The Book of Memory: A Study of Memory in Medieval Culture* (Cambridge: Cambridge University Press, 1990), p. 36.

[109] Carruthers, *Memory*, pp. 17, 31–32. She argues that this Greek tradition of memory lasted until the rise of rationalism of the eighteenth century.

[110] Plato, *Phaedrus* 275d, in *Collected Dialogues* (trans. R. Hackworth; Princeton: Princeton University Press, 1961).

of writing in rhetorical schools. Rather the ancient rhetors organized
their speeches in their minds when they did not write them down, and
thus the written word was primarily at the service of oral presentation. After pointing out Plato's assertion of the potential hindrance to
memory, for instance, Quintilian says:

> [C]oncentration of mind is of the utmost importance...[for memory];
> it is, in fact, like the eyesight, which turns to, and not away from, the
> objects [written characters] which it contemplates. Thus it results that
> after wthat after writing for several days with a view to acquiring by
> heart what we have written, we find that our mental effort has of itself
> imprinted it on our memory.[111]

Here Quintilian describes that the written word can play an assist-
ing role to memory. In another context, he says about the relation of
memorization and the written text in a live performance that the orator
"should never write out anything which we do not intend to commit to
memory."[112] Quintilian argues, in opposition to Cicero who proposes
to take advantage of notebooks,[113] that the orator must memorize the
whole text in advance of the speech rather than just its arguments or
outlines. Yet the implication in the case of either Cicero or Quintilian
is that writing is used to facilitate memory in the speech.[114]

In Greco-Roman schools written texts were certainly used and produced in the life of the schools in order to preserve the teachings and
deeds of a founder or a charismatic teacher. But they were not treated
as having independent authority in forming and preserving the tradition of the schools; rather, it was subordinate to oral teaching stored
in the students' memories and circulated among them.[115] Yet is this

---

[111] Quintilian, *Institutio oratoria* 11.2.10.

[112] Quintilian, *Institutio oratoria* 10.7.32.

[113] Cicero, *De oratore* 2.85.359.

[114] According to Thomas Cole, *The Origins of Rhetoric in Ancient Greece* (Baltimore and London: The Johns Hopkins, 1991), p. 118, the majority of written oratori-
cal texts of the fourth century B.C.E. that survive were composed for other orators
to memorize and perform, whether from memory or manuscript. Martin, *Power of
Writing*, p. 70, argues that "we must admit that, at the time [that is, in Greco-Roman
period]...writing was conceived as a simple means for fixing and memorizing spoken
discourse..." And on the view that the ancient book was *aide-mémoire*, see also Stanford, *Sound of Greek*, p. 3; Gaham, *Beyond the Written Word*, pp. 34–35, 39.

[115] This explains why interpolation of philosophical texts not infrequently occurred.
See Thomas, *Literacy and Orality*, pp. 161–62. Likewise Barton, *Holy Writings*, p. 79
says, "Christian writers in the first two centruires often retain a sense that the Gospels
are not holy texts but the records of living memory. They are corrigible in light of

the case for the early Christians? Note Papias's statement regarding the living voice: "For I did not suppose that information from books would help me so much as the word of a living and surviving voice."[116] This passages has been misunderstood as meaning that Papias contrasts oral tradition with written tradition, preferring the former in general to the latter in general. However, Gamble asserts that what Papias disapproves of here is not so much a book per se as the indirect nature of the information it represents.[117] And it is pointed out rightly by Loveday Alexander that a preference for "a living voice" is a *topos* in the Hellenistic philosophical schools, where the ideal transmission of traditions was thought to be achieved through the personal guidance of a teacher.[118] Seneca, the influential philosopher of the Stoa of the first century C.E., provides good examples for this position; he replies to Lucilius's request to send him philosophical books: "However, the living voice and the sharing of someone's daily life will be of more help than a treatise."[119] Here Seneca expresses oral teaching's superiority over the written text 'in the case of a student who learns things from a teacher.' Accordingly, Papias's preference "living voice" to "information from books" refers to supremacy of person to person oral instruction over the study of written texts. The implication is that in Christian churches written texts were viewed as a reminder of, and thus a supplement, and not an alternative to, the instructions already given orally by teachers.[120]

Regarding Mark's written Gospel, a brief but important point can be made from the observations above. We have already noted earlier the early Christians' perception of Mark's Gospel as a "memoir" or as "notes" of oral teaching. In addition to that, it must be argued that the emergence of Mark's written Gospel never discouraged Mark and his original audience's use of Jesus' teaching as stored in their memories.[121] Rather we may assume that in oral communication or teaching,

---

fresh information, and especially of eyewitness testimony or reliable reporting of it. The vehicle for this testimony is seen as primarily oral in character."

[116] Eusebius *Ecclesiastical History* 3.39.4.

[117] Gamble, *Books*, pp. 30–32.

[118] Alexander, "Living Voice," pp. 230–37.

[119] Seneca, *Moral Epistles* 6.5 (LCL; trans. Richard M. Gummere; Cambridge, Massachusetts: Harvard University Press, 1917) cited by Alexander, "Living Voice," pp. 230–37.

[120] This is reminiscent of Plato, *Phaedrus* 275d observed above.

[121] It is not new among modern biblical scholars for the Gospels to be compared with ancient "*bioi*" or biographies. One of the important purposes of ancient biography was to preserve the memory of the dead founder of a community, Aune, *New*

one important role of the written Gospel was to serve as a memorandum of what one already knew.[122]

Testament, pp. 36, 62; Richard Burridge, *What Are the Gospels? A Comparison with Graeco-Roman Biography* (Grand Rapids, Michigan: Eerdmans, 2nd edn, 2004), pp. 209, 211–12, 298–99.

[122] How the early Christians perceived the written Gospels is worth noting. Many of the Fathers cite the Jesus traditions not only from the written Gospels, but also from the so-called *agrapha* on an equal authority with the Gospels. In particular, Irenaeus and Justin did not speak of the Gospels as distinctive written documents from oral tradition; but for Clement of Alexandria, *Stromateis* 6. 61.2–3 (trans. John Ferguson; The Fathers of the Church 85; Washington, D.C.: The Catholic University of America Press, 1991) and Tertullian, *Apologeticum* 39.3 (trans. Sister Emily Joseph Daly; The Fathers of the Church 10; New York: Fathers of the Church, 1950) and soon afterward Irenaeus, the New Testament, and thus the Gospels, came to be seen, like Jewish written Scriptures, as a distinctive, holy written text. See Gamble, *Books,* pp. 214–15; Barton, *Holy Writings,* pp. 98–100. This indicates that for the early Christians (at least until Irenaeus and Justin Martyr) the existence of written Gospels did not make any difference to the authority of the Jesus tradition circulated orally. At this point it is relevant to raise the question of how such early Christians in the second century perceived the written Gospels in such an environment. One possible clue to this issue can be illuminated from the studies of the physical form(s) which was used by the second- century church to write early Christian literature. As Colins Roberts and T.C. Skeat, *The Birth of Codex* (London: The British Academy, 1983), p. 47, observe, "when the Christian Bible first emerges into history the books of which it was composed are always written on papyrus and are always in codex form." The comparative evidence is instructive. It is remarkable that whereas more than 98 percent of the remains of Greek books dated before the third century C.E. are scrolls, almost all the earliest Christian books known in the same period include the form of the papyrus codex. The question to ask is: Why then did the codex become the most favoured format for the early Christians' literature? The early Christians' predominant adoption of the codex shows important facts about the uses and functions of the early Christian writings and thus the early Christians' perception of them. Thus, in order to answer the question, it is crucial to remember that in antiquity the codex was not recognized as a proper book but as a vehicle for a notebook or a first draft of oral performance. For example, Pliny the Younger, *The Letters of Pliny* 1.6.1 (LCL; trans. Betty Radice; Cambridge, Massachutes; Harvard University Press, 1969), says how his uncle, when travelling, dictated notes to his secretary on codex or wax tablets, and in 3.4.14–15, 9.10.2, Pliny himself also speaks to Tacitus how he concentrated on writing something using codex notebooks rather than on hunting. Quintilian, *Quintilian,* 10.3.31, suggests wax as the best vehicle to compose a first draft, because "it is easiest to erase, unless weak sight demands the use of parchment instead." Those examples show that written texts in the codex form were in some way more provisional rather than understood as formal books, and the use of codex was focused on a very utilitarian purpose. Thus, it is reasonable to assume that pragmatic motives, such as remembering, preaching and teaching, of Christian communities would have lain behind the innovation that the early Christians copied the Gospels in codex form predominantly. Likewise, it is not surprising that we cannot also detect in the early second-century Christians' use of the Gospels a cultic attitude toward their books (as seen in that of the Jews to written Scriptures) or an aesthetic regard for them (as shown in Greek literary works). All of the observations above allow us to believe that, as Barton, *Holy Writings,* p. 88 claims, early Christians perceived the written Gospel as "a convenient repository of the kind

4. *Memory in the Early Church*

Memory played an essential role in the formation of first-century Christianity. This is obvious in the nature of the Synoptic tradition and the Gospels. We have already explored the way in which, for the early Christians, the Gospels were reminiscences of Jesus, or the first disciples' living memories of Jesus. But what has been highly controversial among modern biblical scholars is how to define the early Christians' memories of Jesus. Many historical critics have argued that the Gospels are largely reflections of the faith of the post-Easter Christian communities and that it is hard to find in them a historical Jesus. But we must be cautious about creating a division between the early Christians' memory of a historical Jesus and their faith in Jesus. James Dunn, in a recent book called *Jesus Remembered*, argues that the quest attempting to find the historical Jesus behind the text of the Gospels and the Synoptic traditions is an illusion that the Enlightenment's ideal of historical objectivity gave birth to.[123] Dunn's main thesis is that since the disciples' memories of Jesus were touched by faith from the outset of Jesus' earthly works, not just after Easter, "there is in fact no gap to be bridged between a Jesus historically conceived and the subsequent tradition which has effected consciousness."[124] Thus Dunn claims, "The Synoptic tradition provides evidence not so much for what Jesus did or said in itself but for what Jesus was remembered as doing or saying by his first disciples, or as we might say, for the impact of what he did and said on his first disciples."[125] If so, it is not surprising that the Gospels should be considered as memories of the historic Jesus.

The issue of memory is not only important for the composition of the Gospels as such, but also for understanding the life of the early

---

of oral Jesus-traditions that they already knew, and were accustomed to pass on in teaching and preaching; and so they wrote them on sheets sewn loosely together, rather than on formal scrolls." On the use of the codex in antiquity, see Frederic G. Kenyon, *Books and Readers in Ancient Greece and Rome* (Oxford: Clarendon, 1951), pp. 91–93; E.G., Turner, *Greek Papyri: An Introduction* (Oxford: Clarendon Press, 1968), pp. 6–7; and for the early Christians' use of codex, see Roberts and Skeat, *Birth of Codex*, pp. 47–51; Colin H. Roberts, *Manuscript, Society and Belief in Early Christian Egypt* (London: The British Academy, 1979), pp. 26–48; Gamble, *Books*, pp. 49–50, 65; Alexander, "Ancient Book," pp. 71–112; *idem*, "Living Voice," pp. 242–45.

[123] Dunn, *Jesus*, esp. pp. 125–30.
[124] Dunn, *Jesus*, p. 128.
[125] Dunn, *Jesus*, p. 130.

Christian communities. Nils Dahl, in his neglected book, *Jesus in the Memory of the Early Church*, points out: "Those who have been led to faith and who have received baptism know already what is necessary for salvation. From that moment they need only recall their initiation and permit this memory to shape their conduct."[126] The early Christians were constantly encouraged to store and remember the Gospels, which consists of the memories of Jesus as well as Christian traditions (e.g., 2 Peter 1.15; 3.2; Revelation 3.3; *1 Clement* 13.1–2; 46.7–8). Over and over again, Paul stresses to his converts to call to memory the traditions that he taught (1 Corinthians 11.2, 15.1–3; 2 Thessalonians 2.5; 2 Timothy 2.8, 14; cf. Romans 15.15). It is well known that the Lord's Supper was central to the gathering of the early church and served to revive the Christians' memories of Jesus' deeds, sayings and death (1 Corinthians 11.24; Luke 22.19).

C. Conclusion

What we have thus far demonstrated is twofold. First, despite the fact that it is in written form, the Gospel of Mark is oral in character, and an oral-aural narrative with respect to the communicative medium. Certainly, few can disagree with the argument that there are important differences between the spoken and written words. But what we have observed so far—the rhetorical environment, the production, and the use of the Gospel of Mark—unmistakably shows that an ancient written text was produced in a close interactive relationship with oral modes. It is legitimate to say, then, that Mark wrote his text as much for the ear as for the eye and that "the transition from the oral to the written gospel in Mark's context was not a transition from sound to silence but from sounds recomposed by a storyteller to sounds read from a manuscript."[127] Second, in the oral-aural contexts of the ancient world, human memory was held in high regard, and the early Christians were encouraged to store information in memory and then retrieve it from there for communication. Under this communicative condition the written Gospels served as aids to memory.

---

[126] Nils Dahl, *Jesus in the Memory of the Early Church* (Minneapolis, Minnesota: Augsburg, 1976), p. 16.
[127] Thomas E. Boomershine, "Peter's Denial as Polemic or Confession: The Implications of Media Criticism for Biblical Hermeneutics," *Semeia* 39 (1987), p. 61.

CHAPTER THREE

MEMORY RESOURCES OF THE MARKAN
ORAL-AURAL NARRATIVE: FRAMES

It has been demonstrated in the previous chapter that as an oral-aural narrative the Gospel of Mark, though gaining admittance into the written document, relied on human memory for its preservation and communication; and the written text was used as an aide to remind of what the audience already knew. This raises questions: On what sort of memory resource or cognitive model was the oral-aural communication of Mark's Gospel based; what kind of cognitive model does best account for such a use of Mark's written text? In an attempt to answer this question, this chapter will introduce the oral features of Mark's Gospel, arguing that the frame is a cognitive model that is able to account appropriately for such traits of the oral-aural narrative discourse. There has been considerable progress in both the humanities (mostly related to the study of oral tradition) and cognitive science (cognitive psychology and linguistics) with respect to the studies of human memory and its role in the comprehension and the remembering of a narrative. This chapter incorporates the results to highlight cognitive aspects that operated in processing the Markan oral-aural narrative.

A. The Oral Features of Mark's Gospel and Frames

The narrative is a product of human memory in that it is fundamentally retrospective.[1] But not every reality that has occurred is a narrative. "To make a narrative, [we] have to isolate certain elements out of the unbroken and seamless web of history with a view of fitting them into a particular construct which [we] have more or less consciously or unconsciously in mind."[2] Scholars in the field of cognitive science have been interested in narrative discourse, particularly to test how

---

[1] Ong, "Remembering," pp. 12–14; *idem, Orality*, pp. 139–41.
[2] Ong, "Remembering," p. 12.

human memory affects story production and comprehension, and have created a hypothesis which is now generally accepted in this field. The hypothesis is detailed in terms of typical knowledge structures, or mental frames, for people to compose, understand, and recall a story. Indeed, not all stories are based on framed knowledge (e.g., a science fiction story). But what follows will show that the characteristics of the Markan narrative which are generally known as "orally based thoughts and expressions" are strongly in favour of frame-based information processing and communication.[3] To define the oral features of Mark's Gospel, we will refer to ideas of Jack Goody and Ian Watt, Walter Ong and Eric Havelock.

1. *Homeostatic Organization*[4]

In oral cultures tradition is retold to serve the present, and each retelling is altered and developed on behalf of the present life of a speech community. In other words, people in oral cultures tend to adjust new experience and information to the present typical knowledge system of the social group. Jack Goody and Ian Watt call this feature of oral memory "homeostatic": What is no longer useful and irrelevant to the present lived experience quickly passes out of sight, whereas new elements are constantly modified to fit into the foundation of the cultural identity.[5] This homeostatic feature of oral memory corresponds exactly to the way in which frames process information. In trying to understand how people in an oral culture remember and transmit their cultural traditions, Goody and Watt postulate, having in mind Bartlett's theory of "schematic" memory:

> The individual memory will mediate the cultural heritage in such a way that its new constituents will adjust to the old by the process of interpretation that Bartlett calls 'rationalizing' or the 'effort after meaning'; and

---

[3] For the terms, see Ong, *Orality*, p. 36; and their application to Mark's Gospel, see Joanna Dewey, "Oral Methods of Structuring Narrative in Mark," *Int* 43 (1989), pp. 32–44; *idem*, "Mark as Interwoven Tapestry: Forecasts and Echoes for a Listening Audience," *CBQ* 53 (1991), pp. 221–36.

[4] With regard to the homeostatic organization of oral cultures, Jack Goody and Ian Watt in "The Consequences of Literacy," in *Literacy in Traditional Societies* (ed. Jack Goody; Cambridge: Cambridge University Press, 1968), pp. 30–31.

[5] Goody and Watt, "Literary," pp. 30–31. See also Ong, *Orality*, pp. 46–49 and Dewey, "Oral-Aural Event," pp. 157–59; *idem*, "The Gospel of John in its Oral-Written Media World," in *Jesus in Johannine Tradition* (ed. Robert T. Fortna and Tom Thatcher; Louisville, London: WJK, 2001), pp. 242–44.

whatever part of it has ceased to be of contemporary relevance are likely to be eliminated by the process of forgetting.[6]

Concerning how people obtain and understand information, cognitive scientists claim that a critical condition for the acquisition of new knowledge is the existence of a stereotyped knowledge framework already stored in the memory through prior experiences. Schank and Abelson, scholars in the fields of artificial intelligence and cognitive psychology, thus say:

> Understanding, then, is a process by which people match what they see and hear to pre-stored groupings of actions that they have already experienced. *New information is understood in terms of old information.* By this view, man is seen as a processor that only understands what it has previously understood....we view human understanding as heavily script-based. A human understander comes equipped with thousands of scripts. He uses these scripts almost without thinking.[7]

It must be noted, accordingly, that the reason that oral communication may be called an assimilating process of new information into the old is because people process information in terms of the frame (or concentional knowledge). Each oral performance provides people with an opportunity to interpret and solve the present issues of life by way of their frames.[8] Thus we may say that in oral cultures frame-based information processing was maximized.

2. *Conservative or Traditionalist*

Oral thoughts and expressions may be said to be fundamentally conventional, so the expectations of novelty are less in an oral-aural narrative.[9] As Foley notes, the orally performed narrative is not the occasion

---

[6] Goody and Watt, "Literacy," p. 30. Likewise, the frame determines whether or not a particular piece of information will be selected for understanding; what is relevant to that frame is readily and efficiently processed, or otherwise may be forgotten.

[7] Schank and Abelson, *Scripts*, pp. 67–68. [italics are mine]

[8] Of course, as Jan Vansina, *Oral Tradition as History* (Madison: University of Wisconsin Press, 1985), p. 121, notes, we must guard against thinking that orality is simply synonymous with fluidity, or in oral cultures the memory of the past absorbs into its present usefulness to the community, losing its voice. There are many mnemonic devices to keep tradition stable, such as rote memory, rhetorical devices, increasing dependence upon written documents, repetitive performance and so on. Nonetheless, as Goody and Watt rightly note, "Literacy," p. 31, oral memory must be characterized as homeostatic in the sense that the concept of remembering in oral culture is fundamentally different from that of modern Western print-culture.

[9] Havelock, *Plato*, pp. 87–96, 146–47.

for the formation of the cultural identity of the community, but rather "manifestations of collective values."[10] This is equally true of Mark's oral-aural Gospel. For whomever the Gospel of Mark was intended,[11] when the Gospels were orally performed for the first time, the audience did not hear anything completely new, but rather something which was already a part of their knowledge. In print culture like modern Western society, writing a book is in many cases an attempt to deliver totally new information. But as already discussed, this is not the case for the environment of oral performance and aural reception. Rather, the Gospel of Mark is based on communally shared memory concerning Jesus' ministry and teachings, not just a single author's creative idea (thus contra Kelber).[12] Frame knowledge can illuminate such a conservative set of mind embedded in an oral-aural narrative discourse. As William Croft and Alan Cruse, cognitive linguists, point out:

> Communities are defined by the social activities that bind the members together. Clark argues that communities in-volve the possession of shared expertise among their members: the specialized knowledge that is acquired by engaging in the activities that define the community... This shared expertise is the conceptual structure that is found in the frame/domains of the concepts symbolized by the specialized vocabulary used by members of the community.[13]

Frames represent typical or prototypical knowledge ("shared expertise," to use Croft and Cruse's term) set up through social and cultural experience and generally shared by members of the community.[14] Thus it is not unlikely to believe that the conventional characteristics of Mark's oral-aural narrative reflect Mark and his audiences' shared frames.

The conventional features of oral-aural narrative are closely associated with its communicative medium of oral production and aural reception. The message in oral-aural communication can easily vanish. Its evanescent nature does not then allow a narrator to attempt

---

[10] Foley, "Oral Audience," p. 148.

[11] For the discussion of this issue, see below.

[12] Dunn, *Jesus*, p. 209. For a recent valuable discussion of interaction between the Gospels traditions and the community, see Bailey, "Oral Tradition," pp. 5–10. And in opposition to Kelber, L.W. Hurtado, "The Gospel of Mark: Evolutionary or Revolutionary Document?" *JSNT* 40 (1990), pp. 15–32, argues Mark as both a conservative redactor and a creative theologian; and see also Marcus, *Mark 1–8*, pp. 59–62.

[13] Croft and Cruse, *Cognitive Linguistics*, p. 18.

[14] Taylor, *Linguistic Categorization*, pp. 83–90.

"intellectual experimentation," but instead encourages the "conservative set of mind."[15] So the speaker performs a message in ways (thoughts
and expressions) with which the audience is already familiar, so that
the audience may understand it readily and quickly. Likewise, many
experimental results from the field of cognitive science consistently
demonstrate faster processing times for a frame-based story than with
a frame-irrelevant story.[16] The implication is that, if the audience has
a domain-related frame, the domain-related information will be processed more quickly. Communication can fail, however, if the hearer
does not have enough background knowledge structures or if a story
consists of too many new and unexpected elements. Yet this type
of mismatch between the audience's frames and the communicated
information is greatly decreased in the case of the oral-aural narrative,
given its conservative nature based on frame knowledge.

   This is an appropriate place to argue that the Markan original audience was assumed as having cognitive ability to elicit frame knowledge
explicitly and implicitly implied in the Gospel of Mark. An efficient
communication between the text (or the speaker) and audience is
essentially based on the audience's ability to evoke relevant frames to
which the audience assumes the text refers. What is crucial for the
present study is, thus, to verify the assumption that Mark's original
audience may have shared and evoked various frames presupposed
in the the text. First of all, "the conservative" features of oral-aural
cultures mentioned above obviously lead us to postulate that Mark's
original audience was intended by the text to be capable of opening
an appropriate frame in order to understand Mark's Gospel. Secondly,
the issue of the Markan orginal audience's ability to open a frame is
closely related to that of who were the intended hearers of the Gospel.
Although there is controversy around just who constituted Mark's specific audience,[17] there is a scholarly consensus in characterizing Mark's

---

[15] Ong, *Orality*, p. 41.

[16] Sanford and Garrod, *Understanding*, pp. 111–18; Rumelhart, "Schemata," p. 47.

[17] Regarding a specific audience of the Gospel of Mark, there are primarily three
locations pointed out by scholars: Galilee, Syria and Rome. For the hypothesis of the
Christians in Galilee, see R.N. Roskam, *The Purpose of the Gospel of Mark in its Historical and Social Context* (Leiden/Boston: Brill, 2004), pp. 94–114; for the hypothesis
of the Christians in Syria, see Marcus, *Mark 1–8*, pp. 33–39; for the hypothesis of
the Christians in Rome, see Hengel, *Mark*, pp. 28–30. But, as William R. Telford,
The Theology of the Gospel of Mark (Cambridge: Cambridge University Press, 1980),
p. 15, says that "while Rome is still the most popular of all these alternatives, the question of provenance is clearly still an open one." Thus, Michael F. Bird, "The Markan

original audience as Christian: Mark's Gospel, including the rest of the three Gospels, was written in the first place for Christians, whether as apologetic or evangelistic works.[18] This consensus leads us to the argument that Mark's story about Jesus could have been fairly readily comprehended on the part of Mark's Christian audiences. Moreover, we must not overlook the fact that, as mentioned in the preceding chapter, the early Christians were already familiar with the Jesus traditions in "communal oral memory" even before they were commited into the written documents.[19] Of course, this is not to deny that Mark selected, reordered, and improved the traditions; indeed these 'editorial' activities are characteristic of oral cultures.[20] Nontheless, again it must be kept in mind that "intellectual experimentation" (to use Ong's term) was hardly encouraged in the communication of oral performance and aural reception.

Finally, there is also textual evidence to show that the original audience's frame knowledge is taken for granted in understanding the Gospel of Mark. Mark 15.21, for example, introduces Simon of Cyrene who is identified by his sons' names, Alexander and Rufus. The implication is that the text assumes that at least Alexander and

---

Community, Myth or Maze? Bauckham's *The Gospel for All Christians* Revisited," *JTS* 57 (2006), pp. 474–86, is quite right to suggest that "the Christian experience that pervades the Gospel [of Mark] may be significantly wider than any [particular] geographical or temporal setting." On the challenge against defining the audience of the four Gospels as particular local churches, see Richard Bauckham, "For Whom were Gospels Written?" in *The Gospels for All Christians: Rethinking the Gospel Audiences* (ed. Richard Bauckham; Grand Rapids, Michigan: Eerdmans, 1998), p. 29. Cf. D.C. Sim, "The Gospels for All Christians? A Response to Richard Bauckham," *JSNT* 84 (2001), pp. 3–27.

[18] For this consensus, see Bauckham, "For Whom," pp. 9–10. However, modern reader-oriented approaches to the New Testament writings state that since we know nothing of the author/speaker, nor his community or historical context, they attempt to invent an "implied reader" 'in' or 'over' the text, not a historical audience but a literarily constructed device, who can impose his or her own reading upon it. See *Semeia* 31(1985): *Reader Response Approaches to Biblical and Secular Texts* and Stephen D. Moore, *Literary Criticism and the Gospels: The Theoretical Challenge* (New Haven: Yale University Press, 1989).

[19] Dunn, *Jesus*, p. 250. The assumption that various 'Christian' subject matters had been already established in the early Christian communities before the appearance of the Gospels can be warranted by evidence from the Pauline letters written earlier than the Gospels (e.g., the Christians' position of Jesus as a divine figure (1 Corinthians 8.6; Philippians 2.6–11), Eucharistic meal (1 Corinthians 11.23–25), Gentiles (Romans 1–10 and Galatians 2.11–15, esp v. 15) the Torah (Galatians 1–6 and Romans 1–10) or ritual purity (Romans 14; Galatians 2.11–21).

[20] On the features of oral composition, see above and below and Chapter Two.

Rufus were already known to the historical audience, since "there is no point in identifying someone by referring to others who are unknown" (and also see "Mary the mother of James the younger and of Joses" at 15.40).[21] And the reason that Mark's Gospel contains a number of cryptic passages (e.g., 4.10–12; 8.14–21; 14.51–52; the abrupt ending at 16.8) can also be explained by the assumption that the Gospel of Mark includes the background knowledge shared by the speaker and his audience, but unknown to modern interpreters. However, we must guard ourselves against concluding the content of a frame simply under the cover of assumptions about Mark's Christian readership; rather the identification of its content must be accompanied by textual evidence (words, parallels, and grammars), semantic, syntactical and pragmatic information, and socio-cultural knowledge.[22]

In this study, accordingly, by Mark's original audience I mean the early Christian audiences who, as living inter-personal Christian communities, were familiar not only with routine life in the Mediterranean world, but also with "Christian" subjects (e.g., Jesus' identity as an eschatological messiah, the kingdom of God, faith, discipleship, healing, preaching, miracle, exorcism, and disputation over the observance of the Torah) which are implicitly and explicitly opened in the Gospel of Mark.[23] The assumption of this study, therefore, is that the explicit and implicit meaning of Mark's Gospel may be best understood when

---

[21] Roskam, *The Purpose of the Gospel of Mark*, p. 15.

[22] On the identification of frames, see Chapter One.

[23] Historical-critical studies, such as form and redactional criticism, have claimed that such a wide variety of subject matters reflect the particular concerns of a specific Christian community, within which and for which the Gospel was written. However, as Dunn, *Jesus*, pp. 251–53, rightly claims, "the suggestion that there were churches who knew only one stream of tradition—Jesus only as a miracle worker, or only as a wisdom teacher, etc.—has been given far too much uncritical credence in scholarly discussions on the Gospels and ought to have been dismissed a lot sooner." In this respect, although he undeniably exaggerates when he argues, the "implied readership [of the Gospels] is not specific but indefinite," Bauckham ("For Whom," p. 30) is certainly right to point out that the earliest Christian movement was in no way "a scattering of isolated, self-sufficient communities with little or no communication between them"; but rather "a network of communities with constant close communication among themselves." For this reason, according to Dunn, *Jesus*, p. 252, "Paul could assume common tradition, including knowledge of Jesus tradition, even in a church which he had never previously visited (Rome)." If so, it is no wonder to assume that Mark's Christian audiences may have been also already acquainted with various Christian foundation traditions and subject matters mentioned above and their background knowledge (i.e., frame) which were being circulated among early Christian communities (such as, for example, the Pauline churches).

we take into account that its intended hearers were believers. This
means that the outsider, that is, the non-believer, who did not have
Christian frames to go by, may have understood its meaning differently from the way Mark's Christian hearers did. Jesus' healing action,
for example, has been understood as approving his eschatological
messiahship for the Christian hearers who had the JESUS frame which
includes information that Jesus is the one who brought the kingdom of
God to birth in the world, whereas for outsiders the same action may
have been seen as showing that Jesus was a magician.

3. *Close to Human Life and Situational*

Of more immediate relevance to the concept of frames is the way oral
language is conceptualized. Ong asserts that "oral cultures must con-
ceptualize and verbalize all their knowledge with more or less close
reference to the human lifeworld, assimilating the alien, objective
world to the more immediate, familiar interaction of human beings."[24]
Ong provides an example, drawing on A.R. Luria. Asked to group
things together (*hammer, saw, log, hatchet*) members of an oral culture
answer: "They're all alike. The saw will saw the log and the hatchet will
chop it into small pieces. If one of these has to go, I'd throw out the
hatchet. It doesn't do as good a job as a saw."[25] This observation suggests that for oral people the concepts of words are acquired, interconnected and preserved through their real life-experiences.[26] As Goody
and Watt note, we don't have dictionary definitions of each word in
oral cultures:

> Instead, the meaning of each word is ratified in a succession of con-
> crete situations...This process of direct semantic ratification, of course,
> operates cumulatively; and as a result the totality of symbol-referent
> relationships is more immediately experienced by the individual in an
> exclusively oral culture, and is thus more deeply socialized.[27]

An oral people's way of understanding (i.e., situational thinking) the
concept of words can be explained in terms of a script-type frame.[28]

---

[24] Ong, *Orality*, p. 42. And see also Foley, "Oral Audience," pp. 148–49.
[25] Ong, *Orality*, p. 51 (here he is drawing on Luria's experiment with the illiterate).
[26] Goody and Watt, "Literacy," p. 29.
[27] Goody and Watt, "Literacy," p. 29.
[28] Havelock, *Plato*, pp. 166–67, esp. 180, says that human memory would operate
much better if an oral narrative or its preserved knowledge is cast in a form with

Cognitive scientists most often use a script-like frame as a reference to a stereotyped knowledge about the sequences of actions or events, prototypical things and participants which are associated with a well-defined situation.[29] The script-like frame is formed from repetitious acts such as the journey to work, or cooking a favourite meal, and allows for the understanding and recalling of concepts interrelated due to the domains or situations. According to frame semantics, for instance, people's concept of the word waiter is not related to simply a service man but to a vast repertoire of knowledge in the RESTAURANT frame, including the waiter's motives and clothing and, which is built up through repeat experiences of going to a restaurant.[30] For this reason frame semantics says that people use encyclopedic information in order to properly understand certain concepts.[31]

This is also the case for Mark. Rhoads, Dewey, and Michie claim that "Mark's style is terse, words are concrete rather than abstract."[32] And it is well known that, as will be discussed, concrete actions and an events-packed narrative is characteristic of the Gospel of Mark.[33] These stylistic characteristics readily operate in a relevant script-like frame that allows the concepts of the words to be understood within a specific situational context.

4. *Additive*

Havelock asserts that for better memory operation an oral-aural narrative expresses its thought "paratactically": "Action succeeds action in a kind of endless chain. The basic grammatical expression which would symbolise the link of event to event would be simply the phrase 'and next'...."[34] Likewise, the Markan narrative consists of a series of events joined by 'and.' "Of the thirteen pericope introductions in Mark 1–2, eleven begin with *kai*."[35] In Mark's oral-aural narrative 'and' links

---

which an ordinary audience can easily identify and to which the audience's "psychological needs" of memory conform.

[29] Schank and Abelson, *Scripts*, pp. 36–68, esp. 41.

[30] Schank and Abelson, *Scripts*, pp. 40–41; and see also Croft and Cruse, *Cognitive Linguistics*, p. 7.

[31] Fillmore, "Frame Semantics," p. 134 and Taylor, *Linguistic Categorization*, pp. 81–98 and Croft and Cruse, *Cognitive Linguistics*, p. 30.

[32] Rhoads, Dewey, and Michie, *Mark*, p. 44.

[33] Dewey, "Tapestry," pp. 221–36 and *idem*, *Oral Methods*, pp. 35–36.

[34] Havelock, *Plato*, p. 180.

[35] Dewey, "Oral Methods," p. 35. We will deal with the relationship of 'and next' structure and frame on the sentential level in Chapter Five.

not only events between pericopes but also those between clauses and sentences (see the example of Mark 6.41 below and Chapter Five). A script-like frame of Schank and Abelson which includes the sequencing of frequently experienced events is a good cognitive system to explain the additive feature of oral narrative.[36] A major function of script-type frames allows stories to be preserved and expressed in the prototypical sequence of events. Scripts can then account for the Markan narrative pattern that consists of a chain of events and actions. Since scripts include the contents and the order of the events as their default values, they are capable of guiding the hearer to expect what follows after one action and to make inferences as to what is not explicitly stated, particularly within a single episode; at retrieval they cue recall of the sequences and components (see Chapter Five).[37]

5. Redundant or Copious

"[R]edundancy characterizes oral thought and speech."[38] This is also the case for Mark's Gospel. Repetition has been noted by many scholars as one of the important narrative patterns of Mark's Gospel.[39] For example, Mark's three meal episodes repeat the same actions in the same order:

Mark 6.41 (Feeding of 5,000)	8.6 (Feeding of 4,000)	14.33 (Last Supper)
καὶ λαβὼν... ἄρτους	καὶ λαβὼν τοὺς... ἄρτους	καὶ... λαβὼν ἄρτον
καὶ... εὐλόγησεν	εὐχαριστήσας	εὐλογήσας
καὶ κατέκλασεν	ἔκλασεν	ἔκλασεν
καὶ ἐδίδου	καὶ ἐδίδου	καὶ ἔδωκεν

No doubt the original Markan audience failed to miss this repetitive pattern which is one of the most distinctive features of oral-aural narrative. But more importantly, according to frame theory, overlapping words, phrases and sentences within and between episodes and throughout the whole story are an indication that there are pre-deter-

---

[36] Schank and Abelson, Scripts, p. 41 and see also Rubin, Memory, p. 24.
[37] Schank and Abelson, Scripts, pp. 37–42.
[38] Ong, Orality, p. 40.
[39] On Mark's repetitive narrative pattern, see Robbins, Jesus, pp. 19–51; Kelber, Gospel, pp. 45–70; Frans Neirynck, Duality in Mark: Contributions to the Study of the Markan Redaction (BETL 31; Louvain: Louvain University Press, 1972); Robert M. Fowler, Loaves and Fishes: The Function of the Feeding Stories in the Gospel of Mark (SBLDS 54; Chico: Scholars, 1981).

mined and stereotyped event sequences stored in the memory with respect to a particular frame.[40] A frame includes its own prototypical elements, such as objects, situations, events, actions, and sequences of actions, when the matching frame occurs. This means that it often determines the repetition of the same actions in the same order. In the example above, for the early Christians the repetitive material opened the EUCHARISTIC MEAL frame which included prototypical sequences of actions—taking, giving thanks, breaking and sharing bread (see also 1 Corinthians 11.23–24).[41] Such repetitive elements were already present in the early Christians' (thus Mark and his audience') socio-cultural heritages, and were expressed in performance. As the audience heard the lexical items, thus, to understand the passages they would have made use of them, assimilating them into his/her own frame for THE EUCHARISTIC MEAL.

B. The Features of Oral Composition of Mark's Gospel and Frames

In this section we will discuss how frames may be helpful in understanding the oral compositional characteristics of Mark's oral-aural narrative, partly using Lord's oral composition theory. I do not use Lord's oral thematic composition theory to prove the orality of Mark's Gospel; this is what we already did in the preceding chapter. But the present study is rather concerned with how a narrative is structured and processed in oral cultures. Indeed, the thematic and episodic organization has been referred to as a process of traditional transmission in *primary* oral cultures.[42] Nonetheless, given that the Gospel of Mark, as pointed out in the previous chapter, was written and performed in a rhetorical culture being influenced by a high degree of orality, it is appropriate to see compositional characteristics of the Gospel of Mark as "textual symptoms" of such oral compositions.[43]

---

[40] Schank and Abelson, *Scripts*, p. 41. On the relation of repetitive pattern and frames, see Deborah Tannen, "What's in a Frame," in *New Directions in Discourse Processing* (ed. Roy O. Freedle; Norwood, New Jersey: Ablex, 1979), pp. 167–68.

[41] On the early Christians' EUCHARISTIC MEAL, see section 4.2.1. in Chapter Four.

[42] Lord, *Singer*, pp. 68–98 and Ong, *Orality*, pp. 139–55.

[43] For the term used and an argument similar to mine, see Piether J.J. Botha, "Mark's Story as Oral Traditional Literature: Rethinking the Transmission of Some Traditions About Jesus," *HTS* 47 (1991), pp. 304–31. And for the study that attempts

1. *Thematic Composition*

In an oral culture people do not know what they cannot recall, so all experiences are intellectualized and verbalized mnemonically.[44] For an oral narrative a thematic organization has been long known as a way to orally-based remembering. What an oral narrative speaker remembers to perform is not word-for-word story,[45] but "themes" (or, "type-scenes" and "typical scenes") which are clusters of ideas or repeated incidents, learned from often repeated human experiences.[46] Accordingly, thematic composition is characteristic of the oral-aural narrative. (Note the ancient text has no word gap, no sentence division, no paragraph shif, so the speaker and audience should rely on mental representation of such discourse 'chunks'[47] as thematic units, paragraphs, sentences, clauses, phrases, words.) Themes or typical scenes in Homeric tradition, according to Homerists, include action sequences (e.g., contests, meals, journeys, visits and funeral rites), speech acts (e.g., rebukes, challenges, exhortations, prayers, and boasts) and procedures (e.g., dressing, harnessing horses).[48] Each theme contains a given set of repeated elements of details, "not all of which [however] are always present, nor always in the same order, but enough of which are present to make the scene a recognizable one."[49]

---

to apply oral themes to the analysis of a Pauline letter (to the Philippians), see Casey W. Davis, *Oral Biblical Criticism: The Influence of the Principles of Orality on the Literary Structure of Paul's Epistle to the Philippians* (JSNTSup 172; Sheffield: Sheffield Academic Press, 1999), pp. 92–161; John D. Harvey, *Listening to The Text Oral Patterning in Paul's Letters* (Grand Rapids, Michigan: Baker, 1998).

[44] Ong, *Orality*, pp. 33–36.

[45] On the fluidity of oral memory, see Yates, *Memory*, pp. 1–49, esp. 10–19; C.C. McCown, "Codex and Roll in the New Testament," *HTR* 34 (1941), pp. 219–50; Ong, "Text," pp. 8–9; Lentz, *Orality and Literacy*, pp. 92–93; Thomas, *Literacy and Orality*, pp. 123–27; Burton L. Mack, "Elaboration of the Chreia in the Hellenistic School," in *Patterns of Persuasion in the Gospels* (ed. Burton L. Mack and Vernon K. Robbins; FF; Sonoma, California: Polebridge, 1989), pp. 36–37; Shiner, *Proclaiming the Gospel*, pp. 109–114.

[46] Lord, *Singer*, pp, 68, 78, 98; *idem*, "The Gospels as Oral Traditional Literature," in *The Relationship Among the Gospels: An Interdisciplinary Dialogue* (ed. W.O. Walker; San Antonio: Trinity University Press, 1978), p. 39. Lord, *Singer*, p. 68, says, "Following Parry, I have called the groups of ideas regularly used in telling a tale in the formulaic style of traditional song the 'theme' of the poetry."

[47] On frame's chunking role, see glossary.

[48] Minchin, *Homer*, p. 32.

[49] A.B. Lord, "Perspectives on Recent Work on Oral Literature," in *Oral Literature* (ed. J.J. Duggan; Edinburgh: Scottish Academic Press, 1975), pp. 21–23. For example, in Homeric works the theme of arriving contains: (1) the visitor's being welcomed by his host, (2) the visitor's being washed and fed, (3) the visitor telling who he is

When it comes to the study of the Synoptic Gospels, as discussed earlier, the concept of the thematic pattern of narrative shares certain common ground with that of "forms" in form criticism.[50] For this reason Rhoads, Dewey, and Michie call Mark's episodes repeated in a similar pattern "type-scenes."[51] Despite an important shortcoming regarding the argument for the drastic rupture between pre- and post-Easter traditions, form criticism claims that the Synoptic tradition was preserved and transmitted in various forms reflecting life situations or settings of the early church. In an attempt to seek the "oral forms" of communication remained in the Gospel of Mark, Werner Kelber in his book *The Oral and Written Gospel*, asserts that exorcism stories (Mark 1.23–28; 5.1–20; 9.14–29) or "polarization stories" (to use Kelber's term) repeat in three predictable event sequences, having their "subevents" which Kelber calls "a series of auxiliary features:"

    I.   Confrontation
        a) meeting of exorcist and possessed
        b) the demon's warding-off formula
        c) the exorcist's rebuke and silencing
    II. Expulsion
        a) command to exit
        b) demon's violent exit
    III. Acclamation
        a) choral formula
        b) propagation of cure[52]

The three exorcism stories in Mark's Gospel have a global theme on a higher level—exorcism itself as shown above—and on a lower level its components (Confrontation, Expulsion, Acclamation, and each of their subdivisions) which repeat in the same thematic events and sequential order.

---

and what his ties are to the host, and (4) the visitor's being presented with gifts. See Rubin, *Memory*, p. 19.

[50] On the explanation of the various "forms" occurring in the Gospels, see Rudolf Bultmann, "The Study of the Synoptic Gospels," in *Form Criticism. A New Method of New Testament Research* (trans. Frederick C. Grant; New York: Willett, Clark and Company, 1934), pp. 7–75, and Dibelius, *Tradition*. Botha, "Mark's Story," pp. 319–22, rightly points out the similarity of form criticism's "form" and oral compositional "theme."

[51] Rhoads, Dewey, and Michie, *Mark*, p. 51.

[52] Kelber, *Gospel*, p. 52.

Since a script or frame is "a predetermined, stereotyped sequence of events that defines a well-known situation,"[53] the frame may explain the repetitive pattern of "themes" or "forms" dealing with the events of life in the oral-aural narrative. With respect to the nature of the script-like frame, Schank and Abelson suggest:

> The form of memory organization upon which our arguments [for script] are based is the notion of episodic memory. An episodic view of memory claims that memory is organized around personal experiences or episodes rather than around abstract semantic categories. If memory is organized around personal experiences then one then *one of the principal components of memory must be a procedure for recognizing repeated or similar sequences.* When a standard repeated sequence is recognized, it is helpful in 'filling in the blanks' in understanding. *Furthermore much of the language generation behavior of people can be explained in this stereotyped way.*[54]

For this reason the frame has been argued by Homerists as the closest concept to theme. Thus Minchin, a Homeric scholar, says:

> [T]he typical scene (such as dressing, or preparing a meal), which Lord has declared to be a chunk of discourse committed to memory by an apprentice singer with performance in mind, may in fact be a scripted entity which encapsulates a standardized record of routine activities and which the singer to be, like anyone else, will have learned early in his life.[55]

Certainly, as discussed in Chapter One, there is no need here to assume a form-critical paradigm that the "forms" or script-type frames were created in the course of community development. From the perspective of frames, the speaker and audience process the story in terms of an already existent pattern of event sequences in the mental frame, which is formed through their repeated cultural and linguistic experience. This is the reason that in Mark's oral-aural narrative a series of stories dealing with similar situations has a thematically repeated sequence of events (thus in the exorcism stories, Confrontation, Expulsion, and Acclamation and each with its subevents).[56] Consequently, this frame enables the speaker and listener's memory tasks to be easier because

---

[53] On the definition of script, see Schank and Abelson, *Scripts*, p. 41.

[54] Schank and Abelson, *Scripts*, pp. 18–19. [italics are mine]

[55] Minchin, *Homer*, pp. 14–15.

[56] Likewise, Botha, "Mark's Story," p. 320, identifies those confrontation stories as an example of Mark's "thematic composition."

it has well-known and predictable sequences of events, and so, within the frame, one component stereotypically leads to another.

2. *Episodic Structure*

The basic structure of an oral-aural narrative is episodic.[57] Ong says that, in a primarily oral culture, episodic structure is the most convenient way for the speaker to handle a lengthy narrative.[58] This is also true of the Gospels, which are the products of a semi-oral culture (or "rhetorical culture" to use Robbins' term). It has recently been studied that pericopes or episodes in the Gospel of Mark serve as a basic narrative unit for the stories to be interconnected in varying ways, such as concentric patterns and three-step progressions.[59] Dewey characterizes Mark's oral narrative as "a loose concatenation of series of episodes" strung together in overlapping and interwoven ways rather than a single linear development.[60] This is, according to Dewey, the reason why many scholars fail to find a single linear structure in the Gospel of Mark.[61] If the oral-aural narrative is structured episodically, it is natural to assume that a audience's oral narrative processing is based on its episodic units.

In what ways then do frames aid the audience's episodic processing of oral-aural narrative? We will discuss in detail this topic in the chapters to follow. Here a brief observation will be made in relation to this question. Frame theory provides a theoretical foundation for the cognitive processing of episodic structure in Mark's oral-aural narrative.[62] My argument is that frames have their prototypical components

---

[57] Havelock, *Plato*, pp. 173–75, says that "The fundamental units of the tribal encyclopedia [oral narrative] are sets of doings," "happenings," "episodes," "little stories or situations"; and see also Ong, "Oral Remembering and Narrative Structures," in *Analyzing Discourse: Text and Talk* (ed. Deborah Tannen; Washington, D.C.: Georgetown University Press, 1981), pp. 12–19.

[58] Ong, "Oral Remembering," p. 16.

[59] For example, see Rhoads, Dewey, and Michie, *Mark*, pp. 51–55; Robbins, *Jesus*, pp. 7–10.

[60] Dewey, "Tapestry," pp. 221–36.

[61] Dewey, "Tapestry," p. 224.

[62] For cognitive evidence with respect to the mnemonic effect of episodic structure, see Teun A. van Dijk, "Episodes as Units of Discourse Analysis," in *Analyzing Discourse: Text and Talk* (ed. Deborah Tannen; Washington, D.C.: Georgetown University Press, 1981), pp. 181, 190–92; John B. Black "Episodes as Chunks in Narrative Memory," *VLVB* 18 (1979), pp. 309–10; Valerie Abbott, John B. Black and Edward E. Smith, "The Representation of Scripts in Memory," *JML* 24 (1985), pp. 179–99.

associated with situational information such as characters, location, and time, thus allowing the audience to process an episode as a conceptually or semantically unified unit. In particular, as will be mentioned, since a frame is a set of hierarchically and causally interrelated concepts of stereotyped situations, once the frame is opened by the core elements of a frame (about the opening of a frame, see the chapter to follow), its components are consequently processed as part of a semantically cohesive unit; at retrieval the constituents of the episode are remembered together. In this processing, the frame not only provides a framework for understanding the material of the episode, but also serves to bond the material into an independent chunk.[63]

3. Recall of the Gist of a Story

In oral cultures every performance is new. As they encounter new audiences in every performance, performers make the story a communication event for the audiences by fitting it to the audience's context. The implication is that the story in oral-aural environments includes elements of both stability and variability.[64] But it is important to keep in mind once again that for an oral-aural narrative, stability does not necessarily mean verbatim reproduction; recall of the gist and general structure is enough. Cicero says that "a memory for words [word for word memory]...for us is less essential....but a memory for things [arguments memory] is the special property of the orator."[65] As for the oral-aural Gospels, Birger Gerhardsson also notes:

> In the hermeneutical debate today, there are reasons for thinking once more about the early church Fathers' theme...that the gospel is a spoken word (*viva vox*). The double point of departure is that books surely are permitted and important...but that the gospel was from the beginning a markedly oral word, which should be written 'in the heart' of the

---

[63] Indeed, though causal processing is a fundamental aspect of human cognition of events, the stories of Mark's Gospel are not interlinked with each other in a strict linear plot development *as a whole*, as expected in a modern novel; but they are joined together paratactically. But here it is very important to guard against assuming that this is also the case for *the relationship between the events within an episode*. We will investigate that a causal relationship is an appropriate human cognitive process complete and satisfying in itself to explain the flow of the events within the episode or paragraph.

[64] Rubin, *Memory*, pp. 6–7.

[65] Cicero, *De oratorie* 2.85.359.

listeners...To achieve this aim, it was vital that the message was living, flexible speech.[66]

Despite a general agreement as to the nature of oral memory, little attention has been paid to establishing what the gist is and how it can be abstracted from an oral-aural narrative discourse. Defining the gist of an oral narrative memory as "commonly the sequence of structure that makes the event meaningful to the person who initially perceives and then recalls," Richard Bauckham argues that the gist is an important component of the eyewitness's memories, and that frame is an appropriate type of memory to account for the gist.[67] As noted by Baukham, frame is informative in defining the gist of the oral-aural narrative. Robert Howard suggests:

> Schemata are very important in remembering. Yet, first, we need to distinguish between two types of remembering. Verbatim recall is the recall of information learned by rote....Meaningful recall is usually recall of the gist or the main ideas, rather than their exact wording. Schemata [frames] affect recall of meaningful material....[68]

But how do frames affect the recall of the gist? David Rumelhart, a scholar in the fields of cognitive psychology and artificial intelligence, suggests that mental frames determine what we acquire from incoming information.[69] We do not remember the event in itself; instead, we tend to recall information filled or 'instantiated'[70] in terms of frames, forgetting the data inappropriate to the frame.[71] Here Rumelhart seems to identify information processed by the frame as the gist of the information or story. Accepting frames' summarizing role of information, we will further account for the specific ways in which the frame can affect the form of what we acquire. In doing so, I will primarily refer to the cognitive scientist's idea that "people remember events high in the story hierarchies better than those at lower levels" (for a full discussion, see the chapters to follow).[72]

---

[66] Birger Gerhardsson, "Oral Tradition (New Testament)," in *A Dictionary of Biblical Interpretation* (ed. R.J. Coggins and J.L. Houlden; London: SCM, 1990), p. 500.

[67] Bauckham, *Eyewitnesses*, pp. 333–34, 344–45 (the quotation from p. 334).

[68] Howard, *Concept*, p. 44.

[69] Rumelhart, "Schemata," pp. 49–50.

[70] See the glossary on the term instantiation.

[71] Rumelhart, "Schemata," pp. 49–50.

[72] Schank and Abelson, *Scripts*, pp. 42–46, 160–67; Abbott, Black and Smith, "Scripts," p. 193; Mandler, *Scripts*, p. 67.

C. Conclusion

Drawing on Foley's concept of "immanence," Dewey rightly observes that the original audience's processing of the Markan oral-aural narrative is not based on the text alone, but on his or her prior knowledge of traditions and social contexts:

> [T]he oral story builds on traditions known to both the performer and the audience. As John Miles Foley has shown, references in oral literature are generally metonymic, recalling the larger tradition rather than some specific objective reality. The part stands for the whole and reminds the hearers of a whole complex of traditions with which they are already familiar.[73]

Cognitive scientists make the same point regarding frame theory, as mentioned earlier. Human acquistion of incoming information is not just dependent on the information alone, but on the existing background knowledge organized through past situation, hence frame knowledge.

As discussed, frame-based information processing is a universal cognitive phenomenon of human beings. So what I am attempting to show is how the oral features and structures of the Gospel of Mark are closely associated with the operation of frame-based memory. Consequently, from the relation of the Gospel's orality and frames two conclusions must be drawn. First, oral thoughts and expressions which the Gospel of Mark shows can be easily explained in terms of frame-based memory representation. Second, the frame can be an appropriate cognitive model to illuminate the thematic composition, episodic organization and gist memory of the Markan oral-aural narrative.

It is time, now, to turn our attention to frame theory itself. The next chapter will introduce varying and specific ways in which such a frame helps organize and comprehend narrative discourse.

---

[73] Dewey, "John," p. 244. But frame theory is outside of the concern of her study.

CHAPTER FOUR

FRAME THEORY

In the conclusion of the preceding chapter, I have stated that the frame is a cognitive model to explain the compositional characteristics of Mark's oral-aural narrative, thus opening the way to the use of frame theory for investigating Mark 2.1–3.6. But before proceeding to such a study, this chapter will introduce in detail the properties of frame theory that are relevant for analyzing the structure and contents of Mark's oral-aural narrative. We have already surveyed how frames form in the mind; so the present chapter will focus on their nature, type, and function. The ultimate concern of this exploration is to establish theoretical foundations for analyzing how the Controversy Stories (Mark 2.1–3.6) are organized in terms of frames whereby the aural audience can readily comprehend and remember them.

A. The Nature of Frames

Although there are a few attempts to define the structure of frames in the literature of frame theory, George Lakoff explores the principles on which the frames or ICMs (Idealized Cognitive Model) are organized. His analysis of the structures of ICMs is particularly significant in that it allows us to see how a global frame, including its subframes, in the Controversy Stories organizes information into a structured network. Our next focus is to explore various types of frames, which have their own prototypical components.

1. Structure

Lakoff says, "Each ICM has an ontology and a structure. The ontology is the set of elements [or concepts] used in the ICM. The structure consists of the properties of the elements and the relations obtaining among the elements."[1] Since every culture, according to Lakoff,

---

[1] Lakoff, *Women*, p. 285.

may have its own contents of knowledge, the entities (to use his term "ontology") of each ICM are "idealized" in terms of cultural experiences; however, their representative patterns are structured universally primarily on the basis of bodily experiences.[2] Indeed, the structures are general cognitive processes proposed by cognitive psychologists.[3] But cognitive linguists, as discussed in Chapter One, believe that linguistic construal operations are instances of general cognitive abilities. Thus, frame-based information processing is inseparably related to general cognitive processes. What is then the function of such a structural property of the ICM or frame? For Lakoff a frame is a cognitive model by which to organize our knowledge and experience.[4] To understand a concept means that we are capable of structuring the concept into an existing knowledge or frame. But Lakoff argues further that the reason such concepts in the frame are meaningful is that they are structured in our bodily experience or "embodied."[5] Calling this preconceptual structuring principle of the frame "kinesthetic image schemas," he says:

> One of Mark Johnson's basic insights is that experience is structured in a significant way prior to, and independent of, any concepts. Existing concepts may impose further structuring on what we experience, but basic experiential structures are present regardless of any such imposition of concepts. This may sound mysterious, but it is actually very simple and obvious, so much so that it is not usually considered worthy of notice.[6]

I will describe below the major structuring properties of the frame that are relevant for the investigation of the ways in which his con-

---

[2] Lakoff, *Women*, pp. 68–69, 268, 282–83: Lakoff basically classifies ICMs into four types: "images-schematic"; "prepositional"; "metaphoric"; "metonymic" and the four types of models are constantly used as structuring principles of knowledge. And Lakoff, *Women*, p. 68, says, "Each ICM is a complex structured whole, a gestalt, which uses four kinds of structuring principles."

[3] Croft and Cruse, *Cognitive Linguistics*, pp. 40–73, esp. 45–46.

[4] Lakoff, *Women*, pp. 68, 153–54.

[5] Lakof, *Women*, pp. 277–67.

[6] Lakoff, *Women*, p. 27, citing Mark Johnson's book, *The Body in the Mind* (Chicago: University of Chicago Press, 1987), refers to the image-schematic structure as one of five basic types of frames, as noted above. See *idem, Women*, p. 284. But apparently, he keeps using it as a key principle to organize the elements of other frames. See *idem, Women*, pp. 86, 282–83.

temporary audience may have organized the Controversy Stories into "units."[7]

"Image schemas," according to Lakoff, "are relatively simple structures that constantly recur in our everyday bodily experience: CONTAINERS, PATHS, LINKS, FORCES, BALANCE, and in various orientations and relations: UP-DOWN, FRONT-BACK, PART-WHOLE, CENTRE-PERIPERY, etc."[8] A summary of Lakoff's suggestion is as follows:

1) The CONTAINER Schema:
Bodily experience: We constantly experience our bodies both as containers and as things in containers (e.g., rooms).
Structural elements: INTERIOR, BOUNDARY, EXTERIOR.
Basic logic: Everything is either inside a container or out of it—P or not P.
Sample metaphors: The visual field is understood as a container, e.g., things *come into* and *go out of sight*. Personal relationships are also understood in terms of containers: One can be *trapped in a marriage* and *get out of it*.

2) The PART-WHOLE Schema
Bodily experience: We experience our bodies as WHOLES with PARTS. In order to get around in the world, we have to be aware of the PART-WHOLE structure of other objects.
Structural elements: A WHOLE, PARTS, and a CONFIGURATION.
Basic logic: If A is a part of B, then B is not a part of A. It cannot be the case that the WHOLE exists, while no PARTS of it exist. However, all the PARTS can exist, but still not constitute a WHOLE. If the PARTS exist in the CONFIGURATION, then and only then does the WHOLE exist.
Sample metaphors: Families (and other social organizations) are understood as wholes with parts.

3) The LINK Schema
Bodily experience: Throughout infancy and early childhood, we hold onto our parents and other things, either to secure our location or theirs.
Structural elements: Two entities, A and B, and LINK connecting them.

---

[7] The term "unit," after being brought by M.A.K. Halliday into discourse analysis, has been used as a category to account for "segments of spoken or written text that consist of recurrently meaningful patterns and/or operate as components of meaningful patterns." See Carl H. Frederiksen, "Semantic Processing Units in Understanding Text," in *Discourse Production and Comprehension*. Vol. 1 *in the series, Discourse Processes: Advances in Research and Theory* (ed. Roy O. Freedle; Norwood, New Jersey: Ablex, 1977), p. 58.
[8] Lakoff, *Women*, p. 267.

Basic logic: If A is linked to B, then A is constrained by B, and dependent upon B.
Symmetry: If A is linked to B, then B is linked to A.
Metaphor: Social and interpersonal relationships are often understood in terms of links. Thus, we *make connections*
and *break social ties* (e.g., slavery and freedom).

4) The CENTRE-PERIPHERY Schema
Bodily experience: We experience our bodies as having centres (the trunk and internal organs) and peripheries (fingers, toes, hair). The centres are viewed as more important than the peripheries. Similarly, the centre defines the identity of the individual in a way that the peripheral parts do not.
Structural elements: An ENTITY, a CENTRE, and a PERIPHERY.
Basic logic: The periphery depends on the centre, but not vice versa.

5) The SOURCE-PATH-GOAL Schema
Bodily experience: Every time we move anywhere there is a place we start from, a place we wind up at, a sequence of contiguous locations connecting the starting and ending points, and a direction.
Structural elements: A SOURCE (starting point), a DESTINATION (end point), a PATH (a sequence of contiguous locations connecting the source and the destination), and a Direction (toward the destination).
Basic logic: If you go from a source to a destination along a path, then you must pass through each intermediate point on the path.
Metaphors: Purposes are understood in terms of destinations, and achieving a purpose is understood as passing along a path from a starting point to an endpoint. Complex events in general are also understood in terms of a source-path-goal schema; complex events have initial states (source), a sequence of intermediate stages (path), and a final stage (destination).

Other image schemas include an UP-DOWN schema, a FRONT-BACK schema, a LINEAR ORDER schema, etc.[9]

In addition to the function of image-schemas that structure our experience of space, Lakoff claims that they determine the structure of the "conceptual space" too.[10] He thus maintains:

- Categories (in general) are understood in terms of CONTAINER schemas
- Hierarchical structure is understood in terms of PART-WHOLE schemas and UP-DOWN schemas

[9] Lakoff, *Women*, pp. 272–75.
[10] Lakoff, *Women*, p. 283.

- Relation structure in categories is understood in terms of LINK-schemas
- Radial structure in categories is understood in terms of CENTRE-PERIPHERY schemas
- Foreground-background structure is understood in terms of FRONT-BACK schemas
- Linear quantity scales are understood in terms of UP-DOWN schemas and LINEAR ORDER schemas[11]

For our study, the importance of Lakoff's idea of the structuring principles of frames is immense. In particular, this is greatly helpful for narrative organization and comprehension. A story indeed consists of various frames, but it usually includes one global frame and its subframes. The story dominated by the global frame represents its components in the part-whole or hierarchical structure; thus, a global frame is a whole, and its components or subframes are parts. Alongside the relationship of a global frame to its components, the connection between the components may be made in the link structure. The container structure of a frame is also useful in creating a paragraph or episode boundary. The container structure, which consists of interior, boundary, and exterior enables, the audience to infer the boundary of a global frame-based episode within which the coherence of information can be made. In such a frame-based text sentences are not heard in isolation but as part of a bound whole. Therefore, by chunking it into meaningful or coherent units, frame structures enable frame-based information to be comprehended and communicated quickly and efficiently.

2. Types and Components

I am concerned here with introducing the divergent types of frames and their components. This introduction aims to demonstrate that frames are cognitive models capable of processing diverse information.[12]

---

[11] Lakoff, *Women*, p. 283.

[12] Most of what is said here about the types of frames synthesizes insights derived from Schank and Abelson, *Scripts*, pp. 61–66; Shelley E. Taylor and Jennifer Crocker, "Schematic Bases of Social Information Processing," in *Social Cognition: The Ontario Symposium*. Vol. 1 (ed. E. Tory Higgins, C. Peter Herman, and Mark P. Zanna; Hillsdale, New Jersey: Erlbaum, 1981), pp. 89–134; David L. Hamilton, "Cognitive Representations of Person," in *Social Cognition: The Ontario Symposium*. Vol. 1 (ed. E. Tory Higgins, C. Peter Herman, and Mark P. Zanna; Hillsdale, New Jersey: Erlbaum, 1981), pp. 135–59; Reid Hastie, "Schematic Principles in Human Memory," in *Social*

2.1. *Thing Frame*[13]

The thing frame involves inventory and spatial location information for an object and place. To use Rumelhart's example, the FACE frame consists of several components or subframes which are called "slots."[14] So here frame knowledge includes information that a face has two eyes, two ears, one nose and two lips, chin, etc.; and the EYE frame also has as its subframes or slots—pupil, iris, eyelid etc.—which are opened by the EYE frame, rather than by the FACE frame. Frames also contain information about the relationships that normally hold between the components.[15] For example, in the FACE frame, the face has two eyes on its front side, the ears above the nose, the lips below the nose and so on. Also consider the HOUSE frame, a place frame: Its slots include a roof on its top, walls surrounding it, a flat floor, doors, and windows.[16] The thing frame also involves information on the function of the object belonging to it; for instance, the kitchen is a place for cooking. Jean Mandler suggests twofold benefits of this kind of thing frame in story processing. First, the thing frame provides inventory information that is usually expected to appear in a specific place; second, it enables the hearer/reader to depict "the typical spatial layout of a scene."[17] The elements of the thing frame are represented in terms of the part-whole or hierarchical structure. Consider the FACE frame again. The face is a whole with eyes, lips, nose and eyes as parts. The parts are hierarchically linked to the whole: The nose concept cannot be processed without an assumption of the concept of the human face to which it belongs. Strictly speaking, the word nose can only be understood against the FACE frame.

Cognition: The Ontario Symposium. Vol. 1 (ed. E. Tory Higgins, C. Peter Herman, and Mark P. Zanna; Hillsdale, New Jersey: Erlbaum, 1981), pp. 39–88; Jean M. Mandler, *Stories, Scripts, and Scenes: Aspects of Schema Theory* (Hillsdale, New Jersey.: Erlbaum, 1984); Howard, *Schemata*, pp. 45–48.

[13] Scholars usually use the "scene frame" to refer to the information of landscape and place. For example, see Mandler, *Scripts*, pp. 15–17; Hastie, "Human Memory," pp. 55–56; and Howard, *Schemata*, pp. 45–46. But Hoyle, "Scenarios," p. 29, instead of the scene frame, uses the term "thing frame" to include broad concepts, such as person, scene and place. This book will employ the term "thing frame" following Hoyle but we will also use the person frame distinct from the thing frame.

[14] Rumelhart and Ortony, "Representation of Knowledge," pp. 106–109. On the terms "slots," see Schank and Abelson, *Scripts*, p. 41.

[15] Rumelhart and Ortony, "Representation of Knowledge," pp. 106–109.

[16] Mandler, *Stories*, p. 15.

[17] Mandler, *Stories*, p. 16.

2.2. Person Frame

The person frame in general includes, within a person's personality, such slots as interests, motivation of behaviour, and so on.[18] The person frame is often classified into three types. The first type is the person we know generally through our repeated experiences of him or her, and represents knowledge of one's likes and dislikes, and traits. The second type is the person we know best, which includes knowledge of his or her strengths, weaknesses, and personal traits. The person frame of the third type has to do with social, ethnic, and occupational groups (e.g., volunteers, drunkards, Asians, politicians, street persons, a bus driver, clergy).[19] When we encounter a person in a story world or in the real world, we draw upon our cognitive representation of that kind of person, that is, the person frame, to understand the behaviour of the person.[20] And since the person frame includes knowledge of what would be the individual's typical behaviour in certain situations, it allows us to make predictions of how she or he is likely to act. (Note, for example, that our understanding and expectation of animal stories is largely based on the stereotypical personality frames for the wolf, pig, fox, etc.).[21] The person frame is represented structurally in terms of the link schema. Studies from experiments by social cognitive scientists show that when given lists of behavioural descriptions of an individual, people tend to group materials into "some conceptually good figure on the basis of their schematic conceptions of personality types"; and at recall within the person frame, relevant materials which are so organized have a better mnemonic effect than irrelevant materials.[22] Besides the link structure, the source-path-goal relation affects the organization of the person frame. The impression made by the typical behaviour of the social groups (e.g., purpose-driven actions) plays a driving role in organizing person frame-relevant materials into a goal-directed sequence: A source (starting point), path (on the way to achieve purpose[s]) and goal (achievement of purpose[s]).[23]

---

[18] Hamilton, "Cognitive Representations," p. 151.
[19] Taylor and Crocker, "Schematic Basis," p. 91; Hasti, "Human Memory," pp. 58–71; Howard, *Schemata*, pp. 47–48.
[20] Hamilton, "Persons," pp. 149–52.
[21] For an appropriate example of animal stories, see Minsky, "Framework," pp. 232–37.
[22] Taylor and Crocker, "Schematic Bases," p. 95; Hastie, "Human Memory," pp. 64–69.
[23] Taylor and Crocker, "Schematic Bases," pp. 111–14.

2.3. *Event Frame or Script-Type Frame*

An event frame, or "script-like frame" (using Schank and Abelson's term) has, as its prototypical entities, the sequence of events, location, agents and props.[24] A simple example is the VISITING A FAMILY DOCTOR'S OFFICE frame here in Canada: One feels sick, comes into the office, registers, waits one's turn, sees the doctor, receives the prescription, and comes out. The frame is processed in a more or less fixed order. Such a sequence of actions provides us with a set of expectations about what will happen next and about what entities are likely to be involved in each stage. A frame-based event has not only its prototypical event sequences but also participants and their role slots (e.g., a doctor, patients, registrar(s), bed(s) in the doctor's office). When visiting a family doctor's office or encountering the event discourse, one automatically maps it onto the participant and role slots in the event frame, understanding what the actions of the participants mean and the functions of the props. For instance, because of the frame knowledge regarding the slots for the participants and props' roles, we do not wonder about a registrar asking us to present our health insurance card, and are not surprised to see a (medical) bed in the doctor's office.

Events in script-like frames are organized in a hierarchical (or part-whole) and causal structure (for details, see below).[25] Also, they are linked together in memory in terms of goal-directed relation usually based on a temporal sequence; and the goal sequence is represented by source-path-goal structure:

> The beginning state = the source
> The middle state = the path
> The final state = the goal.[26]

2.4. *Story Frame: Knowledge of Typical Text Structures*

The frames I have surveyed above specify typical knowledge associated with "person," things, including places, objects, and events. Yet the

---

[24] Schank and Abelson, *Scripts*, pp. 41–50.

[25] Lakoff, *Women*, p. 286

[26] Lakoff, *Women*, pp. 285–86, originally suggests the structure of an event-like frame as follows:
> "the initial stage = the source
> the final stage = the destination
> the events = locations on the path."

type of frame in question has to do with the arrangement of the frame knowledge into a story, that is, the common form of a story which is called "story-schemata" or "story grammar."[27] As van Dijk posits, "the reader/hearer has serious expectations about the discourse type and therefore about the schema, [story frame] so that his discourse knowledge enables him to actualize the respective categories."[28] Such story processing of the reader/hearer becomes apparent by virtue of cognitive scientists' experiments. Using the experimental results of human text memory, Perry Thorndyke and Frank Yekovich, cognitive scientists, show how the hearer/reader uses the story schemata or story frame to comprehend and remember narratives. When requested to recall a story that deviates from the normal, expected sequence, they usually "relocate the events in the narrative and recall it in a typical order."[29] Thus, Thorndyke and Yekovich conclude: "These findings indicate that the violation of culturally-accepted structural conventions in stories interferes with the processing of the story information."[30] What is then the common, or 'expected,' sequence of a story-frame? Thorndyke and Yekovich state that for the audience/reader "in general, the more explicit the temporal, causal, and intentional relationships among events in a story, the more comprehensible the story is."[31] The implication is that the typical relationship imputed to event sequences represented by the story frame can be characterized by temporal sequence and causality. On this basic assumption, scholars in this field have attempted to provide various prototypical "grammars" (or "rewrite rules") for encoding narrative structures.[32] This insight from

---

[27] For several discussions of "story-frame" or "rewrite rules" for story, see David E. Rumelhart, "Notes On a Schema for Stories," in *Representation and Understanding: Studies in Cognitive Science* (ed. Daniel G. Bobrow and Allan Collins; New York: Academic Press, 1975), pp. 211–36; P.W. Thorndyke, "Cognitive Structures in Comprehension and Memory of Narrative Discourse," *CP* 9 (1977), pp. 77–110; Mandler, *Stories*, pp. 17–113.

[28] Teun. A. van Dijk, *Macrostructures: An Interdisciplinary Study of Global Structures in Discourse, Interaction, and Cognition* (Hillsdale, New Jersey: Erlbaum, 1980), p. 242.

[29] See Perry W. Thorndyke and Frank R. Yekovich, "A Critique of Schema-Based Theories of Human Story Memory," *Poetics* 9 (1980), pp. 28–29.

[30] Thorndyke and Yekovic, "Schema," pp. 28–29.

[31] Thorndyke and Yekovich, "Schema Theory," p. 32.

[32] For example, Mandler, *Scripts*, p. 24, proposes a rule, Story → Setting and Episode; Episode → Beginning cause Development cause Ending, and so on. And P.W. Thorndyke, "Cognitive Structures in Comprehension and Memory of Narrative

cognitive science is also adapted by Richard Bauckahm to account for
the eyewitnesses's memories behind the Gospels:

> When it comes to memories of events, we must take special account of
> story schemata, which are derived not so much from our direct experi-
> ence of events as from hearing and reading stories and unconsciously
> learning the kinds of narrative structures that are commonly employed
> to tell a meaningful story, whether real or fictional.... In perception and
> recall we are constantly narrativizing experience—by selection, connec-
> tion, and explanation of items—and must employ such narrative struc-
> tures as are available to us as established schemata in our memories. This
> is the only way to make sense of events in the way that stories do.[33]

However, we must be cautious about directly adapting such story formats as those of the Markan Controversy Stories without any regard
for the characteristics of the story. Rather, as mentioned above, a
global event frame makes an impact on the structure of discourse by
means of its typical sequence of events which are in a causal chain and
goal-directed plot. So the expected sequences of the event in the global
LEGAL CONTROVERSY frame (Provocative Events, Charge, Defence and
Verdict, see Chapter Five) must be taken into consideration to determine the structure of the story frame in Mark 2.1–3.6.[34]

Robert Longacre suggests a "narrative template" according to
which Mark's stories are made as follows: "Stage, Inciting Incident,
Mounting Tension, Climax, Denouement, Closure."[35] In my judge-
ment, Longacre's story frame is, though with variation, the best fit
for analyzing the narrative flow of Mark's Controversy Stories, since
Longacre's model appropriately corresponds to and explains the organization of conflict event sequences in Mark 2.1–3.6. Thus, the suggestion is that the cognitive frame for the story format of the five episodes
in Mark 2.1–3.6 may be identified on the basis of Longacre's model with
some variation. (For a specific application to each episode, see Chapter
Six: Preparing Stage, Inciting Incident, Mounting Tension, Climax,
Closure). In Mark's Controversy Stories the purpose of the Preparing
Stage is "to lay the foundation for creating the storyworld time, place,

---

Discourse," *CP* 9 (1977), pp. 77–110, suggests, for a rule for "story": Story → Setting
+ Theme + Plot + Resolution; and a rule for an "episode": Episode → Subgoal +
Attempts + Outcome.

[33] Bauckham, *Eyewitnesses*, p. 346.
[34] Likewise, Thorndyke and Yekovich, "Schema Theory," p. 28.
[35] Longacre, "Narrative Analysis," pp. 140–41.

circumstances and participants (not necessarily the ones dominating the ensuing story)."[36] The section of Inciting Incident introduces a series of "unexpected and routine-breaking" events.[37] With regard to the expected event sequences in the LEGAL CONTROVERSY frame, the Provocative chunk represents the events in the Inciting Incident. The Mounting Tension section representing the Charge chunk involves the antagonist's action that complicates the preceding story, thus causing tension. In the Climax section, representing the Defence chunk, the tension is heightened by the protagonist's response. The Closure section, or Verdict chunk, brings in the resolution of the tension by means of specific events or the participants' evaluative words.

B. FRAMES' FORMAL PROPERTIES AND INFORMATION PROCESSING

It has been confirmed among frame theoreticians that frames are not only units or structures for organizing data but also structures that contain conventional knowledge.[38] In order to know how frame-based information processing operates, it is therefore necessary to keep in mind such properties. The aim of this section is twofold: One is to survey the ways in which frames structure information into semantically coherent chunks; the other is to investigate how frames help the audience/reader efficiently comprehend incoming information.

1. *The Organization of Information*

A human's understanding of information or event is fundamentally based on his or her ability to structure it in cognitive terms. As Kathleen Callow, a linguist and translator, says:

> [M]an's past experience is stored in his mind in areas, and it is stored in the form of units within units. He has the capacity to see very complex events as in some way a unit. At the same time he has the capacity to see the constituent parts as themselves unities. Without this capacity, memory as we know it could not exist and coherent thoughts could not take place. It is not simply that our minds would be confused and

---

[36] Longacre, "Narrative Analysis," p. 141.
[37] Longacre, "Narrative Analysis," p. 141.
[38] Minsky, "Framework," pp. 211–12; van Dijk, "Semantic Macro-Structure," pp. 18–22; Marshall, *Schemas*, pp. 22–23.

disorganised, it is rather that thinking as we know it could not occur at all. One of the essential human capacities that makes thought possible is the recognition of units relating variety together, and variety conjoining to form a unity.[39]

Since frames have their own structuring principles and prototypical components, frames can chunk information into a conceptually or semantically consistent narrative discourse unit. Once the incoming information is matched to a frame, the elements come to be organized in a manner that mirrors the frame and its structures.

1.1. *A Frame Can be Opened by its Core Constituents and Title*

Hearing/reading a text is not an act of passive information reception or "a pipeline transfer of material called 'information' from one place to another."[40] Rather it requires an audience/reader to be actively involved in using relevant frames, in order to interpret the input. Sanford and Garrod say that the listener or reader processes the text in two different stages: "First, he must use the text to identify an appropriate domain of reference, loosely corresponding to what the text is about, and second, he must use the identified domain of reference to interpret the subsequent text as far as this is possible."[41] The mere possession of a relevant frame is not of use for this information or story comprehension. The frame must be activated when hearing/reading a story for an audience/reader to make available from memory more general or typical background knowledge. A mismatch between a frame and the incoming information will then result in losing the input, and thus in miscommunication. Of critical importance is, as a result, to open the appropriate frame which corresponds to the input.[42] In cognitive linguistic terms linguistic items play a key role in leading the audience to open a frame because, as Fillmore claims, "in the process of using a language, a speaker 'applies' a frame to a situation, and shows that he intends this frame to be applied by using words recognized as grounded in such a frame."[43]

---

[39] Callow, *Man*, p. 28.
[40] Ong, *Orality*, p. 176.
[41] Sanford and Garrod, *Understanding*, p. 109.
[42] Rumelhart, "Schemata," pp. 47–48.
[43] Fillmore, "Frame Semantics," p. 120.

But a question arises here: How are words capable of opening conceptual knowledge structures, or frames? A frame is assumed to consist of a set of interrelated concepts; so, in order to answer this question it is necessary to explain the relation of the concepts and words. According to the theoretical constructs of cognitive linguists, "concepts correspond to meanings of linguistics units."[44] A linguistic expression or a word is not a concept, but it is a label to a concept. The central principle of frame semantics is, as Timothy Clausner and William Croft note, that concepts labelled by words "do not occur as isolated, atomic units in the mind, but can only be comprehended (by the speaker as well as the analyst) in a context of presupposed, background knowledge structures [frames]."[45] As Fillmore says:

> Nor would we expect to find *father, mother, son, daughter, brother, and sister* separated from each other, or *buy, sell, pay, spend,* and *cost,* or *day, night, noon, midnight, morning, afternoon, and evening.* These words form groups that learners would do well to *learn together,* because in each case they are lexical representatives of some single coherent schematization of experience of knowledge [that is, frame].... And since the knowledge which underlies the meanings of the words in each group is generally acquired all at once, it would seem natural to expect students to learn the words together.[46]

The observation above leads to a hypothesis that the activation of a frame, which is an organizer of a set of concepts labelled by words, may be caused by the words or phrases referring to the core elements in the frame. By the words referring to the core elements, I mean the lexicons at the basic level in what is called by Rosch "prototype theory."[47] According to Rosch *et al.*, there are three levels of categorization: Superordinate, basic, and subordinate, and people primarily use, whether in linguistic or conceptual categorization,[48] the basic level category to understand, and describe and communicate objects, and events.[49] As Sanford and Garrod note:

---

[44] Croft and Cruse, *Cognitive Linguistics*, p. 14.
[45] Clausner and Croft, "Domains," p. 2.
[46] Charles Fillmore, "Frames and the Semantics of Understanding," *QS* 6–7 (1985–86), p. 223.
[47] Eleanor E. Rosch, Carolyn B. Mervis, Wayne Gray, David Johnson and Penny Boyes-Braem, "Basic Objects in Natural Categories," *CP* 8 (1976), pp. 382–439.
[48] Lakoff, *Women*, pp. 58–67.
[49] Rosch *et al.*, "Basic Objects," pp. 388–93. An appropriate example of three levels of categorization is as follows (basic categories that people prefer to describe an object in most contexts are bolded):

Suppose a speaker or a writer wishes to refer to 'a tank' which he has in his communication plan. He will probably refer to it as 'a tank' and not as 'a vehicle'. The reason is that the listener or reader will have an idea of the properties of tanks, the sorts of things they can do, the situations in which they are to be found, etc., in his long-term memory. A 'tank' enters into a more constrained set of typical situations than does a 'vehicle'.[50]

Keeping those basic premises in mind, it is time to turn to specific ways for frames to be evoked. The opening of a frame can take place in various ways in story comprehension and recall.

1.1.1. *Bottom-Up Processing*[51]

Bottom-up processing occurs when an audience/reader encounters the prototypical components (e.g., event sequences, participants, and props) from within a frame, which is usually of the basic level category (to use Rosch's term). For instance, for the one who has information that a fish has gills, a living thing with gills certainly opens the FISH frame; that is, the word gills evokes the FISH frame in a bottom-up processing.[52] This bottom-up processing is quite similar to Schank and Abelson's model of script-opening by "headers" (i.e., frame-related information). Schank and Abelson suggest four types of headers (bolded) to activate script-type frames: The Precondition Headers (e.g., "John **was hungry**," in the RESTAURANT frame); The Instrumental Headers ("John took the **subway** to the restaurant," in the RESTAURANT frame); The Locale Headers ("John went to **the soccer field**," in the SOCCER frame); The Conceptualization Header ("John went to visit his friend Mary who was **a waitress**. While he was waiting for her, he **ordered a hamburger**," in the RESTAURANT frame).[53] Take an example from Mark 6.41 which, as in 8.6 and 14.22, the same meal actions repeat in the same order:

superordinate	basic level	subordinate
a. vehicle	**car**	hatchback
b. fruit	**apple**	Granny Smith
c. animal	**dog**	spaniel
d. cutlery	**knife**	bread knife
e. furniture	**table**	card table.

[50] Sanford and Garrod, *Understanding*, p. 119.
[51] Rumelhart and Ortony, "Representation of Knowledge," pp. 127–30.
[52] Lakoff, *Women*, p. 53.
[53] Schank and Abelson, *Scripts*, pp. 47–50.

Framed actions	Mark 6.39, 41	8.6	14.18, 22
(Sitting	καὶ…ἀνακλῖναι	καὶ…ἀναπεσεῖν	καὶ ἀνακειμένων)
Taking bread	καὶ λαβὼν…ἄρτους,	καὶ λαβὼν…ἄρτους	καὶ…λαβὼν ἄρτον
Blessing	καὶ…εὐλόγησεν	εὐχαριστήσας	εὐλογήσας
Breaking	καὶ κατέκλασεν	ἔκλασεν	ἔκλασεν
Distributing	καὶ ἐδίδου	καὶ ἐδίδου	καὶ ἔδωκεν

The prototypical sequence of meal actions (parts) induced the first-century Christian audience, who had the post-resurrection perspective, to evoke the EUCHARISTIC MEAL (whole).[54] Indeed, the meal actions in the first and second episodes may seem to invoke the frame related to a general meal situation, but evidence leads us to believe that the EUCHARISTIC MEAL frame is implicitly opened. In particular, two things must be mentioned to support this argument. First, the meal actions of 6.41 and 8.6 correspond exactly with those of the Last Meal of 14.44 from which the Eucharistic institution originates. It is not impossible then to assume that the parallel meal actions evoked the EUCHARISTIC MEAL frame on the part of Mark's historical audience. Second, this can be confirmed when we compare those passages with 1 Corinthians 11.23–24 in which, after giving the title of the meal κυριακὸν δεῖπνον ("the Lord's Supper," 11.20), Paul mentions the details of the meal in the same sequence of actions, though with the omission of the actions of sitting and giving bread: ἔλαβεν ἄρτον, καὶ εὐχαριστήσας, ἔκλασεν.

1.1.2. *Top-Down Processing*
In a top-down fashion, a whole frame may be opened by its central element at the basic level in a taxonomic hierarchy.[55] Such a nucleus, which usually occurs at the beginning of an episode, can be called the pivot of a frame.[56] In story comprehension and at recall, the pivot enables the audience/reader to activate the frame's whole components instantiated in a story. This is because a script-type frame is processed

---

[54] Marcus, *Mark 1–8*, p. 420; Donahue and Harrington, *Mark*, p. 211; France, *Mark*, p. 262.
[55] Rumelhart and Ortony, "Representation of Knowledge," pp. 127–30.
[56] Sanford and Garrod, *Understanding*, pp. 112–13.

in a hierarchical organization whose top level is represented by its title, clustering the other components into its sublevels.[57] Certainly, the opening of a frame by its key element may operate on the event and thing frames. First of all, an event frame may be evoked by its core action and event. Mark 4.35–41, for example, begins with (I have underlined the key properties in the frame),

> Καὶ λέγει αὐτοῖς ἐν ἐκείνῃ τῇ ἡμέρᾳ ὀψίας γενομένης·
> διέλθωμεν εἰς τὸ πέραν. Καὶ ἀφέντες τὸν ὄχλον <u>παραλαμβάνουσιν αὐτὸν</u>
> ὡς ἦν <u>ἐν τῷ πλοίῳ</u> (vv. 35–36)

The bolded expression ("they took him...in the boat") certainly opens in Mark's Gospel the 'SEA TRIP' frame whose central component includes an embarking action of 'getting into the boat.'[58] In story comprehension, once an event frame is opened by its pivot (whole) at the beginning of the story, any details or specific information (parts) mentioned in the follow-up scene may be easily expected and accessed as the default components of the frame. In the example above, accordingly, the SEA TRIP frame is already opened in the audience's mind by its central event (i.e., the embarking action) at the onset of the story. Hence the subsequent information, such as, λαῖλαψ μεγάλη ἀνέμου ("a great storm of wind," in v. 37), τὰ κύματα ("the waves," in v. 37), and τῇ πρύμνῃ ("the stern" in v. 38), is readily processed as typical events and components within the frame;[59] whereas Jesus' sleeping "on

---

[57] On experiments related to recall effect of frame, see Taylor and Crocker, "Schematic Bases," pp. 98–99; and Joseph W. Alba and Lynn Hasher, "Is Memory Schematic?" *PB* 93 (1983), pp. 206–207.

[58] The embarking action as a pivot of the SEA TRIP frame is underlined:
Mark 4.1 (4.35–36): αὐτὸν <u>εἰς πλοῖον ἐμβάντα</u> καθῆσθαι ἐν τῇ θαλάσσῃ (<u>παραλαμβ-</u>
<u>άνουσιν αὐτὸν</u> ὡς ἦν <u>ἐν τῷ πλοίῳ</u>)
5.18 (5.21): <u>ἐμβαίνοντος</u> αὐτοῦ <u>εἰς τὸ πλοῖον</u>...παρεκάλει αὐτὸν ὁ δαιμονισθεὶς (διαπεράσαντος τοῦ Ἰησοῦ [ἐν τῷ πλοίῳ]
6.32: ἀπῆλθον <u>ἐν τῷ πλοίῳ</u> εἰς ἔρημον τόπον.
6.45 (6.51): <u>ἐμβῆναι εἰς τὸ πλοῖον</u> (ἀνέβη πρὸς αὐτοὺς εἰς τὸ πλοῖον')
8.10: <u>ἐμβὰς εἰς τὸ πλοῖον</u>...ἦλθεν εἰς τὰ μέρη Δαλμανουθά
8.13: <u>ἐμβὰς</u> ἀπῆλθεν εἰς τὸ πέραν.
With a variation of 6.32 in which the action is implied, the entire SEA TRIP frame in Mark's Gospel is opened by the expression of embarking on a boat. This indicates that the expression 'getting into a boat' stands for the whole SEA TRIP frame and its components.

[59] Of course, as pointed out in note 54, the rest of the SEA TRIP frame in the Gospel of Mark does not represent very much its typical events and elements; instead, only its pivot ("getting into a boat") is mentioned in brief (but note Mark 6.45–52).

the cushion" (v. 38a) in a stormy sea is unexpected, thus surprising, in light of the same frame.[60]

Next, for the thing frame a name of a thing (e.g., synagogue and sabbath in the Gospels) would serve as the frame title, and for the person frame a name of a group or person (e.g., firefighters and the pharisees) will be its title.[61] In this case the title of the place, object, and person frames opens not just a thing and a person per se, but also activates its other default information. Mark 1.29–31, which refers to Jesus' healing of Simon's mother-in-law, for example, begins with the expressions (the place frame title is bolded): εὐθὺς ἐκ τῆς συναγωγῆς ἐξελθόντες ἦλθον εἰς **τὴν οἰκίαν** Σίμωνος καὶ ᾿Ανδρέου. By referring to the title (τὴν οἰκίαν) of the place frame, which is related to a spatial setting of this episode, the first sentence easily enables the audience to evoke the HOUSE frame which includes information regarding its role as a dwelling place for the family members and its members who live in the house; and then the open frame knowledge guides the audience to process and comprehend the following story against the frame. So, first of all, the occurrence of Simon and Andrew conjoined by καὶ would be fairly understandable without a further explanation (note that Mark has already told us that they are brothers in 1.16). Next, though not explicitly stated that there was Simon's mother-in-law in his house, the audience is not surprised to hear about Simon's mother-in-law's sudden entrance into this episode because a person's mother or mother-in-law is a prototypical participant of the HOUSE frame in the ancient world.[62] Thirdly, because the household was the primary place for the sick to be cared for in first-century Mediterranean cultures,[63] in Mark 1.30 the information of the sick person "lying in bed (κατέκει)" may be anticipated by the open HOUSE frame as typical. Finally, the default values in the open HOUSE frame make it

---

Schank and Abelson call this kind of frame "fleeting script [frame]." For a further explanation of this type of frame, see below.

[60] On the unexpectedness in the frame, we will discuss in detail below.

[61] Hoyle, "Scenario," p. 37.

[62] On the household custom in Jesus' day that a three-generational household (the parent generation, the next generation that consists of some adult siblings having children of their own) all lived in the same house, see Moxnes, *Putting Jesus in His Place*, pp. 30–31.

[63] John Pilch, *Healing in the New Testament: Insights from Medical and Mediterranean Anthropology* (Minneapolis: Fortress Press, 2000), pp. 66–67.

possible to interpret the clause διηκόνει αὐτοῖς as "she served *at table* them."[64]

It is not necessary, however, to call up all the details of a frame whenever the title of a frame is encountered. There are, as Schank and Abelson note, "fleeting scripts [frames]":

> John took a bus to New York
> In New York he went to a museum
> Then he took a train home.[65]

Although BUS, MUSEUM-GOING, and TRAIN in these passages represent the titles of the frames respectively, they say: "It is unlikely that people would fill in the default paths of each of these scripts if exposed to a story.... What is more likely is that they simply remember that the script occurred by establishing an indicator to the entire script."[66]

Before exploring another way for frames to be opened, it is significant to keep in mind that the top-down and bottom-up processings usually operate together in opening a relevant frame. Rumelhart says:

---

[64] In fact, Mark often refers to a house as a place in which healing happens. In Mark's Gospel the word "house" is mentioned as the title of the HOUSE frame, or as a setting of an episode (1.29; 2.1; 2.15; 3.20–30, 31–35; 5.19; 5.34–43; 7.24,30; 9.33; 10.10; 11.17; 14.3). What follows shows the constituents of the HOUSE frame occurring in the Gospel of Mark:
  - Participants: Healer and teacher (such as Jesus); guests (2.15); the disciples (1.29; 2.15; 5.37); a mother-in-law (1.30); friends (5.19); a daughter (5.35); mourners (5.38); women (7.25; 14.3); children (7.27; 7.30; 9.36); dogs (7.27); wife (10.11); husband (10.12); mother and brothers (3.31); sisters (3.35); a crowd (being taught) (3.32)
  - Events: healing (1.29–31; 2.5, 11; 5.35–43; 7.24–30, esp. 30); eating (1.31; 2.15; 7.27–28; 14.3); teaching or preaching (2.2; 5.19; 10.10); debating 'the outsider' (2.6–11; 2.16–17); weeping for the dead (5.38–39); debating 'the insider' (9.33–37); praying (11.10)
  - Props: table (7.28); bed (7.30); ointment (14.3).
  Certainly, this HOUSE frame seems to include unfamiliar components for modern readers (e.g., preaching, teaching, healing, and so on). But for the first-century Christians those things would not be unexpected things in the internal life of a Christian household, because, as most scholars agree, the early Christians gathered together as a house church, and worship, teaching, preaching and table fellowship or the Lord's Supper were parts of such a gathering (Acts 2.42, 46–47; 1 Corinthians 11.20–21, 12.28, 14.26). See Meeks, *Urban Christians*, pp. 74–110. And for an introduction of the concept of household in the first-century world, see Halvor Moxnes, *Putting Jesus in His Places: A Radical Vision of Household and Kingdom* (Louisville: WJK, 2003).
[65] Schank and Abelson, *Scripts*, p. 47.
[66] Schank and Abelson, *Scripts*, p. 47.

Schemata-directed processing is assumed to proceed in roughly the following way: some event occurs at the sensory system. The occurrence of this event "automatically" activates certain "low-level" schemata (such schemata might might be called feature detectors). The low-level schemata would, in turn, activate in a data-driven [bottom-up] fashion certain of the "higher level" schemata (the most probable ones) of which they are constituents. These "higher level" schemata would then initiate conceptually driven processing by activating the subschemata not already activated in an attempt to evaluate its goodness of fit.[67]

1.1.3. *Metonymic Model*

A whole frame can be opened by an element within a frame which stands for the whole frame. George Lakoff proposes: "Given an ICM [frame] with some background condition (e.g., institutions are located in places), there is a 'stand for' relation that may hold between two elements A and B, such that one element of the ICM, B, may stand for another element A. In this case, B = the place and A = the institution."[68] And this metonymic process of frames is highly dependent on the language user's cultural knowledge of the language. An example is provided by Croft and Cruse:

  a. Paris is a beautiful city (location).
  b. Paris closed the Boulevard St. Michel (government).
  c. Paris elected the Green candidate as mayor (population).[69]

It is clear in the sentences that the PARIS frame includes many concepts (location, government, and population) other than its literal denotation, and its title Paris serves to evoke other elements within the frame, being aided by its context. Here is an example from Mark 12.14 in which the Pharisees and Herodians ask Jesus (the person frame is bolded): ἔξεστιν δοῦναι κῆνσον **Καίσαρι** ἢ οὔ; δῶμεν ἢ μὴ δῶμεν; Because of the audience's background knowledge that Caesar is a Roman emperor and thus stands for Roman authorities, the word Καίσαρι opens the semantic information of the institution of the Roman government to which the tax is paid. In other words, as a person frame title, CAESAR here serves to evoke its prototypical

---

[67] Rumelhart, "Schemata," p. 42.
[68] Lakoff, *Women*, p. 78; and see also William Croft, "The Role of Domains in the Interpretation of Metaphors and Metonymies," in *Mepaphor and Metonymy in Comparison and Contrast* (ed. René Dirven and Ralf Pörings; Berlin: Mouton de Gruyter, 2002), pp. 177–87.
[69] Croft and Cruse, *Cognitive Linguistics*, p. 48.

information (i.e., Caesar is a Roman emperor, or the institution of Roman government) to understand the clause appropriately.

Lakoff provides another example of metonymic mapping, quoting Richard Rhodes' book, "Semantics in a Relational Grammar":

> He asked speakers of Ojibwa [a Native American Language of Central Canada] who had come to a party how they got there. He got answers like the following (translated into English):
> – I started to come
> – I stepped into a canoe.
> – I got into a car.[70]

Lakoff concludes, "What Rhodes found was that in Ojibwa it is conventional to use the embarkation point of an ICM of this sort to evoke the whole ICM."[71] This metonymic model is crucial for our present study of the Gospel of Mark. First of all, this provides a theoretical basis for the assumption that, as will be discussed in Chapters Four and Five, event frames at the level of the *koine* Greek clause are metonymically represented by main verbs. Also, the meaning of a word in the Controversy Stories is in many cases best understood in terms of this metonymic model. For example, in Mark 2.14 when Jesus calls Levi to be his disciple, the phrase ἀκολούθει μοι occurs. Here the words expressing the starting point of being a disciple of Jesus are used to stand metonymically for the whole DISCIPLESHIP frame, which includes prototypical elements, such as being with Jesus as a master, learning, teaching, preaching the gospel, healing, and exorcism (Mark 3.14–15; 4.10–11, 34; 6.7, 12–13, 30).[72]

1.1.4. *Preceding Discourse-Based Model*
It is well known among discourse analysts that a listener/reader's processing of current occurrences or passages is greatly constrained by their preceding discourses.[73] A similar cognitive process happens

---

[70] Lakoff, *Women*, pp. 78–79.

[71] Lakoff, *Women*, p. 78.

[72] With regard to exorcism, in particular, see Mark 9.14–29, esp. 19 which shows that Jesus was disappointed to hear that the disciples failed to exorcise. This clearly shows that exorcism was regarded by people and Jesus as part of the DISCIPLE frame. That is, Jesus was disappointed at the disciples because he assumed his disciples were able to do exorcism according to the DISCIPLE frame, but the expected event did not happen. And the father of the boy being possessed by a demon came to the disciples because he believed the disciples could heal his boy in accordance with his DISCIPLE frame. Without this DISCIPLE frame, thus, this passage cannot be understood.

[73] Brown and Yule, *Discourse Analysis*, pp. 47–50.

when the hearer/reader opens a relevant frame for the interpretation of the current text. Sanford and Garrod state that "indeed, selection [of a frame] can be viewed as the outcome of an accumulation of evidence from various sources, both from the current text and from the memory structure for previously encountered text."[74] This is common, in particular in processing narrative discourse based on a series of events and actions. "Previously encountered text" may refer both to words within a single episode and between episodes. First of all, to illustrate the way in which information accumulated within a single episode helps the opening of a frame for incoming information, once again consider Mark 4.35–41. In verse 38 Jesus' disciples said to Jesus, διδάσκαλε, οὐ μέλει σοι ὅτι ἀπολλύμεθα; What do the disciples mean by ἀπολλύμεθα ("we perish")? The SEA TRIP frame is already opened by its title, that is, the key properties in the frame, ("they took him...in the boat") at the start of the story (v. 36), and information that the disciples were confronting a "great storm of wind" (vv. 35–36) was mentioned. As a result, the reference to ἀπολλύμεθα may well be sufficient to evoke a frame relating to drowning in a sinking boat.

Next, the second type of opening frame by virtue of information accumulated between episodes can be well explained by Mark's three exorcism stories (1.21–28; 5.1–20; 9.14–29). In the preceding two stories Jesus rebuked (ἐπετίμησεν, 1.25, but missed in the second story) and commanded the demon to exit (1.25; 5.8); hence the reference to Jesus' command (φέρετε αὐτὸν [the demon-possessed boy] πρός με, 9.19b) in the third story could much more easily lead the audience to expect Jesus' responding pattern of rebuking and casting the demons out (9.25) (i.e., prototypical actions in the EXORCISM frame).[75] Regarding the demon's reaction to Jesus, likewise, the audience's general expectation about the demon's violent behaviour was already met in the preceding stories (1.26; 5.2–4). Hence, such mental processes of the preceding discourse information may determine in the third story the audience's prediction of what type of specific defaults among many properties or actions in the DEMON-POSSESSED PERSON frame will be mentioned; that is, the demon's same violent reaction (9.20 and see also vv. 18, 26).

---

[74] Sanford and Garrod, *Understanding*, p. 129.
[75] On the typical actions in the EXORCISM frame, see Chapter Three.

1.2. *Frames Delimit Information Semantically*

What makes a text coherent, and more than just a list of discrete sentences? This question is a major concern of discourse analysis.[76] The argument is that frames are active cognitive devices that make a story coherent. A frame contains a set of generalized semantic data which are in a mutually linked and predictable relation. Thus, frame-based text processing allows the audience/reader to comprehend the text coherently.[77] Stanford and Garrod give an example of the restaurant frame to show how frames serve to bind the elements of the text which are introduced into it:

> (16) Feeling hungry, John went into a restaurant
> (16') The waiter brought him the menu.
> How does sentence (16') come to be connected to its antecedent? Neither the action itself, nor *the waiter*, nor *the menu* as individual items are mentioned in (16). If the reader has a script, there is no problem. Not only can the processor refer to the words mentioned explicitly in (16), but it can also refer to those roles, props, and actions in the activated script. And in the restaurant script we find *the waiter, the menu*, and the complete conceptualization underlying the action described by (16'). In other words, the script expands the domain of reference in a limited, context-dependent way.[78]

In the example above, the RESTAURANT frame plays the role of bringing together otherwise disengaged items to create a semantically coherent unit by providing its typical elements (e.g., events, characters, and props).

The frames, besides such brief sentences, contribute to organizing information at the level of larger discourse units such as paragraphs or episodes and thematic units. In order for a series of events to form a coherent story, there must be an interactive relationship between such elements as time, place, characters and events (see Chapter Five). Frames, particularly event frames, contain a conventionally interlinked set of situational information, including actions, agents and their rela-

---

[76] For example, see Frederiksen, "Structure and Process," pp. 313–22. A quotation from p. 314, says: "The property that makes a discourse more than a collection of unrelated simple sentences is coherence. A major objective of discourse studies is to explain what makes a text coherent."

[77] Teun A. van Dijk, "Semantic Macro-Structures and Knowledge Frames in Discourse Comprehension," in *Cognitive Processes in Comprehension* (ed. Marcel A. Just and Patricia A. Carpenter; Hillsdale, New Jersey: Lawrence Erlbaum, 1977), p. 18.

[78] Stanford, and Garrod, *Written Language*, p. 54.

tions and roles; hence, they are able to semantically organize a series of events into a coherent story. Once the global frame, which is dominant at the level of the larger discourse units, is opened as a topic, for the coherent processing of information the audience keeps track of its continuity (thus, frame continuity) and change ("frame switch")[79] within the text, monitoring the textual information. As far as the core elements of the global frame are topical throughout the story or discourse unit, the audience processes information within it as semantically bound by the global frame.[80] By contrast, the audience/reader ceases to monitor certain passages in terms of the same frame, that is, a frame switch occurs, if the information in the global frame is seriously changed.[81]

In addition to elements such as events, agents, and props, there are other significant cues to determine if a current frame may be of any further use as a supportive background structure for larger discourse units, in particular a paragraph or episode. Those are spatial-temporal makers going beyond the frame range and introduction of predicates which do not fit the frame. A global frame, especially a script-like frame, contains prototypical information about the "spatio-temporal range over which they operate."[82] So if a lexeme which signals events beyond the stretch of limited space and time is used, that may indicate that the frame has changed.

For instance, there is a distinctive frame switch between Mark 1.14–15 and 1.16–20 (the relevant frame pivot is bolded; the core triggers of the frames are underlined; the agents and locations are italicized):

Μετὰ δὲ τὸ παραδοθῆναι τὸν Ἰωάννην
ἦλθεν ὁ Ἰησοῦς εἰς τὴν Γαλιλαίαν κηρύσσων τὸ εὐαγγέλιον τοῦ θεοῦ
καὶ λέγων ὅτι πεπλήρωται ὁ καιρὸς καὶ ἤγγικεν ἡ βασιλεία τοῦ θεοῦ·
μετανοεῖτε καὶ πιστεύετε ἐν τῷ εὐαγγελίῳ. (1.14–15)

---

[79] For the terminology, see Catherine Emmott, *Narrative Comprehension: A Discourse Perspective* (Oxford: Clarendon, 1997), pp. 133–74 (the quotation from p. 121). Although Emmott uses the term frame in a somewhat different way (i.e., "a mental store of information about the current context, built up from the text itself and from inferences made from the text"), the concept "frame switch" is still appropriate for our study in that it explains the audience/reader's cognitive processing of a narrative unit, such as an episode or paragraph.
[80] van Dijk, *Text and Context*, pp. 159–60.
[81] Emmot, *Narrative Comprehension*, p. 133.
[82] Stanford and Garrod, *Written Language*, p. 146.

Καὶ παράγων παρὰ τὴν θάλασσαν τῆς Γαλιλαίας <u>εἶδεν</u> Σίμωνα καὶ
'Ανδρέαν...
καὶ <u>εἶπεν</u> αὐτοῖς ὁ 'Ιησοῦς· <u>δεῦτε ὀπίσω μου</u>...
καὶ εὐθὺς ἀφέντες τὰ δίκτυα <u>ἠκολούθησαν</u> αὐτῷ.
Καὶ προβὰς ὀλίγον <u>εἶδεν</u> 'Ιάκωβον... καὶ 'Ιωάννην
καὶ εὐθὺς <u>ἐκάλεσεν</u> αὐτούς.
καὶ ἀφέντες τὸν πατέρα αὐτῶν Ζεβεδαῖον ἐν τῷ πλοίῳ μετὰ τῶν
μισθωτῶν <u>ἀπῆλθον ὀπίσω αὐτοῦ</u>. (1.16–20)

The first episode opens the global event frame for PREACHING[83] in
which Jesus' role matches the slot for the preacher, and Galilee fills
the slot for the location in which the preaching occurs. And the
PREACHING frame organizes the events in Mark 1.14–15 into a goal-
directed sequence: Jesus' coming (the beginning stage or the source)
and preaching/saying (the end stage or the goal).[84] Though Jesus keeps
being referred to as a principal actor, there are apparent indications of
a frame shift in 1.16–20. The PREACHING frame and its semantic structures are discarded as the audience processes 1.16–20 in which the
CALLING TO DISCIPLESHIP frame[85] is activated in terms of the underlined triggers (thus bottom-up processing). In that frame, Jesus fills
the slot for a master, not a preacher, and Simon, Andrew, James, and
John fill the slot for the disciples. The Sea of Galilee corresponds to the
location in which the action of the calling of disciples occurs. And the
frame sets up its own sequence of goal-directed events:

> The Beginning stage (source): Passing along by the Sea of Galilee
> The Middle stage (path): Seeing/Calling
> The End Stage (goal): Following

The observation above shows, on the one hand, that the global frame
is a supportive background structure that enables the audience to
organize each episode into a semantically coherent unit. On the other
hand, it affirms that the frame helps mark off episodic boundaries,
assigning its prototypical slots and roles to the elements in the episode
(e.g., consider Jesus' role as a preacher and a master respectively).[86]

---

[83] For the prototypical event sequences (coming, gathering and preaching) in the
PREACHING frame and its parallel event sequences in Mark's Gospel, see below.

[84] Here the path or the middle stage (people's gathering) is implicit, see below.

[85] For the prototypical event sequences (seeing, calling, and following) of the CALL-
ING TO DISCIPLESHIP frame in Mark's Gospel and its parallel event sequences, see
Chapter Six.

[86] Stanford and Garrod, *Written Language*, pp. 149–52, show in their experiment
that, for frame-dependent entities, comprehending and recalling time is shorter than
for the entities beyond the frame range.

1.3. *Frames Determine the Structure of Information by Providing Event or Action Sequences*

Teun van Dijk proposes that "a frame is an ORGANIZATIONAL PRIN-CIPLE relating to a number of concepts which by CONVENTION and EXPERIENCE somehow form a 'unit' which may be actualized in various cognitive tasks, such as language production and comprehension, perception, action, and problem solving."[87] Accordingly, the cognitive scientist postulates that people store and remember information of routine experiences or frame-related information in sequential form.[88] Event frames or script-like frames represent this type of memory. The concern here will be with the influence of such framed action sequences on the organization of the narrative discourse unit. As shown in the examples of Mark 1.14–15 and 16–20, the former episode is based on the prototypical event sequences ("coming" and "preaching," in v. 14) in the PREACHING frame; the latter episode consists of the prototypical event sequences of the CALLING TO DISCIPLESHIP frame ("seeing" in vv. 16 and 19, "calling" in vv. 17 and 20, and "following" in vv. 18 and 20). Such a framed knowledge of connected sequences of events is a basic structure of storyline; and on the basis of frames' sequential events the audience may recognize and expect how a framed episode begins or develops and when it ends. In this respect, it can be said that memory for an episode operates on the basis of well organized structural knowledge.

However, the sequence of actions an event frame holds, as Schank and Abelson propose, is not immutable, but quite variable:

> Thus the restaurant script must contain a tremendous amount of information that encompasses the enormous variability of what can occur in a restaurant. There must also be a 'fast food restaurant' track, a cafeteria track, etc. in the restaurant script, that includes the entering, ordering and paying scenes, but has a different set of possibilities than the fancy restaurant. In the 'fast food track', paying can occur immediately after ordering and before eating; eating may occur inside or outside the restaurant; the person who takes the order must be approached by the patron rather than going to where the patron is seated.[89]

This means that the typical sequences of events in a frame may be to some extent accommodated, depending on particular types of "tracks"

---

[87] van Dijk, *Text,* p. 159.
[88] Schank and Abelson, *Scripts,* pp. 36–46.
[89] Schank and Abelson, *Scripts,* p. 40.

(to use Schank and Abelson's term) in the frame. The internal variation of patterns or tracks within an event frame can explain how it is
possible for the audience to understand without difficulty the stories
which, though based on the same kind of event frame, contain different sequences of events.

The sequential structure of the event frame is, as discussed above, a
useful cognitive model particularly for organizing Mark's action-oriented oral narrative pattern. (I will explore later how the prototypical
sequence of events in the LEGAL CONTROVERSY frame determines the
structure of each story in Mark 2.1–3.6 and helps the cognitive processing of the information in it.) From the cognitive perspective, it is a
mental frame that underlies an association of a chain of events in the
episodes of Mark's Gospel. The framed sequence of an episode existed
in Mark's mind and was expressed in linguistic forms to be communicated to the audience. In turn, given that Mark's Christian audiences were well versed in the stereotyped sequences of an event frame
through their social experience and linguistic knowledge in Greek,[90] it
is quite natural to assume that the audiences were readily capable of
organizing the cognitive structure of the event sequences as they heard
a specific episode.

1.4. *Frames Organize Information into Chunks Hierarchically and Causally*

The frame is not an undifferentiated, linear chain, but rather a hierarchically organized chunking set.[91] Hence, when hearing/reading a story,
an audience/reader integrates new information into a specific domain-
related frame, and the information stored is segmented together into its
closely interrelated subunits corresponding to its sequences of events. I
will explore how such chunking operates within the example of going
to a family doctor's office here in Canada. Arguing that frame-based

---

[90] Mark's Christian audiences' linguistic knowledge in Greek can be supported by
the fact that, as Porter, *Greek New Testament*, pp. 139–71 asserts, Greek was the *lingua
franca* of the Greco-Roman world and the Gospel of Mark was written, and probably
performed, in Greek. Of course, this may be true regardless of the possibility that
the provenance of the Gospel may be Palestine, since in first-century Palestine Greek
was spoken not only by upper-class people, but also by lower-class. For this, see J.N.
Sevenster, *Do you know Greek? How much Greek could the First Jewish Christians have
known* (NovTSup 19; Leiden: E.J. Brill, 1968), pp. 96–191.

[91] Gordon H. Bower, John B. Black, and Terrence I. Turner, "Scripts in Memory
for Text," *CP* 11 (1979), p. 184. And see also Thorndyke and Yekovich, "Schema
Theory," p. 27.

information is divided hierarchically, Abbott, Black and Smith say that "at the top of this hierarchy for an event is an action which summarizes the whole event" (e.g., going to a family doctor's office).[92] The present book calls this action a 'frame title.' Again, "The overall event is broken into superordinate actions [scene titles]" (e.g., entering the office, registering, and waiting).[93] This book terms the actions at this level as 'scene headers.' Finally, "[e]ach superordinate node is then broken down into a detailed set of *scene actions*," a term which we will follow.[94] The scene, according to Schank *et al.*, plays a crucial role in the cognitive representation of stereotypical events: "The smallest conceptual structure that coherently organizes a set of expectations is a *scene*. A scene is a memory structure which groups together action and states relating to a shared purpose, and usually in a shared setting in time and space."[95] This hierarchical chunking of the GOING TO A FAMILY DOCTOR'S OFFICE frame, or part-whole structure, can be presented as follows:

A Frame Title

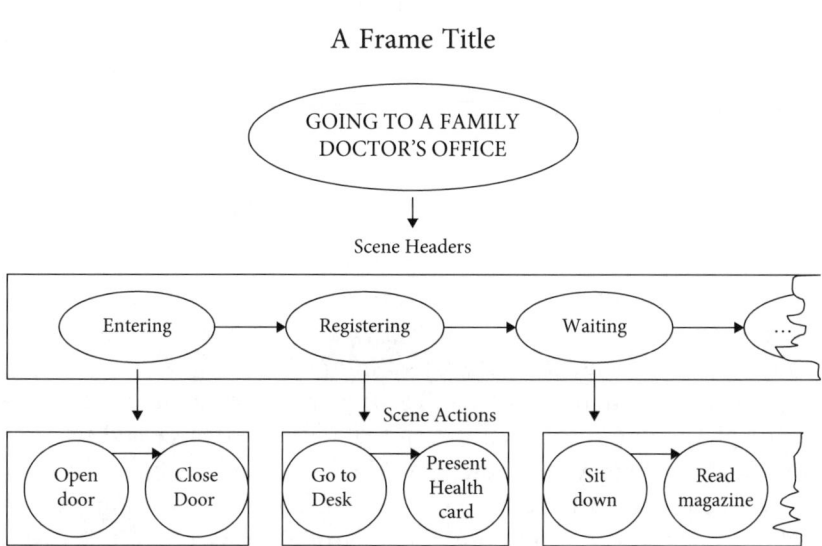

Figure 1: The GOING TO A FAMILY DOCTOR'S OFFICE Frame

---

[92] Valerie Abbott, John B. Black, and Edward E. Smith, "The Representation of Scripts in Memory," *JML* 24 (1985), p. 183.
[93] Abbott, Black, and Smith, "Memory," p. 183.
[94] Abbott, Black, and Smith, "Memory," p. 183.
[95] Schank, Birnbaum, and Mey, "Semantics," p. 320 [the originals' italics]. Schank and Abelson, *Scripts*, pp. 43–44 call "scenes" the chunks that divide actions in scripts into an interrelated set (e.g., entering, ordering, eating, paying bill and going out in the example of GOING TO A RESTAURANT).

The hierarchical structure of the script-like frame may be understood in terms of the part-whole structure. The frame title, and each higher-level structure, is a whole, and each of the events or actions at the lower order is its parts. In addition to part-whole structure, each action is linked in causal chains and goal sequences with the one preceding and the one succeeding in time, though the 'scene actions' represented by different 'scene headers' are linked to one another via the network of their own scene headers.[96] This causal relation connects related actions into a set as a whole, and they are all directed to the top-goal of seeing the doctor.

Such a hierarchical (or part-whole) and causal organization of frames, as will be discussed, is very important in understanding the cognitive processing of each episode in Mark 2.1–3.6 in terms of a global frame. Once the global frame is opened, the information at the paragraph or episode level is bounded as a whole in terms of the global LEGAL CONTROVERSY frame title; and in an operation organized as such, the 'scene headers' serve as a framework for segmenting and understanding detailed information within the paragraph.[97] Next, since the events between each scene are causally interlinked, the audience can predict what will follow next and later recall them inferentially as an episode in a causally interconnected set.

1.5. *A Global Frame Assigns Other Frames into its Subframes*

A frame tends to interact strongly with other frames.[98] And this is how narrative comprehension usually operates. A thing frame is interwoven with an event frame, whether a sub-frame or beyond its boundary, to provide its background information of place and object. A person frame may be interactive with the event frame to describe actors played out in the event. Despite the meshing of several types of frames in a single episode, the story does not result in incomprehension. This is primarily because of a global frame which is topical and upholds the semantic structure of an episode as a whole. While many

---

[96] Abbott, Black, and Smith, "Memory," p. 183; see also Schank and Abelson, *Scripts*, pp. 22–35, esp. 45.

[97] Bower, Black, and Turner, "Scripts," pp. 186–88; Sanford and Garrod, *Understanding*, p. 81.

[98] Schank and Abelson, *Scripts*, p. 58, say, "When two scripts are active at once they compete for incoming items of information. Sometimes the events that fit in one affect the events of the other."

cognitive linguists have focused on frames at the level of sentence (e.g., Fillmore's case frame), Minsky turns our attention to the global frame operating on the level of paragraph, a larger frame.[99] Minsky says,

> Thus in understanding a discourse, the synthesis of a verb-structure with its case assignments may be a necessary but transient phase. As sentences are understood, the resulting substructures must be transferred to a growing "scene frame" to build up the larger picture. An action that is the chief concern of one sentence might, for example, become subsidiary to a characterization of one of the actors in a larger story-frame.[100]

The global frame (to use Minsky's term, "superframe")[101] operating at the paragraph level, as discussed above, not only determines the structure of the episode, but also leads the audience to process coherently a large amount information contained in subframes "in meaningful hierarchies."[102] Consider the example of PARTY provided by van Dijk: "If the party frame is topical, then parts of other frames [e.g., getting peanuts for the guest in the SUPERMARKET frame] may be activated, especially those parts that denote conditions, components, or consequences of the 'topic' frame."[103] Such sub or "minor" frames often includes "fleeting" frames (to use Schank and Abelson's term).[104] Fleeting frames, as mentioned, do not require a recall of all frame details in processing a story; instead it is enough that they invoke the conditions, components, or consequences which are most appropriate to the processing of the global or topic frame. In the example of Mark 1.14–15 in which the global PREACHING frame is opened, the place, "Galilee," where Jesus went to preach, is here used to evoke only the information regarding a specific location of *a preacher*, rather than its own geographical or administrative information.

1.6. *Frames Allow Metaphorical Links*

Metaphor, according to cognitive linguistics, is used as a means of expressing one thing, "a target domain," (the object compared by the metaphor) in terms of another, "a source domain" (the metaphorical

---

[99] Minsky, "Framework," p. 236.
[100] Minsky, "Framework," p. 236.
[101] Minsky, "Framework," p. 236, says, "As the story proceeds, information is transferred to superframes whenever possible, instantiating or elaborating the scenario."
[102] Porter, *Greek New Testament*, p. 70.
[103] van Dijk, "Semantic Macro-Structures," p. 23.
[104] Schank and Abelson, *Scripts*, pp. 46–47.

expression itself).[105] William Croft calls this comparing process "domain mapping."[106] This metaphorical mapping is "so ordinary that we use it unconsciously and automatically, with so little effort that we hardly notice it."[107] The implication is that metaphor operates only on the basis of the language user's background knowledge 'beyond' the literal meaning of a metaphorical expression. Yet in many cases the images in the source domain seem to have nothing to do with the elements in the target domain or these being compared with it. Thus a question arises: How can the audience map between the source domain and the target domain as the text intended? On what basis do elements in the target domain come to be perceived as similar to those in the source domain? The thing that makes it possible for the audience to metaphorically process the target domain in terms of the source domain is the background knowledge interacting between the two domains.[108] This interactive knowledge is apparently stored in the audience/reader's mind through cultural and social experience.[109] In this regard Lakoff proposes that metaphorical mapping is often based on culturally experienced similarities between the target domain and the source domain.[110] Consider Lakoff and Johnson's example, "TIME [target domain] IS MONEY [source domain]":

---

[105] Lakoff and Johnson, *Metaphors*, pp. 3–6, esp. 5.

[106] Croft, "The Role of Domains," pp. 161–77.

[107] George Lakoff and Mark Turner, *More Than Cool Reason: A Field Guide to Poetic Metaphor* (Chicago: University of Chicago Press, 1989), p. xi.

[108] Lakoff and Johnson, *Metaphor*, pp. 147–55.

[109] The importance of language users' cultural and social experience in metaphorical processing is not ignored in recent biblical scholarship. With a similar understanding of metaphor to that of cognitive linguistics, Gerald A. Klingbeil, "Metaphors and Pragmatics: An Introduction to the Hermeneutics of Metaphors in the Epistle to the Ephesians," *BBR* 16 (2006), pp. 273–93, attempts to explore in Ephesians metaphorical components such as 'family,' 'body,' 'position,' 'building,' 'fluid manipulation,' 'legal terminology,' 'sacrifice,' 'light manifestation,' including their submetaphors. Situating his understanding of metaphor in pragmatics, which, as he understands, is concerned with how world knowledge is reflected in linguistic and grammatical uses in communicative situations, Klingbeil ("Metaphors," p. 273) defines metaphors as "complex literary devices that require familiarity with the world view and historical context of the respective author of a particular ancient text and also communicate on an experiential level."

[110] Lakoff and Johnson, *Metaphors*, p. 154. And Zoltán Kövecses, *Metaphor in Culture: Universality and Variation* (Cambridge: Cambridge University Press, 2005), p. 67, also says, "a culture uses a set of different source domains for a particular target domain, or conversely, a culture uses a particular source domain for the conceptualization of a set of different target domains." See also William Croft, "The Role of Domains in the Interpretation of Metaphors and Metonymies," *CL* 4 (1993), pp. 335–70.

Time in our culture is a valuable commodity. It is a limited resource that
we use to accomplish our goals. Because of the way that the concept of
work has developed in modern Western culture, where work is typically associated with the time it takes and time is precisely quantified, it
has become customary to pay people by the hour, week, or year. In our
culture TIME IS MONEY in many ways: telephone message units, hourly
wages, hotel room rates, yearly budgets... These practices are relatively
new in the history of the human race, and by no means do they exist
in all cultures. They have arisen in modern industrialized societies and
structure our basic everyday activities in a very profound way.[111]

Transferring elements from the target domain to the source domain
can be further illuminated when we take into consideration that both
of the domains frequently share a particular area of experience. Taylor
provides a relevant example for this: "MORE [target domain] IS UP
[source domain]. As you add objects to a pile, the pile gets higher.
This experience establishes a natural association between quantity and
vertical extent."[112]

The demon-possessed man in Mark 1.24, for instance, says to Jesus:
ἦλθες ἀπολέσαι ἡμᾶς; Here the question "You came to destroy us?"
refers to a battle between two antagonistic parties. But how does the
audience know that this sentence is not about a real military act or
physical fighting between them? This is possible because of the audience's knowledge of the target domain (exorcism, or 'spiritual' battle)
which was part of their cultural and social experiences.[113] With the
intention of comprehending this sentence, the audience processes a
metaphorical mapping from the source domain (military battle) to
the target domain (exorcism). (For examples of the mapping from the
MILITARY BATTLE domain to the EXORCISM domain in the narrative,
consider, in particular, Mark 3.23–27, which shows Jesus' direct mapping from the military domain to his exorcism domain; and 5.9, in
which the demons inside a Geresane man identify themselves with
"military" (λεγιὼν):[114] In Mark's exorcism stories, then, Jesus is an
attacker, that is, the one who tries to cast out the demons; the demonic

---

[111] Lakoff and Johnson, *Metaphor*, p. 8.
[112] Taylor, *Linguistic Categorization*, p. 138.
[113] For the early Christians' understanding of confrontation with evil powers in
terms of battle, see 1 Corinthians 15.24–28; Ephesians 6.10–17; Galatians 5.16–17;
Revelation 12.7–17.
[114] See Wright, *Jesus*, pp. 446–63, on Jesus' use of the language of cosmic battle to
refer to the specific activities in which he himself engaged.

foes are destroyed, that is, removed from human beings and/or a ter-
ritory (1.26, 34; 5.10–13; 7.30; 9.26). Sometimes the attacker's action
or command accompanies violent protests on the part of the enemy
(1.26, 27; 5.5, 7; 13, 9.26); the conflicts always result in the attacker's
victory, namely, Jesus' success in removing the demons from a person
or place. Thus the metaphorical mapping of EXORCISM in terms of
MILITARY BATTLE may be as follows:

Table 1: Mapping of MILITARY BATTLE and EXORCISM frames

	Source Domain	Target Domain
Frame Title	military battle	exorcism
Participants	two groups of people	Jesus and Demons
Action:		
the beginning	confrontation between two groups	confrontation between Jesus and demons
the middle	fighting	Jesus' commanding to cast the demons out and the demons' violent protests
the final	winning or losing	the demons being cast out and men being set free

1.7. *Frames Determine Grammatical Choices*

It was examined earlier that lexical items play a role in evoking frames
which guide the audience's processing of subsequent texts. This is also
the case for grammatical categories in the text. As Fillmore states, a
frame determines the use of grammatical categories or patterns and
thus "grammatical material observable in the text 'evokes' the relevant
frames in the mind of the interpreter by virtue of the fact that...these
grammatical structures of categories exist as indices of these frames."[115]
Take an example of Sanford and Garrod:

(22) Mary dressed the baby
(22') *The clothes* were made of pink wool.[116]

Even if the words "the clothes" with the definite article in 22' is information being introduced for the first time, it is not difficult to find

---

[115] Fillmore, "Frame Semantics," pp. 123, 124, says that lexical and grammatical
materials in the text are "indices" of frames.
[116] Sanford and Garrod, *Understanding*, p. 105. [the italics are the original author's]

that there are cohesive relationships between 22 and 22'. This is in fact due to the frame evoked by the verb "dressed" in the first sentence, the frame knowledge that dressing someone involves putting clothes on someone. Frame theory assumes that shared knowledge between the speaker (or the text) and audience allows the speaker (the text) to use specific grammatical indicators (in this case the definite article before "clothes") in order to communicate, and on the basis of such grammatical clues the audience links incoming input to prototypical knowledge or knowledge already opened in the mental frame.[117] Thus, recognizing such grammatical indicators is essential in understanding how the text aids the audience's information process in terms of using immediate text knowledge or retrieving from long-term memory.[118]

It has been known that part of the informational structure of discourse can be divided into "given" information (i.e., what has already been known to the hearer/reader in a text) and "new" (what is introduced to the the hearer/reader for the first time).[119] This means that efficient discourse processing may operate depending on such a "given-new contract" of language, an implicit communication contract made between the speaker/writer and the hearer/reader.[120] On the assumption that the

---

[117] Fillmore, "Frame Semantics," p. 124. Also Tannen, "Frame," pp. 166–79. Tannen makes the comparison of narratives told by Greek and American subjects about Wallace Chafe's six-minute short movie about a pear picker and then shows how frame knowledge is reflected in grammatical and linguistic features in which the subjects try to retell the story. She points out the sixteen linguistic and grammatical features as evidence of frames: (1) omission, (2) repetition, (3) false starts, (4) backtrack, (5) hedges and other qualifying words or expressions, 6) negatives, (7) contrastive connectives, (8) modals, (9) inexact statements, (10) generalization, (11) inference, (12) evaluative language, (13) interpretation (14) moral judgment, (15) incorrect statements, (16) addition.

[118] Talmy Givón, *Syntax: An Introduction.* Vol. 1 (Amsterdam/Philadelphia: Benjamins, 2001, orig. 1984), p. 459, states, "When speakers mark a referent in discourse as definite, using various anaphoric and/or definite grammatical devise, they aim to ground it into some pre-existing mental representation in the hearer's mind."

[119] See Brown and Yule, *Discourse Analysis*, pp. 153–79.

[120] For the term "given-new contract," see Haviland and Clark, "What's New?," pp. 512–21; Herbert H. Clark and Susan E. Haviland, "Comprehension and the Given-New Contract," in *Discourse Production and Comprehension* (ed. Roy O. Freedle; Norwood, New Jersey: Ablex, 1977), pp. 1–40, esp. 3–4. On the importance of hearer-old information for the cohesive processing of oral text, see Joseph E. Grimes, "Narrative Studies in Oral Texts," in *Current Trends in Textlinguistics* (ed. Wolfgang U. Dressler; Berlin. New York: Walter de Gruyter, 1978), pp. 125–26: "...cohesion...tells us how we relate what we are saying to the hearer. The speaker has to decide as he goes along how the things he is saying relate to what he thinks his hearer already knows." For Grimes the cohesive devices of oral text are redundancy, anaphora (including direct references like the use of a pronoun, and indirect reference like "animal" to refer back

text uses some "hearer-old markers" (a term which this we will use)[121] when they believe that the referent is already known or familiar to the hearer on the basis of frame knowledge, the present study will survey particularly how, in order to help the audience's discourse processing, New Testament Greek grammar signals that kind of information. By hearer-old I mean that the referent can be retrieved from some generic or cultural knowledge of hearers of a speech community.[122] In doing so, I will primarily refer to ideas from Richard Hoyle, who, in his pioneering work "Scenarios, Discourse and Translation," analyzes various grammatical items in the New Testament text in terms of frame theory. Indeed, Richard Hoyle's work is not yet published except in the form of a Ph.D thesis, so using his theory may seem to be open to criticism. However, three major reasons may be suggested in defence of employing his theory, particularly in explaining the relation of New Testament Greek grammar and frames. First, Hoyle's analysis of New Testament grammar is thoroughly based on the frame theory generally acknowledged in the fields of cognitive linguistics and psychology and discourse analysis.[123] Thus his approach to the grammatical categories of New Testament Greek in terms of frames is fully supported by cognitive science. Second, Hoyle not only bases his research into the use of frame in New Testament Greek on modern linguistics, but also attempts to dialogue with important issues discussed among modern New Testament grammarians (e.g., verbal aspect theory and the use of the Greek article and so on).[124] Third, whereas, as pointed out earlier, biblical scholars whose work involves precise judgments about words and grammars are slow in taking advantage of valuable insights from modern linguistics, Hoyle is the first biblical scholar to combine frame theory, a modern semantic theory, and the Greek grammar of the New Testament.[125] So, no doubt Hoyle's work can provide an appropriate

---

to "horse"), and cataphora i.e., reference that "alerts the hearer to something that is yet to come").

[121] That terminology is used by Hoyle, "Scenarios," pp. 88–95.

[122] In fact, Givón, *Syntax*, pp. 459–64, claims that there are three kinds of bases on which the text assumes that the hearer can identify some information as hearer-old: A referent may be identifiable on the part of the hearer when (1) it is "culturally-shared generic-lexical knowledge"; (2) it can be inferred in "the current speech situation"; (3) it can be inferred in the "shared current text."

[123] See Hoyle, "Scenarios," pp. 9–80.

[124] See Hoyle, "Scenarios,"pp. 88–234.

[125] Of course, in a book, *Biblical Words and Their Meaning: An Introduction to Lexical Semantics* (Grand Rapids, Michigan: Zondervan, 1983), Moisés Silva is con-

starting point for us to examine the New Testament grammatical indicators in the light of frame theory.

But, because the present work is primarily concerned with the role
of frames in interpreting Mark's Controversy Stories, I will not attempt
a complete analysis of New Testament Greek grammar. Instead, my
focus will be narrowed to grammatical indicators directly related to
the frames in the Controversy Stories.

1.7.1. *The Predicative Participle and Main Verb*

It is generally acknowledged that there are three types of uses of the
Greek participle: Substantive (i.e., like a noun), predicative (like the
function of a finite verb describing the subject's action), and adjectival.[126] The present study is concerned with the predicative function
or adverbial function of the participle in the participial clause and its
relation to the main verb. One of Hoyle's key arguments is that, in
the Greek New Testament, main verbs (verb forms with a person and
number suffix, as indicative, subjunctive, optative, imperative verbs)
mark new information or events in a narrative, but participles in particular aorist participles (not marking person suffix), which are adverbial, refer to information already mentioned in the co-texts (i.e., the
immediate text).[127] Note, for instance, Mark 6.36 (the main verb is
bolded and the aorist participle is underlined):

ἀπόλυσον αὐτούς,
ἵνα <u>ἀπελθόντες</u> εἰς τοὺς κύκλῳ ἀγροὺς καὶ κώμας ἀγοράσωσιν ἑαυτοῖς
τί φάγωσιν.

The aorist participle ἀπελθόντες ("going away") is used to describe the
information already presented in the co-text by the main verb ἀπόλυσον
("send away") and thus the crowd's action of going away expressed by
the participle can be logically inferred and expected from Jesus' action

---

cerned with making use of modern linguistic theories in discovering the meaning of
the New Testament language. But his focus remains on lexical semantics.

[126] See Porter, *Idioms*, pp. 181–87. Scholars' terms vary; BDF, §§ 411–421, cat-
egorizes particles in terms of Attributive (including attributive or substantive use),
Adverbial (circumstantial), supplementary (predicative completion of the idea of the
main verb); and E.D. Burton, *Syntax of the Moods and Tenses in New Testament Greek*
(Chicago: University of Chicago, 1943), pp. 163–77, employs the terms Substantive,
Adjective, and Adverbial participles.

[127] Hoyle, "Scenarios," pp. 88–94. On the definition of co-text, see Stanley E.
Porter, "Discourse Analysis and New Testament Studies: An Introductory Survey," in
Discourse Analysis and Other Topics in Biblical Greek (ed. Stanley E. Porter and D.A.
Carson; JSNTSup 113: Sheffield: JSOT Press, 1995), p. 19.

of sending the crowd away expressed by the main verb. Importantly, besides presenting predictable information from the main verbs in the co-text, aorist participles are also used to refer to information occurring initially in the immediate text.[128] In that case, the participles, as prototypical components in the events of main verbs, represent knowledge stored in the audience's long-term memory in relation to the frames of the main verbs. Consider, for example, Mark 1.31: καὶ προσελθὼν ἤγειρεν αὐτὴν κρατήσας τῆς χειρός. The aorist participle προσελθὼν ("coming") preceding the main verb and κρατήσας ("taking") following the main verb are prototypical actions in the RAISING frame invoked by the main verb ἤγειρεν ("he raised") in that the former is prerequisite for raising someone and the latter represents a specific manner of it. This hypothesis is partly confirmed by verbal aspect theory which proposes that the aorist tense-form indicative (perfective aspect) is used to describe background events in narrative discourse, and present/imperfect-tense form indicatives (imperfective aspect) and non-indicatives (in particular, participle and infinitive) are usually used to describe "context" or develop verbal concepts of the main events.[129] Thus, the argument of the present study remains that participles, particularly aorist participles, in the New Testament texts are used to identify information already known to the audience's event frame invoked by main verbs, whereas the main verbs serve to introduce hearer-new information. Therefore, the audience's activation of the event frame of the main verbs in independent clauses allows a ready processing of Greek clause structure consisting of main verb and participle or vice versa (for details, see Chapter Five).

1.7.2. The Article

In English the use of the definite article for an item introduced in discourse, as observed above, is a crucial indication of a frame being activated in the immediate surrounding text. The New Testament Greek article is frequently used for an item if and when it is already known to the audience or as a hearer-old marker, either through the pre-

---

[128] Hoyle, "Scenarios," pp. 94–5.
[129] Porter, *Verbal Aspect*, pp, 92, 105–106; and on the use of the participle and infinitive as subordinate to the main events, *idem, Idioms*, pp. 181–203. On the theory of verbal aspect of the Greek New Testament, see *idem, Verbal Aspect*, pp. 75–109. Instead of traditional categorizing of the verb tenses, Porter proposes that the Greek New Testament has three verbal aspects: Perfective aspect (the aorist tense); imperfective aspect (the present and imperfect tenses); stative aspect (the perfect and pluperfect tenses).

viously mentioned discourse or the audience's long-term memory.[130]
Here I am particularly concerned with the case of the latter.[131] Frame
theory proposes that if an item is, though novel in the co-text, part of
the audience's knowledge in long-term memory, the text at times uses
the Greek article to mark that item as hearer-old information (thus
equivalent to "indirect anaphora"[132] or "bridging inference").[133] Stephen Levinsohn, a discourse analyst, says: "The [Greek] definite article
may be used also to refer to particular referents that are associated by
a 'script' with a known entity. For example, once reference has been
made to a father, an arthrous reference to his child is acceptable, even
if previously unmentioned."[134] Hoyle further develops Levinsohn's
position to demonstrate how frame theory may contribute to the study
of the article, using D.A. Carson's much quoted chart of the Greek
article:

	Use I	Use 2
Articular	(a) definite specific Hearer-old item from open scenario [frame]	(c) generic specific Hearer-old scenario [frame] referred to by title, singular or plural (including singular abstract nouns)
Anarthrous	(b) indefinite, that is, qualitative non-specific Hearer-Old item from open or closed scenario [frame]	(d) non-generic (individual) specific Hearer-new item from open or closed scenario [frame][135]

---

[130] Hoyle, "Scenarios," pp. 139–44. On the use of the Greek article for "known, particular" and anaphoric referents, see BDF, pp. 131–32; Porter, *Idioms*, pp. 106–108.

[131] Indeed, the New Testament includes a number of examples which the article
is not marked for items which are already mentioned in the immediate text and part
of the audience's long-term knowledge or for components of an opened frame in the
co-text. Hoyle argues that lack of the article for such items marks their salience in
discourse. Hoyle, "Scenarios," pp. 144–49.

[132] For the terms "indirect anaphora," see Richard Epstein, "Roles, Frames and
Definiteness," in *Discourse Studies in Cognitive Linguistics. Selected Papers from
the Fifth International Cognitive Linguistics Conference Amsterdam, July 1997* (ed.
Karen van Hoek, Andrej Kiibrik and Leo Noordman; Amsterdam, Philadelphia: John
Benjamins, 1999), p. 54. According to Epstein, in the sentence, "I bought a book but
the cover was torn," "the cover" is an indirect anaphora of "a book." Though "the
cover" has not yet been stated previously, the reason the definite article can be used
for "cover" is because of our stereotypical background knowledge that books have
covers.

[133] Clark and Haviland, "Comprehension," pp. 6–7.

[134] Stephen H. Levinsohn, *Discourse Features of New Testament Greek* (Dallas:
Summer Institute of Linguistics, 1992), p. 97 cited by Hoyle, "Scenarios," p. 134.

[135] Hoyle, "Scenarios," p. 134. D.A. Carson, *Exegetical Fallacies* (Grand Rapids: Baker,
1984), p. 83. Carson's original chart is as follow (bold is the original author's):

Both the presence and the absence of the Greek article can be accounted for by frame theory. But I am more concerned with the case in which a frame determines the *presence* of the Greek article. In that case the use of the Greek article may be classified into two types: Generic articular use and definite articular use. First, the generic articular use is applicable to the title of a frame or a frame itself that is available at all times to members of the speech community, though being a new discourse. Thus Mark 1.32 says, Ὀψίας δὲ γενομένης, ὅτε ἔδυ ὁ ἥλιος. In that sentence the word ὁ ἥλιος is marked by the article because the sun is part of the audience's general world knowledge, thus always being retrieved from their long-term memory.[136]

Next, in the case of definite articular use, if and when an item is a prototypical component from within the frame being activated in the co-text, the Greek article is used to refer to the item, though occurring for the first time in the co-text. Mark 1.12–13, for example, says (the frame is bolded and its components are underlined):

Καὶ εὐθὺς τὸ πνεῦμα αὐτὸν ἐκβάλλει εἰς **τὴν ἔρημον**.
καὶ ἦν ἐν **τῇ ἐρήμῳ** τεσσεράκοντα ἡμέρας πειραζόμενος ὑπὸ τοῦ σατανᾶ,
καὶ ἦν μετὰ τῶν θηρίων,
καὶ οἱ ἄγγελοι διηκόνουν αὐτῷ.

In this example the words τοῦ σατανᾶ and τῶν θηρίων have the Greek article, although they are new information in the co-text. Frame theory makes it possible to explain that this is because they are prototypical components, thus known to the speaker and audience, within the WILDERNESS frame which is opened in Mark 1.12–13 (e.g., on the wilderness as a dwelling place of the Satan, see Mark 5.2–18; Matthew 12.43; Str-B 4.515–16; Tobit 8.3; 4 Maccabees 18.8; 2 Apocalypse of Baruch. 10.81; 1 Enoch 10.4–5; cf. Leviticus 16.10; on the wild beasts,

---

	Use I	Use 2
Articular	(a) definite	(c) generic
Anarthrous	(b) indefinite i.e., qualitative	(d) non-generic (individual item).

[136] Additionally, since the expression Ὀψίας δὲ γενομένης in Mark 1.32 refers to the ending point of the sabbath for which the frame has been evoked since 1.21 (εὐθὺς τοῖς σάββασιν εἰσελθὼν εἰς τὴν συναγωγὴν...) it is also possible that the article in "the sun" is a reference to "sun" as a particular component in the original audience's SABBATH frame which contained the knowledge of Jewish law: According to the law the sabbath begins and ends at or around sundown (e.g., Leviticus 23.32; Nehemiah 13.19; Luke 23.54; John 19.31–42).

see Ezekiel 34.5; Numbers 21.5–6; Deuteronomy 7.22).[137] Consequently, the Greek article induces the audience to interpret those nouns as referring to the open WILDERNESS frame, not just to any individual members in question. Hence, the coherence of this discourse relies on the fact that the nouns are semantically related in terms of their association with the WILDERNESS frame. Further, regarding the use of the Greek article, what we should keep in mind is that the phrase is not just content to evoke a specific component in a frame or the frame itself, but also to set up its role in the frame.[138] In the example above, the Greek articles for "Satan" and "wild beasts" guide the audience to relate the concepts of the nouns to their stereotypical roles, that is, hostile and menacing, in the WILDERNESS frame.[139] Note that the Greek article in the nominals τὸ πνεῦμα, τὴν ἔρημον, and οἱ ἄγγελοι indicates that the nouns play an anaphoric role to refer back to the information present in Mark 1.1–3 and 11.

1.7.3. The Rhetorical Question

Rhetorical questions are also gram-matical indicators that encourage the audience to use cognitive frames in comprehending what is implied in that question. The New Testament text, according to John Beekman and John Callow, contains around 1,000 questions, and

---

[137] The wilderness in biblical and postbiblical Jewish and Christian thoughts, as Guelich, *Mark 1–8.26*, p. 38, rightly notes, represents "the place of God's coming deliverance," "the abode of Satan and evil," and "the inhospitable habitat of wild animals." And see Jeffrey B. Gibson, "Jesus' Wilderness Temptation according to Mark," *JSNT* 53 (1994), pp. 4–43; see also D.C. Allison, "Mountain and Wilderness," in *The Dictionary of Jesus and the Gospels* (Downers Grove, Illinois: IVP, 1992), p. 565. Allison argues that the WILDERNESS frame in Mark 1.12–13 contains such conventional knowledge, and Mark and his historical audience's concept of wilderness depended on that knowledge. We can assume that their frame for the WILDERNESS would have been stored through this knowledge of the Jewish Scriptures.

[138] Cf. Epstein, "Roles," p. 56.

[139] In particular, Deuteronomy 8.15 (LXX), 7.22 (LXX) and Ezekiel 34.5 (LXX) describe wild animals as threatening and evil creatures living in the wilderness. Hence, it is more reasonable to believe in terms of the WILDERNESS frame that the wild beasts play a hostile role in Jesus' wilderness experiences than that they do a peaceful one. Likewise, France, *Mark*, p. 86, says, "θηρία are to be understood, where there is no indication to the contrary, as hostile and dangerous to humans, who need protection from them." Contra Richard J. Bauckham, "Jesus and the Wild Animals (Mark 1:13): A Christological Image for an Ecological Age," in *Jesus of Nazareth: Lord and Christ; Essays on the Historical Jesus and New Testament Christology* (ed. Joel B. Green and Max Turner; Grand Rapids: Eerdmans, 1994), pp. 3–21.

among them about 70 per cent are classified as rhetorical questions.[140] Real questions are used for the speaker to elicit information from those addressed. For example, in Mark 8.27, Jesus asks his disciples on the way, τίνα με λέγουσιν οἱ ἄνθρωποι εἶναι; In the following verse his disciples respond to this question by saying, Ἰωάννην τὸν βαπτιστήν, καὶ ἄλλοι. Without usually (while not necessarily) answering the question, a rhetorical question "serves the purpose of *imparting* or *calling attention to* information, not eliciting it."[141] Mark 3.23–24 states (the rhetorical question is bolded):

> Καὶ προσκαλεσάμενος αὐτοὺς ἐν παραβολαῖς ἔλεγεν αὐτοῖς·
> **πῶς δύναται σατανᾶς σατανᾶν ἐκβάλλειν;**
> καὶ ἐὰν βασιλεία ἐφ᾽ ἑαυτὴν μερισθῇ, οὐ δύναται σταθῆναι ἡ βασιλεία ἐκείνη·

In this passages Jesus' question is not answered by the Pharisees and he continues his teaching. The question is used to invoke from the hearer conventional information about the indivisible unity of the demonic realm.

Information implied by the rhetorical question is often a reflection of the language user's stereotypic knowledge.[142] For this reason Beekman and Callow offer that rhetorical questions can be replaced by the forms of a statement.[143] In Mark 12.37, thus, Jesus says, αὐτὸς Δαυὶδ λέγει αὐτὸν κύριον, **καὶ πόθεν αὐτοῦ ἐστιν υἱός;** The expected answer to this question is that Christ cannot be the son of David. This statement of strong negative affirmation is based on two common ideas: One is that "Lord" is a title for ΥΗWΗ or for someone of the highest status; the other is that "to be the son of someone is to be in some sense subordinate or even inferior."[144] The speaker here uses the rhetorical question to express the stereotyped information. Certainly, the statement represented in terms of a rhetorical question is not just part of

---

[140] John Beekman and John Callow, *Translating the Word of God: with Scripture and Topical Indexes* (Grand Rapids, Michigan: Zondervan, 1974), p. 229.

[141] Beekman and Callow, *The Word of God*, p. 238 (the original author's italics).

[142] See Hoyle, "Scenarios," pp. 176–79.

[143] Beekman and Callow, *The Word of God*, p. 238, propose four principal functions of rhetorical questions in the New Testament:
 1. a statement of certitude
 2. a statement of incertitude
 3. a statement of evaluation or obligation
 4. to highlight and introduce a new subject or a new aspect of the same subject

[144] Evans, *Mark 8:27–16:20*, pp. 273–74.

the speaker's common knowledge, but also part of the listener's one, thus being shared between both the speaker and the hearer.[145] The rhetorical question, accordingly, propels the hearer to activate his or her general background knowledge, namely, a frame, about the matter in question so that the hearer may accept the speaker's opinion and attitude. In Mark 2.1–3.6, as will be discussed, rhetorical questions are used to provide various types of statements of things or events, such as affirmation, negation, amazement, evaluation. For these statements to be effectively communicated to the hearer in terms of rhetorical questions, it is necessary that the audience understands and shares the stereotyped knowledge presupposed by the text of the matter in question, otherwise the communication would fail and the hearer would mistake rhetorical questions for real questions.

The Gospel of Mark contains a number of rhetorical questions which illustrate the existence of frames in the storyline. In order for Mark's original audience to understand rhetorical questions in accordance with the way in which they were intended, the audience must accurately judge in which frames the rhetorical questions operate. Thus, in processing and understanding certain issues Mark's original audience would have needed to evoke two different frames: One is the frame of Jesus, or a frame current in early Christianity, and the other is the frame of first-century Judaism.

1.7.4. Contraexpectation Markers

A frame has prototypical ex-pectations of persons, objects, and events which are based on one's prior experience of the world in a given culture. These expectations make it possible for people to interpret and predict objects and events in the world; but, if the violation of expectation occurs, the text can signal it by virtue of contraexpectation markers in discourse, such as surprising verbs (ἐξίστημι), adversative conjunctions (δέ, ἀλλά, καί,[146] εἰ μή) and negative statements (e.g., οὐ, οὐδέποτε, μή etc.). With the negative statement, Deborah Tannen, a linguist, claims, "The use of a negative statement is one of the clearest

---

[145] The speaker, as Hoyle, "Scenarios", p. 174, rightly proposes, assumes as follows when asking a rhetorical question:
  1. the audience knows the correct 'answer' to the 'question'
  2. the audience knows that the speaker knows the answer
  3. the audience knows that the speaker knows that the audience knows
[146] On the role of καί as a contraexpectation marker, see below.

and most frequent indications that an expectation is not being met."[147] In the same way, William Labov, a sociolinguist, claims, "What reason would the narrator have for telling us that something did not happen since he is in the business of telling us what did happen?" He goes on to answer that "…it expresses the defeat of an expectation that something would happen."[148] It will be noted in Chapter Six that this is also the case for Greek negative statements.

Consider two examples below for contraexpectation markers. One is from George Lakoff and the other from Mark's Gospel. "It is June, but it is snowing."[149] In this sentence the use of "but" shows that the user of language's JUNE frame does not expect it to be snowing in June. Similarly, Mark 5.35–36 says (a contraexpectation marker is bolded):

Ἔτι αὐτοῦ λαλοῦντος ἔρχονται ἀπὸ τοῦ ἀρχισυναγώγου λέγοντες ὅτι ἡ θυγάτηρ σου ἀπέθανεν· τί ἔτι σκύλλεις τὸν διδάσκαλον;
ὁ **δὲ** Ἰησοῦς παρακούσας τὸν λόγον λαλούμενον λέγει τῷ ἀρχισυναγώγῳ·
μὴ φοβοῦ, μόνον πίστευε.

The normal HEALING frame leads one to assume that the news of the sick person's death means putting an end to any attempt for healing. But the use of δὲ in this passage draws the audience's attention to the fact that Jesus' following action is a departure from such an expectation: Despite the daughter's death, Jesus does not stop proceeding to healing.

But, unlike the conjuction ἀλλά whose major usage is adversative, Greek conjunctions like καί and δέ may represent a variety of meanings in sentences or discourse.[150] The semantic function of δέ seems relatively simple since, though A.T. Robertson asserts that δέ involves "no essential notion of antithesis or contrast,"[151] most of the New Testament grammarians acknowledge the primary usage of δέ as adversative, with its frequent use as "progressive," "explanatory" (to

---

[147] Tannen, "Frame," p. 147.
[148] William Labov, *Sociolinguistic Patterns* (Philadelphia: University of Pennsylvania Press, 1972), pp. 380–81.
[149] George Lakoff, "The Role of Deduction in Grammar," in *Studies in Linguistic Semantics* (ed. Charles Fillmore and D. Terence Langendoen; New York; Holt, Rinehart and Winston, 1971), p. 66.
[150] Porter, *Idioms*, pp. 205–206, 208, 211, 214.
[151] A.T. Robertson, *A Grammar of the Greek New Testament in the Light of Historical Research* (Nashville: Broadman Press, 4th edn, 1934 [1906]), p. 1184.

use Zerwick's term), "connective," or "emphasis" (in Porter's words).[152] The conjunction καί, according to Robertson, usually contains three main uses: Adjunctive (also), ascensive (even) and the mere connective (and).[153] Despite its most common connective use, καί, as Porter claims, may be sometimes also used in an adversative sense.[154] The question is how we can know whether καί, along with δέ, is used as connective or adversative. Robertson admits that the determination of the meaning of καί "depends wholly on the context."[155] My argument is that the role of the context can be better explained in reference to a frame explicitly or implicitly mentioned in the text. The text uses various contraexpectation markers to help the audience's understanding of a frame-based story; but it is by means of prototypical event sequences in the audience's mental frame that the audience determines whether such markers are used to indicate the violation of expected sequences of certain events.[156]

1.7.5. Agentless Construction and Pronoun

A frame-based text often leaves its components unstated, if they are typical in the frame being opened in the immediate surrounding text, so that the audience may comprehend the text readily or retrieve relevant information by inferential processing. Porter asserts that the subjects of certain verbs (impersonal verbs, in his example) are not specified explicitly because they "take conventionally-understood subjects."[157] With respect to the Greek Gospels, the use of the agentless construction with no anaphoric subject is an indication that the text takes for granted that the audience is able to understand the missing agents

---

[152] BDF, § 447; Maximilian Zerwick S.J., *Biblical Greek* (Rome: Pontifical Biblical Institute, 1963), p. 157; Porter, *Idioms*, p. 208.

[153] Robertson, *Grammar*, pp. 1179–81.

[154] Porter, *Idioms*, p. 211; see also Robertson, *Grammar*, p. 1183.

[155] Robertson, *Grammar*, p. 1181.

[156] Hoyle, "Scenarios," p. 220. For an recent and important work about Greek conjunctions like δέ, τότε, καί, γάρ, σύν, see Stephanie L. Black, *Sentence Conjunction in the Gospel of Matthew: καί, δέ, τότε, γάρ, σύν and Asyndeton in Narrative Discourse* (JSNTSup 216; Sheffield: Sheffield Academic Press, 2002) (in particular, p. 112 for the quotation to follow). With respect to καί, she argues, "καί has a consistent low-level semantic value that allows it to be used in a variety of semantic relationships between conjoined propositions in Matthew's narrative framework—*relationships which are pragmatically worked out by the audience on the basis of linguistic content, context, and knowledge of the world*—but that in fact the meaning conveyed by καί is procedural rather than conceptual or 'logical'." [my italics]

[157] Porter, *Idioms*, p. 78.

by depending on knowledge stored in their mental frames, or make inferences from the frame currently being activated in the immediate surrounding co-text. Our present concern will be focused on three things: Active and passive verbal forms, and the pronoun. First, some active verbal forms are used without specifying their subject explicitly in the co-text. Note Mark 15.27 (the relevant verb is underlined): σὺν αὐτῷ <u>σταυροῦσιν</u> δύο λῃστάς. Because the CRUCIFYING frame, which carries the information of a kind of Roman ultimate punishment, has been opened since Mark 15.15 (Ὁ δὲ Πιλᾶτος...παρέδωκεν τὸν Ἰησοῦν φραγελλώσας ἵνα σταυρωθῇ), 'Roman soldiers' could be evoked as the agents of executing crucifixion.[158] Second, the passive verbal forms can be hardly missed in this regard. The passive voice is a form where "the agent (the person or thing represented as performing the action) is no longer the grammatical subject of the clause."[159] Certainly, not all passive forms are accounted for as a frame-related phenomenon. Some agency is frequently expressed by some prepositional devices (e.g., διά, ὑπό, ἀπό, ἐκ, παρά + genitive).[160] Despite this fact, the hypothesis is that a frame is a cognitive model to help process and understand the semantic agent of a passive verb with grammatically unspecified agency.[161] Consider Mark 1.15 (the relevant verb is underlined): <u>πεπλήρωται</u> ὁ καιρὸς, which indicates no explicit reference to the agent of bringing "the time (ὁ καιρὸς)" to pass. It is obvious that the semantic agent of the passive verb cannot be decided on the basis of this clause alone, but instead it must be supported by the immediate co-text. The clause in question is conjoined by καί, thus in parallel to, the following clause (ἤγγικεν ἡ βασιλεία τοῦ θεοῦ). Of importance is the fact that the latter clause apparently evokes the SOVEREIGNTY OF GOD frame (cf., "the gospel of God," Mark 1.14), which enabled Jews and Mark's Christian audiences to believe that God was certainly

---

[158] Mark 15.16 (Οἱ δὲ στρατιῶται ἀπήγαγον αὐτὸν...) explicitly says that the soldiers are involved in the subsequent tortures inflicted on Jesus (17–20). But it must be noted that a specfic identification (i.e., Romans) of the soldiers is not given in the text.

[159] Porter, *Idioms*, p. 64 (the original is italicized).

[160] Robertson, *Grammar*, p. 820.

[161] BDF, § 130 (1), 313, 342 (1) and Zerwick, *Biblical Greek*, p. 76, claims that the divine passive or theological passive is used in order to avoid directly naming God as agent. However, as Porter, *idioms*, p. 65, points out, the Gospels do not avoid using the expressions "heaven," "God," and "Lord." Hoyle, "Scenarios," p. 167, provides GRAMCORD data for occurrences in Matthew, Mark, Luke, and John respectively: οὐρανός 82, 18, 35, 18; θεός 51, 49, 122, 83; κύριος 80, 18, 104, 52.

a prototypical agent of ruling over not only his covenantal people but also all things, including events, and not least, time itself. (Consider the Jews' and the Christians' shared belief in monotheism.) Consequently, no doubt the SOVEREIGNTY OF GOD frame opened in the co-text helped Mark's Christian audience identify the semantic agent of the passive verb πεπλήρωται as God who is bringing the time to pass.

Third, a frame can identify the referent of a pronoun with no anaphoric noun. Where textual information activates a certain event frame, the audience can evoke a specific participant in that frame, and the pronoun may be used to refer to its prototypical or default participant, though there is no prior explicit lexical mention of the entity. Note Mark 1.21–22 (the relevant pronoun is underlined and the frame is bolded):

> τοῖς σάββασιν **εἰσελθὼν εἰς τὴν συναγωγὴν** ἐδίδασκεν.
> καὶ ἐξεπλήσσοντο ἐπὶ τῇ διδαχῇ αὐτοῦ·
> ἦν γὰρ διδάσκων <u>αὐτοὺς</u> ὡς ἐξουσίαν ἔχων....

The third plural pronoun is used without specifying its prior noun. Here the opening GOING TO THE SYNAGOGUE includes as default information regarding the general congregation of the synagogue service.[162] Mark's Christian audience would hardly have failed to identify the pronoun with the general synagogue congregation in light of the opening frame.

1.7.6. *Participial Noun Phrase*

In addition to verbal function, the Greek participle may be used to define a referent or provide information about the referent. Such a use of the participle is traditionally known as the substantive and adjectival usage of the participle.[163] We, following Hoyle, will call that participial expression a "participial noun phrase."[164] Frames play some role in such a participial use as well. The prototypical information of the referent which is always available from the frame opened in the co-text or the audience's long-term memory tends to be expressed in the participial noun phrase.[165] The actions invoked by the participle are

---

[162] On the SYNAGOGUE frame and its prototypical components, see Chapters Five and Six.

[163] See Burton, *Syntax*, pp. 163–77 and Porter, *Idioms*, pp. 182–86.

[164] See Hoyle, "Scenarios," p. 180.

[165] Concerning the relations of the participial clauses to their main verb, a further discussion will be made in Chapter Six. Hoyle, "Scenarios," pp. 180–84.

often predictable from the frames for the referent or elements modified by the participle. Note the example of Mark 3.22 (the person frame title is bolded and the substantive participle corresponding to it is underlined): Καὶ οἱ γραμματεῖς <u>οἱ</u> ἀπὸ Ἱεροσολύμων <u>καταβάντες</u> ἔλεγον. The information ("the ones who had come down") described by the participial noun phrase with the article is used to represent a specific status of the noun οἱ γραμματεῖς. Here the information about the participial noun phrase is prototypically inferred from the noun οἱ γραμματεῖς it modifies, since the SCRIBE frame, a person frame, includes information that the scribes are Jewish legal experts (see Chapters Five and Six), typically based in Jerusalem which was the centre of Jewish legal authority.[166]

1.7.7. Temporal Clause

The user of the Greek language often expresses hearer-old information, whether in the audience's long-term memory or from the frame opened in the co-text, using a temporal clause introduced by such particles as, ὅσον, ὅταν, ὡς, ὅτε.[167] For this reason the audience has no difficulty in processing and understanding information concerning the temporal clause on the basis of these open frames.[168] Consider the example of Mark 4.31 (the frame is bolded, the temporal particle is italicized and the predictable information in the frame is underlined): ὡς **κόκκῳ σινάπεως**, ὃς *ὅταν* <u>σπαρῇ ἐπὶ τῆς γῆς</u>, μικρότερον ὂν πάντων τῶν σπερμάτων τῶν ἐπὶ τῆς γῆς. The information regarding the temporal clause, that is, "a mustard seed is planted," is easily evoked from the MUSTARD SEED frame.

1.7.8. Evaluative Language

The semantics of evaluative expressions are difficult to account for without reference to frames. A frame has normative knowledge, and hence it enables the speaker and audience to evaluate specific things against it for their fit.[169] Understanding the expression, "Good coffee!"

---

[166] Robert A. Guelich, *Mark 1–8.26* (WBC 34A; Dallas: Word, 1989), p. 174. C.E.B. Cranfield, *The Gospel According to Saint Mark* (CGTC; Cambridge: Cambridge University Press, 1974, orig. 1959), p. 136, says, "καταβάινω is regularly used in biblical Greek of journeying from, and ἀναβάινω of journeying to, Jerusalem or Palestine (e.g., Luke ii.51, Acts xxv.7, 9)."

[167] Hoyle, "Scenarios," pp. 161–65.

[168] On a variety of usages of the Greek temporal particles, see BDF, §§ 381–82.

[169] Rumelhart, "Schemata," pp. 38–39 and Lakoff, *Women*, pp. 79–80.

requires one to open the knowledge that as a drink coffee can be valued on the basis of "its taste, its contribution to the drinker's alertness."[170] Of course, such normative or typical knowledge is equivalent to cultural expectations which are usually involved in defining what an entity is supposed to be.[171] The entity would be regarded as a better instance of a frame if it has the central attributes of the frame, thus providing more satisfaction. On the contrary, if the entity does not seem fit for the default value in the frame or stereotypes for it, it leads to a negative judgment or to disappointment. In order to interpret appropriately the evaluative expression, it is necessary to open relevant frames and take into consideration in what frames the text interprets and evaluates things or persons. Regarding the study of Mark's Controversy Stories, I will concentrate on such expressions, including verbs and adjectives such as: δύναμαι, ἔξεστι, εὔκοπος, παλαιός, νέος.[172]

2. The Comprehension of Information

I have explored several different ways in which frames organize information or story. In this section, my focus will be turned to the frames' involvement in information processing and comprehension with particular emphasis on story. Schank and Abelson state:

> By subscribing to a script-based theory of understanding, we are making some strong claims about the nature of the understanding process. In order to understand the actions that are going on in a given situation, a person must have been in that situation before. That is, understanding is knowledge-based. The actions of others make sense only insofar as they are part of a stored pattern of actions that have been previously experienced.[173]

Likewise, understanding discourse, as pointed out previously, means finding a configuration of relevant frames that correspond to the passage in question. Without evoking the relevant frame, comprehension is an extremely difficult task, though not impossible. And once the audience opens the relevant frame corresponding to incoming information, the frame is actively involved in processing and comprehending

---

[170] For the example of 'good coffee,' see Fillmore, "Frame Semantics," p. 129.
[171] Taylor, *Linguistic Categorization*, p. 94.
[172] Fillmore, "Frame Semantics," p. 129, says, "Evaluative adjectives can contain in their meanings reference to the dimensions, scales, or standards according to which something is evaluated..."
[173] Schank and Abelson, *Scripts*, p. 67.

the input by instantiating it in several ways. If so, in what specific ways does the frame help story comprehension?

2.1. Frames Provide Essential Elements of Narrative Comprehension

Literary critics often say that the basic elements of the narrative world, whether in modern literature or ancient, consist of three key elements—setting, event, and character.[174] These features play a key role in the audience/reader's hearing/reading experience of a story. A cognitive frame, as discussed earlier, accommodates five major types of information: Event, person, object, thing, place. The implication is that the frames provide supportive knowledge structures for such a narrative processing based on setting, event, and character.

First, because of its prototypical elements related to objects and geographical location, the thing frame can serve to enable the audience to process background information associated with various settings of a narrative. In the Gospel of Mark, many local settings (e.g., the river, the desert, the sea, mountains, houses, boats, the sea of Galilee, the temple, and the synagogues) are usually integral to processing and understanding of an event in focus.[175] Hence, the characters' particular ways of acting and the descriptions of events occurring in a specific place can be appropriately made sense of in terms of the open place or scene frames which provide specific information about the arrangements of the place and its prototypical properties.

For example, the story of Mark 3.31–35 is a continuation of 3.20–22, in which the HOUSE frame (bolded) has been dominant since the opening clause ἔρχεται εἰς **οἶκον** (v. 20). The HOUSE frame here provides significant background knowledge for the understanding of this story. Mark seems to make a contrast between Jesus' family members "standing outside" (ἔξω στήκοντες v. 31) and the crowd "sitting about him [Jesus]" (ἐκάθητο περὶ αὐτὸν vv. 32, 34). The understanding of such a stark contrast between physical postures (στήκοντες and ἐκάθητο) and spatial locations (ἔξω and περὶ αὐτὸν) between the two groups is apparently made possible against the open HOUSE frame which involves a prototypical knowledge of the horizontal and vertical dimensions of house building. Further, since the concept of house

---

[174] In relation to the narrative elements of the Gospel of Mark, see Rhoads, Dewey, and Michie, *Mark*, pp. 63–136.
[175] Rhoads, Dewey, and Michie, *Mark*, pp. 63–72.

may represent a physical and mental boundary distinguishing between 'insider' (household) and 'outsider' (non-household) and has a family as bounded participants, the HOUSE frame makes it possible to infer that when Jesus declared those around him as ἀδελφός μου, ἀδελφὴ and μήτηρ (v. 35), he intended to make up a new family circle that does the will of God.

Second, the event frame or script-like frame also contributes significantly to understanding Mark's story. Agonistic interaction between characters is at the core of the oral-aural narrative.[176] The events or plots of the Gospel of Mark, as David Rhoads and Donald Michie point out, have a characteristic of conflict between Jesus and other characters (Jewish religious authorities, the disciples and evil spirits).[177] The conflict usually arises when the pattern of behaviour in a specific location and time that is taken for granted by one is thought to have been violated by another. Since the event frame involves stereotypic information of action sequences or what the participants are supposed to do in a particular situation, it is an indispensable cognitive resource for the audience to understand and evaluate appropriately various conflict-generating situations.[178]

For instance, Mark 8.27–38, particularly verses 32 and 33, deals with the conflict between Jesus and his disciple, Peter. In order to understand this conflict, what is crucial is to open what we may call the TEACHING THE DISCIPLE frame; this frame may be easily opened by the expressions ἐπηρώτα τοὺς μαθητὰς αὐτου (v. 27) and ἤρξατο διδάσκειν αὐτοὺς (v. 31), and subsequent sentences largely associated with Jesus' instruction (vv. 34–38). The typical participants in the TEACHING THE DISCIPLE frame generally constitute a master who has the responsibility to teach and encourage good actions and thoughts, and to correct and discourage bad actions and thoughts in his pupils; disciples who have a social position of subordination in learning through imitation and instruction; and specific teachings that the disciples are supposed to understand and follow.[179] Such a frame

---

[176] Ong, *Orality*, pp. 43–45.

[177] The conflicts, for example, arise between Jesus and his disciples, Jewish religious authorities, evilpowers, namely Satan or demons. See Rhoads, Dewey, and Michie, *Mark*, pp. 78–97.

[178] We will discuss later how frame deviations facilitate frame-based story comprehension rather than interrupt it.

[179] Vernon K. Robbins, "Plucking Grain on the Sabbath," in *Patterns of Persuasion in the Gospels* (ed. Burton L. Mack and Vernon K. Robbins; Sonoma, California:

and its prototypical components, first of all, guide the audience appropriately to understand the clashing between Jesus and Peter by providing relevant background knowledge. Mark 8.31–33 presents that as a master, Jesus teaches that his messianic role comprises suffering, being rejected, being killed, and resurrection, whereas as a disciple, Peter's thought of Christ constitutes τὰ τῶν ἀνθρώπων ("things of men"), perhaps prosperity and power. The present frame enables the audience to interpret that the disciple misunderstands the master's teaching of his messianic role, thus leading to an expectation that the master will correct or "rebuke" (ἐπετίμησεν, v. 33) the disciple(s)' error. Thus, because of the TEACHING THE DISCIPLE frame, the audience may understand Jesus' rebuking of his disciples (vv. 33–38) as a process of correcting and making them good disciples, rather than opposing them as in the case of Jesus' conflict with Jewish religious authorities. By contrast, in light of the TEACHING THE DISCIPLE frame, Mark's original audience must have understood the disciple's rebuke of the master (ἤρξατο ἐπιτιμᾶν αὐτῷ, v. 32) as a surprising action; so it serves to heighten tension between the master and the disciple(s).

Finally, as Schank rightly points out, "the language understanding process is heavily reliant on predictions based on understanding the goals and intentions of the actors in a story."[180] Frames are remarkably helpful in processing and perceiving the behaviours and roles of various characters in such an oral-aural narrative as Mark's Gospel. An oral-aural narrative has a feature of stereotypic characters. Havelock claims:

> If the saga is functional, if its purpose is to conserve the group mores, then the men who act in it must be the kind of men whose actions would involve the public law and the family law of the group. They must there-

---

Polebridge, 1989), p. 111. On the TEACHING THE DISCIPLE frame and the way its prototypical elements present in other passages of the Gospel of Mark, see Mark 9.9–13, 30–37, 38–50; 10.13–16, 23–31, 32–34, 35–45; cf. 4.10–20. With respect to the relationship of master and disciple, although there are many differences between the model of Jesus and his disciples and the Jewish and Greco-Roman one, all three models share a commonplace in that they are primarily concerned with the prototypical relation of teaching and learning or obedience. On the master-disciple relations produced in ancient Jewish and Greco-Roman cultures, see Martin Hengel, *The Charismatic Leader and His Followers* (Edinburgh: T. and T. Clark, 1981); Robbins, *Jesus*.

[180] Roger C. Schank, "Predictive Understanding," in *Recent Advances in the Psychology of Language: Formal and Experimental Approaches* (ed. Robin N. Campbell and Philip T. Smith; New York and London: Plenum, 1978), p. 99.

fore be 'political' men in the most general sense of that term, men whose acts, passions, and thoughts will affect the behaviour and the fate of the society in which they live so that the things they do will send out vibrations into the farthest confines of this society, and the whole apparatus becomes alive and performs motions which are paradigmatic.[181]

Likewise, the portrayal of the characters present in the Gospel of Mark has to do mostly with performing typical acts. They are described as doing, saying, and responding to certain situations in stereotypic ways.[182] Thus, as Kelber observes regarding Mark's healing stories, "none of the characters are developed into individual personalities. The sick persons or their supplicants are virtually exchangeable figures, for 'what is preserved [in oral narrative] has to be typical.' What matters is the functioning of roles, not the delineation of characters."[183] Mark's stereotypic characterization of the agents may be called the framing of characters. In other words, this typical description of the characters exactly corresponds to person frame-based information processing because, as observed earlier, the person frame consists of typical knowledge of participants and their roles in a given situation. Thus, the person frame apparently plays an essential role on the part of the audience in anticipating their behaviour and identifying their intention (for the example of person frame in Mark's Gospel, see below).

2.2. Frames Enable Expectation

It has been assumed that oral narrative is structured to induce the audience to use their predictive ability in perceiving and interpreting events and things in the story world.[184] In doing so, a primary focus has been put on literary devices such as repetition, ring composition, and chiastic pattern. The argument is that a mental frame serves to

---

[181] Havelock, *Plato,* pp. 167–68.

[182] Havelock, *Plato,* p. 87. Havelock says that the way the characters in oral narrative act is "the way in which the society does normally behave (or does not) and at the same time the way in which we, its members, who form the poet's audience, are encouraged to behave."

[183] Kelber, *Gospel,* p. 51.

[184] J. Notopoulos, "Continuity and Interconnexion in Homeric Oral Composition," *TPAPA* 82 (1951), pp. 81–101; Havelock, *Plato,* p. 147; *idem,* "Oral Composition in the Odeipus Tyrannus of Sophocles," *NLH* 16 (1984), p. 182; Minchi, *Memory,* pp. 181–202. Concerning Mark's Gospel, see Dewey, "Oral Methods," pp. 40–42; Robbins, *Jesus,* pp. 7–14; see also James R. Edwards, "Markan Sandwiches: The Significance of Interpolations in Markan Narratives," *NovT* 31 (1989), pp. 193–216.

guide the audience's expectation-driven narrative processing.[185] Teun van Dijk says:

> Frames are not merely chunks of knowledge, but units of conventional knowledge according to which mutual expectations and interactions are organized...Thus, on the one hand the concepts of a 'restaurant' or a 'party' form a net-work of necessary properties. On the other hand the frames associated with these concepts involve a whole series of objects, events, and actions that are typical parts of restaurant or party episodes.[186]

In a frame-related story comprehension, such a web of interconnected semantic data in the frame sets up many common expectations in the listener. So, as the audience hears a story, they can generate expectations about what is going to happen next and what they are likely to hear about next on the basis of such frame knowledge.[187] There are specific ways for this predictive ability of the frame to operate.

2.2.1. Stereotype and Expectation

Predictability of a frame results from its stereotypic attributes. The frame is formed through any repeat experience in a specific social and cultural environment, and thus it represents a stereotypical knowledge of things, events, and persons. This means that once the frame is opened to account for incoming information, due to its "social stereotypes"[188] or "default assignments,"[189] it enables the audience to predict what elements the input involves and how they will come about. In order to see how it operates, it is necessary to give our attention to each type of frame. First, the stereotyped knowledge stored in the person frame permits the audience to anticipate what typical role he or she plays in a given situation. Consequently, the expectation of such a role allows the audience to guess in advance how that situation will develop. When characters act in accordance with stereotypes for them, the confirmation of the expectations will take place on the part of the

---

[185] Tannen, "Frame," pp. 137–38, defines a frame or script as a "structure of expectation."

[186] van Dijk, "Semantic Macro-Structure," p. 21.

[187] Tannen, "Frame," pp. 137–81, esp. 160–79; Artheur C. Graesser, *Prose Comprehension Beyond the Word* (New York: Springer-Verlag, 1981), p. 34.

[188] Lakoff, *Women*, pp. 85–86.

[189] Minsky, "Framework," pp. 212–13.

audience, but it may come as a surprise to the audience when they act differently from what has been expected.

There is an example from Mark 7.24–30 (the story of the Syrophoenician woman's faith). The story begins by opening the MOTHER frame for the woman (γυνὴ) not least because of the expression γυνὴ...ἧς εἶχεν τὸ θυγάτριον αὐτῆς in verse 25. Thus when hearing information that the woman heard of Jesus (v. 25), the open MOTHER frame enables the audience to predict what she will do with a daughter having an unclean spirit. A family member's plea for other sick members was culturally expected in the first-century Mediterranean "health care system" (e.g., Mark 1.29–31; 5.21–24, 35–43; 9.17–29).[190] Accordingly, the MOTHER frame may lead the original audience to expect that she will beg Jesus to cure her demon-possessed daughter, and this expectation would turn out to be correct when the audience heard the subsequent inputs (ἐλθοῦσα προσέπεσεν πρὸς τοὺς πόδας αὐτου, in v. 25b and ἠρώτα αὐτὸν ἵνα τὸ δαιμόνιον ἐκβάλῃ ἐκ τῆς θυγατρὸς αὐτῆς, in v. 26b). However, in verse 26a, Mark's historical audience was informed of her other social status in turn: Ἑλληνίς, Συροφοινίκισσα τῷ γένει, thus opening a GENTILE WOMAN frame.[191] Because the GENTILE WOMAN frame included a social stereotype where no relationship was ever made between a Gentile woman and a Jewish teacher (John 4.9, 27; Acts 10.28;[192] Galatians 2.11–15; 3.28), the woman was expected to change, in some ways, her attitude towards Jesus, a Jewish teacher, just as Jesus responded to her in verse 27.[193]

---

[190] Pilch, *Healing*, pp. 67–68.

[191] D.E. Nineham, *Saint Mark* (Middlesex: Penguin, 1963), p. 200. Nineham says, "to Mark's readers this word ["a Greek"] will have had religious, rather than racial connotations—'a pagan', 'a Gentile'." And Guelich, *Mark 1–8.26*, p. 385, says, "While 'Greek' may at times imply cultural standing of one 'hellenized' or Greek speaking and educated and thus of the upper class...to refer to the 'Greeks' in the early Christian mission meant primarily to contrast religiously the Jews and 'the Greeks' with the latter synonymous with 'non-Jews' or 'pagans' (e.g., Romans 1:16; 2:9, 10; 3:9; 10:12; 1 Corinthians 1:24; 10:32; Galatians 3:28; Colossians 3:11);" and also Guelich says that "A Syrophoenician by birth" refers to her "citizenship," putting stress on her Gentile origins in terms of the word "by birth."

[192] Most clearly, Acts 10.28 says, "he [Peter] said to them [Conelius's family members], 'You yourselves know how unlawful it is for a Jew to associate with or to visit any one of another nation" (RSV).

[193] On Jews' avoidance of Gentiles, particulary in table fellowship customs, see Philp F. Esler, *Community and Gospel in Luke-Acts: The Social and Political Motivations of Lucan Theology* (SNTSMS 57; Cambridge: Cambridge University Press, 1987), pp. 73–86.

This cognitive flow affects the understanding of the conjunction δὲ in verse 26, which introduces the woman's social status (the contraexpectation marker is bolded): ἡ **δὲ** γυνὴ ἦν Ἑλληνίς, Συροφοινίκισσα τῷ γένει.[194] RSV translates δὲ as "now." But the MOTHER and GENTILE WOMAN frames-based processing of verses 25–26 strongly supports the contraexpectation use (i.e., 'but') of δὲ in verse 26. The information invoking her Gentile status (v. 26) must have led the audience to consider her prior approach to Jesus for help (v. 25) as an uncommon action; hence, no doubt the conjunction δὲ in verse 26 is used to guide the audience's mental process to the Gentile woman's audacious action, which was initiated despite her Gentile status. Thus, in the subsequent story, the audience must have been astonished to hear that she, against a conventional expectation for the Gentile woman and despite Jesus' stereotypic response to a Gentile woman (v. 27), does not withdraw from her role as a mother, and her request for her daughter to be healed. (vv. 26, 28). Likewise, this semantic flow allows us to translate the conjunction (καί) introducing the following clause (v. 26b) as a contraexpectation too; that is, καὶ ἠρώτα... "*nevertheless* she was begging..."[195] Moreover, the word τοῖς κυναρίοις is here used in a pejorative sense by Jesus (note that the evaluative adjective οὐ... καλὸς is used in verse 27, denoting that throwing children's food to a dog is a deviation from the stereotype of feeding children) and she accepts the way Jesus uses the word. The use of the word "dog" in a metaphorical reference for Gentiles or intentionally to insult other people, in fact, was a cultural expectation in the Old and New Testament world and ancient Jewish society (*1 Enoch* 89.42, 46, 47, 49; 1 Samuel 17.43; Isaiah 56.10–11; Matthew 7.6; Philippians 3.2; 2 Peter 2.22; Revelation 22.15). If so, it also was not unexpected in terms of the open GENTILE WOMAN frame that the Greek woman is referred to as a dog.[196]

Second, with respect to the thing frame, it is important to note that the default values of the frame, as already observed, involve not only the typical spatial layout of the place or object but also its inventory of information. People anticipate a certain place to be arranged in certain

---

[194] On the adversative use of δὲ in this clause, see John Donahue and Daniel Harrington, *The Gospel of Mark* (Collegeville, Minnesota: Liturgical Press, 2002), p. 233.

[195] See BDAG, καὶ 1. η on the meanings of καί, such as "and yet," "and in spite of that," "nevertheless."

[196] On such a stereotypic use of the dog in the first-century Jewish world, see Gerd Theissen, *The Gospels in Context Social and Political History in the Synoptic Tradition* (trans. Linda M. Maloney; Edinburgh: T. and T. Clark, 1992), p. 62 note 1.

ways; hence, they can expect how characters in a story will act in that place. Likewise, the information about the typical inventory of an object and place prepares the audience for what specific items are likely to be referred to in a situation associated with the things. In the example above (Mark 7.24–30), Mark says that Jesus entered a house at the beginning of the episode; so, the HOUSE frame (bolded) is activated from the outset and used as a setting of the story: Καὶ εἰσελθὼν εἰς **οἰκίαν** (v. 24b). As a result, the entities of the household, such as τοῖς κυναρίοις ("the little dogs" or "the pups"), τῆς τραπέζης ("the table"), τῶν παιδίων ("children") mentioned in verses 27–28 are expected to occur. (Note that all three nouns have the Greek article, though the words are new information in this episode.)[197] Further, since the uses of a place and object are culture specific, the audience is able to use the stereotypic knowledge of such things to predict how they are used for a particular purpose in a given situation. Then, Mark 7.24c shows that the reason Jesus went into a house was to remain hidden from the public: οὐδένα ἤθελεν γνῶναι. Verse 24c, which explains the reason for Jesus entering the house, is predictable and makes sense, given that verse 24b opens the HOUSE frame, including the information of the role of the house as a private space.

Finally, as a predetermined data structure, the event frame involves agents, locations and actions as its typical components.[198] The event frame is anticipated to proceed in accordance with stereotyped norms: what sort of participants emerges in that event (agents); what one does and how one does it (actions) and where or in what specific situation it happens (locations). See below an example of the PREACHING/TEACHING frame in the Gospel of Mark. This figure shows that in the Gospel of Mark there are firmly expected contents (agents, actions, and locations) and regular action sequences (entering, gathering, and preaching/teaching) of the PREACHING frame. Although the second action of gathering in that sequence is omitted frequently, the missing data can be drawn by inference on the part of the audience because preaching/teaching is presupposed to take place before a group of

---

[197] It may be said that the words, "the dogs," "the table," "the children," themselves evoke the HOUSE frame, apart from "a house" referred to as a setting of the story. But it must be kept in mind that the audience is already prepared for the HOUSE frame by verse 24, in which Jesus went into a house.

[198] In this respect, the event frame operates in close relation to the person and thing frame.

people. (I will deal with this inferential process below.) To be sure, there are many lexical variations for each action and different locations and agents (e.g., different preachers and locations for preaching/ teaching to take place) in the contents of the frame, and the variations are quite natural in a narrative that consists of a hybrid of divergent events. Nonetheless, what is important is that the prototypical slots (agent, action, and location) in the frame play an underlying role in expecting and understanding details associated with the PREACHING/ TEACHING frame.

2.2.2. *Goal-Directed Sequence and Expectation*

When processing a frame-relevant story, people impose the organizational principles of the frame on incoming information in an attempt to understand it. What is directly associated with the predictability of the frame, as noted above, is its goal-directed structure that consists of three states, usually in temporal sequences: Source (the beginning stage), path (an intermediate state of connecting the source and the goal) and goal (the final state). Consider, for instance, the following two sentences used by Schank: "John wanted to go to Hawaii. He called his travel agent." In this example the second sentence is not only understandable because of the TRIP frame, which includes the information, "travel agents can make reservations for trips,"[199] but also is predictable because of the TRIP frame's goal-directed event sequences, which consist of planning to go to some destination (a source), making preparation for achieving the goal for the trip (path), and arriving at the destination (goal). In the PREACHING frame example, the events move in a temporal ordering from entering/going out (i.e., a beginning point), and gathering (an intermediate point), to preaching (a destination). Thus, when hearing and recalling the event of a starting point, it prepares the audience to process subsequent events in terms of goal-oriented relations, enabling the expectation of the intermediate and end points.

Further, the goal structure seems to specify the roles of agents in an event frame or a person frame.[200] The occurrence of default agents and their current behaviours are understood in relation to their given

---

[199] Schank, "Predictive Understanding," pp. 92–94.
[200] Schank and Abelson, *Scripts*, pp. 61–65. They say that the agent of the "personal script" is usually goal-oriented. See also Lakoff and Johnson, *Metaphors*, pp. 70–72; Lakoff, *Women*, p. 275.

Verse	Agent	Actions		Preaching/Teaching	Location
		Entering	Gathering		
1.4-5	John the Baptist	ἐγένετο		κηρύσσων	The Wilderness/ The Jordan River
1.14-15	Jesus	ἦλθεν		κηρύσσων/λέγων	Galilee
1.21	Jesus	εἰσελθὼν		ἐδίδασκεν	The Synagogue
1.38-39	Jesus	ἄγωμεν		ἐκήρυξο	All Galilee/Synagogue
1.45	The Healed Leper	ἐξελθὼν		ἤρξατο κηρύσσειν	City
2.2	Jesus	εἰσελθὼν	συνήχθησαν πολλοι	ἐλάλει αὐτοῖς τὸν λόγον	beside the sea
2.13	Jesus	ἐξῆλθεν	ὁ ὄχλος ἤρχετο	ἐδίδασκεν	Beside the sea
3.14	The Disciples	ἀποστέλλη αὐτοὺς		κηρύσσειν	[All Galilee]
4.1	Jesus		συνάγεται....	ἤρξατο διδάσκειν	Beside the sea
5.20	The Healed Gerasene Man	ἀπῆλθεν		ἤρξατο κηρύσσειν	Decapolis
6.2	Jesus	ἔρχεται		ἤρξατο διδάσκειν	The Synagogue
6.6	Jesus	περιῆγεν		διδάσκων	Village
6.12	The Disciples	ἐξελθόντες		ἐκήρυξαν	[All Galilee]
6.33-34	Jesus	ἐξελθὼν	πολλοι... προῆλθον	ἤρξατο διδάσκειν	The wilderness
7.36	General people			ἐκήρυσσον	[All Galilee]
10.1	Jesus	ἔρχεται	συμπορεύονται... ὄχλοι ἐδίδασκεν		Judea
11.15	Jesus	ἔρχονται			The Temple
12.35	Jesus			ἔλεγεν διδάσκων	The Temple
13.10	All Believers			κηρυχθῆναι	All the Nations
14.9	All Believers			κηρυχθῇ	The Whole World

purposes or roles. So what the agents do next with a specific purpose may be anticipated without a great deal of effort (e.g., a customer entering a restaurant predicts his or her ordering and eating). In the example of the stories of the two feedings involving the EUCHARISTIC MEAL frame, Jesus is set up as a host, and hence, his command "to recline" (Mark 6.39; 8.6; cf. 14.18)[201] sets up an expectation of the subsequent series of actions Jesus takes: "Take," "bless" or "give thanks," "break" and "give" (Mark 6.41; 8.6; 14.22). These successive actions are all connected and predictable by virtue of the host's goal of providing a meal for his guests, and the last action ("give") and the expression of 6.42 and 8.8, "they all ate and were filled," confirm this prediction. In this way, reference to the agent's purpose in the frame makes all subsequent actions predictable and understandable on the part of the audience.

In summary, on the one hand, the predictive ability of the frame facilitates the expectation of how events develop and persons act, envisioning a state toward which they will likely move. Consequently, the audience's memory load of story processing may be alleviated by virtue of the frame that makes him or her prepared mentally for understanding subsequent data. The predictive function of the frame, on the other hand, helps arouse suspense in the audience while hearing a story around whether or not expected events will, in fact, take place. To be sure, most real stories contain deviations from expected events and characters' failures to attain goals. And the tension is heightened when the events that occur in a given situation seem not to be coherent with our existing world knowledge. In other words, without having a typical knowledge that allows us to assume certain behaviour sequences and things as normal in a particular situation, it would be unlikely that people would find such an interruption interesting or cause for suspense (see below). About this Lakoff says, thus, "stereotypes are used in certain situations to…make judgements…Thus, for example, if all one knew about someone was that he was a bachelor, one might be surprised to find that he loves housework and does it

---

[201] The terms ἀνακλῖναι ("to recline") in the Greco-Roman world denoted the usual posture for a formal banquet and a festival meal in Jewish society. See Joachim Jeremias, *Eucharistic Words of Jesus* (Philadelphia: Fortress, 1966), pp. 48–49. In Mark such words, κατακεῖσθαι (2.14), ἀνακλῖναι (6.39), ἀνέπεσαν (6.40), and ἀνακειμένων (14.18) are also used in an eating situation, except for the reference to the sick lying down in bed κατέκειτο (1.30).

well, likes to care for children, etc."[202] If so, it is hardly deniable that the frame contributes to arousing suspense in the audience even in real story processing.

2.3. Frames Enable Making Inferences

A text is a medium by which the speaker communicates with the audience. But the text is implicit in that it does not carry all information about the situations or things in question to the audience, though necessary for the coherent processing of text.[203] This is the reason why inference is so essential to constructing a coherent interpretation of a given text.[204] The importance of inferential processing is all the more true of oral-aural narrative. Angela Hildyard and David Olson, in their experiments, show that while the reader of written discourse relies on the sentence per se and all the specified details, that is, "what was said" in the text whether relevant or irrelevant, the listener to a great extent makes use of their inferential processing to understand "what was meant," attending to "statements which are central to the theme of the message."[205]

Frames come into play in such an inferential processing of a text. As John Black and Gordon Bower point out:

> A text such as a narrative or a set of instructions is a selective rendering of a continuum of myriad events having differing levels of description. The writer mentions only a few high-points, where critical state-changes occur or where goals are achieved. He leaves out what he considers to be predictable...and he writes assuming that his audience will have the necessary knowledge so that they can imagine and fill in the full scenario from the major points and abbreviated description he gives of it.[206]

---

[202] Lakoff, *Women*, p. 86.

[203] Of course, it is not necessary or in fact possible for the text to describe every detail of things and courses of actions. As van Dijk, *Text*, p. 109, points out, "The level of description depends on the topic of conversation and, in a wider sense, on the purposes of the communicative act."

[204] Brown and Yule, *Discourse Analysis*, pp. 266–65, say, "the more interpretive 'work' the reader (hearer) has to undertake in arriving at a reasonable interpretation of what the writer (speaker) intended to convey, the more likely it is that there are inferences being made."

[205] Their experiments were made with school children, but they say their findings are also true of adults. See Angela Hildyard and David R. Olson, "On the Comprehension and Memory of Oral vs. Written Discourse, in *Spoken and Written Language: Exploring Orality and Literacy*" (ed. Deborah Tannen: Norwood, New Jersey: Ablex, 1982), pp. 19–22.

[206] John Black and Gordon Bower, "Story Understanding as Problem-Solving," *Poetics* 9 (1980), p. 225.

It must be noted that "the necessary knowledge" left unspoken is the very frame itself. With respect to narrative processing, making inferences is one of the key functions of frame. The frame enables the audience to understand clearly what is stated implicitly, fill in the omitted elements between and within sentences, and guess the meaning behind the participants' actions. If so, an important question arises: What sort of information can the frames make inferences from? In other words, what sort of knowledge is left out so that the frames may fill in the missing data?

2.3.1. *Cultural Knowledge and Inference*
Common cultural knowledge shared between the speaker and audience is often taken for granted and is thus left out.[207] Such cultural information often involves participants' motivation of actions, the significance of events and the features of persons and objects. Since frames are culture specific, they can draw an inference of cultural knowledge implicitly stated in the text. For instance, Mark 15.1–2 says (a relevant person frame is bolded):

> ...πρωὶ συμβούλιον ποιήσαντες οἱ ἀρχιερεῖς μετὰ τῶν πρεσβυτέρων καιγραμματέων καὶ ὅλον τὸ συνέδριον,
> δήσαντες τὸν Ἰησοῦν ἀπήνεγκαν καὶ παρέδωκαν **Πιλάτῳ**.
> Καὶ ἐπηρώτησεν αὐτὸν ὁ **Πιλᾶτος**·...

The meanings of the priests' act of handing Jesus over to Pilate and his inquiry of Jesus remains obscure until the audience is aware of who and what Pilate is. In this and in subsequent passages the word "Pilate" not only opens a name of an individual but also a Roman governor to Judea who has an authority to put someone to trial and sentence him to death. However, the text does not provide any information about Pilate, though this is the first reference to him in the whole discourse. This demonstrates that the text takes it for granted that the hearer can easily infer the person frame by referring to their PILATE frame, believing that such information of Pilate as a Roman governor is a type of knowledge already known to the audience's long-term memory.

The cultural feature of frame knowledge and its inferential ability can then explain the reason why certain passages are easy for some people to understand, whereas they find it so difficult. Understanding a text necessarily includes inferential processing and it operates natu-

---

[207] Sperber and Wilson, *Relevance*, p. 38; Callow, *Man*, pp. 130–31.

rally for those who have the same cultural heritage or world knowledge as the text. For those with a different cultural background, however, extra details are necessary. In Mark 14.30, for instance, Jesus predicts the time that Peter will deny him using three temporal expressions (in italic type): σὺ σήμερον ("*today*") ταύτῃ τῇ νυκτὶ ("*this night*") πρὶν ἢ δὶς ἀλέκτορα φωνῆσαι ("*before the cock crows twice*") τρίς με ἀπαρνήσῃ ("You will deny me three times"). These temporal words, which Mark seems to indicate are times over a period of a single day, appear odd to modern Westerners for two reasons. The first is that modern Westeners do not use the crowing of the cock as a time signal. The other is that while we have the DAY frame containing reference to a period of time from 12:00 a.m to 12:00 p.m, Jesus in Mark's Gospel uses σήμερον to refer to a time period from the evening (14.17) to the following dawn. The conceptual coherence between the three temporal expressions, however, must have been drawn inferences readily in terms of Mark's ancient audience's DAY frame. This is because the frame contained not only the concept that a day begins at sundown and ends at sunset, but also knowledge of the regular nocturnal time-keeping of cocks.[208]

2.3.2. *Default Values and Inference*
As a pre-existent knowledge structure, a frame comprises default infor-mation. So, in a frame-based story, what is left unspoken is the data which the audience can fill in with best guesses in terms of the default values. Schank and Abelson propose that once a frame is instantiated, "we expect it to be ended in normal fashion," believing that "if some-thing non-standard had occurred it probably would have been men-tioned explicitly."[209] Consider Schank and Abelson's example of the RESTAURANT frame:

John went to a restaurant.
He asked the waitress for coq au vin.
He paid the check and left.[210]

Even if this example does not state explicitly the actions that the wait-ress delivered the food he ordered and John ate it, the activation of

---

[208] For the concept of the Jewish day, see Taylor, *Mark*, p. 550; Cranfield, *Mark*, p. 429. And on the ancient Jews' use of the crowing of the cock as a timekeeping sign, see H. Kosmala, "The Time of the Cock-Crow," *ASTI* 2 (1963), pp. 46–52.
[209] Schank and Abelson, *Scripts*, pp. 51, 60.
[210] Schank and Abelson, *Scripts*, p. 38.

the final sentence allows us to infer that the preconditions of paying for the meal are met.

In addition to making inferences regarding missing data, the default values of the frame are also helpful in discovering the relevant meanings of ambiguous words and establishing the referents of terms, as in the case of deciding that coq au vin is a food the restaurant can supply. Consider Mark 1.29–31, which is structured according to the default or typical event patterns characteristic of the HEALING frame (see below on the HEALING frame in Mark 1–3): The healer's moving into a place (1.29), introducing the sick (1.30a), preparing healing (1.30b), healing action (1.31a), confirming healing (1.31b and c). (For the first four healing stories and their default event patterns in Mark's Gospel, see below.)

Table 3: The HEALING Frame in Mark 1–3

Prototypical Event Sequences	Verses			
	1.29–31	1.40–45	2.1–12	3.1–6
The Healer's Moving into a Place	ἦλθον εἰς τὴν οἰκίαν (1.29)	(Galilee) (1.29)	εἰσελθὼν... Καφαρναοὺμ ἐν οἴκῳ ἐστίν (2.1)	εἰσῆλθεν... εἰς τὴν συναγωγήν (3.1a)
Introducing the Sick	ἡ δὲ πενθερὰ Σίμωνος κατέκειτο πυρέσσουσα (1.30a)	ἔρχεται πρὸς αὐτὸν λεπρὸς (1.40)	ἔρχονται φέροντες πρὸς αὐτὸν παραλυτικὸν (2.3)	ἦν ἐκεῖ ἄνθρωπος ἐξηραμμένην (3.1b)
Preparing Healing	λέγουσιν αὐτῷ περὶ αὐτῆς (1.30b)	λέγων αὐτῷ ...καθαρίσαι (1.40)	ἀπεστέγασαν τὴν στέγην ... χαλῶσι τὸν κράβαττον (2.4)	λέγει... ἔγειρε εἰς τὸ μέσον (3.3)
Healing Actions	ἤγειρεν αὐτὴν κρατήσας τῆς χειρός (1.31a)	λέγει...θέλω, καθαρίσθητι (1.41)	λέγει... ἀφίενται σου αἱ ἁμαρτίαι; (2.5, 11)	λέγει... ἔκτεινον τὴν χεῖρα (3.5a)
Confirming Healing	ἀφῆκεν αὐτὴν ὁ πυρετος καὶ διηκόνει αὐτοῖς. (1.31a,b)	ἀπῆλθεν ἀπ᾽ αὐτοῦ ἡ λέπρα καὶ ἐκαθαρίσθη (1.42)	ἠγέρθη... ἐξῆλθεν ἔμπροσθεν πάντων (2.12)	ἐξέτεινεν καὶ ἀπεκατεστάθη ἡ χεὶρ αὐτοῦ (3.5)

Peter's mother-in law fills the slot for the sick and Jesus that of the healer. Accordingly, the original audience would infer "lying down (κατέκειτο)" as lying in bed due to her health problem, rather than at the table for eating,[211] and the disciples' reporting of her (περὶ αὐτῆς) as 'her being ill' would then represent a request for healing, though the sentence does not explicitly state the specific content of the report. Raising the sick person by hand (ἤγειρεν αὐτὴν κρατήσας τῆς χειρός), to be sure, does not open the HEALING frame for modern western readers/audiences, who usually think of a treatment of medicine as a means of curing. Yet Mark's original audience would hardly fail to derive the physical (usually manual) touching as a component of the HEALING frame, namely, an attempt to heal.[212] And the sick person's immediate action of serving them, probably on the table (διηκόνει αὐτοῖς) was also understood by Mark's audience as a confirmation of the HEALING frame. This is because for the ancients healing did not denote just a curing of physical abnormalities from the biomedical perspective but also a restoration of social state or activity from the socio-cultural standpoint (e.g., Mark 1.44; 2.11–12; 5.30–34; 4.43; 10.52).[213] The ancient HEALING frame, thus, enables the audience to interpret that Jesus' healing includes not only the physical curing but also the restoration of Simon's mother-in-law to her conventional social role, that is, serving at the table.

---

[211] Note that in Mark's Gospel the verbs κατάκειμαι (2.4, 15; 14.3) and συνανάκειμαι (2.15; 6.22) for a corresponding actions are used to denote a posture at the table or eating, as mentioned above.

[212] For the examples to show that the manual touching between Jesus and the sick person is used as a process of healing, see Mark 3.10; 5.23, 28; 6.56; 7.32; 8.22. And for the examples of Mark's HEALING frame, in which the verb ἔγειρω is used, see Mark 2.9, 11; 5.41; 9.27.

[213] Pilch, *Healing*, pp. 12–16, 59. Pilch rightly notes that whereas modern Westerners tend to view physical disease from a "biomedical perspective that sees abnormalities in the structure and/or function of organ systems," the ancients in the first-century Mediterranean culture thought of it as illness from a "sociocultural perspective" that "is concerned with personal perception and experience of certain socially disvalued states that include, but are not limited to, disease" (see p. 59). Likewise, as will be discussed, Jesus' proclamation of forgiving the paralytic's sins (2.1–12) must be understood as demonstrating the wholeness of Jesus' healing, which includes the sinner's spiritual restoration to God.

2.3.3. *A Causal Chain and Inference*

Events in stories are often causally interconnected with each other in temporal sequences, just as our everyday routines are.[214] As Callow says:

> Thus we experience and talk about our referential world in terms of these two related parameters, time and causality. All events can be ranked on a chronological scale in terms of their time relation to other events—all events are caused by preceding events, and in turn cause other events that follow them. Obviously, these two parameters are related since effects are always later on the time scale than their causes.[215]

Accordingly, in some sense, to understand a story is to make the connection between sentences which include such events. Yet, as pointed out, the text at times does not spell out every detail of the causal connection between the events or the sentences. Specific frames are needed in order to generate such a connection by inferential process.[216] As Schank and Abelson put it:

> The restaurant script is a giant causal chain. Although the details have been left out, each action in the above script results in conditions that enable the next to occur. To perform the next act in the sequence, the previous acts must be completed satisfactorily.[217]

For example, consider the sentences:

> Mary entered a restaurant.
> She ordered a lobster.
> And she left a large tip.[218]

The RESTAURANT frame allows us to infer a possible reason for the action in the third sentence: She was happy with the way a waiter served her. *As a result*, she was willing to leave an unexpectedly generous tip. Without the RESTAURANT frame or shared cultural conventions associated with a tip, it is hardly possible to understand and

---

[214] Lakoff, *Women*, pp. 54–55.

[215] Callow, *Man*, p. 253.

[216] A similar point is made by George Lakoff, "Deduction," pp. 63–70, who says that the inferential process in and between many sentences may be made possible by certain presuppositions. Note his example, "(3) John called Mary a virgin and then she insulted him. The pronouns...can be stressed in (3) only if it is presupposed that to call someone a virgin is to insult that person" (p. 63).

[217] Schank and Abelson, *Scripts*, p. 45.

[218] Schank and Abelson, *Scripts*, p. 45.

make such a causal connection between the third sentence and the other sentences. Consider another example provided by Schank and Abelson:

> (3) John cried because Mary said she loved Bill.
> Sentence (3) is a meaningful, well constructed English sentence. Yet, it is literally quite silly. Certainly John didn't cry because of the event of Mary speaking. What 'speaking' does cause is 'thinking', which can cause 'sadness' which can be a reason for 'crying'. Since people don't really misunderstand sentences such as (3), there is little reason for speakers to worry about their imprecision.[219]

Even if Schank and Abelson do not refer to this example in relation to the frame, the FALLING IN LOVE frame is possible background knowledge to explain what caused John to be sad. The FALLING IN LOVE frame generates the inferences that Mary was initially John's girl-friend, but Mary did not love John anymore because she now loved Bill.[220]

Consider an example from Mark 10.23–26 (the relevant frame is bolded):

> v. 23: ὁ ᾽Ιησοῦς λέγει τοῖς μαθηταῖς αὐτοῦ· πῶς δυσκόλως **οἱ τὰ χρήμα-τα ἔχοντες** εἰς τὴν τοῦ θεοῦ εἰσελεύσονται
> v. 24: οἱ δὲ μαθηταὶ ἐθαμβοῦντο ἐπὶ τοῖς λόγοις αὐτου...
> v. 25: εὐκοπώτερον ἐστιν κάμηλον διὰ [τῆς] τρυμαλιᾶς [τῆς] ῥαφίδος διελθεῖν ἢ **πλούσιον** εἰς τὴν βασιλείαν τοῦ θεοῦ εἰσελθεῖν
> v. 26: τίς δύναται σωθῆναι;

In this passage, it is not difficult to find that the disciples' astonish-ment (vv. 23, 26) was caused by Jesus' critical remarks of the rich with respect to entering the Kingdom of God (vv. 23, 24b–25). To be sure, though Jesus' view of wealth causes the disciples' sense of perplexity, there is no textual indication to explain the causal relation-ship between Jesus' view of the rich man and the disciples' bewilder-ment. Yet the WEALTH frame opened by the person frame title (οἱ τὰ χρήματα ἔχοντες v. 23 and πλούσιον v. 25), by providing its stereo-typic knowledge, enables the audience to infer the causal relationship implicitly left between verses 23 and 24, and 25 and 26. This means

---

[219] Schank and Abelson, *Scripts*, p. 23.
[220] Schank and Abelson, *Scripts*, pp. 24–30, suggest five types of "causal syntax": (1) "Actions can result in state changes"; (2) "States can enable actions"; (3) "States can disable actions"; (4) "States (or acts) can initiate mental states"; (5) "Mental states can be reasons for actions."

that for ancient Jews the RICH MAN frame contained the prototypical information that "wealth was a sign of divine blessing while disease and poverty were signs of judgment" (e.g., Deuteronomy 30).[221] No doubt Jesus' warning against the wealthy clashed with his Jewish hearers' (and the disciples') stereotype of wealth, thus resulting in such amazement. There are in these passages two contraexpectation markers, ἐθαμβοῦντο ("they were amazed") and ἐξεπλήσσοντο ("they were exceedingly astonished") which signal that the disciples' conventional knowledge of the wealthy was violated by Jesus' views. Also, the disciples' question ("Then who can be saved?") in verse 25 proves the violation of such a typical expectation of the wealthy; that is, 'if it is difficult for the rich to enter the kingdom of God, no one may be saved!'[222] The text left out such detailed information because it assumed his audience was able to infer in terms of the RICH MAN frame such causality between Jesus' pronouncements and the disciples' astonishment and questioning.[223]

2.4. *Frame Deviation Enhances Interest in and Remembering of Information*

People often think of certain events or happenings taking place around them as unusual or ridiculous (e.g., for Canadians it would be quite surprising to see the blossoms of plants and trees in February or even March!). This way of thinking is made possible, as pointed out above, because they know what is generally taken for granted in a certain situation. Such a judgment is then a reflection of the fact that their normal expectation (or frame) is violated.[224] Frames determine what information is expected and unexpected. I have already discussed the fact that in real stories a storyteller does not make accounts of routine activities which only follow the predictable course. Such a story would be uninteresting to us. To be an interesting story, it must contain unexpected happenings or disrupted sequences of routine actions, that is, violations of the frames.[225] Heightened interest may be aroused

---

[221] Evans, *Mark 8.27–16.20*, p. 101. See also Cranfield, *Mark*, p. 331.
[222] France, *Mark*, p. 405.
[223] Thus, Callow, *Man*, p. 131, says that shared verbal conventions are "clearly essential to successful communication."
[224] Howard, "Schemas," p. 39.
[225] Roger Schank, "Interestingness: Controlling Inferences," *AI* 12 (1979), pp. 273–97, points out three informational requirements to arouse interestedness in the hearer/reader in discourse processing: Interest may be generated when frame-related

when hearing/reading about a character who cannot achieve his or her purposes simply by following the frames. Of course, if a story contains too much unexpected information, its processing takes longer, and this can make it impossible for the audience/reader to follow the course.[226] My argument, however, is that if a story has unexpected events within the bounds of a frame, these events or an episode including them lead the audience to give them a significant status and prominence in a discourse, and thus a special mnemonic effect.[227] Reid Hastie, a scholar in the field of social cognition, claims:

> [T]he expectedness of an [schema-related] event may determine the amount of mental resource that will be allocated to comprehend an event. The more resources, the more links (of any type) will be formed from schema to event. Important unexpected events are hypothesized to receive the greatest amounts of comprehension resources and would be relatively well-remembered.[228]

Schank and Abelson suggest several types of deviations from scripts (frames in our term), such as "obstacles," "errors," and "distractions" and when the deviations occur, what sort of corrections may be made possible.[229] There is a helpful summary of them which is provided by Bower, Black and Turner, cognitive psychologists:

---

expectations are violated; frame-related information is missing; and salient themes (e.g., death, violence, sex etc.) are referred to.

[226] On various cognitive and textual properties, including the reader/hearer's knowledge structure, which contribute to eliciting interest in a story, see Sanford and Garrod, *Understanding*, pp. 171–72, 74–75; Suzanne Hidi and William Baird, "Interestingness—A Neglected Variable in Discourse Processing," *CS* 10 (1986), pp. 179–94.

[227] A similar argument is made by Richard Bauckham, *Eyewitnesses*, pp. 331, 336, who, in an attempt to propose frame as a memory type that makes it possible for the eyewitnesses to remember best various events in the Gospels, states that if certain events are unexpected, unusual and unique, they increase mnemonic effect. On the mnemonic effect of deviations from frames, see also Bower, Black, and Turner, "Scripts," pp. 209–10; Sanford and Garrod, *Understanding*, pp. 81–82; and regarding the special prominence of unexpected material in a general discourse, see Callow, *Man*, pp. 180–84, esp. 180, 184. This point is supported by an experiment from cognitive psychology. Gilles Einstein, Scott Lackey and Mark A. McDaniel, "Bizarre Imagery, Interference, and Distinctiveness," *JEP* 15 (1989), pp. 137–46, show in their experiments that mnemonic power of bizarre images greatly increases in the context in which normal or usual images occur in common, but its mnemonic effect does not happen in the context in which the other bizarre images are common. This suggests that certain frame-unrelated data in the context in which a larger frame dominate will be especially focused on and remembered by the audience.

[228] Hastie, "Memory," p. 78.

[229] Schank and Abelson, *Scripts*, pp. 51–57.

In obstacles, some enabling condition for an imminent action is missing (e.g., You can't read the French menu), so some corrective action is taken (e.g., ask the waiter to translate for you). In errors, a script action leads to an unexpected or inappropriate outcome. For example, you order a hamburger, but the waitress brings a hot dog. The standard corrective action is to repeat the action: order the hamburger again. Distractions are unexpected events or states which set up new goals for the actor, taking him temporarily or permanently outside the script. For example, the waiter may spill soup on the customer, initiating a visit to the restroom for cleaning up.[230]

Frame deviations are particularly illuminating in understanding Mark's five conflict stories in Mark 2.1–3.6, not the least because the stories are all focused on how Jesus and his disciples' actions deviated from his contemporary Jewish legal experts' existing knowledge structure or expectations. When it comes to Mark's original audience, processing of such conflict stories, on the one hand, would give rise to suspense, surprise and interest in them; on the other hand, it would serve to confirm their existing (Christian) frames.

2.5. The Textual Expressions of Frames Bear a Particular Perspective

"All language represents conceptual content from some point of view."[231] Callow says:

> It is quite impossible for us to attend to all our mental content simultaneously; our minds have a single stream of consciousness, and we select a very limited amount of material to form the content of our thinking at any given time. The rest of our stored mental network remains quiescent, held in reserve.[232]

This is also true of frame-based language production and processing. A frame-based text is normally described from the perspective of particular participants or things from within a frame.[233] As Taylor notes,

---

[230] Bower, Black, and Turner, "Memory," p. 210.
[231] Epstein, "Frames," p. 66. Likewise, the importance of a speaker's perspective in linguistic expression has also been pointed out by the verbal aspect theory of Greek. Several scholars have shown how a speaker or writer's perspective on an action is grammaticalized in the Greek New Testament by "the selection of a particular tense-form in the verbal system." See Porter, *Idioms*, pp. 20–21; *idem, Verbal Aspect*, ch. 2; and Fanning, *Verbal Aspect*, chs. 1 and 2.
[232] Callow, *Man*, p. 30.
[233] Charles Fillmore, "The Need for a Frame Semantics Within Linguistics," *Statistical Methods in Linguistics* 76 (1976), pp. 13–19; and Schank and Abelson,

It frequently happens that different uses of a word whose semantic structure is rather complex tend to highlight different components of frame-based knowledge. Thus, if I say that my birthday falls this year on a Monday, I am using the word *Monday* to refer simply to a position in the sevenday week. Suppose, on the other hand, that I compain of a Monday morning feeling. What is at issue here is not primarily the position of Monday in the week, but rather the fact that Monday follows the weekend. What is perspectivized is only one component of the Monday frame, ie. the reluctance with which one returns to work after the leisure of the weekend.[234]

Understanding the text as "schematized" by a certain frame involves evoking and processing appropriately its "foregrounded" prototypical items and their roles.[235] Of course, foregrounding a particular element in the frame does not necessarily mean making other elements unimportant; rather the rest is held in view even while the particular perspective on certain elements comes to the fore.[236] In other words, an understanding of foregrounded events or things accompanies an understanding of other backgrounded elements or the frame itself.[237] Such an operation of foreground and background not only involves the major elements or participants of the frame but also their sub-elements or sub-participants. Fillmore provides an example:

HE SOLD HER THE PARROT FOR $300.
SHE BOUGHT THE PARROT FOR $300.
SHE SPENT $300 ON THE PARROT.
SHE PAID HIM $300 FOR THE PARROT.
THE PARROT COST HER $300.
HE CHARGED HER $300 FOR THE PARROT.
All of the associated scenes are built up from the same cognitive schema [frame], the commercial transaction; but they differ in that they foreground and background different segments [the BUYER, the SELLER, the MONEY, and the GOODS] of that schema.[238]

The example above shows how a framed text is intended to induce the audience to comprehend it from the perspective of particular participants in the frame.

Scripts, p. 42. Schank and Abelson say, "A script must be written from one particular role's point of view." And see also van Dijk, "Semantic Macro-Structure," pp. 24–25.

[234] Taylor, *Linguistic Categorization*, p. 90.
[235] Croft and Cruse, *Cognitive Linguistics*, pp. 40–73.
[236] Fillmore, "Scenes-and-Frames," pp. 59–60.
[237] Callow, *Man*, pp. 31–33.
[238] Fillmore, "Linguistics," p. 20.

As an example from Mark's Gospel, 1.29–31 in which the HEALING frame is opened will be dealt with again, particularly to show how the frame's prototypical participants (the healer, the sick person, disease and healing actions) are foregrounded and backgrounded as the story proceeds. In verse 29 (ἐξελθόντες ἦλθον εἰς τὴν οἰκίαν Σίμωνος) the healer's movement is foregrounded. Verse. 30 contains two clauses: ἡ δὲ πενθερὰ Σίμωνος κατέκειτο πυρέσσουσα, καὶ εὐθὺς λέγουσιν αὐτῷ περὶ αὐτῆς; so, the audience is led to focus on the sick person and then move to the helper of the sick person when the subject shifts from Peter's mother-in-law lying down, to the indefinite agents (probably the disciples) reporting to Jesus about her. By backgrounding the sick and the helpers, the perspective is turned to the actions of the healer, Jesus, when verse 31 describes Jesus as the agent of actions invoked by two aorist participles (προσελθὼν, "coming forward" and κρατήσας, "grabbing") and one main verb (ἤγειρεν, "he raised"). And then the focus shifts to the disease responding to the healer's actions (ἀφῆκεν αὐτὴν ὁ πυρετός), and finally the sick and her actions are foregrounded again in verse 31: διηκόνει αὐτοῖς. Further, when verse 31 states that Jesus takes her "by the hand" (κρατήσας τῆς χειρός), the "hand," which is a subframe or a prototypical component of the PERSON frame, is foregrounded at the moment of the healing, backgrounding Jesus and the other parts of the sick person's body.

C. CONCLUSION

Frames have their own organizational principles to structure concepts within them. Thus, incoming information can be understandable or meaningful because it is structured in terms of frames' structuring principles. When it comes to story processing, six major types of frames are useful: Event, person, object, thing or place, and stories, which have their own prototypical components and structures. Since frames contain not only a variety of structuring principles but also a set of interrelated and mutually predictable concepts, they are capable of organizing and helping comprehend incoming information or stories. First of all, the organizational functions of frames are as follows:

- Frames can be opened by their core elements and titles.
- They bind the input or stories into semantically coherent units in terms of their prototypical concepts interrelated by human experience.

- Frames determine the structure of the story by providing their typical events sequences.
- Frames organize a story hierarchically and causally.
- A global frame plays a role of assigning other frames present in the story into its subframes.
- Frames are capable of interconnecting metaphorical expressions in the story into other story information.
- Frames determine in various ways grammatical choices of New Testament Greek, so that the audience's textual processing and understanding may greatly increase in terms of the frames evoked by the grammatical categories.

Besides organizing information, frames help the hearer/reader understand the story by providing basic elements for narrative processing, such as places, objects, persons, and events, by making expectation possible, and by making inferences. It is also because of frames, which consist of typical information and event sequences, that many unexpected events in real stories give rise to suspense and interest in the audience. Finally, when frame-based knowledge is expressed in a clause or sentence, it tends to perspectivize one component of the frame.

PART TWO

THE APPLICATION OF FRAME THEORY TO MARK'S
ORAL-AURAL NARRATIVE

CHAPTER FIVE

FRAMES AND THE ORGANIZATION OF THE
CONTROVERSY STORIES (MARK 2.1–3.6)

I have thus far explored the characteristics of Mark's oral-aural narrative, the properties of frames, and frame theory's relevance for the narrative. On the basis of such observations, in this chapter and the chapter to follow I will test in what specific ways frame theory may be used as a heuristic tool of leading us to a better understannding of Mark's Controversy Stories (2.1–3.6) as a part of oral-aural narrative.

I acknowledge that there is some repetition between Chapters 5 and 6 since both of the chapters deal with the same passage structured in terms of the global LEGAL CONTROVERSY frame as a whole and the hearer's cognitive processing of that passage, although making different arguments. There is an important reason, nonetheless, why Chapters 5 and 6 should be included as separate chapters. It is a commonplace among scholars who are interested in the Gospels as story that the hearer/reader's understanding of a narrative involves both *what* it says (i.e., the content of a story) and *how* it is told (the structure of a story).[1] Accordingly, a discussion of how frames serve the original hearer to come to an understanding of Mark 2.1–3.6 in cognitive terms should necessarily include issues concerning ways in which the audience comes, through the use of frames, to an understanding of both *what* the narrative is about and *how* it is told. Thus Chapter Five is focused on frames' comprehension processing associated with how the narrative says; Chapter Six will show frames' processing related to what.

The main concern of the present chapter is to demonstrate the frames' function in organizing the three units of narrative discourse in Mark 2.1–3.6 such as a thematic section, paragraph or episode, and clause or sentence on the part of the hearer. First of all, I will show that frames help organize Mark 2.1–3.6 into a larger thematic unit. The next focus will be on the frames' role in marking paragraph or episode

---

[1] See Rhoads, Dewey, and Michie, *Mark*, pp. 1–9.

boundaries, and finally the frames' function of chunking information at the level of clause will be discussed in order to define what the remembered gist of each episode might be.

A. The Frame Organization of Mark 2.1–3.6 into a Larger Thematic Unit

How a text is understood is inseparably related to how the text structures its information.[2] It has been stated in Chapter Three that thematic structure often consisting of clusters of repeated incidents is a vital component of oral narrative composition. The argument of this book is that the global LEGAL CONTROVERSY frame which operates at the macro-level of Mark 2.1–3.6 makes it possible for the five episodes within it to be structured and understood as a thematically cohesive unit. But "[m]emories must be told in forms corresponding to socially available schemata if those who tell their memories are to be successful in communicating with others."[3] It is therefore important to show that the LEGAL CONTROVERSY frame was part of the early Christian audiences' mental frame, and thus they were ready for cognitive processing of that unit. I will first survey the social environment in which their everyday knowledge and experience associated with legal conflict would have been formed. And then I will show how the prototypical components in the global LEGAL CONTROVERSY frame occur coherently in the five episodes. Finally, besides Mark 2.1–3.6, Mark's other legal controversy stories will be examined briefly in order to verify that the LEGAL CONTROVERSY frame is an organizational structure of Mark's story related to legal conflict between Jesus and Jewish religious leaders.

1. Controversy or Conflict and the Early Christians

As already discussed, frames are formed from numerous previous social and cultural experiences within a specific situation. Thorndyke and Yekovich say:

> As we accumulate additional experiences with a concept, our expectations for the expected properties, or slot fillers, of the concept become

---

[2] Brown and Yule, *Discourse Analysis*, p. 94.
[3] Bauckham, *Eyewitnesses*, pp. 46–47.

more clearly defined. For example, consider how our BIRTHDAY PARTY schema develops.

Over the years, repeated attendance at birthday parties leads us to develop and modify our knowledge of party formats and traditions.[4]

This is the case for the early Christian audiences' LEGAL CONTROVERSY frame. The ancients, according to anthropologists, "lived in an agonistic world in which individuals, cities, and peoples were constantly battling."[5] In particular, the agonistic tone is characteristic of oral cultures and narrative: "Many, if not all, oral or residually oral cultures strike literates as extraordinarily agonistic in their verbal performance and indeed in their lifestyle."[6] There may be several causes explaining such a polarized culture of the ancient world (e.g., "common and persistent physical hardships of life" and "[i]gnorance of physical causes of disease and disaster").[7] Above all, a context of struggle is not unrelated to the honour-based culture of the first-century Mediterranean world. As Malina proposes:

> In the first-century Mediterranean world, every social interaction that takes place outside one's family or outside one's circle of friends is perceived as a challenge to honor, a mutual attempt to acquire honor from one's social equal. Thus gift-giving; invitations to dinner; debates over issues of law... all these sorts of interactions take place according to the patterns of honor called challenge-response. Because of these constant and steady cures in Mediterranean culture, anthropologists call it an agonistic culture.[8]

Given such a first-century Mediterranean culture, it is in no way an exaggeration to say that conflict was part of Mark and his audiences' routine experience in their social interaction.

In particular, the situation of the early Christians and their literature was directly subject to such an agonistic culture. The dispute between the early church and Jews or Jewish Christians over the law and *halakah* observance was not an issue confined only to a specific community, but rather a universal phenomenon occurring in the early church which still did not consider its identity as separate and distinct

---

[4] Thorndyke and Yekovich, "Schema Theory," p. 28.

[5] Jerome Neyrey, *Honor and Shame in the Gospel of Matthew* (Louisville, Kentucky: WJK, 1989), p. 44; see also Bruce Malina, *New Testament World: Insights from Cultural Anthropology* (Louisville, Kentucky: WJK, 2000), p. 36.

[6] Ong, *Orality*, pp. 43–45 (the quotation from p. 43).

[7] Ong, *Orality*, pp. 44–45.

[8] Malina, *New Testament*, p. 36.

from Judaism.[9] To be sure, this controversy was initiated by Jesus' conflict with the Jewish religious leaders in his ministry, and turned to more distinctive issues as the early church became influential in Judaism.[10] And such an agonistic culture was deeply reflected in early Christian literature, especially the Pauline writings (e.g., Galatians and Romans) and the Synoptic Gospels,[11] as well as the Gospel of John.[12] With respect to the conflict stories in the Synoptic Gospels, Aland Hultgren argues:

> [I]n the first-century church there was an active tendency on the part of certain traditionists to present material in the form of spirited dialogues between Jesus and his opponents on certain issues. It appears that there was actual ly a primitive church consciousness of presenting materials in what we have designated the conflict story form. One can support this claim not only by the studies above, but also by the fact that con-

---

[9] For an excellent study of this issue, see James D.G. Dunn, *The Partings of the Ways: Between Christianity and Judaism and their Significance for the Character of Christianity* (London: SCM; Philadelphia: Trinity Press International, 1991).

[10] Wright, *Jesus*, pp. 369–442 and also see James D.G. Dunn, *Jesus, Paul and the Law: Studies in Mark and Galatians* (Louisville, Kentucky: WJK, 1990), pp. 10–86.Compare Bultmann, *Synoptic Tradition*, p. 53; E.P. Sanders, *Jesus and Judaism* (Philadelpia: Fortress, 1985), pp. 212–37, who claims that many disputes between Jesus and his Jewish religious leaders in the Synoptic Gospels do not go back to the historical Jesus, but are a retrojection of the post-Easter Christians into the lifetime of Jesus. However, this radical distinction between "historical" Jesus and the early church must be criticized. In particular, it has been wrongly assumed by many biblical scholars that controversy or conflict between Christianity and Judaism erupted at around 80 C.E. when at Jamnia Jewish Christians were barred from attending the synagogue service. Thus, according to W.D. Davies and D.C. Allison, *A Critical and Exegetical Commentary on the Gospel According to Saint Matthew*. Vol. 1 (ICC; Edinburgh: T. and T. Clark, 1988), pp. 133–38, the conflict stories in the four Gospels do not reflect Jesus' day, nor even that of the church up to 70 C.E., but project the situations of controversies of post-Jamnia council back into Jesus' day. And also see W. Horbury, "The Benediction of the Minim and Early Jewish Christian Controversy," *JTS* 33 (1982), pp. 19–61. But this picture of Jamina council and its impact on the parting of Christianity and Judaism has been increasingly regarded as "entirely mythological" by more cautious scholars, such as Wright, *the People of God*, pp. 161–66; *idem, Jesus*, pp. 373–75. And also see Dunn, *Partings of the Ways*, pp. 231–32; John J. Collins, *The Scepter and the Star: The Messiahs of the Dead Sea Scrolls and Other Ancient Literature* (New York: Doubleday, 1995), p. 20.

[11] On the Gospel of Matthew, see Davies and Allison, *Matthew*, pp. 138–47; and on Luke's Gospel, see Joseph A. Fitzmyer, *The Gospel According to Luke I–IX* (AB 28; New York: Doubleday, 1981), pp. 57–59.

[12] See J. Louis Martyn, *History and Theology in the Fourth Gospel*, rev.ed. (Nashville: Abingdon, 1979), Part I.

flict stories were collected together...in the pre-Marcan stage of their transmission.[13]

There is widespread agreement as to the pre-Markan collection of Mark 2.1–3.6. One of the important insights of form criticism is that the reason such a collection of conflict traditions was put together and preserved is because of its value to the earliest Christians who were in conflict with Jews, whether non-Christian Jews or Jewish Christians. This means that in regard to issues associated with the law and *halakah*, the early Christians used the traditions "to explain or defend themselves against criticism from without."[14] Certainly, thus, for the early Christians, including Mark's Christian audiences, the controversy over legal issues was part of social experiences ("collective memory," to use Halbwach's word)[15] from the birth of the early church. Given that frame knowledge forms from repetitious, similar social interactions with the environment, it is not difficult, therefore, to believe that such a context of dispute would lead the early Christians to the formation of the LEGAL CONTROVERSY frame.

2. *The* LEGAL CONTROVERSY *Frame of Mark 2.1–3.6*

Stephen Levinsohn makes the point that "[a] text such as a Gospel or Epistle typically 'coheres' or enjoys an overall 'thematic *continuity*'...even though it has *local discontinuities* such as changes of spatiotemporal setting, changes in the cast of participants and changes of topic."[16] Indeed, this thematic organization corresponds to the compositional feature of oral narrative which clusters similar

---

[13] Arland Hultgren, *Jesus and His Adversaries* (Minneapolis: Augsburg, 1979), p. 50. Dunn, *Paul*, pp. 27–36 (quotation from p. 29), argues that the pre-Markan traditions of Mark 2.1–3.6 influenced Paul's thinking on the law: "the tradition behind Mark 2.15–3.6 provides an invaluable bridge between Jesus and Paul and shows a little of the development in Christian thinking on the law which must have prepared the way for the decisive contribution of Paul."

[14] Whereas H.W. Kuhn, *Ältere Sammlungen im Markusevangelium* (SUNT 8; Göttingen: Vandenhoeck und Ruprecht, 1971), pp. 53–98, says that the life setting of such controversy stories is an internal dispute among early Christianity with the Judaism of Jewish Christianity, Hultgren, *Jesus*, pp. 162–65, considers it as a controversy between Jewish Christians and Judaisms. In both cases our thesis remains valid: the debate over legal issues was the critical life setting the early Christians confronted.

[15] See chapter one on "collective memory."

[16] Levinsohn, *New Testament Greek*, p. 13.

materials by virtue of "associative thinking."[17] Mark 2.1–3.6 has been commonly thought by form critics to consist of five "apophthegms" (or "controversy dialogues")[18] "pronouncement" stories,[19] or "*chreia.*"[20] This shows that the composition of Mark 2.1–3.6 represents the characteristic of the oral mind that organizes materials in plural form ("polla")[21] or "cluster like-density."[22] For this reason Kelber claims that a cluster of the Markan Controversy Stories represents "a technique of information gathering that betrays the cognitive processes of oral operations."[23]

If so, an important question for my present purpose is what makes Mark 2.1–3.6 thematically coherent, despite its five episodes, each of which has a different topic. It has been commonly said that there is the theme or "form" of controversy in Mark 2.1–3.6.[24] James Dunn says:

> All five of the narrative sections [Mark 2.1–3.6] focus on controversies between Jesus and his critics, particularly the Pharisees. In all five the principal issue seems to be the authority claimed by Jesus, implicitly or explicitly, in matters of healing and forgiveness, consorting with sinners, fasting and the Sabbath, a claim disputed or obviously disallowed by Jesus' critics on legal grounds. The variation in the ways in which both these criticisms and the authority of Jesus are expressed in no way lessens but rather enriches the thematic unity of the whole.[25]

---

[17] Kelber, *Gospel*, p. 80. Kelber's other example for this "associative thinking" includes Mark's parabolic stories crowded into Mark 4, sayings in Mark 4 and 13, "heroic and polarization stories" in Mark 1–9 and "didactic stories" in Mark 10 and 12. And for Mark's thematic composition, including 2.1–3.6, see also Botha, "Mark's Story," pp. 319–22.

[18] Bultmann, *Synoptic Tradition*, pp. 11–69, refers to the category of *apophthegms* as including the controversy dialogues, scholastic dialogues and biographical apophthegms, and classifies the five stories in Mark 2.1–3.6 as controversy dialogues.

[19] Vincent Taylor, *The Formation of the Gospel Tradition* (London: Macmillan, 1935), pp. 30, 63–87; *idem, Mark*, pp. 91–92.

[20] Sanders and Davies, *Synoptic Gospels*, pp. 146–62.

[21] The characteristics of oral expression and composition, according to Havelock, *Plato*, p. 180, are "a knowledge of 'happenings' (*gignomena*) which are sharply experienced in separate units and so are pluralised (*pollar*) rather than being integrated into systems of cause and effect. And these units of experience are visually concrete; they are 'visibles' (*horata*)."

[22] Kelber, *Gospel*, p. 80.

[23] Kelber, *Gospel*, p. 80.

[24] See Bultmann, *Synoptic Tradition*, pp. 11–69.

[25] Dunn, *Paul*, p. 13.

The assumption that the form (or theme) of controversy consists of its specific components leads scholars to identify the subunits or sequences of events underlying Mark 2.1–3.6 for the purpose of demonstrating the thematic characteristic of the unit. Having found analogies for this form in Jewish (rabbinic) literature, Bultmann asserts that the controversy dialogues consist of three parts: First, an action of Jesus or his disciples; second, an opponent's attack by accusation or question; and third, Jesus' reply to the attack by a counter-question.[26] Taylor and, following him, Robert Tannehill propose relatively simple structures of the pronouncements stories in that they consist of brief narratives introduced by a question or description of events and a "pronouncement" of Jesus.[27] And Tannehill attempts to support his argument by providing many analogies from Hellinistic literature.[28] Arland Hultgren makes a claim in a similar fashion to Bultmann's view that the form of the conflict stories has a three-part structure: Introductory narrative, opponent's question or attack, and dominical saying.[29] Vernon Robbins attempts to explore the features of Greco-Roman judicial rhetoric in the Plucking of Grain on the Sabbath, thus the Controversy Stories. Following George Kennedy's idea of ancient rhetoric, first of all, Robbins suggests that the essential acts of judicial rhetoric taking place in the courtroom include "a statement of the case, arguments, counter-arguments, and a verdict."[30] And then on the basis of the model of rhetoricians' four stages of judicial rhetoric—introduction, statement of case, refutation, and conclusion—he analyzes the Synoptic passages.[31] Finally, from the anthropological perspective, Bruce Malina and Jerome Neyrey attempt to analyze the dispute between Jesus and his opponents in terms of the ongoing, agonistic contest for acquiring honour.[32] In particular, Malina suggests four typical steps in a challenge-riposte exchange for such an analysis:

---

[26] Bultmann, *Synoptic Tradition,* pp. 39–42.

[27] Taylor, *Formation,* p. 30 and Robert Tannehill, "Synoptic Pronouncement Stories: Form and Function," in *SBL Seminar Papers* (ed. Paul J. Achtemeier; Chico, California: Scholars Press, 1980), pp. 51–56; *idem,* "The Pronouncements Story," pp. 1–13.

[28] Tannehill, "The Pronouncements Story," pp. 6–12.

[29] Hultgren, *Jesus,* pp. 52–58.

[30] Robbins, "Plucking Grain," p. 108.

[31] Robbins, "Plucking Grain," pp. 110–41.

[32] Malina, *New Testament,* pp. 34–37, 42–44; Bruce Malina and Jerome Neyrey, "Honor and Shame in Luke-Acts: Pivotal Values of the Mediterranean World," in *The*

(1) claim to honour; (2) challenge to that claim; (3) riposte to the challenge; and (4) public verdict by onlookers.[33]

Every attempt appears legitimate in its own right. Yet if we take it seriously that Mark's Gospel is an oral-aural narrative that relied on human memory, it is imperative to account for how such forms would help in cognitive terms the audience's easy and quick processing and recall of Mark 2.1–3.6 as a whole. Most of the scholars, except Taylor and Tannehill, seem to acknowledge that there is a series of repeated thematic patterns associated with controversy situations in Mark 2.1–3.6. In fact, to look at it from the perspective of frame theory, since a frame or script-like frame is "a predetermined, stereotyped sequence of actions that defines a well-known situation," the scholars' idea that the conflict stories consists of, to some degree, fixed event sequences supports the notion that the early Christians apparently used consistent and framed knowledge structures to process and understand such stories. Thus, the argument is that the LEGAL CONTROVERSY frame, including its prototypical event sequences, operates in Mark 2.1.3–6 as a global cognitive model which make it possible to understand the whole unit in a thematically cohesive way.

But how do we know there is such a frame operating in this unit?[34] There is a key criterion to identify the global frame operative at the macro-level of Mark 2.1–3.6. If the five episodes repeat fixed sequences of events, this would show there is a specific patterning of frame-based information processing. Thus consider action sequences of the LEGAL CONTROVERSY frame in Mark 2.1–3.6 below:

Social World of Luke-Acts (ed. Jerome Neyrey; Peabody, Massachusetts: Hendrickson, 1991), pp. 36–38, 49–51; Neyrey, *Honor and Shame*, pp. 44–52.

[33] Malina, *New Testament*, pp. 33–36.

[34] In addition to the suggestion to follow, in order to answer this question it is worth remembering here the two more fundamental points discussed in the preceding chapters. First, one of the basic assumptions of cognitive linguistics is that linguistic expressions are reflections of a speaker's cognitive processing of events or things; and for successful communication the text takes for granted that the audience shares the same cognitive processing of information. Then the textual expression of Mark 2.1–3.6 shows how the speaker and audience processed the information. Second, an oral-aural narrative appropriately accounts for human cognitive processing in that it heavily relies on memory for its communication and is used as an aid to memory.

Table 4: The LEGAL CONTROVERSY Frame in Mark 2.1–3.6

Verse	Provocative Action	Charge	Defence	Verdict
		Prototypical Event Sequences		
.1–12	vv. 1–5 ἀφίενται σου αἱ ἁμαρτίαι	vv. 6–7 τί οὗτος οὕτως λαλεῖ; βλασφημεῖ	vv. 8–11 …ἐξουσίαν ἔχει …ὁ υἱὸς τοῦ ἀνθρώπου ἀφιέναι ἁμαρτίας	v. 12 ἠγέρθη καὶ… πάντας… δοξάζειν …τὸν θεὸν
.13–17	vv. 13–15 ἐσθίει μετὰ τῶν ἁμαρτωλῶν καὶ τελωνῶν	v. 16 ὅτι μετὰ τῶν τελωνῶν καὶ ἁμαρτωλῶν ἐσθίει;	v. 17 οὐκ ἦλθον καλέσαι δικαίους ἀλλὰ ἁμαρτωλούς	(implied)
.18–22	v. 8a not fasting (implied)	v. 18b οἱ δὲ σοὶ μαθηταὶ οὐ νηστεύουσιν;	vv. 19–22 …οἶνον νέον εἰς ς ἀσκοὺς καινού	(implied)
.23–28	v. 23 …ἐν τοῖς σάββασιν… ἤρξαντο ὁδὸν ποιεῖν τίλλοντεςτοὺς στάχυας	v. 24 τί ποιοῦσιν τοῖς σάββασιν ὃ οὐκ ἔξεστιν;	v. 25 ὁ υἱὸς τοῦ ἀνθρώπου καὶ τοῦ σαββάτου	(implied)
.1–6	v. 1 healing on the sabbath (implied)	v. 2 παρετήρουν αὐτὸν εἰ τοῖς σάββασιν θεραπεύσει αὐτόν, ἵνα κατηγορήσωσιν αὐτοῦ.	vv. 3–5a ἔξεστιν τοῖς σάββασιν ἀγαθὸν ποιῆσαι. ἢ κακοποιῆσαι…	vv. 5b–6 ἀπεκατεστάθη ἡ χεὶρ αὐτου… οἱ Φαρισαῖοι… συμβούλιον ἐδίδουν κατ᾽ αὐτοῦ ὅπως αὐτὸν ἀπολέσωσιν

The figure above shows that in all five episodes the same thematic events, namely, provocative event or action, charge, defence and verdict, recur in a relatively fixed order, though having internal variation (see below). It is possible to say then that the five conflict stories' narrative patterns are repetitive enough to be an event-type frame or script because textual structure is a representation of mental or conceptual structure. We call such stereotyped event sequences the prototypical components in the global LEGAL CONTROVERSY frame, and assert that it is this framed or scripted material that enables the audience to structure and process the conflict stories as a thematically coherent unit. We will now survey in detail how the global LEGAL CONTROVERSY frame operates consistently through the five stories, specifically focusing on its prototypical event sequences.

2.1. Provocative Events

All of the five stories begin with disputable legal issues—forgiveness of sins (Mark 2.5), table fellowship with tax collectors and sinners (2.15), not fasting (2.18), making a path by plucking the grain on the sabbath (2.23) and healing on the sabbath (3.1)—in which Jesus and his disciples are involved due to words (2.5) or behaviour (2.15, 18, 23; 3.1–2).[35] All these legal topics were, as will be dealt with in detail, ones with which the first-century Jews and Christians (e.g., Gal 2.11–18) were greatly concerned.[36] In the first episode, pronouncing the forgiveness of the paralytic's sins, Jesus challenges the most fundamental religious belief of Jews that forgiveness is a prerogative of God.[37] In the second episode, Jesus and his disciples have table fellowship with religious and social outcasts like sinners and tax collectors, which must be regarded as highly provocative in light of ritual purity laws.[38] What the third episode shows is that Jesus' disciples are depicted as making an insufficient commitment to *halakah* by not participating in the

---

[35] Cf. E.P. Sanders, *Jewish Law from Jesus to the Mishnah: Five Studies* (London: SCM; Philadelphia: Trinity Press International, 1990), pp. 131–254 and *idem, Jesus and Judaism*, pp. 35, 209, 264. To be sure, in the third and fifth episodes the disciples and Jesus' disputable actions are not directly introduced in the provocative stage but in the charge stage. I will argue below, nonetheless, that in this case the provocative nature is implicit even in 2.18a and 3.1 on the part of the audience.

[36] On the importance of such legal issues in the *Sitz im Leben* of the early church and first-century Judaism, see Emil Schürer, *The History of the Jewish People in the Age of Jesus Christ* (175 B.C.–A.D. 135). Vol. 2 (Edinburgh: T. and T. Clark, 1979), pp. 388–487; Jacob Neusner, *From Politics to Piety: The Emergence of Pharisaic Judaism* (Englewood Cliffs, New Jersey: Prentice-Hall, 1973), pp. 81–96; George F. Moore, *Judaism in the First Centuries of the Christian Era: The Age of the Tannaim*. Vols. 1 and 2 (Cambridge: Havard University Press, 1966); Kuhn, *Ältere Sammlungen*, pp. 53–98; Hultgren, *Jesus*, pp. 151–61; Dunn, *Paul*, pp. 16–28.

[37] Moore, *Judaism*. Vol. 1, pp. 497–552.

[38] Neusner, *Politics*, pp. 78–96, esp. 78–80. Indeed, the first and second episodes have respectively a lengthy healing story preceding Jesus' provocative proclamation of forgiveness of sins, and a story of the calling of Levi preceding Jesus' table fellowship with sinners and tax collectors; and thus the opening of the LEGAL CONTROVERSY frame may be difficult at this point. Yet, as will be discussed below, the healing and calling stories play a part in preparing the audience for the subsequent legal dispute between Jesus and his opponents by introducing issues with potential for controversy.

practice of fasting.[39] Finally, by making a road and/or plucking the grain and healing the man with a withered hand respectively, Jesus' disciples and Jesus in the fourth and fifth episodes provoke the dispute as to the observance of the sabbath laws.[40]

2.2. *Charge*

The provocative events are followed immediately by Jesus' opponents' hostile questioning or accusation (Mark 2.6–7, 16, 18b, 24; 3.2). The questions are focused on the *reason* for Jesus and his disciples' particular behaviours and typically begin with interrogative pronouns and particles as follows (bolded):

2.7   **τί** οὗτος οὕτως λαλεῖ;
2.16 **ὅτι**[41] μετὰ τῶν τελωνῶν καὶ ἁμαρτωλῶν ἐσθίει;
2.18 **διὰ τί**[42] οἱ μαθηταὶ Ἰωάννου καὶ οἱ μαθηταὶ τῶν Φαρισαίων
      νηστεύουσιν, οἱ δὲ σοὶ μαθηταὶ οὐ νηστεύουσιν;
2.24 **τί** ποιοῦσιν τοῖς σάββασιν ὃ οὐκ ἔξεστιν;[43]

This type of question is missing in the final episode in which their unspoken accusation is explained by Mark. The opponents are identified by group titles such as scribes (Mark 2.6), the Pharisees (Mark 2.18, 24; 3.6) and "the scribes of the Pharisees" (Mark 2.16). It is true, however, that the third episode does not explicitly identify the agent questioning Jesus regarding his disciples' not fasting; instead, verbs with no explicit agent (underlined) are used: ἔρχονται καὶ λέγουσιν αὐτῷ (Mark 2.18). And Jesus' hearer is described in the third plural pronoun (underlined): εἶπεν αὐτοῖς ὁ Ἰησοῦς). Who is the semantic agent of the verb and to whom does the pronoun refer? I believe frame theory can answer this question. Since scribes (2.6), "scribes of the Pharisees" (2.16) and the Pharisees (2.24; 3.6) have filled the slot for an accuser in the LEGAL CONTROVERSY frame throughout the stories,

---

[39] Moore, *Judaism*. Vol. 2, pp. 257–66, esp. 260.

[40] For the ancient Jews' concern with the law regulating sabbath observance and the dispute between Jesus and the Pharisees regarding the law, see David Flusser, *Jesus* (Jerusalem: Magnes Press, The Hebrew University, 1997, originally published 1968), pp. 56–63 and Moore, *Judaism*. Vol. 2, pp. 21–39.

[41] On the interrogative use of ὅτι, see Robertson, *Grammar*, 730, 917; Porter, *Idioms*, p. 280.

[42] On the interrogative function of the phrase διὰ τί in New Testament Greek, see BDF, § 299.

[43] Marcus, *Mark 1–8*, p. 212.

it is legitimate to believe that the same agents (the Pharisees or the scribes here), are implied in the pronoun and intended to be processed as the semantic subjects of the agentless verbs. In the same way the accusers of the fifth episode are also mentioned in the verb with no specific agent (underlined): καὶ <u>παρετήρουν</u> αὐτὸν εἰ τοῖς σάββασιν θεραπεύσει αὐτόν, ἵνα <u>κατηγορήσωσιν</u> αὐτοῦ (3.2). And verse 4 shows that Jesus answers the agent referred to by the third plural pronoun (underlined): λέγει <u>αὐτοῖς</u>. Though there is no antecedent noun, in order to identify the entity of the pronoun the audience draws on his or her mental LEGAL CONTROVERSY frame which has information regarding its prototypical accuser instantiated by the Pharisees or the scribes. In doing so, the audience is able to identify the implicit accuser with the Pharisees or scribes. So it is like frame opening based on preceding discourse (see Chapter Four). Besides, when we take into consideration that this dispute takes place in a synagogue, it is not difficult to infer that the Pharisees are implied as the semantic agent of such a hostile watching. This is because the Pharisees were prototypical participants in the SYNAGOGUE frame.[44] This is confirmed in 3.6, in which Mark describes the Pharisees turning up suddenly and going out of the synagogue.

The text does not, however, provide enough information about the scribes and the Pharisees (who they are and what they intend to do); instead the necessary information is presupposed in it. This is also the reason why for modern interpreters their presence and role as Jesus' opponents in Mark 2.1–3.6 may look unfamiliar.[45] Yet frame theory claims that the text assumes the original audience to have shared knowledge of them (thus note the Greek article, a hearer-old marker, before the initial information τῶν γραμματέων (Mark 2.6), οἱ Φαρισαῖοι (Mark 2.15) in the immediate context). In New Testament times, the Pharisees had high standing among and a great influence on the people even in the period prior to 70 C.E.; they were perceived as interpreters of the Law (Josephus, *Jewish War* 2.119–68; *Jewish Antiquities* 18.11–25) or meticulous preservers of the "traditions of elders" (Mark 7.3; Josephus, *Jewish Antiquities* 13.297, 408).[46]

---

[44] On the SYNAGOGUE frame and its participants, see below.

[45] Hultgren, *Jesus*, p. 56; and Marcus, *Mark 1–8*, p. 219.

[46] Josephus, *Jewish Antiquities* (LCL; trans. Ralph Marcus and Louis H. Feldman; Cambridge, Massachusetts: London/Harvard University Press, 1998) and *idem, Jewish War* (LCL; trans. H.J. Thackeray; Cambridge, Massachusetts: Harvard University Press, 1997). I do not agree with Sanders, *Jesus and Judaism*, p. 178, who argues

As for the scribes, E.P. Sanders claims that most scribes were Levites and priests;[47] and their role was largely associated with legal exegesis (Nehemiah 8.7–9; 2 Chronicles 17.7–9; Ezra 7.6; Josephus, *Life* 196–98)[48] and judicial inquiry (Mark 3.22; 14.53–55). Further, as noted above, the early Christians were involved in an increasing dispute with Jewish communities; so the information that the Pharisees and Jewish scribes were scrupulous legal experts was part of their culture-based, conventionalized knowledge. For Mark and his historical audience, thus, what was necessary for processing the information associated with the Pharisees and scribes in the Controversy Stories was stored in their mental frames for PHARISEE and SCRIBE. These person frames enabled the audience to understand the legal experts' entering and questioning, after seeing Jesus and his disciples' provocative conduct, and to be able to infer their intention in questioning Jesus and his disciples as to their behaviour of challenging or accusing (see below).[49] In this way, for Mark's audience the PHARISEE[50] and SCRIBE frames

that the Synoptic depiction of the Pharisees confronting Jesus as to legal issues is "unrealistic" and rather a retrojection of the early church's later controversies with Judaism. Arguing against Sanders' extreme skepticism about the historical reliability of Mark's depiction of the Pharisees, Dunn, *Jesus*, pp. 61–88, rightly demonstrates that the Pharisees' high regard for scrupulous observance of ancestral traditions about Sabbath, dietary law and ritual purity, as Mark portrays them, dates to the period prior to 70 C.E.

[47] E.P. Sanders, *Judaism: Practice and Belief 63 B.C.E–66 C.E.* (London: SCM; Philadelphia:Trinity International Press, 1992), pp. 170–82.

[48] Josephus, *Life* (LCL; trans. H.J. Thackeray; London: Heinemann; Harvard University Press, 1965), cited by Marcus, *Mark 1–8*, pp. 523–24.

[49] Note, as discussed in the Chapter Four, the person frame tends to understand frame-relevant information in purposive terms. For other examples in Mark's Gospel which associate the Pharisees and the scribes with Jesus' opponents with respect to Jewish legal issues, see below.

[50] Sanders forcibly argues that it is highly unlikely that Jesus engaged in controversy with the Pharisees over legal matters such as those in the controversy stories in question. For Sanders the Pharisees in Jesus' day "did not control the religious life of Judaism in such a way as to make non-Pharisees feel excluded and grateful for the offer to join the kingdom of God. All the evidence, further, is against the assumption that the Pharisees would feel hostile to including ordinary people in the kingdom." No doubt Sanders' statement is exaggerated because much evidence shows that the Pharisees were frequently in extreme conflict with the religious opponents, such as the Sadducees and the Qumran community. Thus, in explaining his justification in describing "Jesus' opponents-in argument as Pharisees," Flusser, *Jesus*, p. 69, says, "In those days [Jesus' day], if one said 'Pharisee,' one immediately thought of a religious hypocrite. On his deathbed, the Sadducean King Alexander Jannaeus warned his wife not against the true Pharisees, but against the 'painted ones, whose deeds are the deeds of Zimir, but who expect to receive the reward of Phinehas.' The Sadducean king spoke of 'the painted ones.' The Essenes called the Pharisees 'the whitewashed.'"

would play a role in driving the stories into a controversial vein, thus directly opening the LEGAL CONTROVERSY frame.

2.3. Defence

All five stories depict Jesus immediately responding to his critics' question or accusation (Mark 2.8–11; 2.17; 2.19–22; 2.25–28; 3.3–5). As pointed out in the preceding section, the opponents' charge is generated by both Jesus and his disciples' conduct: In the first and last instances the challenge results from Jesus' statement and action; in the second story the disciples are questioned over Jesus' meal practice; and in the third and fourth stories Jesus is questioned due to the disciples' not fasting (probably involving Jesus himself) and doing "works" on the sabbath. Yet Jesus is described as the only one who reacts to the questions or accusations in all these episodes. In doing so Mark narrows the conflict into an issue between Jesus and his opponents. Following up with his critics' objection to his and his disciples' particular actions, Jesus' reaction is focused on explaining justification for the conduct. There are framed defensive procedures that shape Jesus' speech:

Table 5: Prototypical Elements in Jesus' Defence

Verse	Counter-question	Pronouncement	Healing
2.8–11	vv. 8–9	v. 10	v. 11
	τί ταῦτα διαλογίζεσθε	ἐξουσίαν ἔχει ὁ υἱὸς	ἔγειρε ἆρον τὸν κράβαττον
	ἐν ταῖς καρδίαις ὑμῶν; τί ἐστιν εὐκοπώτερον ...ἢ...;	τοῦ ἀνθρώπου ἀφιέναι ἁμαρτίας ἐπι τῆς γῆς	σου καὶ ὕπαγε εἰς τὸ οἶκον σου
2.17		v. 17 οὐ χρείαν ἔχουσιν οἱ ἰσχύοντες ἰατροῦ ἀλλ' οἱ κακῶς ἔχοντες· ...ἦλθον καλέσαι... ἁμαρτωλούς.	
2.19–22	v. 19a μὴ δύνανται οἱ υἱοὶ τοῦ νυμφῶνος...; νηστεύειν;	vv. 19b–22 ...οὐ δύνανται νηστεύειν ...τότε νηστεύσουσιν ἐν ἐκείνῃ τῇ ἡμέρᾳ. οὐδεὶς ἐπίβλημα ῥάκους ἀγνάφου ἐπιράπτει ἐπὶ ἱμάτιον	

Table 5 (*cont.*)

Verse	Counter-question	Pronouncement	Healing
		οὐδεὶς βάλλει οἶνον νέον εἰς ἀσκοὺς παλαιούς· οἶνον νέον εἰς ἀσκοὺς καινούς.	
2.25–28	vv. 25–26 οὐδέποτε ἀνέγνωτε τί ἐποίησεν Δαυὶδ ὅτε χρείαν ἔσχεν καὶ ἐπείνασεν αὐτὸς καὶ οἱ μετ᾽ αὐτου...;	vv. 27–28 τὸ σάββατον διὰ τὸν ἄνθρωπον ἐγένετο... ὥστε κύριος ἐστιν ὁ υἱὸς τοῦ ἀνθρώπου καὶ τοῦ σαββάτου	
3.3–5	v. 4 ἔξεστιν τοῖς σάββασιν ἀγαθὸν ποιῆσαι ἢ κακοποιῆσαι...;		v. 5a ἔκτεινον τὴν χεῖρα

Jesus' defence, except in the second episode that has only a pronouncement, is expressed through a consistent pattern which begins with counter-question and ends with pronouncement and/or healing action (in the case of the healing story). And with the exception of the first and final stories, in both of which Jesus' counter-question carries the form of a 'comparison question' (τί ἐστιν εὐκοπώτε ρον...ἢ..., 2.9 and ἔξεστιν...ἢ..., 3.4), each story includes parable (in the second and third) and Scripture quotation (in the fourth) as part of the content of Jesus' defence. Once the LEGAL CONTROVERSY frame is opened by the opponents' critical question or accusation at the charge stage, the audience is likely to process such actions taken by Jesus in defensive terms and put him in the slot for a defendant. This is because the LEGAL CONTROVERSY frame is structured in goal-directed sequences. Scholars have stressed the importance of the final sayings of Jesus in Mark 2.1–3.6, even calling the stories as a whole a pronouncement story. [51] It must be noted, however, that the global LEGAL CONTROVERSY frame operates at the macro-level of Mark 2.1–3.6 and thus the pronouncements are placed as a part of Jesus' defence at the close of the dispute between Jesus and the opponents.[52]

---

[51] Taylor, *Formation*, pp. 30 and Robert Tannehill, "Synoptic Pronouncement Stories," pp. 51–56; *idem*, "The Pronouncements Story," pp. 1–13.
[52] See Bultmann, *Synoptic Tradition*, p. 41.

This means that they are to be processed and interpreted in light of the LEGAL CONTROVERSY frame.

2.4. *Verdict*

It is explicitly expressed in the first and the final episodes (Mark 2.1–12 and 3.1–6) that the conflicts between Jesus and his opponents result in making a judgment regarding what Jesus did. Such a verdict is a final stage of the prototypical event sequences in the LEGAL CONTROVERSY frame.

With respect to Jesus' healing of the paralytic (2.1–12), Mark concludes the story with two kinds of verdicts of Jesus' behaviour: God and the onlookers' vindication; and the final episode which ends with two contrasting verdicts: God's vindication and the Pharisees' guilty verdict of Jesus (see the chart below):[53]

Verse	God's Vindication	The Onlooker's Vindication	The Pharisees' Guilty Verdict
2.12a	...ἠγέρθη...	ὥστε ἐξίστασθαι πάντας καὶ δοξάζειν τὸν θεὸν...	
3.5c	...ἀπεκατεστάθη ἡ χεὶρ αὐτου		...οἱ Φαρισαῖοι... συμβούλιον ἐδίδουν κατ' αὐτοῦ ὅπως αὐτὸν ἀπολέσωσιν

Indeed, there seems to be no direct reference to God's vindication of Jesus in either of the concluding stages. But there is textual evidence to show that Mark's Christian audience may have recognized that God is involved in the verdict of Jesus. In both of the stories the climax of healing actions is described in the passive verbs with no specific agent of healing: ἠγέρθη (2.12a) and ἀπεκατεστάθη (3.5c). My argument is that God may be elicited with the help of the co-texts as the most relevant semantic agent of the verbs to refer to healing in Mark's Christian audiences' mental frame. (I will discuss this in detail in Chapter Five.) What both concluding remarks show, thus, is that whereas Jesus' conduct is ultimately vindicated by God and the onlookers, the Pharisees as his accuser decide to sentence Jesus to death for what he did.

---

[53] Cf. Neyrey, *Honor and Shame*, pp. 44–48.

The rest of the episodes seem to provide no explicit information in the texts concerning a verdict. Yet if a frame is referred to as operative in a text, we should assume its prototypical actions, unless otherwise specified, to be accomplished.[54] Part of the reason for such an omission of the components of the frame, as discussed earlier, is because the text supposes that the audience is familiar with the frame and hence draws inferences about the missing portions or defaults. If so, frame theory allows us to say that, in the case of the instances with no explicit reference to a verdict, the verdict is implicit at the close of the conflict dialogue. This means that the audience who possesses the LEGAL CONTROVERSY frame would readily process the specific verdict by virtue of inference (thus, see below on the examples of explicit reference to the verdict stage in Mark' other controversy stories). The inferential content of the verdict, of course, depends on whose side one is on. But no doubt Mark's historical audience's verdict was a grant of vindication to Jesus and his ministry, just as with the crowd in the first story.

3. The Other LEGAL CONTROVERSY Stories in Mark's Gospel

Before drawing a conclusion, it is valuable to compare Mark 2.1–3.6 with Mark's other controversy stories in his Gospel (see the chart below). In doing so, my concern is to explore whether the parallel conflict stories repeat the same prototypical event sequences as those of the LEGAL CONTROVERSY frame in Mark 2.1–3.6 (see the chart below). My discussion is confined to the controversy stories dealing with legal issues. The observations below show that, as in Mark 2.1–3.6 there is in Mark's other legal conflict stories a consistent, thematic patterning that builds up their structure. The controversial tone of the stories is prepared by Jesus and his disciples' provocative actions (Mark 7.1–14; 11.27–33), by the introduction of his typical adversaries (Mark 10.2; 12.13) or the controversial issue (Mark 12.18). The provocative scenes are immediately followed by Jesus' opponents' challenging with the *halakic* issues (Mark 7.5; 10.2; 12.19–23), religious authority (Mark 11.27–28) or religious-political issues (Mark 12.14–15). Note in all the stories the opponents' challenge is in question-form. Jesus' prototypical opponents are typically filled by legal experts like the Pharisees (7.1–14; 10.2–9; 12.13–17), scribes and the high priests (3.22–30; 7.1–14;

---

[54] Schank and Abelson, *Scripts*, pp. 36–40.

11.27–33), and the Sadducees (12.18–27). After the hostile question or accusation, Jesus' defensive reaction repeats in counter-question (10.3; 11.29; 12.15, 24) and/or in quoting Scripture (7.6–14; 10.6–8; 12.26). And the tension between Jesus and his opponents greatly increases by the religious authorities' answer and Jesus' response to that (10.2–9; 11.27–33).

Table 6: Other LEGAL CONTROVERSY Frames in Mark's Gospel

		Prototypical Event Sequences			
Verse	Provocative Event/ Issue	Charge/ Challenge	Defence/ Response	Response by Inquirer	Response by Jesus
7. 1 | 13	vv. 1–2 οἱ Φαρισαῖοι καί τινες τῶν γραμματέων ἰδόντες…τινὰς τῶν μαθητῶν αὐτοῦ ὅτι κοιναῖς χερσίν, τοῦτ᾽ ἔστιν ἀνίπτοις, ἐσθίουσιν τοὺς ἄρτους	v. 5 διὰ τί οὐ περιπατοῦσιν οἱ μαθηταί σου κατὰ ἣν παράδοσιν τῶν πρεσβυτέρων; (question)	vv. 6–13 καλῶς ἐπροφήτευσεν Ἡσαΐιας περὶ ὑμῶν τῶν ὑποκριτῶν (Scripture quotation)		
10.2 | 9	v. 2 Introduction of Φαρισαῖοι	v. 2 εἰ ἔξεστιν ἀνδρὶ γυναῖκα ἀπολῦσαι, πειράζοντες αὐτόν, (question)	v. 3 τί ὑμῖν ἐνετείλατο Μωϋσῆς; (Scripture quotation) in counter-question)	v. 4 Μωϋσῆς βιβλίον ἀποστασίου γράψαι καὶ ἀπολῦσαι. (Scripture quotation	vv. 5–9 …ὃ οὖν ὁ θεὸς συνέζευξεν ἄνθρωπος μ᾽ χωριζέτω…
11.27[55] | 33	vv. 15–18 …εἰσελθὼν εἰς τὸ ἱερὸν ἤρξατο	vv. 27–28 οἱ ἀρχιερεῖς καὶ οἱ γραμματεῖς	vv. 29–30 τὸ βάπτισμα τὸ Ἰωάννου ἐξ	vv. 31–32 οὐκ οἴδαμεν	v. 33 οὐδὲ ἐγὼ λέγω ὑμῖν ἐ᾽

[55] As every commentator admits, Mark 11.19–25 (the Story of the Cursed Fig Tree) is inserted between 11.15–18 and 11.27–33 both of which deal with 'the controversy over Jesus' authority to disrupt the temple,' Thus the chief priest and scribes' challenge of Jesus' right to do "these things" is directly linked to Jesus' temple cleansing activities. See Cranfield, *Mark*, p. 361; Morna D. Hooker, *The Gospel According to Saint Mark* (Peabody, Massachusetts: Hendrickson, 191), p. 271; Evans, *Mark 8:27–16:20*, pp. 199–200.

able 6 (*cont.*)

		Prototypical Event Sequences			
Verse	Provocative Event/ Issue	Charge/ Challenge	Defence/ Response	Response by Inquirer	Response by Jesus
	ἐκβάλλειν τοὺς πωλοῦντας καὶ τοὺς ἀγοράζοντας...	καὶ οἱ πρεσβύτεροι... ἔλεγον... ἐν ποίᾳ ἐξουσίᾳ ταῦτα ποιεῖς; (question)	οὐρανοῦ ἦν ἢ ἐξ ἀνθρώπων; (counter-question)		ποίᾳ ἐξουσίᾳ ταῦτα ποιῶ.
2.13 7	v. 13 ...τινας τῶν Φαρισαίων καὶ τῶν Ἡρῳδιανῶν αὐτὸν ἀγρεύσωσιν λόγῳ	vv. 14–15 ...ἔξεστιν δοῦναι ...κῆνσον Καίσαρι ἢ οὔ; (question)	vv. 15–17a τίνος ἡ εἰκὼν αὕτη καὶ ἡ ἐπιγραφή;... τὰ Καίσαρος ἀπόδοτε Καίσαρι καὶ τὰ τοῦ θεοῦ τῷ θεῷ (counter-question)		
2.18 7	v. 18 ἔρχονται Σαδδουκαῖοι πρὸς αὐτόν, οἵτινες λέγουσιν ἀνάστασιν μὴ εἶναι,	vv. 19–23 ἐν τῇ ἀναστάσει... τίνος αὐτῶν ἔσται γυνή; (question)	vv. 24–27 οὐ διὰ τοῦτο πλανᾶσθε μὴ εἰδότες τὰς γραφὰς μηδὲ τὴν δύναμιν τοῦ θεοῦ; ...περὶ δὲ τῶν νεκρῶν ὅτι ἐγείρονται οὐκ ἀνέγνωτε ἐν τῇ βίβλῳ Μωϋσέως (counter-question)		

Finally, though not being indicated in the chart, Mark 12.13–17 explicitly mentions that the conflict ends with the opponents' positive evaluation toward Jesus' reply (ἐξεθαύμαζον). The LEGAL CONTROVERSY frame would enable the listener to infer in such an expression Jesus' avoidance of his opponents' hostile trap. Indeed, such an concluding remark or verdict occurs only here in the five stories just mentioned; but it should be noted that, as shown above, Mark 2.12 and 3.6 as well as in the other controversy stories (Mark 3.29; 14.64) show the some kind of verdict following a controversy or conflict is not unusual in Mark's Gospel.[56] Consequently, the omission of the verdict in other instances does not mean that the audience did not remind of it; rather, for an oral-aural narrative such an omission is often desirable.[57] A more possible explanation for the missing verdict stage may be made in light of frame theory. Since the verdict stage is a prototypical component in the LEGAL CONTROVERSY frame, his audience would be able to make inferences about the omitted portion, using their mental frame.

With respect to a thematic structure of Mark 2.1–3.6, now some conclusions can be drawn from the observations above. First of all, the five episodes in Mark 2.1–3.6 all recur with the identical thematic events and sequential order, and this is, though with variation, also the case for Mark's other controversy stories in his Gospel. Such stereo-typed narrative patterns of the conflict stories can be best explained by the recycling of the global LEGAL CONTROVERSY frame. Next, the underlying patterns of Mark 2.1–3.6, which have been known as "forms" or thematic compositions of controversy or conflict, are in fact the outlines of cognitive frames which organized Mark and his historical audience's memory storage of the controversy situation. We must believe that, as already pointed out, for such an effective cognitive processing the text assumes the original audience to be well versed in the LEGAL CONTROVERSY frame, which reflected real-life dispute or verbal exchange over some issue, and thus its prototypical event sequence; so the text relied on this familiarity to communicate

---

[56] Thus, note Mark 14.64b in which the high priest, elders and scribes also make a guilty judgment against Jesus (οἱ δὲ πάντες κατέκριναν αὐτὸν ἔνοχον εἶναι θανάτου, "and they all condemned him to be worthy of death"), when hearing Jesus' defence of his own identity as τὸν υἱὸν τοῦ ἀνθρώπου ἐκ δεξιῶν καθήμενον τῆς δυνάμεως καὶ ἐρχόμενον μετὰ τῶν νεφελῶν τοῦ οὐρανοῦ ("the son of man sitting at the right hand of the power and coming along the clouds of the heaven"). An excellent book about Jesus' trial in Mark 14.61–64, see Darrell L. Bock, *Blasphemy and Exaltation in Judaism and the Final Examination of Jesus* (WUNT 2.106; Tübingen: Mohr Siebeck, 1998). And also see Mark 3.29. At the close of Beelzebul controversy with the scribes, Jesus finally judges the scribes who charge himself of demonic collusion as commit-ting the charge of having committed the unpardonable sin and thus being subject to "eternal condemnation" (ἔνοχός ἐστιν αἰωνίου ἁμαρτήματος).

[57] Rubin, *Memory*, pp. 22, 25–26.

with the hearer. As Sanford and Garrod say, "In terms of the dominant scenario hypothesis, repeated use of a scenario (through repeated subsidiary references to it) should bolster the status of its token in [linguistically] explicit focus and hence in long-term memory."[58] The LEGAL CONTROVERSY frame then serves as the organizational principle for unifying the five stories in Mark 2.1–3.6 into a single thematic unit primarily by means of their identical cognitive structures.[59] And in this way the listener's task of understanding and remembering the oral-aural narrative is made easier because of that unit's familiar structure in which each story is told.

B. Frames' Organization of Paragraph or Episode

It has been pointed out in Chapter Three that oral memory is also episodic and the Markan oral narrative consists of an association of series of episodes. It is then time to focus on the issue of the paragraph or episodic structure of Mark 2.1–3.6. The five stories in Mark 2.1–3.6 are not only in a thematic composition, but are also organized in a paragraph or episodic unit. This section will survey how frames help the cognitive processing and understanding of information in the paragraph or episode, clustering it into a coherent structure. We will begin this by defining what a paragraph or episode is by the helpf of some insights from discourse analysis.

1. *What is a Paragraph or Episode?*

One of the basic assumptions of discourse analysts is that the speaker/writer structures a spoken or written text for communication with the hearer/reader; and the structure is well represented both by microstructures, such as words, phrases, sentences, and even paragraphs or episodes, and by a macrostructure which, being made up of microstructures, conveys the large thematic ideas.[60] In these discourse structures a paragraph or episode, on the one hand, serves as a part of

---

[58] Sanford and Garrod, *Understanding*, p. 183.

[59] Thorndyke and Yekovich, "Schema Theory," p. 38, say, "The narrative structure created during comprehension of the first story could be activated and used to encode the information from the second story." Thus, it is obvious that the identically structured stories such as those of Mark 2.1–3.6 facilitate comprehension.

[60] Porter, *Idioms*, pp. 299–300.

a larger discourse; on the other hand, it constitutes a group of sentences.[61] This shows that an episodic structure plays a crucial role in organizing discourse, in particular by unifying the series of sentences in it into a coherent unit. The text then marks the division of the text into separate chunks or paragraphs so that the audience may recognize that a new episode is beginning and hence that the last episode has ended. What kind of markers do we then expect to find at the beginning of a new episode? There is a general consensus that in narrative, whether oral or written,[62] paragraph boundary signals usually include time, place, and characters.[63] Thus, van Dijk characterizes paragraph or episodes "as coherent sequences of sentences of a discourse, linguistically marked for beginning and/or end, and further defined in terms of some kind of 'thematic unity'—for instance, in terms of identical participants, time, location or global event or action."[64]

2. Frames Help Bind Episodic Units by Defining their Boundary Markers: Place, Character, and Thing Frames

Cognitive linguists have shown the importance of human cognitive processing in understanding the coherence of information within the

---

[61] R.E. Longacre, "The Paragraph as a Grammatical Unit," in *Syntax and Semantics: Discourse and Syntax* 12 (ed. Talmy Givón; New York: Academic Press, 1979), p. 116.

[62] Of course, it has been known that in storytelling of oral narrative the speaker divides between one paragraph and another by using such prosodic characteristics as pauses and pitch. For example, see Leo Noordman, Ingrid Dassen, Marc Swerts, and Jacoues Terken, "Prosodic Markers of Text Structure," in *Discourse Studies in Cognitive Linguistics* (ed. Karen Van Hoek, Andrej A. Kibrik, and Leo Noordman; Amsterdam/Philadelphia: John Benjamins, 1997), pp. 133–48. But it must be noted that there is a correspondence between the textual paragraph boundary markers and such a prosodic characteristic in packaging the information in paragraph units. For example, Chafe shows in his study that the speaker tends to make a relatively lengthier hesitation at the point where, if the narrative were written, we would expect to find a linguistic signal of paragraph shift. See Wallace Chafe, "The Deployment of Consciousness in the Production of a Narrative," in *The Pear Stories* (ed. Wallace Chafe; Norwood, New Jersey: Ablex, 1980), pp. 43–44; *idem*, "The Flow of Thought and the Flow of Language," in *Syntax and Semantics*. Vol. 12: *Discourse and Syntax* (ed. Talmy Givón; New York: Academic Press, 1979), pp. 176–80. This indicates that linguistic markers of paragraph boundary can be used as signals to show how speakers' and listeners' mental processing operates when speaking and hearing a narrative.

[63] See Longacre, "Paragraph," pp. 115–120; Chafe, "Flow of Thought," pp. 150–80; Alexander Georgakopoulou and Dionysis Goutsos, *Discourse Analysis. An Introduction* (Edinburgh: Edinburgh University Press, 1997), pp. 65–66.

[64] van Dijk, "Episodes," p. 177.

episode or paragraph.[65] For the understanding of a text the audience constructs cognitive representations of the episodic context, using information such as temporal and spatial background, consistent participants and events while the subsequent text is told. Thus, Wallace Chafe claims that without such information, when events within particular contexts are spoken, "the listener's self" as "the user of consciousness" is "uncomfortable and disoriented."[66] Then he goes on to say that information about the setting "needs to be placed at the beginning of a narrative... Once established in that manner, it can be retained in peripheral consciousness as background orientation for the particular, localized events which may then be focused on."[67] Chafe rightly points out the importance of the monitoring role of human consciousness built up from the background information in story comprehension. But such human consciousness is the event-like mental frame. Evoked by those boundary markers or constituents of episode, event frames enable the audience to process an episode coherently and help define the boundaries of episodes. With respect to such a frame's role in marking episode divisions, the present section is concerned with place, time, and character change markers, and in the next section I will discuss how the LEGAL CONTROVERSY frame's prototypical event sequences instantiated by each episode contribute to such a cognitive representation of the episodic context.

Little background information, in fact, is spelled out in a text; instead it is mentioned frequently with brief lexical indications to specific elements. This means that in order to understand the subsequent events, the listener must infer detailed information from prototypical knowledge about spatial and temporal background and participants. And this information does not need to be mentioned in every sentence or whenever the text mentions new information, at least within the boundary of the episode. This is because the frame previously opened by the setting and character information helps make sense of subsequent events. Spatial or temporal reference at the beginning of the episode opens a specific scene frame in the mind of the audience and

---

[65] For example, see Emmott, *Narrative Comprehension*, pp. 103–94; Tuen A. van Dijk and W. Kintsch, *Strategies of Discourse Comprehension* (New York: Academic Press, 1983), pp. 163, 338–39.

[66] Chafe, "Consciousness," pp. 41–42.

[67] Chafe, "Consciousness," p. 42.

enables the audience to process and understand incoming information against that frame.[68] This is also true of character information.
Specific titles of characters open the person frame, and so in light of
the open person frame, the audience not only assumes that there is
a beginning of a new episode dealing with a topic or theme different
from the previous one, but also understands the characters' actions
to follow and their reaction to specific happenings. But Mark 2.1–3.6
represents Jesus, his disciples (except for the first and final episode)
and the scribes and the Pharisees as on-going actors who recur in all
the epsidoes. So their role as the boundary markers seems less significant. We need to focus, instead, on the more minor characters that are
directly involved in individual episodes.

2.1. *The First Episode (Mark 2.1–12)*

The spatial background and the topic character (i.e., characters to
appear anew in each episode) are clearlyindicated to mark the boundaries of the first episode.

2.1.1. *A Setting Marker: The* HOUSE *Frame*
The spatial layout of the present episode is referred to at the beginning
of this episode as ἐν οἴκῳ (v. 1). The chart of the HOUSE frame is as
follows:

Verse	Frame Title	Default Elements	Prototypical Happenings
v. 1	ἐν οἴκῳ		
v. 2		τὴν θύραν	συνήχθησαν πολλοι ἐλάλει... τὸν λόγον
v. 4a		τὴν στέγην	
v. 6			ἐκεῖ καθήμενοι
v. 12			ἐξῆλθεν

What we must remember is that even if the lexicon of the "house"
(οἶκος) is only mentioned once here, the HOUSE frame—a place
frame—operates throughout the episode, serving the audience as

---

[68] For the frame-opening power of the information of spatio-temporal setting, character, and things, see Chapter Four; and also see Sanford and Garrod, *Understanding*,
pp. 129–31.

background information to understand the subsequent events. Thus, τὴν θύραν (v. 2), and τὴν στέγην are expressed with the Greek article, a hearer-old marker, even if both words are new information in the immediate text. The use of the Greek article in those cases indicates that the text takes it for granted that the audience already knows and easily understands the information by referring back to the open HOUSE frame because they (the door and roof) are parts of its proto-typical components. Likewise, the participants' particular behaviours can be made sense of only in light of the open HOUSE frame. Verse 2, first of all, shows Jesus teaching the word (τὸν λόγον) and many people gathering into the house. It may be assumed that teaching and the crowd's gathering have nothing to do with stereotype of the HOUSE frame. Yet as far as Mark's Christian audience is concerened, these elements may have been understood as prototypical in the HOUSE frame, provided that a house was a place in which the early Christians used to get together as ἐκκλησία for worship, teaching and fellowship (1 Thessalonians 1.1; 2 Thessalonians 1.4; 2.14; Galatians 1.2; 1 Corinthians 7.17; 11.16; 14.33, 34; 16.1; Colossians 4.15; Philemon 2; Rome 16.23; cf. Acts 16.15, 40).[69] Next verse 6 presents the scribes in a certain physical position (underlined): ἦσαν δέ τινες τῶν γραμματέων ἐκεῖ καθήμενοι. We may wonder where they were sitting. And verse 12 presents the paralytic going out (ἐξῆλθεν), after being healed by Jesus. From where did he go out? Because the open HOUSE frame contains the knowledge of typical spatial use of a house including the actions of coming, sitting, and going out, though no explicit reference to the house is mentioned in each case, these sentences are understandable. The observations show that the HOUSE frame allows 2.1–12 to be a spatially coherent episode.

2.1.2. A Character Marker: The PARALYTIC Frame
Charting the PARALYTIC frame, we find:

Verse	Frame Title	Default Elements	Prototypical Actions
v. 3	παραλυτικὸν	σου αἱ ἁμαρτίαι	
v. 4b		τὸν κράβαττον	αἰρόμενον ὑπὸ τεσσάρων

---

[69] See note 399 on the early Christians' HOUSE frame.

(*cont.*)

Verse	Frame Title	Default Elements	Prototypical Actions
v. 5			ἀφίενταί σου αἱ ἁμαρτίαι
v. 9		τὸν κράβαττον	ἔγειρε καὶ ἆρον σου... καὶ περιπάτει
v. 11		τὸν κράβαττον	ἔγειρε ἆρον... σου καὶ ὕπαγε εἰς τὸν οἶκόν σου
v. 12		τὸν κράβαττον	ἠγέρθη καὶ εὐθὺς ἄρας... ἐξῆλθεν

After presenting the spatial setting of the subsequent events in verses 1–2, Mark signals the beginning of a new episode by virtue of the introduction of a new topical participant (to use Longacre's terms, "a thematic participant"),[70] namely, the paralytic (bolded): καὶ ἔρχονται φέροντες πρὸς αὐτὸν **παραλυτικὸν** αἰρόμενον ὑπὸ τεσσάρων (v. 3); and he marks the end of the episode by taking him off the stage (the relevant verb is underlined) καὶ ἠγέρθη καὶ εὐθὺς ἄρας τὸν κράβαττον ἐξῆλθεν ἔμπροσθεν πάντων (v. 12). The word referring to a person in terms of the kind of disease he has opens the PARALYTIC frame, a person frame, activating stereotypic information associated with the sick person: τὸν κράβαττον (vv. 4b, 9, 11, 12), αἰρόμενον ὑπὸ τεσσάρων (v. 4b), ἀφίενταί σου αἱ ἁμαρτίαι.[71] Above all, the PARALYTIC frame determines what is to happen as a result of his coming into the story: The forgiveness of sins (v. 5) and specific actions associated with healing (vv. 9, 10, 11, 12).

Under the influence of form criticism, scholars have divided Mark 2.1–12 into a composite of two different stories such as a miracle or healing story (vv. 1–5a, 10b–12) and a story of forgiveness (vv. 5b–10a).[72] A similar view is apparent in Johannes Louw and Eugene Nida's dictionary based on semantic domains. The dictionary, on the one hand, categorizes ἁμαρτία (88.298) into the semantic domains of Sin, Wrongdoing, Guilt (L 88.289–88.318) in Moral and Ethical Qualities and Related Behavior (88); and ἀφίημι (40.8) into the semantic domain

---

[70] Longacre, "Paragraph," p. 118: Longacre says, "In narrative discourse, a narrative paragraph is built around a thematic participant, occasionally a small set of thematic participants."

[71] Indeed, as will be discussed, the PARALYTIC frame is a subframe of the HEALING frame.

[72] Bultmann, *Synoptic Tradition*, pp. 14–15; Taylor, *Mark*, pp. 191–92. Cf. Cranfield, *Mark*, p. 96.

of Forgiveness (B 40.8–40.13) in Reconciliation, Forgiveness (40); on the other hand, it places παραλυτικός (23.171) or ἀσθένεια (23.143), into the semantic domain of Sickness, Disease, Weakness (I 23.142–23. 184) in Physiological Processes and States (23). Form criticism's view and such categorizations as Louw and Nida's lexicon show that they fail to recognize that sins and the forgiveness of them and the illness of the paralytic and his healing were interconnected concepts in the ancient Jewish culture, so that personal sin may have been conventionally perceived to be a cause of illness or disease (Numbers 12.6–9; John 5.13).[73] This idea can be supported by textual evidence (a hearer-old marker is underlined): ἀφίενται σου <u>αἱ ἁμαρτίαι</u> (v. 5) has a hearer-old marker, the Greek article, this can best be explained by the text's assumption that its audience may process the information by referring back to the open PARALYTIC frame. Thus the hearer may make perfect sense of the co-occurrence of the forgiveness of sins and of healing through the prototypical knowledge opened by use of παραλυτικόν; thus the PARALYTIC frame contributes to processing this unit as a semantically coherent single episode.

2.2. The Second Episode (Mark 2.13–17)

Many scholars have believed that there are in Mark 2.13–17 two distinct stories(a calling story [vv. 14] and a controversy story [vv. 15–17]).[74] Different spatial setting markers (παρὰ τὴν θάλασσαν in v. 13 and ἐν τῇ οἰκία in v. 15) in this unit seem to support this. But the same topic character, tax collector, occurring between the two stories makes this theory difficult. I propose that the global LEGAL CONTROVERSY frame operative in Mark 2.13–17 enables the second episode to be processed as a single episode (see section 2.3).

---

[73] Geza Vermes, *Jesus the Jew: A Historian's Reading of the Gospels* (Philadelphia: Fortress, 1973), pp. 58–61; and for the ancient Jews' concept of the relationship of illness and sins, see Plich, *Healing*, pp. 47–48. Hooker, *Mark*, p. 85, suggests a good example from a Talmudic saying (*B. Nedarim* 41a): "No one gets up from his sick-bed until all his sins are forgiven." But see John 9.3–4 in which when questioned about "who sinned, this man or his parents, that he was born blind," Jesus says, "It was not that this man sinned, or his parents, but that the works of God might be made manifest in him" (RSV). This shows that the interconnection of sins and disease or illness was conventional, but not necessary, at least in John' s Gospel.

[74] Taylor, *Mark*, pp. 201–208; William Lane, *The Gospel According to Mark* (Grand Rapids, Michigan: Eerdmans, 1974), pp. 99–102.

2.2.1. Setting Markers: The SEASHORE *and the* HOUSE *Frame*
At the beginning of the second episode, Jesus, an on-going character, went by the sea where he met the crowd and taught. The beginning of the new episode is signalled by the new location marker (underlined): καὶ ἐξῆλθεν πάλιν <u>παρὰ τὴν θάλασσαν</u> (Mark 2.13). As a result, the spatial setting shifts from the house to the seashore. Such a SEASHORE frame, a place frame, because of its sense of geographical spaciousness, prepares the audience for comprehending the information to follow: πᾶς ὁ ὄχλος ἤρχετο πρὸς αὐτόν. Besides the setting of the event in verse 13, the frame plays a specific role in understanding the occurrence of a particular character in the story.[75] Then, verse 14 shows that Jesus encountered a tax collector, Levi, as "he passed by (παράγων)" the seaside. Information that the seaside is described as a place to meet a toll collector is not surprising in light of the place frame for SEASHORE at Capernaum since the custom booth was historically located at the seaside near Capernaum.[76]

Verse 15 signals the shift of the background place frame in which Jesus is described as probably going into Levi's house (ἐν τῇ οἰκίᾳ αὐτοῦ) opening the HOUSE frame. A chart of the HOUSE frame is as follows:

Verse	Frame Title	Prototypical Happenings
vv. 15/5a	τῇ οἰκίᾳ	κατακεῖσθαι
v. 15b		συνανέκειντο
v. 16		ἐσθίει (2x)

Then the subsequent story is focused on meal practices such as "reclining at the table" (κατακεῖσθαι and συνανέκειντο, v. 15) and "eating" (ἐσθίει, v. 16) which are highlighted not only in Jesus' having table fellowship with the tax collectors and sinners, and but also in the scribes of the Pharisees' accusing of him (vv. 15–16). The introduction of the eating issue is prepared by and rendered understandable in light of the HOUSE frame because having a meal is one of the typical acts occurring in a house (Mark 1.29–31; 14.3, 12–26). The SEASHORE

---

[75] Contra Marcus, *Mark 1–8*, p. 223.
[76] Taylor, *Mark*, p. 203; France, *Mark*, pp. 131–32; Donahue and Harrington, *Mark*, p. 101.

frame serves to set up a spatial setting for Jesus' calling of Levi, a tax collector, into discipleship; and now the HOUSE frame provides the background information for a place of Jesus' table fellowship with tax collectors and sinners.[77]

2.2.2. A Character Marker: The TAX COLLECTOR Frame

Despite the fact that there are two different spatial settings in this episode, it should be noted that as long as key topic participants are indicated as being present within an episode the audience's cognitive processing of it is semantically bounded. Charting the TAX COLLECTOR frame, we find:

Verse	Frame Title	Generic/metaphorical Reference	Default Element	Prototypical Actions
v. 14			τὸ τελώνιον	καθήμενον ἐπὶ τὸ τελώνιον
v. 15b	τελῶναι	ἁμαρτωλοί		
v. 16	τελωνῶν (2x)	ἁμαρτωλῶν (2x)		
v. 17		ἁμαρτωλούς οἱ κακῶς[78]		ἔχοντες [χρείαν …ἰατροῦ]

In the second episode, Levi serves to link verses 13–14 ("calling story") and verses 15–17 ("controversy story"); and in this linking the TAX COLLECTOR frame plays an important role (the person frame's trigger, or prototypical action, is underlined): Λευὶν…καθήμενον ἐπὶ τὸ τελώνιον. τὸ τελώνιον refers to a workplace and so an action of sitting at a custom booth. This is clearly stereotypic of a tax collector or a tax officer, and someone sitting on τὸ τελώνιον apparently activates the TAX COLLECTOR frame, a person frame. This can be supported by use of a grammatical indicator. The new information τὸ τελώνιον has a hearer-old marker, the Greek article; a possible explanation is that the text presumes that the tax office's role as a workplace for a tax collector

---

[77] Of course, the theme of table fellowship is semantically related to the CALLING TO DISCIPLESHIP frame; see Chapter Six.

[78] On metaphorical mapping of ἁμαρτωλοὶ and οἱ κακῶς, see section 5.2.3 in this chapter.

is semantically known to the audience through long-term memory. Thus, the open TAX COLLECTOR frame evoked by its prototypical action καθήμενον ἐπὶ τὸ τελώνιον, "sitting at the tax (toll) booth," naturally prepares the audience for the occurrence of tax collectors and sinners who are topic participants in the subsequent story.

But Levi's presence in the follow-up story (or among Jesus' meal associates) (vv. 15–17) may be doubted, given the text does not seem to make any explicit reference to Levi.[79] This doubt may be resolved by looking at the issue of just whose house it is where Jesus' table fellowship takes place. Verse 15 says the meal takes place ἐν τῇ οἰκίᾳ αὐτοῦ and indeed the pronoun used (αὐτοῦ) is ambiguous enough to refer to both Jesus and Levi. But the frame-based processing allows the audience to identify the referent of the pronoun with Levi. The assignment of the "his" reference depends on the background knowledge of who can play a role of host since the role of entity described by the pronoun is that of a host (note "his house"). Mark 1.29–31 showed that after being called by Jesus (Mark 1.16–17), the disciples (Simon and Andrew) played a role of hosting Jesus in their house to have table fellowship; hence, it is highly possible to believe that the CALL-ING TO DISCIPLESHIP frame[80] and the knowledge of its participant's (a disciple's) role that are activated in this passage just as in 1.16–20 enable the audience readily to assign the role of the host described by the pronoun to the disciple, Levi, called by Jesus, rather than Jesus. Of course, though it is not impossible to assign the hosting to Jesus, we need to remember that the Gospel of Mark shows little evidence to show that Jesus has a house in Capernaum.[81]

Indeed, in verses 15 and 16, the word τελῶναι repetitively occurs being conjoined by καί with ἁμαρτωλοί (the title of person frame is bolded): πολλοὶ **τελῶναι** καὶ ἁμαρτωλοί; συνανέκειντο τῷ Ἰησοῦ... ἐσθίει μετὰ τῶν ἁμαρτωλῶν καὶ **τελωνῶν**...μετὰ τῶν **τελωνῶν** καὶ ἁμαρτωλῶν ἐσθίει; In the conjoined nouns **τελῶναι** regularly comes first, except

---

[79] Thus, Guelich, *Mark 1–8.26*, p. 98, says, "after his call, he plays no further role in the story (2.15–17)." And also see Elizabeth S. Malbon, "TH OIKIA AYTOY: Mark 2.15 in Context," *NTS* 31 (1985), pp. 282–92. She argues that Jesus has a meal with the outcasts in his own house.

[80] For this frame, see Chapter Six.

[81] For scholars in favour of the assignment of the pronoun reference to Levi, see Marcus, *Mark 1–8*, p. 225. Yet, as Gundry, *Mark*, p. 127, says, "Perhaps Mark thinks that since Simon followed Jesus but Jesus entered Simon's house and ate there (1.29–31), it ought to be clear enough by precedent that Levi follows Jesus but Jesus goes to Levi's house for a meal."

for the second case.[82] Such conjoined nouns indicate that they refer to the single entity. H.W. Smyth points out that the Greek καί, besides its copulative function, serves to add "the whole" to "a part," namely, "the universal" to "the particular," or vice versa. [83] It can be then best explained that the second group (ἁμαρτωλοί) of the conjoined nouns is a generalization of τελῶναι or tax collectors are a subset of sinners.[84] There is, in fact, no reference to the tax collectors in Jesus' final defensive pronouncement, but only the sinners (bolded): οὐκ ἦλθον καλέσαι δικαίους ἀλλὰ ἁμαρτωλούς (v. 17). This may seem to disprove the tax collectors' role as a topic character in this episode. However, it must be remembered that for the first-century Jewish audience, tax collectors and sinners were stereotypically associated with one another to represent the semantically same concept or a single frame, that is, "blatant violators of the Mosaic covenant."[85] This can be supported in grammatical terms. In verse 16, Mark makes use of one Greek article for both the nouns conjoined by καί: τῶν ἁμαρτωλῶν καὶ τελωνῶν. Carson says, "If one article governs two substantives joined by καί, it does not necessarily follow that the two substantives refer to the same thing, but only that the two substantives are grouped together to function in some respect as a single entity."[86] If so, it becomes evident that, in the second episode, the tax collectors and sinners are used interchangeably to refer to the single semantic information or frame (deliberate violators of the Mosaic covenant). This means that, though no explicit lexeme of the tax collector is used, the tax collectors are also semantically implicit in the concept of "sinners" in Jesus' final pronouncement too. Accordingly, it is likely that, regardless of the switch of the setting information, the topic TAX COLLECTOR frame,

---

[82] This is, according to Dewey, *Public Debate*, p. 83, because of Mark's "chiastic order (eats, sinners, tax collectors/tax collectors, sinners, eats)."

[83] Herbert W. Smyth, *Greek Grammar* (Cambridge, Massachusetts: Harvard University Press, 1956), § 2869. And also see BDAG, καί 1.a.γ. For example, consider οἱ ἀρχιερεῖς καὶ τὸ συνέδριον ὅλον ("the high priest and all the rest of the council") in Matthew 26.59.

[84] Marcus, *Mark 1–8*, p. 226.

[85] See Sanders, *Jesus and Judaism*, pp. 174–211, esp. 178, for the following quotation: "Thus we know in general terms who the wicked were, and we can readily understand why 'tax collectors' and 'sinners' go together in several passages in the Gospels: they were all traitors. Tax collectors, more precisely, were quislings, collaborating with Rome. The wicked equally betrayed the God who redeemed Israel and gave them his law. There was no neat distinction between 'religious' and 'political' betrayal in first-century Judaism."

[86] Carson, *Exegetical Fallacies*, pp. 84–85 (cited also by Hoyle, "Scenarios," p. 210).

including its explicit and implicit information, helps cluster 2.13–17 into a semantically coherent episodic unit.

2.3. The Third Episode (Mark 2.18–22)

Mark 2.18–22 is an apparently new episode distinct from the preceding one (2.13–17). This is evident at least from the shift of the topic participants (bolded): Καὶ ἦσαν **οἱ μαθηταὶ Ἰωάννου** καὶ **οἱ Φαρισαῖοι** νηστεύοντες (v. 18a). The tax collectors and sinners of Mark 2.13–17 disappear at the beginning of the fourth episode; instead John the Baptist and the Pharisees are indicated as its new participants. Nonetheless, the characters play no further role in the story after being mentioned briefly in the introductory narrative and in the question of Jesus' opponents at the beginning of the episode (v. 18a and b). And the text does not express in what spatial and temporal setting the controversy takes place. In other words, the setting and character markers do not contribute to determining the boundaries of the third episode. Instead, since there is a dominant topic of conflict between Jesus and his opponents over fasting throughout the episode, we will be concerned in section 2.3 to follow with the role that the LEGAL CONTROVERSY frame instantiated by that topic plays in a semantically coherent processing of the episode.

2.4. The Fourth Episode (Mark 2.23–28)

Although a topic character does not appear in it, the fourth episode clearly marks its temporal and spatial settings at the beginning of the story.

2.4.1. Setting Markers: The SABBATH Frame and the GRAINFIELD Frame

Verse 23 says (the temporal and spatial setting markers are underlined): Καὶ ἐγένετο αὐτὸν <u>ἐν τοῖς σάββασιν</u> παραπορεύεσθαι διὰ <u>τῶν σπορίμων</u>. As a frame title τοῖς σάββασιν clearly opens the SABBATH frame for the audience. Consider the chart of the SABBATH frame:

Verse	Frame Title	Prototypical Question
v. 23	ἐν τοῖς σάββασιν	
v. 24	τοῖς σάββασιν	τί ποιοῦσιν…ὃ οὐκ ἔξεστιν
v. 27	τὸ σάββατον (2x)	
v. 28	τοῦ σαββάτου	

What should be noted is a hearer-old marker, the Greek article, preceding the noun τοῖς σάββασιν, whose article is used to encourage information already known to the audience's long-term memory of sabbath. In this episode, the SABBATH frame contributes to the semantic coherence of this episode, not only by virtue of the linguistic repetition of its title (vv. 24, 27–28), but also by opening its prototypical information of sabbath regulations in which no work should be done. The observance of such sabbath laws, along with ritual purity and circumcision, is one of the principal distinguishing marks of the ancient Jews as the people of God (Exodus 16.22–30; 34.21; 35.2–3; Numbers 15.32–36; Nehemiah 10.31; 13.15–22; Jeremiah 17.21–22; 1 Maccabees 2.29–41; *Jubliees* 50.6–13; CD 10.14–11.18).[87] With respect to the disciples' behaviour, the reason that the use of the legal question in verse 24 (τί ποιοῦσιν … ὃ οὐκ ἔξεστιν) may be understandable is because of the frame's prototypical knowledge of the sabbath laws.[88] Likewise, such SABBATH frame knowledge enables interpretation of the meaning of Jesus' appeal to the Son of Man's authority as "lord of the sabbath" in verse 27. Jesus claims here that the Son of Man has authority beyond all 'the sabbath laws,' not just the sabbath as a day.[89]

The geographical location of the episode, the grainfields, opens the GRAINFIELD frame, a scene frame, as the background setting of this controversy story. Consider the chart of the GRAINFIELD frame:

Verse	Frame Title	Default Element	Prototypical Action
vv. 23/23b	τῶν σπορίμων	τοὺς στάχυας	ὁδὸν ποιεῖν τίλλοντες τοὺς στάχυας (ἔφαγεν)—implied

---

[87] It is well known that the Pharisaic and rabbinic tradition was vitally concerned with delineating what could and could not be done on the sabbath. See Schürer, *The History of the Jewish People*. Vol. 2, pp. 467–75 and Sanders, *Jewish Law*, pp. 6–23.

[88] Most of the modern commentators on Mark's Gospel infer that issues such as sabbath laws and observance are apparently involved in the conflict between Jesus and the Pharisees in this episode (and also 3.1–6), though the text includes no direct assertive explanation of the relationship of "sabbath" to "laws." This shows that the modern commentators themselves unwittingly presuppose and make use of SABBATH frame knowledge opened by the lexical items like τοῖς σάββασιν and τί ποιοῦσιν … ὃ οὐκ ἔξεστιν. For those commentaries, see Taylor, *Mark*, pp. 214–24; Lane, *Mark*, 114–26; Guelich, *Mark 1–8.26*, pp. 117–41; France, *Mark*, pp. 142–52.

[89] For a detailed argument for this, see Chapter Six.

The opening of the GRAINFIELD frame can be supported by the textual evidence that, though initially occurring in the episode, the word "grainfield" has the Greek article τῶν σπορίμων. In this case the Greek article is there to open the prototypical knowledge stored in the audience's long-term memory associated with a grainfield. Consequently, the frame enables the audience to understand the subsequent events coherently. In verse 23b "heads of grain" is also marked with the Greek article τοὺς στάχυας, even though it is used as new information in the episode. Here, the article apparently refers to the heads of grain that are prototypically present in the open GRAINFIELD frame, namely, the grain grown in the field. Moreover, the GRAINFIELD frame helps to understand Jesus' use of the David example (the eating issues are underlined):

τί ἐποίησεν Δαυὶδ ὅτε <u>χρείαν ἔσχεν</u> καὶ <u>ἐπείνασεν</u> αὐτὸς καὶ οἱ μετ' αὐτοῦ, πῶς εἰσῆλθεν εἰς τὸν οἶκον τοῦ θεοῦ ἐπὶ Ἀβιαθὰρ ἀρχιερέως καὶ <u>τοὺς ἄρτους</u> τῆς προθέσεως <u>ἔφαγεν</u>, οὓς οὐκ ἔξεστιν <u>φαγεῖν</u> εἰ μὴ τοὺς ἱερεῖς, καὶ ἔδωκεν καὶ τοῖς σὺν αὐτῷ οὖσιν;

When the Pharisees charge Jesus' disciples with plucking grain on the Sabbath, Jesus defends his disciples by appealing to David's precedent of eating "the bread of the presence" and giving it to his companions. Yet it seems quite strange on the surface that Jesus refers to David's action of eating and sharing with his fellows, given the text does not mention that the disciples ate the heads of grain after reaping them.[90] However, the GRAINFIELD frame stored in the audience's mind would lead them to make a semantic connection between the disciples' plucking of the heads of grain and Jesus' reference to the David case. Frame theory proposes that the action sequences of the frame mentioned in the text must be assumed to proceed to its completion, unless they are otherwise marked. This means that the disciples' action of "plucking heads of grain" in verse 23, which is a prototypical action in the GRAINFIELD frame, allows the audience to make inferences that its next action stage (eating) was done on the part of the disciples. Jesus' use of the David example, which includes the issue of eating, for the defence of his disciples' conduct is not unexpected. The frames for

---

[90] Thus, Guelich, *Mark 1–8.26*, p. 123, says that nothing comparable exists between Jesus' conduct and David's in that whereas David's behaviour "involved illegally eating the showbread, the disciples' conduct involved illegal work on the sabbath. Consequently, the only apparent common ground lies in the doing of something forbidden by law."

SABBATH and GRAINFIELD, thus, would help the audience process the fourth story as a semantically bounded episodic unit.

2.5. *The Fifth Episode (Mark 3.1–6)*

While Mark 3.1–6 and 2.23–28 are linked together in a temporal setting of the sabbath, thus in continuation of the SABBATH frame, the present story evidently marks the shift of episodic boundary by means of a new physical location of the synagogue and introduction of a new topic participant, a man with a "withered" hand.

2.5.1. *A Setting Marker: The SYNAGOGUE Frame*
We find the chart of the SYNAGOGUE frame as follows:

Verse	Frame Title	Default Elements	Pototypical Participants	Prototypical action
v. 1a	τὴν συναγωγήν	τοῖς σάββασιν		εἰσῆλθεν … εἰς
v. 3		τὸ μέσον		
v. 6			οἱ Φαρισαῖοι	ἐξελθόντες

The text provides lexical items to help a cognitive processing of the physical setting of the episode (the place frame title is bolded): εἰσῆλθεν … εἰς **τὴν συναγωγήν**. The lexeme τὴν συναγωγήν, with the Greek article, evokes the SYNAGOGUE knowledge stored in the original audience's mental frame (e.g., the synagogue building, the typical events happening, the participants in the events, and a visiting day). The open SYNAGOGUE frame enables the audience to expect that the sabbath (τοῖς σάββασιν) will be mentioned in the text (v. 2). This is because it is prototypical knowledge that the sabbath was a regular day for attending a synagogue (e.g., Mark 1.21; 6.2).[91] The SYNAGOGUE frame operative in this story helps us to understand the sick person's particular way of acting according to its typical spatial layout. In verse 3, Jesus commands: ἔγειρε εἰς τὸ μέσον. The text does not spell out into the middle (τὸ μέσον) of what place the man should "stand up." Though it is new information in the immediate text, the word τὸ μέσον has the Greek article, a hearer-old marker. The use of the article here

---

[91] Moore, *Judaism*. Vol. 2, p. 38. Consider that "going to church" prototypically opens information of Sunday as a visiting day of the church.

may be readily explained when we take it into consideration that the SYNAGOGUE frame is already opened at the beginning of the episode, and it is prototypical knowledge in the frame that a synagogue building has a middle part. In narrative discourse processing, the hearer-old marker leads the audience to associate τὸ μέσον with a specific place in the mental SYNAGOGUE frame. If so, no doubt the audience's mental frame that those attending a synagogue sat on stone benches around the walls or squatted on the floor enabled understanding of Jesus' command as implying that the man with a crippled hand should walk into *the middle of the synagogue so that all participants may see him.*[92] This is also the case for verse 6. Although verse 6 καὶ ἐξελθόντες οἱ Φαρισαῖοι does not explicitly mention from where they went out, the open SYNAGOGUE frame fills in the missing information in the text, thus meaning that 'the Pharisees went out *from the synagogue.*' The Pharisees, moreover, suddenly pop up in 3.6, implying that their exisence has been presupposed throughtout the story. This is not surprising in light of the SYNAGOGUE frame, given the frame involves religious leaders like the Pharisees as its prototypical participants (cf., a correlation of ἡ συναγωγή and οἱ γραμματεῖς in Mark 1.21–22 and 12.38–39) and thus the Pharisees are assumed throughout the episode.[93] Note the Greek article as a hearer-old marker before the words οἱ Φαρισαῖοι (v. 6); this shows their presence is already known by the audience's long-term memory.

2.5.2. *A Character Marker: "The Man with A Withered Hand" Frame*
Note the chart of "the Man with a withered hand" frame:

Verse	Frame Title	Prototypical Actions
v. 1b	ἄνθρωπος ἐξηραμμένην ἔχων τὴν χεῖρα	
v. 2		θεραπεύσει αὐτόν

---

[92] Guelich, *Mark 1–8.26*, p. 134.
[93] With regard to the Pharisees in time of Jesus, Schürer, *The History of the Jewish People*. Vol. 2, p. 402, says, "…the Pharisees maintained their leadership in spiritual matters…. They held the greatest authority over the congregations, so that everything to do with worship, prayer, and sacrifice took place according to their instructions." As Moore, *Judaism*. Vol. 1, p. 287, says, "The synagogue in the hands of the Pharisees was doubtless the chief instrument in the Judaizing of Galilee."

(*cont.*)

Verse	Frame Title	Prototypical Actions
v. 3	τῷ ἀνθρώπῳ τῷ τὴν ξηρὰν χεῖρα ἔχοντι	
v. 5		ἔκτεινον τὴν χεῖρα
v. 5b		ἐξέτεινεν καὶ ἀπεκατεστάθη ἡ χεὶρ αὐτοῦ

Mark 3.1b marks the beginning of a new episode by introducing a new topic character into a story (the person frame title is bolded): καὶ ἦν ἐκεῖ **ἄνθρωπος ἐξηραμμένην ἔχων τὴν χεῖρα**. The description of the character with a specific type of disease opens the semantic information, or frame, of the sick person as a subunit of the HEALING frame. Such semantic information leads the audience to the expectation of Jesus' acts of healing in the subsequent story; and this is exactly what the Pharisees expect in a storyline, as shown in verse 2 (the trigger of the HEALING frame is bolded): παρετήρουν αὐτὸν εἰ...**θεραπεύσει** αὐτόν. Thus, because of the frames for SICK PERSON and HEALING, Jesus' commands (ἔγειρε εἰς τὸ μέσον in v. 3 and ἔκτεινον τὴν χεῖρα in v. 5) and the man's action (ἐξέτεινεν in v. 5b) can be said to have the semantic cohesion to represent the processes of healing; otherwise the meaning of such actions does not make sense at all.

3. Frames Bind Episodic Units in Terms of their Prototypical Event Sequences

We have already argued that the properties or slots that characterize the LEGAL CONTROVERSY frame in Mark 2.1–3.6 consist of such event sequences as provocative events, charge, defence and verdict, and as a result, they play a part in organizing the whole of the five episodes into a single thematic unit. Here I will be concerned with how such prototypical event sequences of the LEGAL CONTROVERSY frame help structure each episode in that thematic unit into a semantically bounded entity, thus serving as episodic boundary markers. As Fillmore claims:

> [K]nowing that a text is, say, an obituary, a proposal of marriage, a business contract, or a folktale, provides knowledge about how to interpret particular passages in it, how to expect the text to develop, and how to know when it is finished. It is frequently the case that such expectations combine with the actual material of the text to lead to the text's correct interpretation. And once again this is accomplished by having in mind an abstract structure of expectations which brings with it roles, purposes,

natural or conventionalized sequences of event types, and all the rest of the apparatus that we wish to associate with the notion of 'frame.'[94]

This section will assert that the LEGAL CONTROVERSY frame is a cognitive structure whereby one may process and interpret the information of each episode in that thematic unit, and, in particular, its prototypical event sequences organize individual episodes in causal (link structure) and hierarchical (part-whole structure) terms. The frame's sequential events enable the audience to recognize and expect not only when a framed episode begins and ends, but also how it develops.

3.1. The First Episode (Mark 2.1–12)

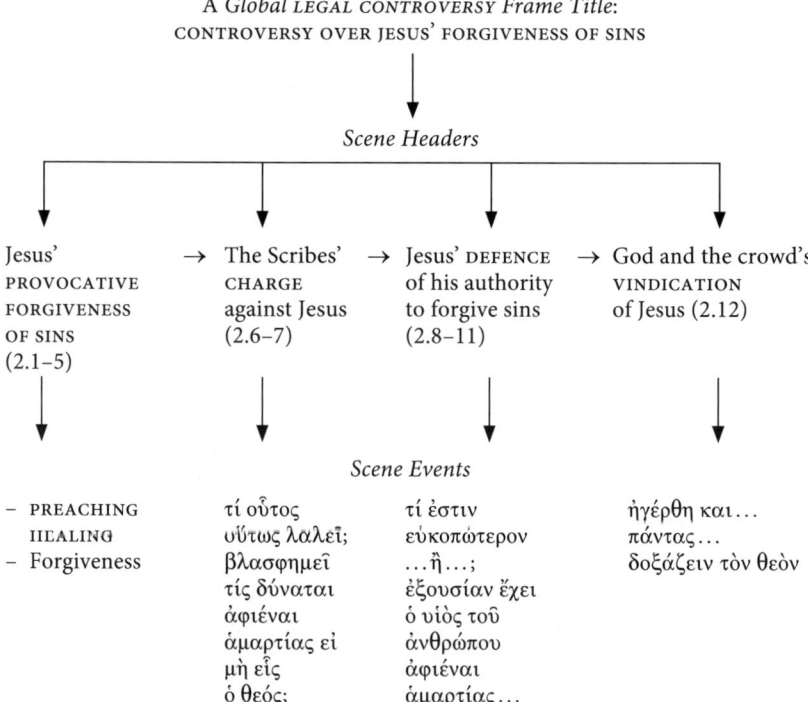

A *Global* LEGAL CONTROVERSY *Frame Title:*
CONTROVERSY OVER JESUS' FORGIVENESS OF SINS

Scene Headers

| Jesus' PROVOCATIVE FORGIVENESS OF SINS (2.1–5) | → The Scribes' CHARGE against Jesus (2.6–7) | → Jesus' DEFENCE of his authority to forgive sins (2.8–11) | → God and the crowd's VINDICATION of Jesus (2.12) |

Scene Events

| – PREACHING HEALING – Forgiveness | τί οὗτος οὕτως λαλεῖ; βλασφημεῖ τίς δύναται ἀφιέναι ἁμαρτίας εἰ μὴ εἷς ὁ θεός; | τί ἐστιν εὐκοπώτερον …ἢ…; ἐξουσίαν ἔχει ὁ υἱὸς τοῦ ἀνθρώπου ἀφιέναι ἁμαρτίας… | ἠγέρθη καὶ… πάντας… δοξάζειν τὸν θεὸν |

Figure 2: Instantiation of the LEGAL CONTROVERSY Frame in Mark 2.1–12

---

[94] Fillmore, "Frame Semantics," p. 117.

The figure above shows that the prototypical slots (provocative events, charge, defence and verdict) of the LEGAL CONTROVERSY frame are well 'instantiated'[95] by the properties of the story in the first episode. The LEGAL CONTROVERSY frame instantiated in Mark 2.1–12 is represented in a hierarchical structure which, as a global frame title CONTROVERSY OVER JESUS' FORGIVENESS OF SINS, contains its four scene headers (or event sequences): Jesus' provocative action of forgiving sins, the scribe's charge, Jesus' defence of his authority to forgive sins, and God and the onlookers' verdict. And then each scene header has its 'subevents,' including subframes that are embedded into the header at a higher level. Next, the instantiated event sequences are connected with each other in a causal chain (link structure). The paralytic's visiting (vv. 1–4) *enables* Jesus to pronounce the forgiveness of sins (v. 5). And such forgiveness *causes* the scribe to charge Jesus with blasphemy (v. 7). In turn, the scribes' charge *leads to* Jesus' defence of his authority for forgiveness (vv. 7–11). Finally, Jesus' defence *results in* God and the crowd's vindication of Jesus (v. 12).

3.1.1. *Provocative Action: Jesus' Pronouncement of Forgiveness of Sins (Mark 2.1–5)*

In the first stage, Jesus is depicted as pronouncing boldly the forgiveness of the paralytic's sins: τέκνον, ἀφίενταί σου αἱ ἁμαρτίαι (v. 5). The meaning of this announcement should be understood against the background knowledge or frame associated with the forgiveness of sins in first-century Jewish culture, a knowledge that forgiveness is God's prerogative (Exodus 34.6–7; Isaiah 43.25; 44.22).[96] So the audience's

---

[95] For the term instantiation, see glossary.

[96] Some scholars have argued that here the conflict between Jesus and the scribes is not about Jesus' behaving as God, dispensing forgiveness, but Jesus' claim for his authority beyond the officially established and authorized channels of forgiveness of sins in first-century Palestinian Judaism, that is, the temple sacrifice and priesthood. This postulation has been made mainly by proponents of what is called "new covenantism." See Sanders, *Judaism*, pp. 240, 273; Dunn, *Partings of the Ways*, pp. 45–46; Wright, *Jesus*, pp. 434–44. However, what we can say in light of frame theory is that for Mark's original audience the temple sacrifice and priesthood could be components (or default values) in the FORGIVENESS OF SINS frame. But in the subsequent text (in particular, in the scribe's charge and Jesus' defence) the most evocative information is Jesus' taking up of an exclusively divine prerogative, that is, God's role of forgiving sins. Furthermore, noting the passive voice, ἀφίενται. E.P. Sanders, *The Historical Jesus* (London: Penguin, 1993), pp. 213–24, asserts that the historical Jesus did not try to take the place of God by pronouncing the forgiveness of the man's sins since "the text does not have Jesus say, 'I forgive your sins' but 'your sins are forgiven',

mental frame for FORGIVENESS OF SINS must have regarded such a statement as highly provocative given the Jews' concern for guarding the uniqueness of God. Jesus' pronouncement of forgiveness of sins in this episode serves as a condition for the LEGAL CONTROVERSY frame due to its confrontational nature relative to Jewish religious belief, and so it is transferred to the first scene header in the LEGAL CONTROVERSY frame, that is, a provocative event. To be sure, in addition to such a statement of Jesus, there is in the first stage a lengthy narrative (vv. 1–4) which consists of two frames (PREACHING and HEALING). The two frames both serve to develop the story toward Jesus' announcement by providing relevant background information. The PREACHING frame, as already discussed, consists of its prototypical actions, such as an agent's (preacher's) entering, people gathering, and the agent's preaching (or teaching) (vv. 1–2).[97] By providing information about the crowding people the PREACHING frame, along with the HOUSE frame (see Chapter Six), helps the hearer understand the reason for the paralytic initiating an unexpected way of approaching Jesus. The other is the HEALING frame, which is opened by reference to the sick (a core component in the HEALING frame) and his visiting (the relevant frame components are underlined): καὶ <u>ἔρχονται</u> <u>φέροντες</u> πρὸς αὐτὸν <u>παραλυτικὸν</u> αἰρόμενον ὑπὸ τεσσάρων (v. 3).[98] The HEALING frame, by providing its prototypical knowledge of a close link between 'spiritual' sin and physical disease, also enabled the audience to be prepared for Jesus' pronouncement of forgiveness of the paralytic's sins.

3.1.2. *Charge: The Scribes' Charge against Jesus Making a Claim to Forgive Sins (Mark 2.6–7)*

This scene involves the information regarding the scribes' presence and their questioning (the relevant frame is bolded; the frame-related information is underlined and the contraexpectation marker is italicized): ἦσαν *δ'ε* **τινες τῶν γραμματέων** ἐκεῖ καθήμενοι καὶ <u>διαλογιζόμενοι</u> ἐν ταῖς καρδίαις αὐτῶν. There is clear textual evidence

---

in the passive voice." Thus, Sanders says that such a claim "would not be unique or especially offensive." But Sanders' position is not how Mark and his audience understood the story because the text clearly spells out Jesus' authority to forgive (v. 10) and that he is accused as blaspheming (v. 6).

[97] See Chapter Four.

[98] For the sequential events of the HEALING frame in the Gospel of Mark, see Chapter Four.

for cognitive processing of a charge against Jesus in this stage. First of all, the SCRIBE frame, as already discussed, activates social stereotypes related to the interpreter of the law; hence the reference to τινες τῶν γραμματέων occurring right after Jesus' pronouncement of sins would be stimulating enough to activate specifically controversial information within the audience's mental frame regarding Jesus' forgiveness. Next, the evaluative statement in a negative tone, "he is blaspheming," inserted between the two questions (τί οὗτος οὕτως λαλεῖ; and τίς δύναται ἀφιέναι ἁμαρτίας εἰ μὴ εἷς ὁ θεός;) reveals the hidden motive of the questioners. Indeed the appropriate understanding of the expression βλασφημεῖ strongly requires the activation of an appropriate frame for the word, or the role of the expression in a Jewish cultural context, and hence the audience probably needed to draw on the information related to blasphemy: God was revered as the only One God (Deuternomy 6.4–5); forgiveness of sins was God's prerogative; there were people with professional expertise for estimating the commitment of blasphemy (e.g., members of the Sanhedrin).[99] Blasphemy is directly related to the unforgivable sin; the one who affronted the majesty of God deserved the death penalty (Leviticus 24.16; 1 Kings 21.13; 1QS 4.11; CD 5.12; Mark 3.29; 14.64; Philo, *vita Mosis* 2.206; Josephus, *Jewish Antiquities* 4.202).[100] The argument is that this knowledge came together in the frame for βλασφημεῖ and so the frame enabled the audience to interpret that the scribes accused Jesus of affronting God by arrogating his divine prerogatives.[101]

Finally, the conjuction δέ at the beginning of verse six may be best understood as playing the role of a contraexpectation marker. Certainly δέ has different uses other than adversative; so RSV translates δέ as "now." Yet the three things, such as the provocative tone opened by Jesus' proclamation of forgiveness, the occurrence of the legal experts

---

[99] For the judicial role and members of the Sanhedrin prior to 70 C.E., see Schürer, *The History of Jewish People*. Vol. 2, pp. 200–23 (the quotation to follow from pp. 210–13). The key figures in the Sanhedrin in Jesus' day, according to Schürer, included the chief priest and scribes.

[100] Philo, *de vita Mosis* 2.206 (LCL; trans. F.H. Colson; Cambridge, Massachusetts: Harvard University Press, 1935), says: "But if anyone, I will not say blasphemes [βλασφημεῖν] the Lord of Gods and men, but even ventures to utter His Name unseasonably, let him suffer the penalty of death." On the concepts of blasphemy used by the ancient Jews, see Sanders, *Jewish Law*, pp. 57–67; Block, *Blasphemy and Exaltation*; Evans, *Mark 8.27–16.20*, pp. 452–55.

[101] Bock, *Blasphemy and Exaltation*, p. 188.

and subsequent negative comments from the scribes, lead us to believe that verse six beginning with δὲ is in adversative relation to the provious clause(s). This implies that Jesus' action of pronouncing the forgiveness of sins was taken by the scribes as a violation of their frame for FORGING SINS. Hence the information in verses 6-7 can best be processed in terms of such a scene header as the scribes' charge against Jesus making a claim to the forgiveness of sins.

3.1.3. Defence: Jesus' Defence of His Authority to Forgive (Mark 2.8-11)
The third event scene begins with Jesus' counter-questioning the scribes (the repetitive word is underlined):

καὶ εὐθὺς ἐπιγνοὺς ὁ Ἰησοῦς τῷ πνεύματι αὐτοῦ
ὅτι οὕτως <u>διαλογίζονται</u> ἐν ἑαυτοῖς λέγει αὐτοῖς·
τί ταῦτα <u>διαλογίζεσθε</u> ἐν ταῖς καρδίαις ὑμῶν;

In verse 8 the agent of the action shifts from τινες τῶν γραμματέων (verse 6) to ὁ Ἰησοῦς. Given the open LEGAL CONTROVERSY frame, the shift of the agent means that the current part of the story leads the audience to focus on the perspective of a defendant, Jesus.[102] Moreover, the repetitive use of the word διαλογίζομαι in association with Jesus' response, which was also used in the scribes' hostile questioning (διαλογιζόμενοι ἐν ταῖς καρδίαις αὐτῶν in v. 6), encourages the audience to understand Jesus' subsequent sayings and actions as direct responses to the scribes' challenging questions. His subsequent reply consists of the question of what is a simpler thing (v. 9), the Son of Man's authority (v. 10) and the healing of the paralytic (v. 11). Using a rhetorical question, the Markan Jesus refers in the first place to the audience's typical knowledge of which is simpler, to say the word of forgiveness or to heal. It would be normal to accept that it is easier to affirm the forgiveness of sins than to heal a person's sickness in terms of external proof (note the contraexpectation marker δὲ in verse 10 before Jesus' pronouncement of healing, which indicates that Jesus can perform an even harder task of curing the sick); so Jesus' healing of the

---

[102] The importance of subject position in sentence and discourse has been discussed in the fields of discourse analysis and linguistics. In particular, "sentential topic," that is "what a sentence is about," is usually determined by sentential subjects or initial noun-phrases. See John Lyons, *Introduction to Theoretical Linguistics* (Cambridge: Cambridge University Press, 1969), pp. 334-37 and Sanford and Garrod, *Understanding*, pp. 136-39.

paralytic that follows, which is a harder thing, confirms his authority to forgive sins, a simpler thing which he had already done.

Next, Jesus defends his power to forgive by appealing to the authority of the Son of Man. Here, it must be noted that the use of the power of the Son of Man for Jesus' defence depends on the opening of the relevant SON OF MAN frame based on scriptural knowledge. The phrase ὁ υἱὸς τοῦ ἀνθρώπου and his role refer to an apocalyptic figure "like a son of man (υἱὸς ἀνθρώπου, LXX)" in Daniel 7.13–14 who is given divine authority from the Heavenly being to rule earthly nations at 'eschatology.'"[103] Note, first of all, in the phrase ὁ υἱὸς τοῦ ἀνθρώπου, a hearer-old marker, the Greek article, before the nouns means the title was already known to the audience and here draws the audience's attention to the role of the apocalyptic figure in Daniel 7.[104] This opening of the Danielic figure in verse 10 is confirmed by Mark's use of the words, ἐπὶ τῆς γῆς, "upon the earth," υἱὸς ἀνθρώπου, "Son of Man," and ἐξουσία, "authority," as in Daniel 7.13–14, 17. Further, as Wright rightly notes, there is a thematic correspondence between the Markan ὁ υἱὸς τοῦ ἀνθρώπου and the Danielic figure: Just as the Danielic figure plays a role of vindicating "the saints of the most high" in the situation of *controversy* with the pagans in the co-text (Daniel 7.22–28), so the Markan ὁ υἱὸς τοῦ ἀνθρώπου is described as defending his authority in *controversy* with his opponents.[105] Thus, for Mark's audience Jesus,

---

[103] The Son of Man title has been one of the most debated issues in biblical studies for years. Numerous issues surround the discussion, including the title's association with Daniel 7 and whether it is an idiom (thus a circumlocutory expression for a speaker himself that can be replaced by "I") or representative of a title. See, for example, Morna D. Hooker, *The Son of Man in Mark* (Montreal: McGill University Press, 1967); Vermes, *Jesus the Jew*, pp. 16–91; Barnabas Lindars, *Jesus Son of Man* (Grand Rapids: Eerdmans, 1983); Seyoon Kim, *"The 'Son of Man'" as the Son of God* (Grand Rapids, Michigan: Eerdmans, 1985); Chrys C. Caragounis, *The Son of Man* (WUNT 38; Tübingen: J.C.B. Mohr (Paul Siebeck), 1986): I.H. Marshall, "Son of Man," in *Dictionary of Jesus and the Gospels* (ed. Joel B. Green, Scot McKnight and I. Howard Marshall; Downers Grove, Illinois: IVP, 1992), pp. 775–81. The title's association with Danielic figure must be decided in the passage in which the title occurs. The majority of scholars agree that here in Mark 2.10 the title clearly refers to the Danielic figure. See Kim, *"The Son of Man,"* pp. 89–94; Caragounis, *The Son of Man*, pp. 179–88; Hooker, *The Son of Man*, pp. 81–93; Lindars, *Jesus*, pp. 44–47.

[104] The title of the Son of Man occurs 81 times altogether in the four canonical Gospels (14 times in Mark, 30 in Matthew, 25 in Luke, and 12 in John) and in all these cases the Greek article is without exception used for that title. See Larry W. Hurtado, *Lord Jesus Christ. Devotion to Jesus in Earliest Christianity* (Grand Rapids, Michigan/Cambridge, U.K.: Eerdmans, 2003), p. 291.

[105] Wright, *The People of God*, p. 432, claims that "within the original contexts [of the controversy stories] the most natural Jewish way for supporters of Jesus to

as the Son of Man to whom God has granted the power to forgive sins, now exercises that authority over the paralytic. Finally, Jesus demonstrates his authority to forgive sins by physically healing the paralytic.[106] Jesus' use of physical healing as approval for his authority to forgive sins must have made perfect sense in the original audience's HEALING frame, in which illness (effect) and sins (cause) are prototypically interwoven.

3.1.4. *Verdict: God and the Onlooker's Vindication of Jesus (Mark 2.12)*

Once more, the LEGAL CONTROVERSY frame plays the role of a global frame; so it enables to determine the audience's cognitive processing of the meaning of this stage. It is important to keep in mind the notion that a framed text leads the audience to comprehend it from the perspective of particular participants in the frame. And no doubt a particular perspective is reflected in the use of specific lexemes and grammatical structures.[107] This final event stage (Verdict) in the LEGAL CONTROVERSY frame foregrounds the perspectives of God (note the passive ἠγέρθη, see below) and the onlooker (bolded [ὥστε ἐξίστασθαι, **πάντας** καιδοξάζειν τὸν θεὸν]) with those of Jesus and his critics being backgrounded. This shift of the perspective of the participants leads the audience to see and evaluate the conflict from the point of view of participants other than the accuser and the defendant.

I have already discussed that the episode in Mark 2.1–12 ends with God and the onlooker's vindication.[108] Vincent Taylor suggests that the reason for the crowd's glorification of God and thus vindication of Jesus is because of the healing of the paralytic, not the forgiveness of sins. Taylor believes that Mark 2.1–12 is a composite of a healing story and controversy story.[109] Yet, though Jesus' healing may be a direct reason for the crowd's glorification of God, the assumption that

---

tell stories about his controversial actions and words was to tell them in the form of Jewish controversy stories, such as we find...in the book of Daniel"; "In the greatest Danielic controversy and vindication story of all, it is 'one like a son of man' who is vindicated. The gospel stories have this exact same form, and as often as not end with a reference to Jesus as the 'son of man'."

[106] Caragounis, *The Son of Man*, p. 188.
[107] See Chapter Four.
[108] Taylor, *Mark*, p. 199.
[109] Taylor, *Mark*, pp. 191–92.

forgiveness and healing are interconnected concepts in the audience's mental frame leads us to believe that the crowd's glorification and amazement are caused by both Jesus' power to forgive and the physical healing. The implication is that Jesus' right to forgive is also being vindicated by the onlooker.

Jesus' words for healing (ἔγειρε ἆρον τὸν κράβαττον σου καὶ ὕπαγε εἰς τὸν οἶκον σου) in verse 11 are followed immediately by the healing of the man: ἠγέρθη (v. 12). The text makes use of the aorist passive verb in conceptualizing the healing of the man. Who is the semantic subject that Mark had in mind when using the passive verb? There are important reasons to believe that Mark's original audiences may have processed God as the ultimate agent of this healing or curing. Ancient Jews had a religious belief that God is responsible for "wondrous works," such as healing and exorcism.[110] This is reflected in Jesus' thought of his exorcism (Mark 3.23–30; Matthew 12.24–32; Luke 11.14–23): Jesus asserts that he casts demons out by τὸ πνεῦμα τὸ ἅγιον (Mark 3.29; πνεύματι θεοῦ in Matthew 12.28; δακτύλῳ θεοῦ in Luke 11.20).[111] If so, provided mental frame influences the language user's choice of grammatical category, it is not impossible to believe that such a religious belief enabled his audience to process God as the semantic agent of the passive verb. This can be supported by the co-text in which the GOD frame has been opened explicitly and implicitly throughout the episode, as shown in verse 7; and, more relevantly, verse 12, in which the onlookers "glorified God" (καὶ δοξάζειν τὸν

---

[110] Thus, according to Josephus, *Jewish Antiquities* 20.97–99, 167–72; *idem, Jewish War* 2.258–63, many popular leaders or prophets in first-century Palestine attempted to perform signs or miracles, just as Moses performed signs by God's power (*Jewish Antiquities* 20.286). Sander, *Jesus*, p. 171, argues that "their promised signs were doubtless intended to prove that they were who they said, and that God truly acted through them." Similarly, Wright, *Jesus*, p. 191, states that for Jesus and his followers the mighty works he performed would be seen as "signs that the kingdom of Israel's god was indeed coming to birth." And, referring to Jesus Ben Sira's *Ecclesiasticus*, Vermes, *Jesus the Jew*, p. 59, says that for ancient Jews the physician's action of healing does not "originate from the regions of darkness; it is a divine gift"; thus when sick he is "to pray to God, to repent from sin, to resolve to amend his ways, and to offer gifts and sacrifices in the Temple." Cf. Exodus 15.26: "...I will put none of the diseases upon you which I put upon the Egyptians; for I am the Lord, your healer"; Deuternomy 32.39: "See now that I, even I, am he, and there is no god beside me; I kill and I make alive; I wound and I heal..." (RSV).

[111] Cf. Mark's use of passive verbs in his other healing episodes, see Mark 1.31, 34; 3.5, 10; 5.29; 6.56; 7.35.

θεὸν) for Jesus' forgiveness and healing.[112] With the help of the GOD frame evoked by this aorist passive verb, therefore, the last prototypical event sequence in the LEGAL CONTROVERSY frame allows the audience to understand the phrase ἠγέρθη as implying that, by "raising" the paralytic, God vindicates Jesus' divine right to forgive.

3.2. The Second Episode (Mark 2.13–17)

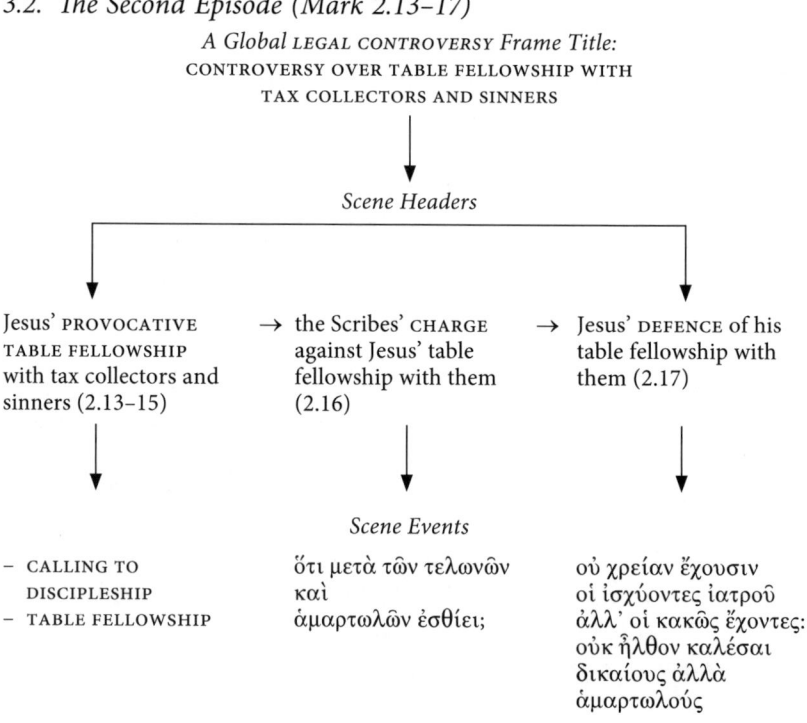

A Global LEGAL CONTROVERSY Frame Title:
CONTROVERSY OVER TABLE FELLOWSHIP WITH
TAX COLLECTORS AND SINNERS

Scene Headers

Jesus' PROVOCATIVE TABLE FELLOWSHIP with tax collectors and sinners (2.13–15)

→ the Scribes' CHARGE against Jesus' table fellowship with them (2.16)

→ Jesus' DEFENCE of his table fellowship with them (2.17)

Scene Events

– CALLING TO DISCIPLESHIP
– TABLE FELLOWSHIP

ὅτι μετὰ τῶν τελωνῶν καὶ ἁμαρτωλῶν ἐσθίει;

οὐ χρείαν ἔχουσιν οἱ ἰσχύοντες ἰατροῦ ἀλλ᾽ οἱ κακῶς ἔχοντες: οὐκ ἦλθον καλέσαι δικαίους ἀλλὰ ἁμαρτωλούς

Figure 3: Instantiation of the LEGAL CONTROVERSY Frame in Mark 2.13–17

---

[112] Timothy Dwyer, *The Motif of Wonder in the Gospel of Mark* (JSNTSup 128; Sheffield: Sheffield Academic Press, 1996), p. 67, says, "Particularly in *2 Maccabees, Joseph and Asenath* and *the Letter of Aristeas*, there is a demonstration that the God of Israel is the true God by the way God does things to astound people. This is potentially very important for Mark, and one must keep in mind the possibility that Mark uses reactions of wonder in such a way to let his readers or hearers know that one proof that God was revealed in the ministry of Jesus is that people responded with wonder and awe at what took place."

The second episode is neatly organized according to the global LEGAL CONTROVERSY frame's prototypical event sequences (note that the verdict is implicit at the end of the episode) and its structuring principles. At the top of the hierarchy there is the title of the global frame, CONTROVERSY OVER JESUS' TABLE FELLOWSHIP WITH TAX COLLECTORS AND SINNERS. The title consists of three scene headers at the lower level: "Jesus' provocative table fellowship with tax collectors and sinners," "the scribes' charge against Jesus' table fellowship with them," and "Jesus' defence of his table fellowship with them." They are evoked when the audience hears input details (scene events) and then serve as frameworks for coherently understanding the events. Also, the instantiated event sequences are causally interrelated with each other. Jesus' calling Levi into discipleship (vv. 13–14) *enables* Jesus to have meal association with tax collectors and sinners, including Levi (v. 15). And Jesus' table fellowship with them *causes* the scribes/Pharisees to charge Jesus (v. 16), and, finally, the scribes/Pharisees' challenge *leads to* Jesus' defence of his association with sinners and tax collectors (v. 17).

3.2.1. *Provocative Action: Jesus' Table Fellowship with Tax Collectors and Sinners (Mark 2.13–15)*

This unit constitutes two major events associated with Jesus' activities: Calling Levi (vv. 13–14) and a meal with tax collectors and sinners (v. 15). Though the above scene header may be called up immediately by Jesus' actions in verse 15, the provocative nature of Jesus' action is first prepared by the CALLING TO DISCIPLESHIP frame opened in verse 14 (the frame's typical events are underlined):

Καὶ…<u>εἶδεν</u> Λευὶν τὸν τοῦ Ἀλφαίου <u>καθήμενον ἐπὶ τὸ τελώνιον</u>,
καὶ <u>λέγει</u> αὐτῷ· <u>ἀκολούθει μοι</u>.
καὶ…<u>ἠκολούθησεν</u> αὐτῷ.[113]

In order for a frame to operate in an appropriate way, certain conditions must be met (e.g., for the SOCCER frame there must be two teams). The CALLING TO DISCIPLESHIP frame presents a condition of conflict for the opening of the LEGAL CONTROVERSY frame because it introduces Levi activating the TAX COLLECTOR frame into

---

[113] For an explanation of the typical components in the CALLING TO DISCIPLESHIP frame, including those in Mark 1.16–20, see Chapter Six.

the story, making available Jesus' intimate fellowship as shown, for example, by Jesus' having a meal with him and other tax collectors.[114]

The text describes Jesus as involved in meal fellowship with tax collectors and sinners in verse 15. In what sense can such table fellowship of Jesus in verse 15 evoke provocative information? Since frame knowledge determines whether certain behaviour is appropriate for a particular case, the frames, such as TAX COLLECTOR and SINNER (person frames) and TABLE FELLOWSHIP (an event frame)[115] must be taken into account for the controversial nature of Jesus' meal practice (the frame titles are bolded and the components triggering the frame are underlined): Καὶ γίνεται κατακεῖσθαι αὐτὸν...καὶ πολλοὶ **τελῶναι** καὶ **ἁμαρτωλοὶ** συνανέκειντο τῷ Ἰησοῦ καὶ τοῖς μαθηταῖς αὐτοῦ:. For the Jewish audience the TABLE FELLOWSHIP frame, which is triggered by κατακεῖσθαι, συνανέκειντο, contained not only the prototypical knowledge of the participants' observance of ritual laws,[116] but also information regarding the social function of a meal as a symbol of identification.[117] So the fact that Jesus has such mealtime companions as tax collectors and sinners whose social stereotype represents open violators of Mosaic laws and thus ritual regulations, would enable the following inference: Jesus not only risks defiling himself but also encroaches on Jewish meal practice according to which no respectable religious teacher was expected to eat with those who disregarded the laws (cf., Ps 1.1; Prov 29.7). For this reason Jesus' conduct would be considered to be provocative enough to be an issue of legal dispute.

3.2.2. Charge: The Scribes/Pharisees' Charge against Jesus Eating with a Tax Collector and Sinners (Mark 2.16)

The "scribes of the Pharisees" (οἱ γραμματεῖς τῶν Φαρισαίων) are introduced as a subject of the participle (ἰδόντες) and verb (ἔλεγον)

---

[114] On the CALLING TO DISCIPLESHIP frame's opening of semantic information regarding Jesus' meal fellowship with the disciples, see Chapter Six.

[115] On the widespread concern with table fellowship among the early Christians, see James D.G. Dunn, *Unity and Diversity in the New Testament: An Inquiry into the Character of Earliest Christianity* (London: SCM, 3rd edn, 2006), pp. 177–83.

[116] On the relation of table fellowship to ritual purity in the pre-70 rabbinic traditions, see Neusner, *Politics*, pp. 80, 83–90 (the quotation from p. 86): "Of the 341 individual Houses' legal pericopae, no fewer than 229, approximately 67 percent of the whole, directly or indirectly concern table fellowship...The Houses' laws of ritual cleanness apply in the main to the ritual cleanness of food, and of people, dishes, and implements involved in its preparation."

[117] On the social aspect of table fellowship, see Joachim Jeremias, *New Testament Theology* (London: SCM, 1971), p. 115.

in raising a question with his disciples about Jesus' meal practice. In doing so, Mark 2.16 draws the audience's attention to the legal experts' role of accusation in relation to Jesus' meal practice. This is primarily because the words οἱ γραμματεῖς τῶν Φαρισαίων apparently open the person frame for professional interpreters of the law on the part of the audience (notice the Greek article, a hearer-old marker, before the nouns occurring for the first time in the immediate text).[118] And the preceding stage has already implicitly opened in the audience's mind the semantic information that Jesus' eating with tax collectors and sinners was in violation of ritual laws, including contemporary Jewish social boundaries. Thus, the intention of the legal experts' questioning cannot be understood so as to elicit information in a neutral sense from Jesus' disciples (i.e., a real question) but rather as taking offence at Jesus' "unlawful" action (a rhetorical question).

It is true, certainly, that the text does not explain the basis of the scribes/Pharisees' charge against Jesus' actions, but presupposes it as background knowledge of the audience. Frame theory must be used to identify the basis of the objection. Verse 16 says (repetitive words are underlined and the relevant person frame is bolded): οἱ γραμματεῖς τῶν Φαρισαίων...ὅτι ἐσθίει μετὰ **τῶν ἁμαρτωλῶν καὶ τελωνῶν**...ὅτι μετὰ **τῶν τελωνῶν καὶ ἁμαρτωλῶν** ἐσθίει. Both of the twice repeated words ἐσθίει and τῶν ἁμαρτωλῶν καὶ τελωνῶν highlight the components of eating and participants in the TABLE FELLOWSHIP frame. This means that what is at issue in the Jewish legal experts' hostile rhetorical question is Jesus' *action of eating* and *the participants*. Hence, the emphatic reference to Jesus' eating food with τῶν ἁμαρτωλῶν καὶ τελωνῶν, which opens the semantic information of the blatant violators of Mosaic laws, is evocative enough to open the RITUAL PURITY frame. For first-century Jews, the frame included information that, in order to keep ritually purified, YHWH's covenantal people should avoid any contact with unclean things (e.g.,

---

[118] The combination of the two groups (οἱ γραμματεῖς τῶν Φαρισαίων) indicates that some scribes belonged to the Pharisaic party. Thus Joachim Jeremias, *Jerusalem in the Time of Jesus: An Investigation into Economic and Social Conditions during the Time of Jesus* (Philadelphia: Fortress 1969), pp. 233–45, says that the majority of Jewish scribes in New Testament times were Pharisees. However, see Sanders, *Judaism*, pp. 170–82, who argues that most scribes were Levites and priests, challenging the equation of scribes with Pharisees. Yet Jeremias and Sanders are in agreement with each other in the assertion that both the Pharisees and scribes were regarded as the prototypical groups concerned with observing and teaching the Law of Moses and *Halakah* or non-biblical traditions.

Numbers 19.15, 18), including food (e.g., Leviticus 11.34, 38), or persons (e.g., Leviticus 5.3; 15.2, 25; 21.17–21).[119] This can be confirmed by Jacob Neusner's striking argument that the strict observance of ritual purity in "pure-eating fellowships" was one of the central features characterizing the Pharisees before 70 C.E.[120] Once this RITUAL PURITY frame is opened, the Pharisees' accusatory question makes perfect sense in terms of an attempt to show disapproval of Jesus' meal practice dubiously evaluated against the frame's fitness (e.g., Mark 7.1–5). It is apparent, thus, that "the scribes of the Pharisees" make a judgment of Jesus' conduct on the basis of "ideal model" (to use Lakoff's term),[121] a model whereby, in order to observe ritual purity, pious Jews should not partake of food with tax collectors and sinners. Consequently, the frames, or the background knowledge, RITUAL PURITY and PHARISEE, along with TAX COLLECTOR and SINNER, lead us to the argument that as professional experts of the Torah the scribes/Pharisees' question is to charge Jesus with disregarding the laws of ritual purity by having table fellowship with such violators of the laws as tax collectors and sinners.[122]

3.2.3. Defence: Jesus' Defence of His Meal Practice (Mark 2.17)

This unit begins with καὶ ἀκούσας ὁ Ἰησοῦς λέγει αὐτοῖς. Given the open LEGAL CONTROVERSY frame, the introduction of Jesus as a subject indicates that Jesus, as a defendant, is foregrounded, and at the same time the Pharisees/scribes backgrounded. Likewise the open LEGAL CONTROVERSY frame allows the inference that Jesus attempts to defend and not just state in a neutral sense his table fellowship with tax collectors and sinners. In his defence, Jesus shifts the point of reference from the Pharisees' concern with ritual purity to the human need for help: οὐ χρείαν ἔχουσιν οἱ ἰσχύοντες ἰατροῦ ἀλλ' οἱ κακῶς ἔχοντες. And then Jesus goes on to validate his association

---

[119] On the first-century Jews' observance of purity laws, see Dunn, *Partings of the Ways*, pp. 38–44, 107–113.

[120] Neusner, *Politics*, pp. 80–90. The quoted words come from Marcus, *Mark 1–8*, p. 230.

[121] Lakoff, *Women*, p. 87.

[122] But Sanders, *Historical Jesus*, p. 236, argues that the legal issue in this episode is not ritual laws but "the commandments of the Jewish law that stipulate how one changes from being wicked to being upright; Jesus regarded himself as having the right to say who would be in the kingdom." For the criticism of Sanders' extreme position, see Dunn, *Partings of the Ways*, pp. 107–11.

with the disreputable in terms of the central purpose of his mission: οὐκ ἦλθον καλέσαι δικαίους ἀλλὰ ἁμαρτωλούς. Nevertheless, while the second clause directly responds to the Pharisees' challenge, the proverb or the physician metaphor (i.e., the source domain) in the first clause seems on the surface less obviously related to Jesus' defence of his meal association with tax collectors and sinners (the target domain). Yet the metaphorical link between the physician proverb and Jesus' defence depends on the semantic information of the HEALING frame opened by ἰατροῦ, a core participant in that frame. The role of the healer or physician in the HEALING frame typically involved the healing of social and spiritual illness, as well as the curing of physical disease;[123] and the preceding episodes, in fact, have shown Jesus both curing physical disease (Mark 1.29-31, 32-34, 40-45; 2.1-12) and calling the sinner to discipleship. So such knowledge of the healer's social and physical functions in the HEALING frame and textual information of Jesus' actions could have enabled the audience in this passage to link Jesus metaphorically with the physician who performed that kind of healing, given that he have had table fellowship with socially disvalued tax collectors and spiritually ill people, namely, sinners. (see the figure below):[124]

Table 7: Mapping of HEALING and CALLING TO DISCIPLESHIP Frames

	Source Domain	Similarity	Target Domain
Frame Title	healing	restoration	calling to discipleship
Participants (Role)	the physician	agent of restoring	I (Jesus)
	(to heal the sick)		(to call the sinners)
	the sick	in need of restorer	sinners (and tax collectors)
	the strong	in no need of restorer	the righteous (the Pharisees)

---

[123] Pilch, *Healing*, p. 63. For the same reason, Hellenistic literature frequently portrayed the philosopher as a physician, regarding vice as the illness; see Dio Chrysostom, *Orations* 32.14–30; Epictetus, *Discourses* 3.23, 30 (LCL; trans. W.A. Oldfather; Cambridge, Massachusetts: Harvard University Press, 1966–1967).

[124] In some sense, the relationship between JESUS and the PHYSICIAN can be seen as a metonymic one i.e., the PHYSICIAN stands for JESUS) in that in Mark's Gospel and in the early Christians' knowledge JESUS was typically associated with a healer of physical disease. In any case, on the mapping process of elements from one domain to another which is made possible on the basis of the co-occurrence of the domains within a particular field of experience, see Chapter Four.

Accordingly, in such a metaphorical link the physician proverb serves to defend Jesus' mission of calling the socially and spiritually sick, tax collectors and sinners, into a proper relationship with God through discipleship.

3.3. *The Third Episode (Mark 2.18–22)*

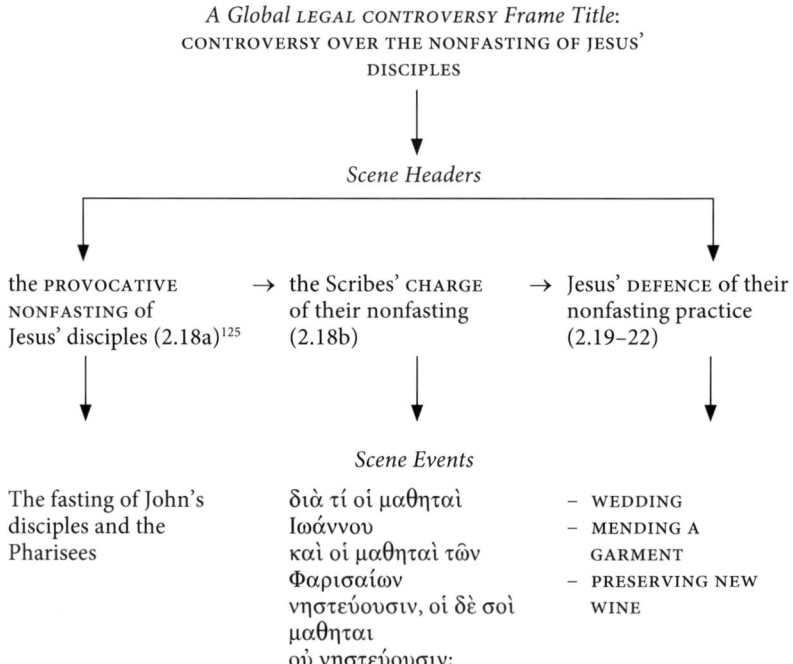

The LEGAL CONTROVERSY frame is also open in the third episode and its event slots are filled in by the properties of the story. The instantiated story can be hierarchically represented. In that representation, a global frame title may be inferred as CONTROVERSY OVER THE NON-FASTING OF JESUS' DISCIPLES; and at the lower level of the title there are three stereotyped event slots: The provocative nonfasting of Jesus' disciples, the scribes' charge against their nonfasting, and

---

[125] Indeed the disciples not fasting are not explicitly but implicitly mentioned in this stage.

Jesus' defence of their nonfasting practice, which are opened by the incoming story and enable the audience to interpret specific scene events at each stage. Likewise, the instantiated event sequences are a causally interconnected whole. The nonfasting practice of Jesus' disciples (2.18a) *causes* Jesus' critics to raise an accusatory question (v. 18b). This censure in turn *leads to* Jesus' defence of his disciples not fasting (vv. 19–22).

3.3.1. Provocative Action: The Non-fasting of Jesus' Disciples (Mark 2.18a)

This scene immediately introduces a topical issue of fasting: Καὶ ἦσαν οἱ μαθηταὶ Ἰωάννου καὶ οἱ Φαρισαῖοι νηστεύοντες. As pointed out above, this scene includes no explicit reference to the non-fasting of Jesus' disciples; instead this information is explicitly given in the next stage of the scribes' charge (v. 18b). As a result, the controversial nature of this scene seems questionable. Since the frame enables causal inference, however, the open LEGAL CONTROVERSY frame leads to the inference that the cause (the non-fasting of Jesus' disciples) of the scribes' challenge (v. 18b) is implicit in verse 18a. If so, in what terms may the non-fasting of Jesus' disciples be seen as provocative? The answer partly relies on the cognitive processing of fasting. The topical word νηστεύοντες is evocative enough to open the event frame or "situational script" (to use Schank and Abelson's term) for FASTING. The FASTING frame has opened the semantic contents:

Frame Title	FASTING (a religious practice of abstaining from eating and drinking)
Participants	Devout Jews
Purpose	Repentance before God
	Self-purification
	Preparation for the coming of the eschatological kingdom of God[126]

---

[126] The ancient Jews fasted for several reasons. As the Mosaic law (Leviticus 16.1–34; 23.26–32; 35.9; Numbers 29.9–11) commands, they kept the Day of Atonement as the day of fasting; and as part of spontaneous fasts they often would fast to express personal repentance; and the Pharisees practised regular weekly fasting (Luke 18.12; Matthew 6.16). For the general reasons for such a fasting practice, see Moore, *Judaism.* Vol. 2, pp. 26–66; for the fact that the ancient Jews fasted in a eschatological hope for the establishment of the kingdom of God (Zechariah 8.19), see Wright, *the People*

Given that Jesus and his disciples were known as the bringers of the eschatological kingdom of God and thus supposed participants (Mark 1.14–15, 16–21; 3.13–19; 6.7–13), no doubt their non-fasting would be judged as a legally disputable issue.[127]

3.3.2. Charge: The Scribes' Charge of the Disciples' Non-fasting (Mark 2.18b)

Jesus' opponents pose a question to Jesus about the non-fasting of his disciples (the prototypical participants in the FASTING frame are underlined and a contraexpectation marker bolded): διὰ τί οἱ μαθηταὶ Ἰωάννου καὶ οἱ μαθηταὶ τῶν Φαρισαίων νηστεύουσιν, οἱ δὲ σοὶ μαθηταὶ οὐ νηστεύουσιν. It is clear that the questioners accuse Jesus' disciples of failing to partake in fasting, and the charge is apparently based on their typical knowledge of who are the expected participants in that practice. This typical knowledge determines the use of δὲ ("but") as a contraexpectation marker here, which connects the fasting of John and the Pharisees' disciples and the non-fasting of Jesus' disciples. This contraexpectation marker indicates that, unlike John the Baptist and the Pharisees' disciples, Jesus' disciples' conduct was unexpected and thus surprising in the scribes' or questioners' frame for FASTING. Thus, the question carries an overtone of complaint.

3.3.3. Defence: Jesus' Defence of the Non-fasting of his Followers (Mark 2.19–22)

The shift of the subject in εἶπεν αὐτοῖς ὁ Ἰησοῦς (v. 19) shows that the defendant is foregrounded, the critics being backgrounded. Jesus goes on to defend his disciples with three short parables or metaphors: Wedding, sewing garments, and preserving new wine. First is Jesus' wedding metaphor (the participants or components in the WEDDING frame are underlined): μὴ δύνανται οἱ υἱοὶ τοῦ νυμφῶνος ἐν ᾧ ὁ νυμφίος

---

of God, pp. 234–35 and idem, Jesus, pp. 433–34; Lane, Mark, p. 109. In particular, the eschatological orientation of fasting may be traced in that of John the Baptist (Matthew 11.19; Luke 7.34) and the Pharisees who were also proponents of apocalyptic movements; see Martin Hengel, Judaism and Hellenism: Studies in Their Encounter in Palestine During the Early Hellenistic Period. Vol. 2 (Philadelphia: Fortress, 1974), p. 253. Cf. S. Lowy, "The Motivation of Fasting in Talmudic Literature," JJS 9 (1958), pp. 19–38.

[127] John B. Muddiman, "Fast, Fasting," in The Anchor Bible Dictionary 2 (ed. D.N. Freedman; New York: Doubleday, 1992), pp. 773–76.

μετ' αὐτῶν ἐστιν νηστεύειν. The point is clear: Just as for the wedding guest to fast during a wedding is unthinkable, so is it absurd for Jesus' disciples to fast while they are with him. Further, the effectiveness of Jesus' defence of his disciples' non-fasting in terms of the wedding metaphor depends on two things. First, it is appropriate to call up the WEDDING frame, an event frame, whose prototypical knowledge contained a time for festive rejoicing, eating and drinking, not fasting. The textual evidence shows that the text assumes the audience to have that knowledge. Note a hearer-old marker, the Greek article, preceding the typical participants in the frame, οἱ υἱοὶ τοῦ νυμφῶνος and ὁ νυμφίος, and a rhetorical question is used to invoke the typical information already stored in the audience's long-term memory for a wedding ceremony (for this reason the text does not explain why fasting is not suitable during a wedding).

Next, the power of Jesus' use of the wedding metaphor in his defence relies on the audience's ability to link metaphorically Jesus and his disciples with the bridegroom and the wedding guests. Though the text does not explicitly mention it, such a metaphorical link may have operated on the basis of the knowledge in the early Christian audience's long-term memory that the kingdom of God inaugurated by Jesus was understood as a wedding ceremony (Matthew 22.1–14; 25.1–13; Ephesians 5.23–33; Revelation 19.7–9; 21.2, 9; John 3.29).[128] Thus it is not hard to imagine that for Mark and his audience, Jesus filled the slot for a bridegroom at a wedding, his disciples for wedding guests, and his practice of eating and drinking for a celebration in a metaphorical processing of the frames for WEDDING (the source domain) and THE KINGDOM OF GOD (the target domain):

---

[128] On the kingdom of God as a key to Jesus' and the early church's proclamation, see Wright, *Jesus*, pp. 198–662; *idem*, *The People of God*, pp. 341–471. For frames' metaphorically linking role, see Chapter Five. In fact, whereas the wedding celebration was made use of by rabbis as a metaphor for the age of messianic redemption in Judaism, the Messiah was not represented as the bridegroom. See Joachim Jeremias, *The Parables of Jesus* (New York: Charles Scribners's Sons, 1963), p. 52 note 13; and Guelich, *Mark 1–8.26*, pp. 110, 116. Thus, Jesus' statement would have hardly been understood by his opponents.

Table 8: Mapping of the WEDDING and
THE KINGDOM OF GOD Frames

	Source Domain	Similarity	Target Domain
Frame Titles:	wedding	a time of rejoicing	the kingdom of God
Participants:	a bridegroom	a protagonist	Jesus
	wedding guests	dependants	the disciples, believers
Event:	feasting	celebration	"eating and drinking" (Mark 2.15–16; cf. Mark 1.13c; 6.34–44; 8.1–10; 14.25; Matthew 11.19; Luke 7.34)[129]

The metaphorical linking of the two frames (or domains) leads to the recognition of Jesus' intention in using the wedding metaphor for the defence of his disciples' non-fasting. The purpose of fasting (i.e., to hasten the age of Israel's renewal and redemption) has been accomplished by Jesus' inauguration of the kingdom of God; so the participants must rejoice in the inaugurated kingdom of God, otherwise it would be ridiculous (cf., Zechariah 8.19).[130]

The following two parables are about not patching an old garment with a new patch and not putting new wine in old wineskins. They seem, on the surface, to deal with themes other than fasting. How then can they be processed semantically as part of Jesus' defence of the non-fasting of his disciples? It is important, first of all, to keep in mind that the open LEGAL CONTROVERSY frame guides the audience to understand these parables under the third event header, because they are still spoken by Jesus, a defendant. Once this is recognized, we need to focus on the flow of semantic information in this episode. The preceding parable showed that the metaphorical link between the frames for WEDDING and KINGDOM OF GOD leads to the inference that the coming of the kingdom of God invalidates

---

[129] On Jesus' practice of eating and drinking as a celebration of the inaugurated kingdom of God, see Jeremias, *New Testament Theology*, pp. 115–16, 169 and Wright, *Jesus*, p. 272.

[130] Wright, *Jesus*, pp. 433–34, says, "It [Mark 2.19] is a claim about eschatology. The time is fulfilled; the exile is over; the bridegroom is at hand. Jesus' acted symbol, feasting rather than fasting, brings into public visibility his controversial claim that in his work Israel's hope was being realized..."

its participants' observance of the old practices of Jewish religion such as fasting. To be sure, it is this semantic information that the present two parables take up and develop, stressing the tension between the old and the new (frame titles are bolded and a contraexpectation marker is underlined): Οὐδεὶς ἐπίβλημα ῥάκους ἀγνάφου **ἐπιράπτει ἐπὶ ἱμάτιον παλαιόν** εἰ δὲ μή…, καὶ οὐδεὶς **βάλλει οἶνον νέον** εἰς ἀσκοὺς παλαιούς: <u>εἰ δὲ μή</u>…, (vv. 21–22). The two epigrammatic sayings serve to evoke typical actions in the frame for MENDING A GARMENT and PRESERVING NEW WINE: People do usually try to incorporate new things (new unshrunk cloth and new wine) to fit old things (old garments and old wineskins).[131] Note the contraexpectation marker εἰ δὲ μή ("otherwise" or "if he does,") which is textual evidence for the frame operation in those parables. Of importance for our present concern is to answer what "the new things" and "the old things" refer to metaphorically. The argument is that, even if no explicit link is made in the text, the audience's mental frame would have processed a metaphorical link between the source domain and the target domain on the basis of their similarities, which are culture specific:

Table 9: Mapping of the MENDING A GARMENT Frame

	Source Domain	Similarity	Target Domain
Frame Title:	sewing unshrunk cloth on an old garment (v. 21)	incompatibility	compromising Jesus' teachings of the kingdom of God and Jewish traditions
Components:	a piece of unshrunk cloth (v. 21)	newness	Jesus' teachings of the kingdom of God
	old garment (v. 21)	oldness	Judaism, Jewish traditions

---

[131] Guelich, *Mark 1–8.26*, p. 114.

Table 10: Mapping of the PRESERVING NEW WINE Frame

	Source Domain	Similarity	Target Domain
Frame Title:	preserving new wine in an old wineskin (v. 22)	incompatibility	compromising Jesus' teachings of kingdom of God and Jewish traditions
Components:	new wine (v. 22)	newness	Jesus' teachings of the kingdom of God
	old wineskins (v. 22)	oldness	Judaism, Jewish traditions

Given the everyday life experience of mending a garment and the early Christian audience's social and religious conflict with Judaism, it would not be difficult to believe that Mark and his audience must have linked metaphorically the incompatibility of the new and the old to that of Jesus' teachings of the kingdom of God and Jewish traditions. If so, the concluding verse ἀλλὰ οἶνον νέον εἰς ἀσκοὺς καινούς, "but [pour] new wine into new wineskins," highlights that the radical newness of the kingdom of God inaugurated by Jesus' teaching and works overrules the old structures of Judaism. Consequently, the two parables should be understood as part of Jesus' defence of the non-observance by his disciples, who are living in the new age of salvation, of the old religious practices such as fasting.

3.4. *The Fourth Episode (Mark 2.23–28)*

The fourth episode also shows that the LEGAL CONTROVERSY frame operates to organize its information. As a result, CONTROVERSY OVER MAKING A PATH BY PLUCKING GRAIN ON THE SABBATH is represented as the title of the LEGAL CONTROVERSY frame operative on the current episode. And then the headers of prototypical event sequences evoked by incoming information serve to divide this conflict story into the three scenes as the story progresses: "the disciples' provocative action of making a path by plucking grain on the sabbath," "the Pharisees' charge against their violation of the sabbath laws," and "Jesus' defence of the disciples' violation of sabbath laws." In addition to hierarchical arrangement, the event sequence instantiated by the LC frame is also causally interconnected. The questionable works of Jesus' disciples on the sabbath (v. 23) *cause* the Pharisees, the legal experts, to take offence both at them and at Jesus. (v. 24). *As a result of* the charge, Jesus defends his disciples (vv. 25–28).

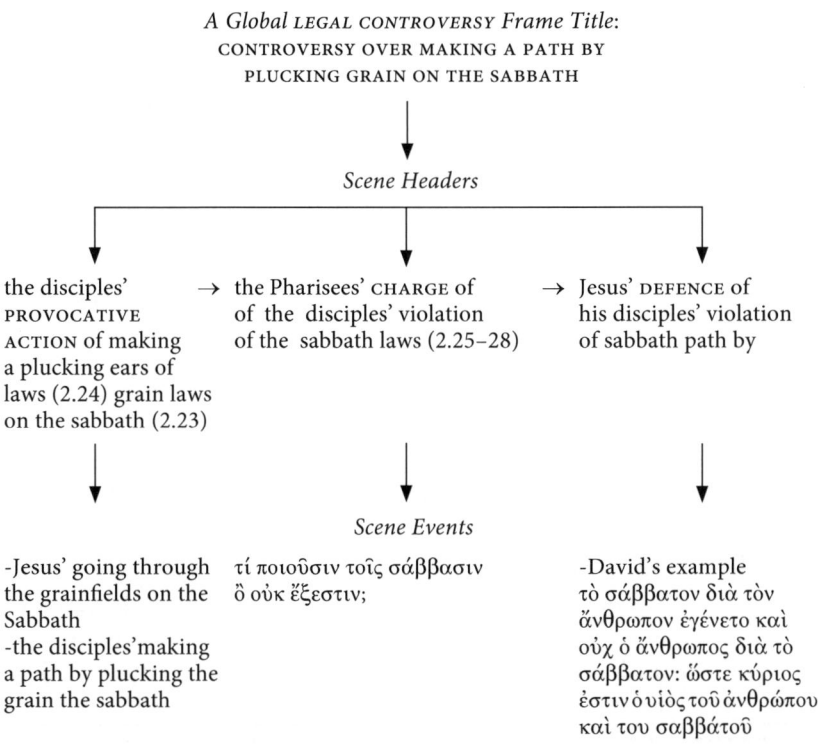

A *Global* LEGAL CONTROVERSY *Frame Title*:
CONTROVERSY OVER MAKING A PATH BY
PLUCKING GRAIN ON THE SABBATH

Scene Headers

the disciples'   →   the Pharisees' CHARGE of   →   Jesus' DEFENCE of
PROVOCATIVE   of the disciples' violation   his disciples' violation
ACTION of making   of the sabbath laws (2.25–28)   of sabbath path by
a plucking ears of
laws (2.24) grain laws
on the sabbath (2.23)

Scene Events

-Jesus' going through   τί ποιοῦσιν τοῖς σάββασιν   -David's example
the grainfields on the   ὃ οὐκ ἔξεστιν;   τὸ σάββατον διὰ τὸν
Sabbath   ἄνθρωπον ἐγένετο καὶ
-the disciples'making   οὐχ ὁ ἄνθρωπος διὰ τὸ
a path by plucking the   σάββατον· ὥστε κύριος
grain the sabbath   ἐστιν ὁ υἱὸς τοῦ ἀνθρώπου
                                                        καὶ του σαββάτου

Figure 5: Instantiation of the LEGAL CONTROVERSY Frame in
Mark 2.23–28

3.4.1. *Provocative Action: The Disciples' Plucking of the Grain on the Sabbath (Mark 2.23)*

Verse 23 introduces Jesus' disciples plucking the grain and making a path[132] through a grainfield on the sabbath day, which will be a topic in the subsequent conflict between Jesus and the Pharisees (the relevant frame title is bolded):...ἐν **τοῖς σάββασιν**...οἱ μαθηταὶ αὐτοῦ ἤρξαντο ὁδὸν ποιεῖν τίλλοντες τοὺς στάχυας. The text does not explicitly explain why the disciples' action would be disputable, but the specific reference to τοῖς σάββασιν as a temporal setting in which the subsequent actions happened, is highly likely to open the audience's mental frame for THE SABBATH—a day on which no work should be done. As discussed earlier, the observance of the laws of the sabbath, which includes that no work was allowed, was, in fact, prototypical information in the SABBATH frame not only for Jews, but also for

---

[132] On the translation of ὁδὸν ποιεῖν as "making a path," see BDAG, ὁδός 1.

Mark and his audience. Thus note the Markan passages, except for the present and following episodes (Mark 3.1–6), which indicate that sabbath laws were being kept when the word τοῖς σάββασιν occurs (the frame titles are bolded):

   1.21, 32: εὐθὺς **τοῖς σάββασιν** εἰσελθὼν εἰς τὴν συναγωγὴν...
            Ὀψίας δὲ γενομένης, ὅτε ἔδυ ὁ ἥλιος, ἔφερον πρὸς αὐτὸν πάντας τοὺς κακῶς ἔχοντας και; τοὺς δαιμονιζομένους:
   15.42: ἐπεὶ ἦν παρασκευὴ ὅ ἐστιν **προσάββατον**, ἤδη ὀψίας γενομένης, ἐλθὼν Ἰωσὴφ [ὁ] ἀπὸ Ἀριμαθαίας... τολμήσας εἰσῆλθεν πρὸς τὸν Πιλᾶτον καὶ ᾐτήσατο τὸ σῶμα τοῦ Ἰησοῦ.
   16.1–2: διαγενομένου **τοῦ σαββάτου** Μαρία ἡ Μαγδαληνὴ καὶ Μαρία ἡ [τοῦ] Ἰακώβου καὶ Σαλώμη ἠγόρασαν ἀρώματα ἵνα ἐλθοῦσαι ἀλείψωσιν αὐτόν.

In all these examples, the texts state that the characters initiated their works before the sabbath began ('going to Pilate,' 15.42), during the sabbath ('goint to synagogue,' 1.21) and after it ended ('going to Jesus to be healed,' 1.32; 'goint to Jesus' tomb,' 16.1–2). Though the texts do not explicitly explain the reason, no doubt the text takes for granted that the audience would understand the characters' actions as attempts to keep the sabbath regulations in reference to the SABBATH frame. This shows that such a sabbath law is prototypical information of the SABBATH frame in Mark's Gospel. It is safe, then, to believe that the disciples' action of making a path by plucking the grain would be taken as provocative enough to incur the disapproval of the religious establishment because, in light of the SABBATH frame, their action would be regarded as a violation of the sabbath laws.

3.4.2. *Charge: The Pharisees' Charge of the Violation of the Sabbath Laws by Jesus' Disciples (Mark 2.24)*

The Pharisees' questioning is directed to Jesus about his disciples' behaviour: καὶ οἱ Φαρισαῖοι ἔλεγον αὐτῷ· ἴδε τί ποιοῦσιν τοῖς σάββασιν ὃ οὐκ ἔξεστιν: The Pharisees' question is more of a challenge to Jesus than a mere quest for information. This is made obvious from the use of the evaluative word ἔξεστιν ("lawful") for what the disciples do. The use of an evaluative word indicates that normative knowledge in the Pharisees' SABBATH frame, in this case *halakic* interpretation of the sabbath laws, enables them to evaluate the disciples' actions in terms of appropriateness. And their negative evaluation (ὃ οὐκ ἔξεστιν, "what is not lawful") clarifies that the legal experts charge them with failing to observe the sabbath laws. Thus we can summarize the event at this stage in terms of the header of the second event scene in the LEGAL CONTROVERSY frame.

3.4.3. Defence: Jesus' Defence of His Disciples' Violation of Sabbath Laws (Mark 2.25–28)

This unit has two parts, each beginning with "Jesus said to them" (vv. 25, 27). In the first part there is the David story, and the second has to do with God's original intent of the sabbath and the Son of Man's authority. The header of the third prototypical event scene guides the audience to interpret each part not just as Jesus' saying but his defence of his disciples against the Pharisaic charge. For his first defence, Jesus provides the David story, in which David and his companions are involved in the illegitimate action of eating the showbread, which is reserved for the priests (Mark 2.25–26). On what basis is the David story relevant for Jesus' defence? It is the behaviour of Jesus' disciples that is objected to and thus focused on in the narrative. So the example of the David story must be used to help justify the unlawful action of Jesus' disciples. Yet in verse 26 the text just states that David "entered the house of God (εἰσῆλθεν εἰς τὸν οἶκον τοῦ θεοῦ)," "ate the bread of the Presence (τοὺς ἄρτους τῆς προθέσεως ἔφαγεν)" and "gave it even to those who were with him (ἔδωκεν καὶ τοῖς σὺν αὐτῷ οὖσιν)." The text itself gives no clue about who David is, though necessary for understanding the present passage.

Besides, the text provides no explicit reason why such an illegal action of David and his companions can be justified; and it gives no information on how the case of David's companions can be relevant to Jesus' disciples. So it is because of the audience' frame knowledge that the text may be processed in a coherent way despite the missing information. Mark 2.25 states οὐδέποτε ἀνέγνωτε τί ἐποίησεν Δαυὶδ...; (the person frame title is bolded). These words certainly open not only knowledge of David in the scriptures (1 Samuel 21.1–6) but also prototypical information of an authoritative archetypal messiah (Mark 10.48; 11.9–10; 12.35–37)[133] in Mark's Christian audiences' mental frame for DAVID.[134] Consequently, this person frame for

---

[133] Here it is worth remembering again that a relevant frame can be opened not only by the current textual information but also by the help of other textual information. Thus, Sanford and Garrod, *Understanding*, p. 129, say that in most cases during hearing and reading, the reader/hearer has "other information at his disposal, such as the title of the book, previous scenarios encountered in the text, and the unique information provided by the text itself which has been interpreted through the previous scenarios. This additional information provides another constraint in the selection of a scenario: indeed, selection can be viewed as the outcome of an accumulation of evidence from various sources, both from the current text and from the memory structure for previously encountered text."

[134] Taylor, *Mark*, p. 216, points out, "The story [of David] is cited...because of the acknowledged greatness of David." The passages quoted above clearly confirm that the

DAVID enabled the audience to understand that on the basis of his own authority, David's unlawful action may be justified and the illegal action of his companions also validated due to their master's authority. Likewise, the audience's mental frame for JESUS as not only the Davidic Messiah (Mark 10.48; 11.9–10; cf. Romans 1.3; Matthew 1.1ff.; Luke 3.23ff.; John 7.41–42; Acts 15.16; Revelation 5.5; 22.16) but also as greater than David (Mark 12.35–37)[135] enabled the inference that the disciples' illegal action can be appropriate because Jesus authorized them to do so.[136]

The next example says (the relevant frame is bolded and its components are underlined): τὸ σάββατον διὰ τὸν ἄνθρωπον ἐγένετο καὶ οὐχ ὁ ἄνθρωπος διὰ τὸ σάββατον. In particular, the clause τὸ σάββατον διὰ τὸν ἄνθρωπον ἐγένετο ("the sabbath was made for the benefit of the man") plays the role of activating or 'perspectivizing' another component, namely, the creation story (Genesis 1.26–2.3; cf. Exodus 20.11),[137] in the SABBATH frame by means of the expressions τὸ σάββατον, τὸν ἄνθρωπον (for the word τὸν ἄνθρωπον, see LXX Genesis 1.26–27), and ἐγένετο, (for the verb ἐγένετο, see LXX Genesis

---

authoritative archetype of a messiah was part of stereotypical expectation of DAVID on the part of Mark's hearer. On the claim that the Davidic profile is so clearly part of the messianic expectation not only in Jewish tradition in Jesus' day but also of the early Christians, see Martin Hengel, *The Zealots: Investigations into the Jewish Freedom Movement in the Period from Herod 1 until 70 A.D.* (trans. David Smith; Edinburgh: T. and T. Clark, 1989), pp. 298–300; Wright, *Jesus*, p. 509; Sanders, *Historical Jesus*, pp. 85–90. In particular, Wright, *The People of God*, p. 310, says, that "the persistence of messianic themes throughout most of the New Testament is all the more powerful a witness to the fact that...such expectation [of Jewish Messiah] certainly existed. The early Christians...redrew it around a new fixed point, in this case Jesus, thereby giving it precision and direction. It is especially striking that the *Davidic* Messiahship of Jesus should be given such prominence" (emphasis is the original author's).

[135] Mark's depiction of Jesus as the Davidic Messiah, see Joel Marcus, *The Way of the Lord: Christological Exegesis of the Old Testament in the Gospel of Mark* (Louisville, Kentucky: WJK, 1992), pp. 130–52. Marcus, *Mark 1–8*, p. 245, says Mark's link of Jesus with the Davidic messiah seems clear in the way in which "he describes the disciples' plucking of grain, since it creates the impression that a path is being cleared for Jesus, as would be done in preparation for a royal visit."

[136] Dewey clearly points out that in using the example of David, Jesus shows that just as David's authority is linked with that of his followers, his disciples also may share his authority. Dewey, *Public Debate*, pp. 97–98. Likewise, Robert M. Fowler, *Let the Reader Understand: Reader-Response Criticism and the Gospel of Mark* (Minneapolis: Fortress, 1991), p. 106, claims: "The function of verse 26 for the reader is to show Jesus defending himself and his disciples by appealing to the paradigm of Israelite royalty par excellence, King David, in an episode in which David took to himself the prerogatives of priesthood."

[137] For a similar frame related to the Genesis story, see Mark 10.2–9.

1.3, 5, 6, 8, 9, 11, 13, 15, 19, 20, 23, 24, 30, 31).[138] Moreover, since the sabbath in the creation story is made *after*, thus, *for the benefit of*, the human,[139] no doubt Jesus has the Genesis order of sabbath creation in mind. It seems, therefore, a natural inference in light of the SABBATH frame including the creation story that for his defence the Markan Jesus chooses the clause in question in order to introduce the original intent of the institution of sabbath, that is, the welfare of humanity. Again, the scene header of this unit allows us to interpret the meaning of Jesus' appeal to the original intent of the sabbath: The divine intent is in no way infringed upon by the disciples' plucking of heads of grain because such an action produces benefits for Jesus and them in accordance with God's original intent of sabbath in that its purpose was to alleviate hunger (which is implicit knowledge activated by the phrase τίλλοντες τοὺς στάχυας [see above]) and to make a path, probably for Jesus (see next chapter).

The question to be asked, however, is who have the right to decide which conduct or works are grounded in the purpose for which God instituted the Sabbath. The final saying, which has to do with the authority of the Son of Man, gives an answer to this question. Mark 2.28 says; ὥστε κύριος ἐστιν ὁ υἱὸς τοῦ ἀνθρώπου καὶ τοῦ Σαββάτου. Mark here again uses a puzzling title ὁ υἱὸς τοῦ ἀνθρώπου, "the Son of Man." Though many scholars refer to the Son of Man here as humanity in general,[140] it is most probable that after Mark 2.10 the ὁ υἱὸς τοῦ ἀνθρώπου opens JESUS. Above all, given that the Son of Man is used in Mark's Gospel as Jesus' self-designation (Mark 8.31, 38; 9.9, 12, 31; 10.33, 45; 14.21a,b, 41), no doubt Mark's original audience had JESUS in mind for it is implicit in the title ὁ υἱὸς τοῦ ἀνθρώπου.[141] If so, a crucial question is how Jesus' use of Son of Man as a self-designation in this situation contributes to his defence. As already discussed,

---

[138] On the translation of ἐγένετο as "was made," see BDAG, γίνομαι 2.

[139] Given that the sabbath denotes resting, it is a quite natural inference from the Genesis order of creation that the sabbath is for human benefit. See a Rabbinic saying attributed to R. Simeon b. Menasyra (180 C.E.): "The Sabbath was delivered to you, and not you to the Sabbath," cited from Guelich, *Mark 1–8.26*, p. 124.

[140] See, for example, T.W. Manson, *The Teaching of Jesus* (Cambridge: Cambridge University Press, 2nd ed., 1935), p. 214; Vermes, *Jesus the Jew*, pp. 180–81.

[141] On the Son of Man as Jesus' self designation, see Marshall, "Son of Man," pp. 775–81; Kim, "The Son of Man," pp. 7–14. Thus France, *Mark*, p. 147, notes: "Mark and his readers lived in a Christian context where ὁ υἱὸς τοῦ ἀνθρώπου...could have only one meaning, and that was as a title of Jesus...it is inconceivable that Mark could have intended, or expected his readers to understand, a different sense for the phrase in this case."

the phrase ὁ υἱὸς τοῦ ἀνθρώπου opens, apart from information about Jesus, a figure "like a son of man" in Daniel 7.13–14 who is given divine authority (ἐξουσία, LXX) over every nation. In Mark 2.28 the opening of the frame for such a Danielic "son of man" may be supported by the fact that ὁ υἱὸς τοῦ ἀνθρώπου claims his authoritative role, as clearly shown in the clause κύριος ἐστιν ὁ υἱὸς τοῦ ἀνθρώπου καὶ τοῦ σαββάτου. Accordingly, as ὁ υἱὸς τοῦ ἀνθρώπου, Jesus declares himself to be Lord over the sabbath so that he may prove he has the authority to allow his disciples' true use of it.

Besides the example of David, therefore, what the cognitive processing of the last two sayings in terms of the LEGAL CONTROVERSY frame shows is that they may be summarized as further arguments for Jesus' authority by which his disciples' infraction of sabbath laws can be justified.

3.5. *The Fifth Episode (Mark 3.1–6)*

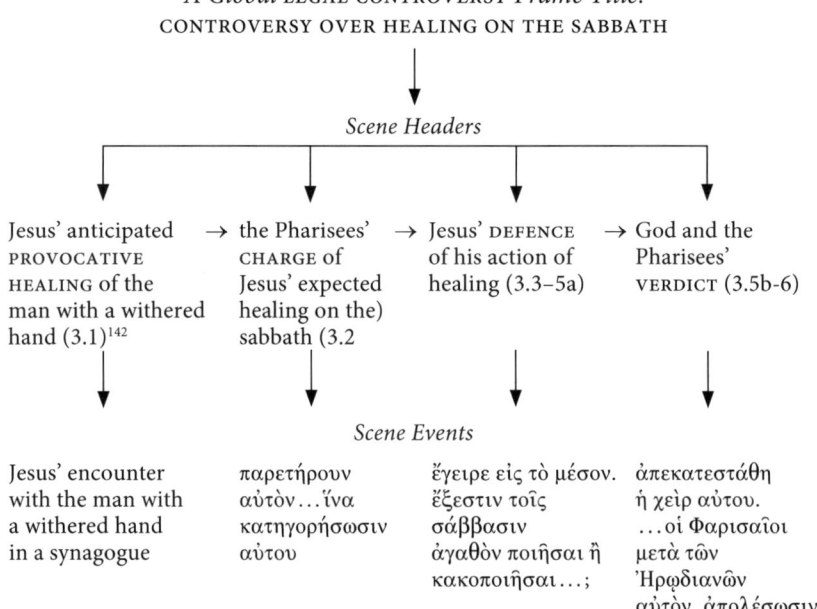

A Global LEGAL CONTROVERSY Frame Title:
CONTROVERSY OVER HEALING ON THE SABBATH

Scene Headers

Jesus' anticipated → the Pharisees' → Jesus' DEFENCE → God and the
PROVOCATIVE   CHARGE of   of his action of   Pharisees'
HEALING of the Jesus' expected healing (3.3–5a) VERDICT (3.5b-6)
man with a withered healing on the)
hand (3.1)[142] sabbath (3.2

Scene Events

Jesus' encounter   παρετήρουν   ἔγειρε εἰς τὸ μέσον.   ἀπεκατεστάθη
with the man with   αὐτὸν...ἵνα   ἔξεστιν τοῖς   ἡ χεὶρ αὐτου.
a withered hand   κατηγορήσωσιν   σάββασιν   ...οἱ Φαρισαῖοι
in a synagogue   αὐτου   ἀγαθὸν ποιῆσαι ἢ   μετὰ τῶν
                                        κακοποιῆσαι...;   Ἡρῳδιανῶν
                                                                αὐτὸν ἀπολέσωσιν

Figure 6: Instantiation of the LEGAL CONTROVERSY Frame in Mark 3.1–6

---

[142] In this stage Jesus' healing is anticipated and thus its provocative nature is implicit. For details, see below.

The above figure shows that the final episode is well structured by the LEGAL CONTROVERSY frame. At the top of this hierarchical representation of the story, its title can be processed as CONTROVERSY OVER HEALING ON THE SABBATH which summarizes the whole event. The overall event is broken into episodes on the basis of the prototypical event sequences (scene headers) of the LEGAL CONTROVERSY frame: Jesus' anticipated provocative healing of the man with a withered hand, the Pharisees' charge against Jesus' expected healing on the sabbath, Jesus' defence of his action of healing, and the God and the Pharisees' verdict. And each scene header is then broken down into detailed events. Next, the overall events in this episode are causally linked to each other. Jesus' encounter of the man with a withered hand in the synagogue (v. 1) *enables* the Pharisees to expect that Jesus will heal the crippled man on the sabbath and to seek grounds for an official accusation concerning the violation of the sabbath laws (v. 2). The Pharisees' accusative attitude *leads to* Jesus' defence (vv. 3–5). On the one hand, Jesus' defence *results in* God's vindication; on the other hand, it *gives rise to* the legal experts' guilty verdict of him (v. 6).

3.5.1. *Provocative Action: Jesus' Expected Healing of the Man with a Withered Hand in the Synagogue (Mark 3.1)*

Indeed Jesus' provocative action of healing occurs as the narrative develops. And this stage seems to display a simple description of Jesus and the man with a withered hand. Nevertheless, the dispute over the observance of sabbath regulations is staged here (the relevant frame is bolded and the frame components are underlined): Καὶ **εἰσῆλθεν πάλιν εἰς τὴν συναγωγήν**. καὶ ἦν ἐκεῖ <u>ἄνθρωπος ἐξηραμμένην ἔχων τὴν χεῖρα</u> (Mark 3.1). First of all, it is important to note that, as mentioned earlier, for Mark's audience Jesus' "entering the synagogue (εἰσῆλθεν...εἰς τὴν συναγωγήν)" implicitly evokes prototypical information about sabbath as a day of regular assembly. (Note the information about sabbath is given in explaining the Pharisees' purpose of watching over Jesus. This indicates that the text supposes that it was already known to the audience that that day was the sabbath). If so, the processing of this verse in provocative terms now depends on the opening of the HEALING frame, which serves as a condition of the LEGAL CONTROVERSY frame. I have already observed that the words ἄνθρωπος ἐξηραμμένην ἔχων τὴν χεῖρα open the HEALING frame due to information about the sick person with a specific disease.

Besides, as pointed out earlier, for the opening of the frame it also must be considered that the HEALING frame of the first four healing episodes in Mark's Gospel, consists of such prototypical set patterns, such as the healer's moving into a place, introducing the sick, preparing healing, healing, confirming healing (see Chapter Four). The information in Mark 3.1 (Jesus' moving into the synagogue in which the man with a withered hand is present) structurally corresponds to the first and second stages of the HEALING frame. The information of Mark 3.1, thus enables the audience to expect that Jesus will heal the man with a withered hand in the subsequent story. If so, no doubt the semantic information of Jesus' impending healing in the synagogue will prepare the audience for another upcoming conflict between Jesus and his opponents regarding healing on the sabbath.

3.5.2. Charge: The Pharisees' Charge of Jesus' Expected Healing (Mark 3.2)

Two elements are crucial for the operation of the second scene header in this verse: καὶ παρετήρουν αὐτὸν εἰ τοῖς σάββασιν θεραπεύσει αὐτόν. First of all, even if the agent of "watching" (παρετήρουν) Jesus is not explcitly mentioned, as discussed above, the Pharisees may be processed as semantic agents of the verb. This is because as religious teachers and experts the Pharisees were default participants in the SYNAGOGUE frame (cf., Mark 1.22; Matthew 23.6, 34; Luke 11.43). This is confirmed in Mark 3.6 in which ἐξελθόντες οἱ Φαρισαῖοι εὐθὺς. Next, verse 2 clearly shows that as legal experts the Pharisees' watching of how Jesus responds to the patient on the sabbath is not out of casual interest, but represents a hostile search for further evidence for a legal charge: ἵνα κατηγορήσωσιν αὐτοῦ.

3.5.3. Defence: Jesus' Defence of Healing on the Sabbath (Mark 3.3–5)

This stage consists of Jesus' three actions: Jesus' command to the patient (v. 3), questioning to the Pharisees (v. 4), and healing (v. 5). In the first part, Jesus proceeds to heal with a command, "Stand up into the middle," just as his opponents expected. Such a command may, as noted above, represent a preparatory stage of healing in light of the HEALING frame; but the global LEGAL CONTROVERSY frame evoked in this episode determines the meaning of such a command in the immediate text. It is important that there is no reference to the sick person's request for healing before Jesus' proceeding to take action for him. As a result, verse 3 is focused on showing that Jesus' telling him to come forward is seen as a response to the opponents' hostile "watching" of his actions.[143] Thus Jesus takes the man with a crippled hand as a test case for the defence of his ministry of healing on the sabbath.

The second part of Jesus' defence consists of the question directly addressed to his critics: "Is it lawful on the sabbath to do good or to do harm, to save life or to kill?" "To do good" and "to save life" on the sabbath, in fact, may have been justified legally by the principle in the Pharisees' frame for OBSERVING THE SABBATH.[144] This can be confirmed by textual evidence. One is Jesus' use of a rhetorical question aimed at invoking typical knowledge in Jesus' original audience's long-term memory. The other piece of evidence is that the Pharisees' silence in response to Jesus' question is marked by a contraexpectation indicator (the relevant conjunction is underlined): οἱ δὲ ἐσιώπων (v. 4). The use of δὲ is textual evidence to show that the Pharisees were expected to express a positive answer to Jesus. It then appears that Jesus attempts to defend his healing of the man's crippled hand by appealing to the scribal definition of "works" permissible on the sabbath. Yet the problem is that the man's withered hand was generally not considered as a life-threatening situation. A different solution is possible in light of the audience's frame-opening based on preceding discourse which includes information concerning Jesus as lord of the sabbath (Mark 2.28):[145] Jesus' groundwork for the healing on the sabbath goes beyond *halakic* interpretation of the sabbath laws to his authority as lord of the sabbath, which allows him to do works that would have been viewed as illegal by the Pharisees. Consequently, for the audience Jesus, as lord of the sabbath, has the right to define the man's crippled hand as equal to mortal danger; and so it can be justified for him to heal the man on the sabbath.

In the last part of the defence Jesus indeed performs healing by a word: λέγει τῷ ἀνθρώπῳ· ἔκτεινον τὴν χεῖρα (v. 5a). Apparently, this is a prototypical component in the HEALING frame. Yet, provided the HEALING frame has been used as a subframe of the LEGAL CONTROVERSY frame in this episode, Jesus' action of healing the withered hand may be processed in terms of its third prototypical

---

[143] Guelich, *Mark 1–8.26*, p. 134.
[144] Sanders, *Jewish Law*, p. 21; Guelich, *Mark 1–8.26*, p. 134.
[145] For preceding discourse-based model to open a relevant frame, see Chapter Four.

scene header as an attempt to approve his authority "to save life," namely, to heal the sick on the sabbath.

3.5.4. *Verdict: God's Vindication and the Pharisees' Guilty Verdict of Jesus (Mark 3.5b–6)*

With respect to Jesus' healing on the sabbath there are two kinds of verdicts, namely God's and the legal experts'. God's verdict is implied in the clause (the passive verb is underlined): καὶ <u>ἀπεκατεστάθη</u> ἡ χεὶρ αὐτοῦ. Here, the agent of healing is grammatically unspecified. However, since for the ancient audience God was, as already pointed out above, a prototypical agent of healing the sick, the semantic subject of the verb may possibly be processed as God. In other words, as a hearer-old marker this passive verb serves to activate the audience's mental frame that God's restoring-eschatological power works through Jesus. So what we must remember is that the meaning of God's healing is not limited to the restoration of the man's crippled hand. Given that the HEALING frame has been used as a subframe of the LEGAL CONTROVERSY frame, it should rather be interpreted as meaning God's approval of Jesus' person and ministry of saving life on the sabbath.[146] The information of the legal experts' condemnation may be opened in the clause: καὶ ἐξελθόντες οἱ Φαρισαῖοι...συμβούλιον ἐδίδουνκατ᾽ αὐτοῦ ὅπως αὐτὸν ἀπολέσωσιν (v. 6). Of course, the decision to destroy Jesus is indicative of "the implacable opposition of official Judaism to Jesus" and an early anticipation of Jesus' death in Mark's narrative as a whole.[147] Yet no doubt the LEGAL CONTROVERSY frame operative on the present episode enables the audience to deduce that the Pharisees who have played the role of Jesus' accusers in the end found Jesus guilty. Therefore, there is a certain irony here: Whereas God authorizes Jesus "to save life" on the sabbath by providing him with the power of healing, the Pharisees conspire to kill God's eschatological agent, Jesus, in order to honour God by means of the observance of the sabbath laws.

In short, episodic structure and memory is characteristic of oral-aural narrative. The importance of such episodic structure in narrative pro-

---

[146] Wright, *Jesus*, p. 395, rightly notes that Jesus' Sabbath controversies are all about his eschatological agenda.

[147] For this interpretation, see Lane, *Mark*, p. 124 and Hooker, *Mark*, p. 108.

cessing has also been stressed by cognitive scientists who propose that people process and recall stories in terms of paragraph or episodic units.[148] Thus in this section an attempt has been made to show two ways in which frames help cognitive processing of the episodic structure of the Markan oral-aural narrative. First, I have shown that frames may enable narrative information to be semantically bound into an episodic unit by defining its boundary markers, such as temporal, spatial information, and characters, and by providing their prototypical information. Next, I have verified that as a global frame the LEGAL CONTROVERSY frame serves not only to organize the five stories in Mark 2.1–3.6 into a single thematic unit, but also to process each episodic unit in it as semantically bounded in terms of its prototypical event sequences instantiated by individual story properties.

Mark 2.1–3.6 has been analyzed so far in accordance with the theory of cognitive scientists that frame or scripted events are represented in memory as hierarchically and causally organized information scenes, and that the audience understands the events on the basis of the scenes. Each story may be summarized in terms of its own global frame title instantiated at a higher level. At a lower level, prototypical event sequences determine the structure of the episode and lead the audience to understand a large amount of information in the paragraph coherently, and transfer it to its scene headers. Since the prototypical event sequences in the LEGAL CONTROVERSY frame are a causally interconnected network, moreover, they enable the audience to understand coherently the relationship between the events of an episode and recognize the beginning (by an introduction of predicates that mark a new provocative event) and the end (by Jesus' defensive reactions or judgmental expressions from God, and the onlookers or Jesus' opponents) of an episode. Because of the global LEGAL CONTROVERSY frame and its prototypical event sequences instantiated by each story, therefore, the audience may view each paragraph information not only as an interconnected entity but also as distinct from the other paragraph one within Mark 2.1–3.6.[149]

---

[148] K. Haberlandt, "Encoding of Story Constituents," *Poetics* 9 (1980), p. 113; Black, "Episodes as Chunks," pp. 309–318.

[149] van Dijk, "Semantic Macro-Structures," p. 6, says that "the coherence of the discourse depends on the coherence of the possible-world fragment or course of events it represents."

C. Frame Organization of Sentences

I have explored in the previous section how the frame helps paragraph or episodic processing in Mark 2.1–3.6. Here we will consider the frame's function of chunking sentence information. Mark's original audience, as already discussed earlier, was not required to remember and reproduce Mark's Gospel verbatim, but the gist was enough. What is of primary interest is, thus, to test how the frame helps identify the gist, or summary, by chunking sentential information.

1. Use by Frames of New Testament Grammatical Categories: Main Verbs and Participial Clauses

As discussed above, a frame is a hierarchical set of concepts which are interconnected by human experiences. The hierarchical structure of a frame makes memory easier by allowing for an economical storage of a story on the part of the audience. Since parts belong in a whole, the access to the actions at the whole (higher) level readily leads to its parts.[150] Thus, all detailed actions at a lower or a part level in a frame-related story need not be stored, because it is conceptually dependent on and thus can be derived from the higher or whole level.[151] As Schank and Abelson propose:

> For the purposes of what is remembered, we are claiming the following: The macro-events [MAINCONS, i.e., main conceptualization] are remembered primarily; the micro-events are remembered (after enough time) equally poorly whether they were inferred and filled into the causal chain, or explicitly stated. This is because when an event is script-based, the actual event can be forgotten. What needs to be remembered is a pointer to the script that defined that event. This pointer is the macro-event itself.[152]

In frame-based story comprehension and recalling, the gist of the story is close to the main events; and other elements at lower levels can be summarized by the main actions as their prototypical contents may be

---

[150] For experimental evidence of this, see Bower, Black, and Turner, "Scripts," pp. 186–87.

[151] Roger C. Schank, "The Structure of Episodes in Memory," in *Representation and Understanding: Studies in Cognitive Science* (ed. Daniel G. Borow and Allan Collins; New York: Academic Press, 1975), p. 241.

[152] Schank and Abelson, *Scripts*, p. 166.

inferred as needed.[153] Accordingly, as Bower, Black, and Turner claim: "'John read the menu, decided on his selection, and told the waiter what he wanted to eat' can be summarized as 'John ordered.'"[154] A similar point is also made in Lakoff's metonymic model that one point or element of a frame can stand for the whole frame; at recall one element of the frame allows people to remember or infer the rest of the elements in the frame.[155]

Such a chunking function of the frame is critical for our present concern with the summary of information at the level of sentence and explains how oral memory for the gist of stories is made possible. I discussed in Chapter Four that in New Testament Greek the event of the main verb stands for other events metonymically or conceptually, and (aorist) verbs in predicative or adverbial participial clauses represent information predictable from their main verbs, whether the information is already mentioned in the co-text or prototypically belong to the event of the main verb. In other words, the Greek New Testament participle involves the information already known to the audience's mental frame for the event of the main verb. This is also the case for the other subordinate clauses. Cognitive scientists' experiments propose that people are most likely to remember the main events or clauses of the passage and less likely to remember subordinate events or clauses.[156] Hoyle explains the prototypical relationship of New Testament Greek main verbs and participial clauses, including subordinate clauses, in light of frames:

> Greek uses a main verb to mark the core event in a scenario [frame], and uses participles, or verbs in subordinate clauses, to refer to other events which are conceptually part of the main verb's scenario [frame]. Thus the cluster of main verb plus related participles represents one mental

---

[153] Schank and Abelson, *Scripts*, pp. 46–48; and Bower, Black and Turner, "Scripts," p. 187. Sanford and Garrod, *Understanding*, p. 81, say: "It can be argued that the MAINCON formulation is not at all arbitrary. The actions of a script can be thought of as goal structures, and the MAINCON the action which is the topmost goal of the hierarchy. So, in the ordering scene, all actions other than ordering itself are subsidiary subgoals enabling the act of ordering to be carried out—calling a waiter, for example. In this way, Schank and Abelson's formulation is a specific version of the idea that main goals are closer to the 'gist' of goal-based discourse than are the subgoals enabling the main goal to be realized."

[154] Bower, Black and Turner, "Scripts," p. 187.

[155] Lakoff, *Women*, pp. 77–80.

[156] D.E. Rumelhart, "Notes," pp. 211–36; P.W. Thorndyke, "Cognitive Structures in Comprehension and Memory of Narrative Discourse," *CP* 9 (1977), pp. 77–110.

scenario [frame], and fills one memory slot in the macro structure of the text.[157]

Indeed, the notion that participial clauses are conceptually dependent on their main verb has been already recognized by many grammarians. For example, C.F.D. Moule simply says: "The ruling consideration in interpreting participles is that they express something which is dependent on the main verb, or a pendant to it."[158] Likewise, though warning not simply to equate a participle with a dependent clause, Porter acknowledges the following: "The verb-modifying participle enters into a number of syntactical relations which have semantic consequences. Some of these may be characterized as temporal relations between events... but others may be analyzed as indicating other sorts of circumstantial relations."[159] And such relations of the predicative participle to its main verb have been given various labels such as concessive, causal, conditional, instrumental, purposeful or resultive and complementary.[160] Here an important question for the present study is what determines these relations. BDF, Moule, and Porter all agree that "context" plays a crucial role in inferring the various relations between the participles and main verbs.[161] Yet it must be noted, as discussed earlier, that the contextual information of a text frequently does not spell out information necessary for us to understand the semantic relation between sentences; instead, the audience's mental frame regarding the contextual information must be taken into account for discourse processing. The argument is that the context which permits the audience to draw inferences does not just lie in the text but in the audience's mental frame as opened by the linguistic input.[162] Accordingly, it is the audience's mental frame that makes an inferential processing between

---

[157] Hoyle, "Scenarios," p. 69. In order to support his hypothesis, Hoyle provides grammatical evidence: "Grammatically, the high frequency of conjunctions at the beginning of each Participle and main verb cluster, together with the low frequency and restricted choice of conjunctions within the cluster, suggests that the scenarios are the building blocks of stories between which relationships may be overtly marked, but within which marking is largely unnecessary" (p. 98). See the analysis of Mark 2.1–3.6 below.

[158] C.F.D. Moule, *An Idiom—Book of New Testament Greek* (Cambridge: Cambridge University Press, 1971), p. 99.

[159] Porter, *Idioms*, p. 190 (the original is italicized).

[160] BDF, § 417; Burton, *syntax*, pp. 169–75; Porter, *Idioms*, pp. 191–93.

[161] BDF, § 417; Moule, *An Idiom*, p. 99; Porter, *Idioms*, p. 190.

[162] T.A. van Dijk, *Discourse and Context: A Sociocognitive Approach* (Cambridge: Cambridge University Press, 2008), pp. x, 16, 56–73.

sentences possible. Brown and Yule assert that when we account for the importance of context in the interpretation of sentences, we should make appeal to notions such as "'shared presupposition', 'encyclopaedic knowledge', 'intention/purpose in uttering' and 'experience of previous similar text,'" all of which are called frames in this book.[163]

All these observations above—the New Testament grammarians' idea of the relations of the predicative participial clauses to their main verb, the importance of context in these relations, and cognitive linguistics' account of context in relation to frame—allow us to confirm the hypothesis that the semantic and pragmatic uses of predicative participial clauses in relation to their main verb are determined by the main verb's event frame. We may summarize the data concerning the syntactic, semantic, and pragmatic relations of the events referred to by the participle to the main verb as follows, drawing on Hoyle and supplementing with verbal aspect theory.

1) If the present participle is placed before the main verb (i.e., the antecedent participle), it pragmatically refers to the process, situation, and event temporally simultaneous with the main verb. In addition, the information regarding the antecedent present participle is used to explain the reason for the main verb's action. This is in conformity with verbal aspect theory. "...when an event is seen as still taking place, especially as overlapping with a current action, or event still to come, the imperfective aspect grammaticalized by the present tense-form is the natural form to use."[164] However, most grammarians acknowledge that the simultaneous temporal meaning of the present participle is often violated and, in many instances, "[a present] participle expressing the notion of completion preceded the finite verb."[165] But what remains valid in all of these instances is that the event of the present participle, whether it represents occurrences concurrent with or preceding

---

[163] Brown and Yule, *Discourse Analysis*, pp. 25–26, 35–58 (the quotation from p. 44). One of the most important contributions of modern semantic theory to linguistic study is the idea that language should be understood in the 'context' in which it is used. See John Lyons, *Structural Semantics. An Analysis of Part of the Vocabulary of Plato* (Cambrideg: Cambridge University Press, 1963), pp. 23–24; Charles Fillmore, "Topics in Lexical Semantics," in *Current Issues in Linguistic Theory* (ed. R.W. Cole; Bloomington: Indiana University Press, 1977), p. 119; and for such an emphasis on context in biblical scholarship, see Anthony C. Thiselton, "Semantics and New Testament Interpretation," in *New Testament Interpretation* (ed. I. Howard Marshall; Grand Rapids: Eerdmans, 1977), 75–104.

[164] Porter, *Idioms*, p. 188.

[165] BDF, § 339; see also Fanning, *Verbal Aspect*, p. 408.

the main verb, can be explained by the frame represented by the main verb in terms of its pragmatic relations to the main verb.

2) If the present participle is placed after the main verb (i.e., the subsequent participle), being non-temporarily related to the main verb's frame, the subsequent present participle is used to mark the pragmatic relationships to the event frame of the main verb such as manner, reason, purpose, and result. Of course, by non-temporal, I do not mean that there is no temporal relationship between the subsequent aorist participle and the main verb. Rather, the author has chosen to mark a non-temporal relationship by putting the participle after the main verb.[166]

3) If the aorist participle occurs before the main verb, it refers to an event that occurs temporally previous to the main verb. Porter argues:

> ...in contexts where issues of time are relevant, syntax seems to be important"; that is, "the syntactical pattern appears to be used to make relative statements about when the process is seen to have occurred...Thus when the [aorist] Participle is placed before the main verb, there is a tendency for the action to be depicted as antecedent.[167]

Porter goes on to say that this is also confirmed by verbal aspect theory: "The aorist tense-form grammaticalizes the perfective aspect, which is often found in contexts...where action is looked upon as complete. Therefore, when an event is seen as preceding another action, or as already complete, the aorist is the natural form to use."[168] It is fair to say that the pragmatic use of the antecedent aorist participle is to provide a preceding event from that of the main verb in the sequential stages of the event frame represented by the main verb, sometimes accompanying implicit reason for the main verb's event.

4) If the aorist participle is placed after the main verb, which occurs relatively less frequently in New Testament Greek and has no instance in the episodes in question, it refers to the event non-temporarily related to the main verb. In this case the aorist participle is used to

---

[166] Cf. Porter, *Verbal Aspect*, p. 381–82 (the quotation from p. 381); *idem, Idioms*, pp. 188–190, states that "when the Participle is placed after the main verb, there is a tendency for the action to be seen as concurrent or subsequent." But even in Porter's observation of the subsequent aorist participle following the main verb, time sequence between the subsequent participle and the main verb is disrupted.

[167] Porter, *Idioms*, p. 188; and see also *idem, Verbal Aspects*, p. 381.

[168] Porter, *Idioms*, p. 188.

mark such pragmatic relationships to the main verb's event frame as manner, means, reason, purpose and result, concessive, amplification, restatement, restrictive setting and condition.[169]

2. The Analysis of Sentences

I here attempt to discover the gist, or summary, of sentences and thus each episode in Mark 2.1–3.6 by chunking sentences according to the event frame of the main verb in independent clauses.

2.1. The First Episode (Mark 2.1–12)

(All of the main verbs are bolded, but the number is in accordance with the main verb in the independent clauses; participles are underlined and they are placed in a different line from the main verb depending on whether they are antecedent or subsequent. Subordinate clauses and the verbs of speaking or thinking expressed by characters other than the narrator are indented, being chunked on the basis of the same kind of grammatical analysis; conjunctions between chunks are italicized.)

1. *Καὶ* <u>εἰσελθὼν</u> πάλιν εἰς Καφαρναοὺμ δι᾽ ἡμερῶν
   ἠκούσθη
        ὅτι ἐν οἴκῳ **ἐστίν.**

The antecedent aorist participle εἰσελθὼν ("entering") refers to a preceding action from the main verb's event frame ἠκούσθη ("it was rumoured"), serving as a prerequisite event for a rumour of Jesus to spread.

2. *καὶ* **συνήχθησαν** πολλοὶ
        ὥστε μηκέτι **χωρεῖν** μηδὲ τὰ πρὸς τὴν θύραν,
3. *καὶ* **ἐλάλει** αὐτοῖς τὸν λόγον.
4. *καὶ* **ἔρχονται**
   <u>φέροντες</u> πρὸς αὐτὸν παραλυτικὸν <u>αἰρόμενον</u> ὑπὸ τεσσάρων.

The subsequent present participle φέροντες ("bringing") denotes a specific manner in which the main verb's event ἔρχονται ("they come") occurs; and the imperfective (the present tense-form) aspect shows that φέροντες is concurrent with ἔρχονται. The present participle αἰρόμενον ("being carried") is used adjectivally to describe the noun

---

[169] Hoyle, "Scenarios," pp. 100–32.

παραλυτικὸν ("a paralytic"), thus being a participial noun phrase. As a hearer-old marker the adjectival participle (αἰρόμενον) expresses the generic information about the physical condition of the paralytic.

> 5. *καὶ μὴ δυνάμενοι προσενέγκαι* αὐτῷ διὰ τὸν ὄχλον
> **ἀπεστέγασαν** τὴν στέγην
> ὅπου **ἦν**,

The antecedent present participle μὴ δυνάμενοι ("not being able to"), syntactically followed by the aorist infinitive προσενέγκαι ("to reach"), refers to a situation or condition of the main verb's action ἀπεστέγασαν ("to unroof the roof"), providing a specific reason for the main verb's action. The paralytic and his fellows' approach to Jesus through the door is still impossible at the same time that they are digging through the roof. Accordingly, the present participle explaining the condition by which they are not able to reach Jesus in the normal way denotes the reason for the main verb's action of "unroofing the roof," which is certainly not a normal way of visiting.[170] Note the phrase δύναμαι plus infinitive forms a "catenative construction,"[171] thus translating in the present case as "not being able to reach him" (see also Mark 2.19).

> 6. *καὶ ἐξορύξαντες*
> **χαλῶσι** τὸν κράβαττον
> ὅπου ὁ παραλυτικὸς **κατέκειτο**.

The antecedent aorist participle ἐξορύξαντες ("digging through") is used to refer to a prototypically preceding action in sequential stages of the event frame for χαλῶσι ("let down") of the main verb. And the speaker's choice of the perfective aspect (the aorist tense-form) for the action of making a hole through the roof (ἐξορύξαντες) also shows that such an action is complete when the paralytic's friends are letting the pallet down. Further, the action ("digging through") regarding the antecedent aorist participle may also explain the reason why the friends can *let* the paralytic *down from the roof.*

> 7. *καὶ ἰδὼν* ὁ Ἰησοῦς τὴν πίστιν αὐτῶν
> **λέγει** τῷ παραλυτικῷ·
> τέκνον, **ἀφίενται** σου αἱ ἁμαρτίαι.

---

[170] Or it may be possible that as an exception of the simultaneous temporal meaning of the antecedent present participle its event (" not being able to reach") refers to the event prededing the event of the main verb ("to unroof the roof").

[171] Cf. Porter, *Idioms*, p. 197.

The antecedent aorist participle ἰδὼν ("seeing") is a prototypical event that temporally and logically occurred prior to the main verb's action λέγει ("he says"). In this case we may say that Jesus's saying results from his watching their action based on faith; so, the participle's action ("seeing") is conceptually subordinate to the main verb's action.

8. ἦσαν δέ τινες τῶν γραμματέων ἐκεῖ
    καθήμενοι καὶ διαλογιζόμενοι ἐν ταῖς καρδίαις αὐτῶν·
        τί οὗτος οὕτως λαλεῖ;
        βλασφημεῖ
        τίς δύναται ἀφιέναι ἁμαρτίας εἰ μὴ εἷς ὁ θεός;

The first subsequent present participle καθήμενοι ("sitting") amplifies the manner in which the scribes appear (ἦσαν, "they were") in the story. The second subsequent present participle διαλογιζόμενοι ("questioning") denotes a specific purpose: They were there to raise a question) This shows that the two actions regarding the subsequent present participle belong in the same frame as the main verb.[172]

9. καὶ εὐθὺς ἐπιγνοὺς ὁ Ἰησοῦς τῷ πνεύματι αὐτοῦ
        ὅτι οὕτως διαλογίζονται ἐν ἑαυτοῖς
    λέγει αὐτοῖς·
        (1) τί ταῦτα διαλογίζεσθε ἐν ταῖς καρδίαις ὑμῶν;
        (2) τί ἐστιν εὐκοπώτερον,
        εἰπεῖν τῷ παραλυτικῷ· ἀφίενταί σου αἱ ἁμαρτίαι, ἢ
        εἰπεῖν: ἔγειρε καὶ ἆρον τὸν κράβαττον σου καὶ
        περιπάτει;

In the real-life occurrence, recognizing is a prototypical prerequisite in the frame for SPEAKING to someone else. Thus, the antecedent aorist participle ἐπιγνοὺς ("recognizing") refers to an event that occurs before the main verb's event λέγει ("he says"). Here ἐπιγνοὺς ("recognizing") is semantically related to the main verb by providing motivation for an act of saying. Note the verb ἐστιν ("it is") is semantically an incomplete main verb without εὐκοπώτερον ("easier"); thus here the semantic main verb is ἐστιν εὐκοπώτερον. Though not affecting the chunking of the main clause, chunk (2) within Jesus' speech has three verbs, ἔγειρε, ἆρον and περιπάτει, all of which are conjoined by

---

[172] This clause is not periphrastic since the grammatical subject (the scribes) is placed between the auxiliary verb and the participle. As Porter, *Idioms*, pp. 45–46, points out, in order for a set of εἰμί and a participle to be periphrastic, there may be no elements between "the auxiliary verb and the participle except for those which complete or directly modify the participle." And see also Mark 2.18 and 3.1a.

καὶ. They are sequential actions in the same event frame for HEALING THE PARALYTIC (for details, see the following chapter); so these highly salient details of the event in the verb's frame mark the significance of the verb's frame because they are commonly recalled and more easily brought to mind.[173]

> ἵνα δὲ **εἰδῆτε**
> ὅτι ἐξουσίαν **ἔχει** ὁ υἱὸς τοῦ ἀνθρώπου
> ἀφιέναι ἁμαρτίας ἐπὶ τῆς γῆς
> 10. **λέγει** τῷ παραλυτικῷ
> σοὶ **λέγω, ἔγειρε ἆρον** τὸν κράβαττον σου καὶ **ὕπαγε**
> εἰς τὸν οἶκον σου.

It has been claimed that this verse is grammatically "clumsy" because λέγει τῷ παραλυτικῷ "awkwardly" follows as the main clause of the ἵνα-purpose clause addressed to the scribes.[174] Thus Cranfield argues the ἵνα-purpose as "Mark's own comment addressed to the readers of the gospel."[175] Yet BDF states that "this use of ἵνα with 'I will say this [in the present instance σοὶ λέγω following the words λέγει τῷ παραλυτικω]' to be supplied is also class."[176] Thus, as is believed by many scholars, if we take λέγει τῷ παραλυτικῷ as Mark's parenthetical statement to show that the following words are addressed to the paralytic, the ἵνα-clause naturally takes the following σοὶ λέγω...σου as its main verb.[177] The turning of Jesus' addressee from the scribes (Mark 2.10) to the paralytic (Mark 2.10b-11) is hinted at in verse 9 (εἰπεῖν τῷ παραλυτικω). Mark's inserted statement may be then best understand as an aside designed to help the audience to know that what follows is directed to the paralytic.[178] So the ἵνα-purpose clause is coherently

---

[173] Note the forms of the three verbs are present imperative, aorist imperative and present imperative. Hoyle, "Scenarios," p. 99, says that "script-type events from a single scenario are sometimes encoded as a series of conjoined main verbs. In narrative, such verbs are typically Aorist, but may be Present in form. These forms, being statistically unusual, are thus 'marked' and indicate extra semantic information. I argue that these forms are used to 'highlight' the scenario in which they belong, i.e., give it extra significance or prominence at discourse level."

[174] Cranfield, *Mark*, p. 100, says, "the verse [v. 10] is very clumsy"; Lane, *Mark*, p. 96, says, "Structurally, there is [v. 10] an awkward change of addressee in the middle of the verse. Jesus *appears* to be addressing the scribes…" (Lane's italics).

[175] Cranfield, *Mark*, p. 100.

[176] BDF, § 470.

[177] Guelich, *Mark 1–8.26*, p. 89; Caragounis, *The Son of Man*, p. 184; France, *Mark*, p. 129.

[178] France, *Mark*, p. 129.

connected to Jesus' word addressed to the paralytic: Jesus pronounces healing to the paralytic in order that the scribes may know that he has authority to forgive.[179] Thus Mark 2.10 and 2.11 can be together clustered into the tenth chunk, which is made possible by the independent main verb (λέγει τῷ παραλυτικῳ), as a continuation of Jesus' speech.

11. καὶ ἠγέρθη
12. καὶ εὐθὺς ἄρας τὸν κράβαττον
    ἐξῆλθεν ἔμπροσθεν πάντων,
           ὥστε ἐξίστασθαι πάντας καὶ δοξάζειν τὸν θεὸν
           λέγοντας ὅτι οὕτως οὐδέποτε εἴδομεν.

The antecedent aorist participle ἄρας ("taking up")[180] is a preceding action in sequential stages of the main verb's event frame for ἐξῆλθεν ("he went out"). Consider in Mark 2.9, 11 and 12 the threefold repetition of the action sequences: ἐγείρω, αἴρω, ἐξέρχομαι with the variations of verse 9 (περιπατέω) and verse 11 (ὑπάγω). Moreover, this chunk has another pattern of main verb plus participle in its subordinate clause, in which the subsequent present participle clause (λέγοντας ὅτι..., "saying that...") is an amplification of the main verb's events: ἐξίστασθαι ("be amazed") and δοξάζειν τὸν θεὸν ("[they all] glorify God"). Note that ὥστε plus infinitive is a result clause, playing the role of a main verb; thus the semantic main verbs of the subordinate clause are ὥστε ἐξίστασθαι... καὶ δοξάζειν (also see Mark 2.2).

The summary below shows what the gist of the first episode may be when sentential information in it is chunked on the basis of the event frames of the independent main verb (note that the main verbs are bolded as an indicator, or "pointer" [to use Schank and Abelson's term], of the frame, and the independent main verb and all verbal tense forms conceptually belonging in such a frame, are underlined, following the bolded indicator of the independent main verb's frame. The content of the verb of speaking is sub-chunked along with the verb of speaking itself, identifying its gist. The global LEGAL CONTROVERSY frame is used to organize the flow of storyline):

---

[179] See Porter, *Verbal Aspect*, p. 362, on the function as the purpose clause of ἵνα in this passage.
[180] Unlike the use of the passive participle αἰρόμενον in Mark 2.3 ("a paralytic carried (αἰρόμενον) by four fellows"), by the use of the active participle ἄρας in Mark 2.12 ("he took up (ἄρας) the pallet") Mark seems to show dramatically that the paralytic's physical, in particular arm-strength, is restored.

CONTROVERSY OVER JESUS' FORGIVENESS OF SINS
Jesus' PROVOCATIVE FORGIVENESS OF SINS
   1. It **was rumoured**------------ He [Jesus] <u>went</u> into, and it **was rumoured**
                                          that he <u>was</u> in a house
   2. Many **gathered together**--- many **gathered together**, so that people
                                          <u>made</u> no room, not even about the door
   3. And he **preached**
   4. They **came** ------------------ they **came**, bringing to him a paralytic
                                          <u>carried</u> by four fellows
   5. And **unroofed**-------------- <u>were not able to reach</u> him, **unroofed** the
                                          qroof where he <u>was</u>
   6. And **let down** -------------- <u>dug through</u>, **let down** the pallet on which
                                          the paralytic <u>lay</u>
   7. Jesus **said**,
        Your sins **are forgiven** --Jesus <u>saw</u> their faith, **said** 'Your sins <u>are</u>
                                          <u>forgiven</u>'

The Scribes' CHARGE against Jesus
   8. Some of the scribes **were** --- some of the scribes **were** there, <u>sitting</u> and
                                          <u>questioning</u> in their hearts, 'Why does this
                                          man <u>speak</u> thus? He is <u>blaspheming</u>. Who
                                          <u>can forgive</u> sins but God alone?'

Jesus' DEFENSE of his authority
   9. Jesus **said**
        (1) why do you **question** thus?
        (2) which **is easier**, your sins **are forgiven**, or
             rise, **take up** your pallet and **walk**?
   ---------------------------------- Jesus <u>recognized</u>, they <u>questioned</u>, and
                                          said, 'Why do you <u>question</u> thus...?
                                          Which is easier... <u>are forgiven</u> or rise,
                                          take up... <u>walk</u>?'

   10. He **said** to the paralytic
         I **said**, **rise**, **take up** your pallet, **go to your house/household**[181]
         ------------------------------ 'So that you [the scribes] <u>may know</u> the Son
                                          of Man <u>has</u> authority <u>to forgive</u>,' He **said** to
                                          the paralytic, '<u>I said</u>, <u>rise, take up</u> your
                                          pallet, go to your house.'

God and the crowd's VINDICATION of Jesus
   11. He **rose/was raised** [by God]
   12. And **went out** -------------- <u>took</u> the pallet <u>up</u>, **went out**, so that they
                                          were all <u>amazed</u>, <u>glorified</u>, <u>saying</u> 'we <u>have</u>
                                          <u>never seen</u> such a thing.'

---

[181] On the translation of οἶκος as house/ household, see Chapter Six.

The verbs in subordinate clauses are grammatically related to each independent main verb and thus semantically dependent upon them. Thus, though there are forty-eight verbal tense forms, the core storyline of the first episode may be summarized in terms of twelve information segments, made possible by the chunking role of the main verbs in relation to the participles and subordinate clauses. In chunks 7, 9, and 10, in which the verbs of speaking are followed by their contents, the contents are expected to be processed as the same core event as the main verb, thus indicating the chunk in conjunction with the main verb.

2.2. *The Second Episode (Mark 2.13–17)*

1. Καὶ **ἐξῆλθεν** πάλιν παρὰ τὴν θάλασσαν:
2. καὶ πᾶς ὁ ὄχλος **ἤρχετο** πρὸς αὐτόν,
3. καὶ **ἐδίδασκεν** αὐτούς.
4. καὶ <u>παράγων</u>
   εἶδεν Λευὶν τὸν τοῦ Ἀλφαίου καθήμενον ἐπὶ τὸ τελώνιον,

The antecedent present participle παράγων ("passing by") refers to an event that is in process at the same time as the main verb's event εἶδεν ("he saw"). In other words, in this clause the present participle indicates the time setting of the action of the main verb: "While passing by, he saw Levi...." The adjectival present participle with the article τὸν...καθήμενον ("sitting") describes what Levi is. As a hearer-old marker, the adjectival participle is used to express common knowledge in the person frame for TAX OFFICER, which is opened by the word τὸ τελώνιον, ("the toll booth").

5. καὶ **λέγει** αὐτῷ:
        ἀκολούθει μοι.
6. καὶ <u>ἀναστὰς</u>
   ἠκολούθησεν αὐτῷ.

The antecedent aorist participle's action ἀναστὰς ("arising") is a preceding action in the event frame for ἠκολούθησεν ("he followed") of the main verb (cf., Mark 1.18 and 20).

7. καὶ **γίνεται** κατακεῖσθαι αὐτὸν ἐν τῇ οἰκίᾳ αὐτοῦ,

In New Testament Greek γίνομαι frequently performs its function as a main verb in conjunction with an infinitive (usually καὶ ἐγένετο + infinitive, see Mark 2.23).[182] Thus in this clause the word γίνεται by

---

[182] J.H. Moulton and W.F. Howard, *A Grammar Of New Testament Greek* Vol. II (Edinburgh: T. & T. Clark, 1919), p. 427.

itself provides very little semantic information as a main verb and so, in the verbal phrase γίνεται κατακεῖσθαι, the semantic main verb is κατακεῖσθαι ("to recline").

8. καὶ πολλοὶ τελῶναι καὶ ἁμαρτωλοὶ **συνανέκειντο** τῷ Ἰησοῦ καὶ τοῖς μαθηταῖς αὐτοῦ·
        ἦσαν γὰρ πολλοὶ καὶ **ἠκολούθουν** αὐτῷ.
9. καὶ οἱ γραμματεῖς τῶν Φαρισαίων <u>ἰδόντες</u>
            ὅτι **ἐσθίει** μετὰ τῶν ἁμαρτωλῶν καὶ τελωνῶν
        ἔλεγον τοῖς μαθηταῖς αὐτοῦ·
        ὅτι μετὰ τῶν τελωνῶν καὶ ἁμαρτωλῶν **ἐσθίει;**

It is certain that SEEING is a prototypical prerequisite in the frame for SPEAKING to someone in a real-life situation. Thus, here the antecedent aorist participle ἰδόντες ("seeing") refers to an event that precedes the main verb's event ἔλεγον ("he said").

10. καὶ <u>ἀκούσας</u>
        ὁ Ἰησοῦς **λέγει** αὐτοῖς
            (1) [ὅτι] οὐ χρείαν **ἔχουσιν** οἱ ἰσχύοντες ἰατροῦ ἀλλ᾽ οἱ κακῶς ἔχοντες·
            (2) οὐκ **ἦλθον** καλέσαι δικαίους ἀλλὰ ἁμαρτωλούς.

The antecedent aorist participle ἀκούσας ("hearing") refers to an action that occurs before the λέγει ("he says") of the main verb. Jesus' hearing of what his opponents have said leads him to respond to it, hence the participle serves as an implicit reason for the main verb's event, "saying." As hearer-old markers the nominal present participles with the Greek article, οἱ ἰσχύοντες ("those who are well") and οἱ κακῶς ἔχοντες ("those who have illness") refer to any prototypical agents ("the healthy" and "the sick") in the HEALING frame opened in this passage (see above and Chapter Six on the HEALING opened here). Or, quite possibly, οἱ ἰσχύοντες and οἱ κακῶς ἔχοντες are metaphorically used to refer back to οἱ γραμματεῖς τῶν Φαρισαίων (v. 16) and τελῶναι καὶ ἁμαρτωλοὶ (vv. 15–16) respectively (see Chapter Six).

Thus, the summary of the second episode may be as follows:

CONTROVERSY OVER TABLE FELLOWSHIP WITH
TAX COLLECTORS AND SINNERS
Jesus' PROVOCATIVE TABLE FELLOWSHIP with tax collectors and sinners
1. he [Jesus] **went out** beside the sea
2. the crowd **came** to him
3. he **taught** them
4. and **saw Levi**------------------------------<u>came along, **saw** Levi</u>
5. and **said follow** me----------------------**said**, '<u>follow</u> me'

6. he **followed** him -----------------------------rose, **followed** him.
7. he **reclined** [at the table] --------------------it came to pass that he
                                                   reclined
8. many tax collectors and sinners **reclined**
   [at the table] with Jesus and his disciples----**reclined**, for they were
                                                   many, followed him

The Scribes' CHARGE against Jesus' table fellowship with them
 9. The Pharisees of the Scribe **said** to the disciples
                Why does he **eat**
                with tax collectors and sinners?
---saw he ate with the sinners
                                                 and tax collectors, **said**,
                                               'Why does he eat....'

Jesus' DEFENSE of his table fellowship with them
10. Jesus **said**
                  (1) those who are well **have** no
                       need of a physician, but those
                       who have illness
                  (2) I **came not** to call the righteous,
                       but sinners
---Jesus heard, **said**, 'those
                                               who are well have no
                                               need...but those who have
                                               illness, I came not to call
                                               the righteous but sinners.

The second episode can be summarized by ten information segments based on the chunking of the main verbs in independent clauses, even though there are twenty-five verbal tense forms. Note that segments 5, 9, and 10, which have the speech verbs as the chunk indicators, contain the subchunk units consisting of the contents of speech verbs too.

2.3. *The Third Episode (Mark 2.18–22)*

    1. καὶ **ἦσαν** οἱ μαθηταὶ Ἰωάννου καὶ οἱ Φαρισαῖοι
       νηστεύοντες.

The subsequent present participle νηστεύοντες, "fasting," denotes an amplification of the main verb ἦσαν ("they were"); the participial information (fasting) may be inferred from a prototypical way of being or living of the Pharisees and John the Baptist's disciples.

2. *καὶ* **ἔρχονται** καὶ **λέγουσιν** αὐτῷ·
   διὰ τί οἱ μαθηταὶ Ἰωάννου καὶ οἱ μαθηταὶ τῶν
   Φαρισαίων **νηστεύουσιν**,
   οἱ δὲ σοὶ μαθηταὶ οὐ **νηστεύουσιν**;

There are in this chunk two main verbs ἔρχονται ("they come") and λέγουσιν ("they say"), which are conjoined by καὶ with the same subject, rather than main verb plus participle or participle plus main verb. This highlights the event frame by having two main verbs as its two indicators or core elements, thus encouraging the audience to pay special attention to the main verb's event frame, in this case the ASKING A QUESTION frame.

3. *καὶ* **εἶπεν** αὐτοῖς ὁ Ἰησοῦς·
   (1) **μὴ δύνανται** οἱ υἱοὶ τοῦ νυμφῶνος
       ἐν ᾧ ὁ νυμφίος αὐτῶν **ἐστιν νηστεύειν**
   (2)   ὅσον χρόνον **ἔχουσιν** τὸν νυμφίον μετ᾽ αὐτῶν
       οὐ δύνανται νηστεύειν.
   (3) **ἐλεύσονται** δὲ ἡμέραι
       ὅταν **ἀπαρθῇ** ἀπ᾽ αὐτῶν ὁ νυμφίος,
   (4) καὶ τότε **νηστεύσουσιν** ἐν ἐκείνῃ τῇ ἡμέρᾳ.
   (5) Οὐδεὶς ἐπίβλημα ῥάκους ἀγνάφου **ἐπιράπτει** ἐπὶ
       ἱμάτιον παλαιόν·
       εἰ δὲ μή, **αἴρει** τὸ πλήρωμα ἀπ᾽ αὐτοῦ
       τὸ καινὸν τοῦ παλαιοῦ
       καὶ χεῖρον σχίσμα **γίνεται**.
   (6) καὶ οὐδεὶς **βάλλει** οἶνον νέον εἰς ἀσκοὺς παλαιούς·
       εἰ δὲ μή, **ῥήξει** ὁ οἶνος τοὺς ἀσκοὺς
       καὶ ὁ οἶνος **ἀπόλλυται**
       καὶ οἱ ἀσκοί·
   (7) ἀλλὰ οἶνον νέον εἰς ἀσκοὺς καινούς.

We may summarize the third episode as follows:

CONTROVERSY OVER THE NONFASTING
OF JESUS' DISCIPLES
The PROVOCATIVE NONFASTING of Jesus' disciples
1. John's disciples and the Pharisees **were**----- John's disciples and the
                                              Pharisees **were** there, <u>fasting</u>

The Scribes' CHARGE of their nonfasting
2. People **came** and **said** (RAISING A QUESTION)
        Why do John's disciples and
        the disciples of the Pharisees **fast**,
        but your disciples do **not fast**

Jesus' DEFENSE of their nonfasting practice
3. Jesus **said**
        (1) can the wedding guests **fast**
        (2) they **cannot fast**
        (3) but the days **will come**
        (4) then they **will fast**
        (5) no one **sews** a patch of unshrunk cloth on
             an old garment
        (6) no one **pours** new wine into old wineskins
        (7) but [**pours**] new wine into new wineskins
-- Jesus **said**, 'Can the wedding guests... <u>fast</u> while the bridegroom is with them?, <u>cannot fast</u>... as long as they <u>have</u> the bridegroom, the days <u>will come</u> when the bridegroom <u>is taken away</u> from them, then they <u>will fast</u>, no one <u>sews</u>... otherwise, the patch <u>would tear</u> away from it, no one <u>pours</u>... otherwise the wine <u>would burst</u> the wine skins'

The third episode consists of three information chunks, though there are twenty explicit verbal tense forms. Chunk 3 has seven subchunks within the speech itself. Note that the main verb of subchunk (7) is implicit. These chunks within the speech may be best stored in memory as core elements of chunk 3 along with the main verbs of speech.

2.4. *The Fourth Episode (Mark 2.23–28)*

   1. *Καὶ ἐγένετο* αὐτὸν ἐν τοῖς σάββασιν **παραπορεύεσθαι** διὰ τῶν σπορίμων,
   2. *καὶ* οἱ μαθηταὶ αὐτοῦ **ἤρξαντο** ὁδὸν **ποιεῖν** τίλλοντες τοὺς στάχυας.

The subsequent present participle, τίλλοντες, "plucking," refers to a manner of making a path which is the main verb's event. Both events represent a single activity. Note that with ἄρχομαι plus infinitive the main conceptual idea is an infinitive verb's event; thus here the main verb's event is ποιεῖν ("to make").

   3. *καὶ* οἱ Φαρισαῖοι **ἔλεγον** αὐτῷ·
               ἴδε τί **ποιοῦσιν** τοῖς σάββασιν
               ὃ **οὐκ ἔξεστιν;**

4. καὶ **λέγει** αὐτοῖς·

    οὐδέποτε **ἀνέγνωτε**

      τί **ἐποίησεν** Δαυὶδ

        ὅτε χρείαν **ἔσχεν** καὶ **ἐπείνασεν** αὐτὸς καὶ οἱ μετ᾽ αὐτοῦ,

        πῶς **εἰσῆλθεν** εἰς τὸν οἶκον τοῦ θεοῦ ἐπὶ Ἀβιαθὰρ ἀρχιερέως

        καὶ τοὺς ἄρτους τῆς προθέσεως **ἔφαγεν**,

          οὓς οὐκ **ἔξεστιν φαγεῖν** εἰ μὴ τοὺς ἱερεῖς,

        καὶ **ἔδωκεν** καὶ τοῖς σὺν αὐτῷ οὖσιν;

Note that in the subordinate clause within the speech, the two main verbs ἔσχεν ("he was in need") and ἐπείνασεν ("he was hungry") are conjoined by καὶ, sharing the same subject. It is obvious that having need and being hungry are prototypically parts of the same event, and hence they may be chunked into a single event frame, that is, the BEING HUNGRY frame. In this case the conjoined events in the main verb mark the significance of the main verb's frame. The participial noun phrase τοῖς σὺν αὐτῷ οὖσιν ("those who are with him") is used to refer back to the preceding textual referent οἱ μετ᾽ αὐτοῦ ("his companions" or literally "those with him" in v. 25), thus being hearer-old information.

5. καὶ **ἔλεγεν** αὐτοῖς·

    (1) τὸ σάββατον διὰ τὸν ἄνθρωπον **ἐγένετο**

    (2) καὶ οὐχ ὁ ἄνθρωπος διὰ τὸ σάββατον·

6. ὥστε κύριος **ἐστιν** ὁ υἱὸς τοῦ ἀνθρώπου καὶ τοῦ σαββάτου.

The particle ὥστε, with which subchunk (3) begins, may be used as an indication that verse 28 is a result clause of verse 27. Yet, in line with E.D. Burton who views Mark 2.28 as "disjoined from the antecedent sentence" and thus an independent clause, this study posits that the ὥστε clause is a conclusion of the whole episode of Mark 2.23-28.[183]

The summary of the fourth episode may be then as follows:

CONTROVERSY OVER MAKING A PATH
BY PLUCKING GRAIN ON THE SABBATH

The disciples' PROVOCATIVE ACTION of making a path by plucking ears of grain laws on the sabbath

1. he **walked** through the grainfields ---- it came to pass that he **walked**
2. the disciples **made** a path ------------- **made** a path, plucking the grains

---

[183] Burton, *Syntax*, p. 100. On the role of verse 28 as a conclusion of the whole of the episode, see Chapter Six.

The Pharisees' CHARGE of the disciples' violation of the sabbath laws
3. the Pharisees **said**
     why **are** they **doing** on the Sabbath ------ **said**, 'Why are they <u>doing</u>…
                                                                    what <u>is</u> not lawful?'

Jesus' DEFENSE of his disciples' violation of sabbath laws
4. he **said**
     have you **never read** what David **did** ---- **said**, '<u>Have</u> you <u>never read</u> what
                                                                    David <u>did</u> he <u>had</u> need and <u>was</u>
                                                                    hungry how he <u>entered</u> and ate
                                                                    and <u>gave</u> it to those who <u>are</u>
                                                                    with him?'

5. and **said**
       (1) the sabbath **was made** for man
       (2) not man [**was made**] for the sabbath
6. the Son of Man **is** lord even of the Sabbath'
     -- **said**, 'The sabbath was made for
                                                                    man… the Son of Man is lord…'

The gist of the fourth episode, which has nineteen explicit verbal tense
forms, may be condensed into six information chunks on the basis of
the information chunking of the five independent main verb frames
and the function of Mark 2.28 as a concluding statement of the whole
episode. Note the verb of speaking in chunk 5 has two subchunks, in
which the main verb of subchunk (2) is implicit.

2.5. *The Fifth Episode (Mark 3.1–6)*

1. *Καὶ* **εἰσῆλθεν** *πάλιν εἰς τὴν συναγωγήν.*
2. *καὶ* **ἦν** *ἐκεῖ ἄνθρωπος*
     ἐξηραμμένην **ἔχων** *τὴν χεῖρα.*

The subsequent present participle ἔχων, "having," is an amplification
of the main verb ἦν, "he was." In other words, "having a withered
hand" is a specific description of a man being present. The perfect
participle ἐξηραμμένην, "withered," defines predicatively the noun
"hand." Here serving as a hearer-old marker, the participle is used to
open a particular kind of disease related to hand or body related to the
referent ("hand") of the noun.

3. *καὶ* **παρετήρουν** *αὐτὸν*
     εἰ τοῖς σάββασιν **θεραπεύσει** *αὐτόν,*
                         ἵνα **κατηγορήσωσιν** *αὐτοῦ.*

4. καὶ **λέγει** τῷ ἀνθρώπῳ τῷ τὴν ξηρὰν χεῖρα ἔχοντι·
   ἔγειρε εἰς τὸ μέσον.

Similarly, as a hearer-old marker, the present participial noun phrase τῷ τὴν ξηρὰν χεῖρα ἔχοντι ("the one who has the withered hand") is used to draw the audience's attention back to τῷ ἀνθρώπῳ who has a specific disease related to a hand, which is already stored in the audience's memory due to the preceding discourse.

5. καὶ **λέγει** αὐτοῖς·
   (1) **ἔξεστιν** τοῖς σάββασιν ἀγαθὸν ποιῆσαι ἢ κακοποιῆσαι,
   (2) [**ἔξεστιν** τοῖς σάββασιν] ψυχὴν σῶσαι ἢ ἀποκτεῖναι;
6. οἱ δὲ **ἐσιώπων**.
7. καὶ <u>περιβλεψάμενος</u> αὐτοὺς μετ' ὀργῆς, <u>συλλυπούμενος</u> ἐπὶ τῇ πωρώσει τῆς
   καρδίας αὐτῶν
   λέγει τῷ ἀνθρώπῳ·
        ἔκτεινον τὴν χεῖρα.

Here the main verb is preceded by the two participles with different verbal tense-forms. The antecedent aorist participle περιβλεψάμενος ("looking around") refers to a preceding action in the sequential stages of the main verb's event frame λέγει ("he says"). Referring to a situation temporarily concurrent with the main verb's action, the antecedent present participle συλλυπούμενος ("being grieved") explains reason for leading Jesus to say ἔκτεινον τὴν χεῖρα. So, it is clear that Jesus' grief for the Pharisees was not only in process at the same time as his speaking to the paralytic but also an implicit reason for a healing pronouncement, whereas his looking around at them was completed at the time of his proclamation of healing. Thus the use of the participles shows that the two-participial information ("looking around" and "being grieved") is prototypically part of the main verb's event frame.

8. καὶ **ἐξέτεινεν**
9. καὶ **ἀπεκατεστάθη** ἡ χεὶρ αὐτοῦ.
10. καὶ <u>ἐξελθόντες</u> οἱ Φαρισαῖοι
    εὐθὺς μετὰ τῶν Ἡρῳδιανῶν συμβούλιον **ἐδίδουν** κατ' αὐτοῦ
    ὅπως αὐτὸν **ἀπολέσωσιν**.

The antecedent aorist participle ἐξελθόντες ("going out") refers to an event occurring prior to the event συμβούλιον ἐδίδουν κατ' αὐτοῦ ("they took counsel...against him"), and thus it is an event in the sequential stages of the main verb's event frame. This means that the participial information prototypically belongs in that of the main verb.

So, we can infer the gist of the story according to the main verb's chunking function as follows:

CONTROVERSY OVER HEALING ON THE SABBATH

Jesus' anticipated PROVOCATIVE HEALING of the man with a withered hand
1. he **entered** the synagogue
2. a man **was** there ---------------------------- a man **was**, having the withered hand

The Pharisees' CHARGE of Jesus' expected healing on the sabbath
3. they **watched** him ------------------------- they **watched** him if he would heal him so that they may make a charge against him

Jesus' DEFENSE of his action of healing
4. he **said stand up** into the middle ----------- **said** to the man who has the withered hand, 'Stand up'

5. and **said** to them
   (1) it **is legal** to do good on the Sabbath or to do evil,
   (2) [it **is legal**] to save life or to kill
   --- **said**, 'It is legal to do good … or to do evil, to save life or to kill'
6 they **were silent**
7. he **said stretch out** your hand -------------- looked around, grieved, **said** to the man 'Stretch out your hand'

God and the Pharisees' VERDICT
8. he **stretched it out**
9. his hand **was restored**
10. the Pharisees **took** counsel against him ---- went out, **took** counsel, in order that they might destroy him

The fifth episode may be condensed into ten information chunks out of twenty-five verbal tense forms, and they may be stored as its gist in memory and on recall serving as frameworks for the storyline. Note that chunk 5 has two subunits, and in chunks 4, 5, and 7, the contents of the speech verbs serve as indicators to the chunks together with the speech verbs themselves.

In brief, our concern thus far has been with how frame theory can contribute to defining the gist of the stories in Mark 2.1–3.6, which may represent the memory of oral-aural narrative. Our basic assumption for this study follows cognitive science's experimental results: People's remembering of narrative depends on events high in the story hierarchies. In particular, for the application of this idea to New Testament Greek sentence processing, I have focused on the semantic and pragmatic relations of the independent main verb to the participle. A Greek main verb marking a discourse-new event represents the core element or event in a frame, and participles or verbs in subordinate clauses are used to mark events prototypically belonging in the main verb's event frame. Thus, the main verb event serves as an indicator to the cluster of main verb and participles. The observations made above have shown that this hypothesis is the case for the sentential analysis of Mark 2.1–3.6. The string of main verbs forms the framework of the story line; and participial information and dependent verbs, which are grammatically and semantically related to independent main verbs, can be clustered into the semantic chunks of the independent main verbs. It is certain, then, that remembering the sequence of main verbs is an efficient reading technique for oral-aural narrative processing.

It is time to explain what relevance the frame chunk consisting of the main verb and participle has for the oral-aural feature of Mark's Gospel. Two factors must be kept in mind. First, we have already noted that the 'and next' kind of organization is a basic grammatical form of expression which represents a compositional characteristic of oral-aural narrative, and thus of Mark's Gospel.[184] The observations above have consistently shown that there is a high frequency of 'and next' organizations with the use of conjunctions such as καί and δέ, at the beginning of each main verb or main verb plus participle cluster. This demonstrates that that chunking unit serves as a basic framework for the 'and next' organization noted in Mark's oral-aural narrative discourse. Second, as discussed earlier, an action-oriented narrative progress is characteristic of Mark's oral-aural Gospel. Since the sequencing of actions or events makes up information regarding the main verb's frame, the semantic chunk of independent main verbs plus participles and dependent verbs is a good way of understanding and remembering such an action-packed narrative flow. Accordingly, it is certain that the main verb's event frame is nearer to the gist or summary of five controversy episodes in Mark 2.1–3.6. The participle's

---

[184] See Chapter Three (esp. 3.1.4).

events, as shown above, are prototypically related to the main verb's event frame; the recall of the main verbs lends the audience ready access to other subordinate events by means of inference. An assumption is that remembering the main verb's events as indicators to the event frame on the sentential level enables the audience to make the gist memory representation.

We have observed thus far that two kinds of frames operate at different discourse levels: Sentences and Paragraphs. Hearers process episodes by means of paragraph-level frame(s) (e.g., the LEGAL CONTROVERSY and the HEALING and so on) and sentences by means of main verb frames. A question may arise here: How do hearers use the two kinds of frames and process the inputs coherently when they are of a different discourse level? To provide a more specific example, the two healing stories (Mark 2.1–12 and 3.1–6) show that the HEALING frame at episode level is opened not primarily by the main verbs (ἔρχονται, 2.3 and ἦν, 3.1) but by participles or participial phrases (φέ ροντες...παραλυτικὸν 2.3 and ἐξηραμμένην ἔχων τὴν χεῖρα, 3.1). Is it a problem that paragraph-level frame openers are not found in main clauses for discourse processing? To put it another way, how do the participles and the main verbs work in opening up frames necessary for discourse processing when the higher level frame's core components are not found in the main verbs? This problem can be resolved when remembering frames' hierarchical processing at discourse level. For story comprehension and recall, as mentioned before, the frame is hierarchically structured at a larger level of discourse too. When the audience hears for the first time what is orally performed, the audience uses all of the input represented not only by main verbs, but also by participles and nouns at the level of sentences so that they can build up a relevant larger or higher level frame (the HEALING or/ and the LEGAL CONTROVERSY) which is necessary to understand discourse at the level of episode. This means that when the main verbs (ἔρχονται, 2.3 and ἦν, 3.1, in the example above) do not represent core information needed to open frames at the higher level of discourse, the hearer alternatively makes every effort to find the relevant higher frame in other grammatical elements like participles (φέροντες, 2.3 and ἐξηραμμένην ἔχων τὴν χεῖρα, 3.1) and nouns (παραλυτικὸν 2.3).[185]

---

[185] On the hearer/reader's searching process to find information relevant in opening frames, see van Dijk, *Macrostructures*, pp. 230–40; Rumelhart, "Schemata," p. 42

Once the larger frame (the HEALING) or/and global frame (the LEGAL CONTROVERSY) has been opened, it, in turn, guides the hearer coherently to link information of the subframes (including main verb frames, ἔρχονται, 2.3 and ἦν, 3.1 in the example above) within the open frame. And when the audience recalls what was already heard (2.1–12; 3.1–6) as a whole, they use the opened episode-level frame(s) as a framework to recall the storyline of the narrative formed by the main verb frames (thus see above for the flow of storyline organized by the global LEGAL CONTROVERSY frame).

Here is another example of the CALLING TO DISCIPLESHIP frame (2.14)(chunked according to main verbs, bolded, participles underlined):

1. καὶ <u>παράγων</u>
   εἶδεν Λευὶν τὸν τοῦ Ἀλφαίου καθήμενον ἐπὶ τὸ τελώνιον,
2. καὶ **λέγει** αὐτῷ· **ἀκολούθει** μοι.
3. καὶ <u>ἀναστὰς</u>
   ἠκολούθησεν αὐτῷ.

In this example the CALLING TO DISCIPLESHIP frame is not apparently opened until the main verb (λέγει) and the speech verb (ἀκολούθει) in the second information chunk and the main verb (ἠκολούθησεν) in the third chunk are expressed. This is not least because while the main verb ("saw") and even the participle ("passing by [seashore]") in the first chunk are prototypical properties in the CALLING TO DISCIPLESHIP frame in Mark's Gospel,[186] they represent less 'typical' information than the main verbs ("call and "follow") in the second chunk.[187] Thus the hearer's comprehension of the first chunk relies on the second and third chunks. When and as the CALLING TO DISCIPLESHIP frame is opened, the main verb and the participle in the first chunk is understood in terms of the opened frame: Jesus' purpose of passing by the seashore and seeing Levi, for example, is to call him to follow his footsteps. Yet no matter how each sentence is well made sense of in its own frame, sentential meaning can

---

and see also Minsky, "Framework," p. 236 on the interactive processing of frames at sentence and paragraph levels.

[186] On the CALLING TO DISCIPLESHIP frae in Mark's Gospel, see section 6.2.1. in Chapter Six.

[187] For Rosch and Mervis' research on prototype effect that shows asymmetries among categorymembers and asymmetric structures within categories, Rosch, Mervis, "Basic Objects," pp. 382–439.

be appropriately understood in light of higher frames at episode level. So when the audience opens the LEGAL CONTROVERSY frame by means of verse 16 καὶ οἱ γραμματεῖς τῶν Φαρισαίων ἰδόντες ... ἔλεγον τοῖς μαθηταῖς αὐτοῦ, the CALLING TO DISCIPLESHIP frame opened in verses 14–15 starts serving as a subframe of the global frame, providing a precondition for conflict between Jesus and the religious leaders (see section 6.2.3. in Chapter Six).

The proposition that frame openers may be represented in other grammatical elements than main verbs is not surprising at all, when it is taken into consideration that a frame, as Schank and Abelson note, usually consists of divergent key components which may enable the audience to open it.[188] And what frames' hierarchical operation at discourse level has shown is that the hearer's discourse processing works in an inseparable relation of episode-level frame and main verb frames' role of forming the building blocks of the story.

D. CONCLUSION

We have demonstrated so far how frames may be helpful in organizing, processing, and remembering the oral-aural narrative discourse units in Mark 2.1–3.6 in cognitive terms on the part of the hearer. First, the global LEGAL CONTROVERSY frame determines the organization of Mark 2.1–3.6 into a single thematic unit as a whole by providing its repeated set patterns of prototypical events. Second, with respect to the frame's episodic processing of Mark 2.1–3.6, two things have been discussed. One is that frames, by defining episode boundary markers such as temporal, spatial information, and characters within an episode, help cognitive processing of the episodic structure of each story in Mark 2.1–3.6. The other is that we have verified that the LEGAL CONTROVERSY frame's prototypical event sequences are instantiated or filled in by the specific information the individual episodes represent, thus enabling each episode to be a semantically bounded unit. In other words, since the LEGAL CONTROVERSY frame instantiated by the input of each episode provides its conceptually interconnected event sequences, the frame's prototypical event sequences enable the audience not only to process each episode in a semantically

---

[188] Schank and Abelson, *Scripts*, pp. 47–50.

coherent way, but also to recognize that there is a beginning of a new episode and hence, at the same time, the end of a previous one by its beginning and ending information. The final concern of this chapter was to define what has been known as the memory for oral-aural narrative. As a result, we have posited that frames, by hierarchically (or in part-whole relation) assigning participles or verb events in subordinate clauses into main verb events, help to identify the gist of each episode. All these observations demonstrate that frames are very helpful in understanding the structures and mental processes related to Mark's oral-aural narrative.

CHAPTER SIX

FRAMES AND THE PROCESSING OF THE CONTROVERSY
STORIES (MARK 2.1–3.6)

In the preceding chapter we have seen that frames play a significant role in organizing the structures of the oral-aural narrative discourse in Mark 2.1–3.6 and in identifying the 'gist' memory of each episode within it on the part of the hearer. This present chapter will examine the ways in which frames help the audience readily and quickly to understand what the text, Mark 2.1–3.6, says. Structurally, this investigation will be made on the basis of the sequential flow of the story frame as discussed in Chapter Four (Stage, Inciting Incident, Mounting Tension, Climax, Closure). With regard to the reference point for an examination, I will rely on the properties of frames that have been observed in Chapter Four, specifically in the section "Comprehension of Information."

A. The First Episode (Mark 2.1–12)

1. *Preparing Stage (Mark 2.1–2)*

Mark 2.1–2 opens the PREACHING/TEACHING frame because of the set expectations of "entering (εἰσελθὼν)," "gathering (συνήχθησαν)" and "preaching the word (ἐλάλει... τὸν λόγον)." Once that frame is opened, Jesus fills the slot for a preacher and the πολλοὶ ("many people") gathered as 'those being taught,' and the house (ἐν οἴκῳ v. 1) is labelled as a location for the preaching to take place.[1] It is worth noting that the term τὸν λόγον has the Greek article, though occurring initially in this

---

[1] That οἶκος is here used just as a public place in which Jesus teaches many people seems strange for modern Western readers. But, as Moxnes, *Putting Jesus in His Place,* pp. 25–28, rightly points out, translating οἶκος in the New Testament as 'home' implying a 'private area,' in contrast to 'public area,' reflects a modern, Western middle-class' perspective; Moxnes goes on to argue that οἶκος in first-century Palestine represented the more public space of 'house.' If so, the fact that, as already noted in Chapter Three, the house is used as a place for a public gathering in the Gospel of Mark is not surprising. In line with Moxnes, we then translate οἶκος in Mark's passages quoted in this study as 'house' or 'household' in an attempt to avoid the modernized concept of οἶκος.

episode. In fact, τὸν λόγον is a normal expectation in the occurrences of the PREACHING frame in the Gospel of Mark (1.45; 4.14, 33; cf. 16.20);[2] besides, there is evidence to show that for the early Christians ὁ λόγος was a default property tied to the frame of PREACHING (Luke 1.2; Acts 4.4; 6.4; 8.4; 10.44; 11.19; 17.11; Galatians 6.6; Colossians 4.3; 2 Timothy 4.2). So the article is used here as a hearer-old marker to refer to the particular word which is activated in the audience's mind due to the current PREACHING frame. In verse 1 ἠκούσθη is a verb with no specific agent, so information regarding who spreads and hears the news is not explicitly mentioned. But in light of the frame for SPREADING RUMOUR in which ordinary people are the typical agents of spreading and receiving rumour by word of mouth, the semantic subject of the passive verb (the agents of spreading or hearing the news about Jesus) can be assumed to be villagers. Thus the identification of many indefinite people (πολλοί, in v. 2) gathering where Jesus is may be understandable in light of the frame (so, note in v. 4 the use of the Greek article for the word τὸν ὄχλον occurring for the first time in the Gospel of Mark).[3]

Mark stresses the overcrowding of people by using the expressions μηδὲ τὰ πρὸς τὴν θύραν. Because of the HOUSE frame opened by the place title οἴκῳ, the initial introduction of τὴν θύραν with the Greek article is not surprising (note it is default information in the open HOUSE frame); and in the flow of the narrative, the Greek article leads the audience to associate the door with the house in which Jesus preaches. More importantly, the HOUSE frame may infer the information about the prototypical function of a door (i.e., letting people enter and exit); so a specific focus (or perspective) on the door among many objects within the frame enables the audience to understand the resultive clause of verse 2: ὥστε μηκέτι χωρεῖν μηδὲ τὰ πρὸς τὴν θύραν as implying that 'no one can

---

[2] Mark 1.45 (the relevant frame is bolded and its prototypical default is underlined): ὁ δὲ ἐξελθὼν ἤρξατο κηρύσσειν πολλὰ καὶ διαφημίζειν τὸν λόγον

4. 1, 14:   Καὶ πάλιν ἤρξατο **διδάσκειν** παρὰ τὴν θάλασσαν
.... ὁ σπείρων τὸν λόγον σπείρει
   4. 33:   Καὶ τοιαύταις παραβολαῖς πολλαῖς ἐλάλει αὐτοῖς τὸν λόγον καθὼς ἠδύναντο ἀκούειν
   cf. 16.20: ἐκεῖνοι δὲ ἐξελθόντες ἐκήρυξαν πανταχοῦ, τοῦ κυρίου συνεργοῦντος καὶ τὸν λόγον βεβαιοῦντος διὰ τῶν ἐπακολουθούντων σημείων.

[3] Consider also the use of πάλιν (underlined) in Mark 2.1: Καὶ εἰσελθὼν πάλιν εἰς Καφαρναοὺμ δι' ἡμερῶν... The word πάλιν seems to reveal that Jesus' visiting of Capernaum would be what the audience might expect (cf., Mark 1.21; 9.33) against background knowledge of Jesus' hometown (Mark 1.9; 6.1; cf. 1.24; 10.47; 14.67; 16.6 in which Jesus is called "the Nazarene").

enter the house anymore' or 'no one can approach Jesus anymore.' This information then prepares the audience for making sense of the paralytic and his friends' strange or unexpected action to follow. In addition, the double negative (μηκέτι... μηδε) strongly indicates that an expected action failed to take place in the house and thus marks surprise.[4] The expectation is that a house, and thus its door, is commonly a place for people to go in and out freely. So the inferential and contraexpectation functions of the expression ὥστε μηκέτι χωρεῖν μηδὲ τὰ πρὸς τὴν θύραν can only be understood in light of the frames for HOUSE and DOOR.

2. Inciting Incident (Mark 2.3–5)

As the paralytic is introduced in verse 3, the PREACHING frame is replaced by the HEALING frame evoked by the references to its core participant (παραλυτικὸν) and his visiting of Jesus. Once the HEALING frame is clearly opened, because of its prototypical event sequences (healer's moving into a place, 2.1; introducing the sick, 2.3; preparing healing, 2.4; healing, 2.5, 11; confirming healing, 2.12) the audience expects them to proceed normally unless the text states otherwise. In this frame the paralytic fills the slot for the sick person and Jesus fills the slot for the healer. Before we examine Jesus' healing activity, it is important to note the fact that Mark gives an account of healing within the context of teaching or preaching. In Jesus' contemporary culture sickness was dealt with as illness not just as disease. John Pilch, for this reason, argues, "Since illness concerns the sociocultural meaning of a sickness experience, it makes good sense to view a teacher as a healer." [5] Indeed teaching and healing are in Mark's Gospel often inseparably related (1.21, 22; 2.13; 4.1, 35; 5.35; 6.2, 6, 30; 9.17, 38). So Mark 1.27 shows that, when Jesus healed the man with an unclean spirit in the synagogue, the crowd cried out (the teaching information is bolded and the healing information is underlined): τί ἐστιν τοῦτο; **διδαχὴ καινὴ κατ' ἐξουσίαν**· <u>καὶ τοῖς πνεύμασι τοῖς ἀκαθάρτοις ἐπιτάσσει, καὶ ὑπακούουσιν αὐτῷ</u>. Thus the fact that the healing of the paralytic occurred in the context of Jesus' teaching must have made good sense in the audience's mental frame that viewed a teacher as a healer.

Before we pay further attention to frames' role in the narrative comprehension, it is also worth accounting for frame operation related to the

---

[4] On Greek negative statement as a contraexpectation marker, see Chapter Four.
[5] Pilch, *Healing*, p. 71.

choice and use of the third person pronoun. In verses 3 and 4, the third person pronoun (bolded) is initially used in this episode apparently in reference to Jesus, though there is in the preceding co-text no linguistic expression which could be treated as the direct antecedent (i.e., a proper name, Jesus) for the pronoun: ἔρχονται φέροντες πρὸς αὐτὸν παραλυτικὸν...μὴ δυνάμενοι προσενέγκαι αὐτω διὰ τὸν ὄχλον. The proper name of Jesus has not occurred since Mark 1.25 and reoccurs at 2.5. This seems to raise a serious problem in relation to a traditional understanding of the use of pronoun, according to which one of the important functions of pronoun is to replace given information.[6] Sanford and Garrod rightly claim, however, that "the degree to which a concept is activated determines the ease with which it can be referred to by an anaphoric pronoun, 'him.'"[7] If so, the translation of αὐτόν as a reference to Jesus in this case depends not only on the hearer's mental representation of Jesus as the main character of his Gospel (Mark 1.1), but also on what is predicated on the subjects of the preceding three verbs (underlined) in verses 1–2: εἰσελθὼν πάλιν εἰς Καφαρναούμ; ἐν οἴκῳ ἐστίν; ἐλάλει τὸν...λόγον. In particular, the expression ἐλάλει αὐτοῖς τὸν λόγον apparently evokes Jesus' stereotypical role, particularly as a teacher or preacher (e.g., Mark 1.14–15, 21–22, 27, 38–39; 2.13; 4.1, 2; 6.2, 34; 8.31; 9.31; 10.1; 11.17; 12.14, 35; 14.49). It must be also noted that verses 3 and 4, which include the pronoun, assign αὐτὸν and αὐτῷ to the role of the healer to whom the paralytic was being brought. As mentioned, Jesus fills the slot of healer in the Gospel of Mark. It seems logical, accordingly, to assume that the text presupposes the hearer to infer that the non-anaphoric pronoun refers to Jesus on the basis of the mental frame for JESUS (involving a preacher and healer). In other words, the belief that his audience has that mental frame for JESUS enables the text to use the hearer-old marker (αὐτόν) to denote Jesus, even in the absence of a corresponding direct antecedent.[8] This assumption can be confirmed when the proper name of Jesus (bolded) is mentioned in verse 5: καὶ ἰδὼν ὁ Ἰησοῦς τὴν πίστιν αὐτῶν.[9]

---

[6] On the substitutional function of pronouns, see Porter, *idioms*, pp. 128–38.
[7] Sanford and Garrod, *Understanding*, p. 194. For frames' role in the anaphoric function of pronoun, see Chapter Four.
[8] On pronoun's function of referring to new information, see Chapter Four; Brown and Yule, *Discourse Analysis*, pp. 218–22.
[9] On the similar use of the third person pronoun in the Controversy Stories, see also Mark 2.13, 15, 18, 23, 24; 3. 2.

The open HEALING frame enables the audience to expect what happens in the story and infer the intention, or purpose, of the participants' behaviour such as φέροντες πρὸς αὐτὸν παραλυτικόν, ἀπεστέγασαν τὴν στέγην, and ἐξορύξαντες χαλῶσι τὸν κράβαττον: To have the sick person healed. Since the PARALYTIC frame, as a subframe of the HEALING frame, involves its prototypical knowledge of the paralytic's physical state of being unable to move normally, it makes the way ("being carried by four men") the paralytic approaches Jesus predictable and understandable: Note αἰρόμενον ὑπὸ τεσσάρων referred to by the adjectival participle, a hearer-old marker; and the noun τὸν κράβαττον followed by the Greek article, a hearer-old marker used here, though it occurs initially. And the original audience's frame for HEALING the sick person may have helped to identify the indefinite agent of the verb ἔρχονται and τεσσάρων who brought and carried the paralytic to Jesus. John Pilch rightly points out that in the "health care system" of first-century Mediterranean culture, family members (e.g., Jairus and a Syro-Phoenician woman in Mark 5.22–24; 7.24–30) and fictive kin villagers (e.g., Mark 1.33 in which the whole city [ὅλη ἡ πόλις] gathered at the door when the sick person was brought to Jesus) played a crucial role in health maintenance or sickness care.[10] By using the indefinite subject τεσσάρων, Mark must have assumed his original audience would readily identify the agents of the verb or the "four men" as family members or fellow villagers, by referring to their mental "health care" (to use Pilch's term) frame.

Verse 4 shows that "due to the crowd (διὰ τὸν ὄχλον)" the paralytic's friends make the choice of the roof as a route to reach Jesus: καὶ μὴ δυνάμενοι προσενέγκαι αὐτῷ διὰ τὸν ὄχλον ἀπεστέγασαν τὴν στέγην. In order to be able to understand the paralytic's attempt to reach Jesus via the roof rather than the door, the audience must open the background knowledge of the roof in the HOUSE frame. The shape of the roof was flat, constructed of wooden props, and its function was not usually for the gathering of people, thus the crowd was not gathered there.[11] For the original audience, however, the way which the paralytic approaches Jesus by digging a hole in the roof must have been unexpected information in the frame for VISITING SOMEONE'S HOUSE. The frame deviation enables the proper translation of the conjunction καὶ (bolded) in verse 4:

---

[10] Pilch, *Healing*, pp. 66–67.
[11] Gustaf Dalman, *Sacred Sites and Ways: Studies in the Topography of the Gospels* (trans. Paul Levertoff; London: SPCK, 1935), p. 69.

v.3   …ἔρχονται φέροντες πρὸς αὐτὸν παραλυτικὸν αἰρόμενον ὑπὸ
      τεσσάρων.
v.4   καὶ μὴ δυνάμενοι προσενέγκαι αὐτῷ διὰ τὸν ὄχλον ἀπεστέγασαν τὴν
      στέγην.

The VISITING SOMEONE'S HOUSE frame enables the audience prototypically to expect that the paralytic and his fellows would meet Jesus just
after coming (ἔρχονται, in v. 3) to the house. Yet verse 4 shows that
contrary to what might be expected in terms of the usual order of visiting a house, they do not see Jesus because of people crowded around
the house. Accordingly, that unexpected action in the frame enables
the audience to translate καί as the adversative conjunction 'but,' a
contraexpectation marker (a signal of semantic discontinuity between
vv. 3 and 4).

The significance of frame deviation for narrative comprehension is
that, when the frame's predictability is interrupted by deviations, the
audience's interest in and tension around the story, and with that their
remembering of it, are heightened. If so, the audience would find surprising and interesting the action of the paralytic's four friends, which
obviously deviated from their typical knowledge regarding visiting the
house. And it is only against this typical background knowledge associated with visiting a house that the audience may understand the actions
as those of faith which cross social and cultural boundaries.

Verse 5, which refers to Jesus seeing "their faith" (ἰδὼν ὁ Ἰησοῦς τὴν
πίστιν αὐτῶν), shows that the perspective of a participant in the HEAL-
ING frame shifts from the sick person to the healer. Such a shift of the
perspective, on the one hand, foregrounds and highlights the role of the
healer; on the other hand, it prepares the audience for the way in which
Jesus as a healer usually responds to the sick person. Jesus' response to
their faith was the statement of forgiveness of the paralytic's sins. Jesus'
pronouncement of forgiveness was intelligible and predictable in the
open frame for HEALING the paralytic, provided sin and disease, or forgiveness and curing, were frequently interrelated concepts for Mark's
original Christian audiences(see Chapter Five). For Jesus' original audience ἀφίενται σου αἱ ἁμαρτίαι would have activated the frames for both
GOD who has the prerogative to forgive (e.g. Mark 11.25)[12] and PRIEST

---

[12] For example, Mark 11.25 states (the relevant clause is underlined): Καὶ ὅταν
στήκετε προσευχόμενοι, ἀφίετε εἴ τι ἔχετε κατά τινος, ἵνα καὶ ὁ πατὴρ ὑμῶν ὁ ἐν τοῖς
οὐρανοῖς ἀφῇ ὑμῖν τὰ παραπτώματα ὑμῶν.

who was a declarer of the forgiveness of sins on behalf of God in the atonement rituals (Leviticus 4.26, 31; cf. Mark 1.44). Although the link of sin and disease was not unexpected, Jesus' action of pronouncing the pardon of sins may have been understood as a deviation in the contemporary Jews' frame opened by ἀφίενταί σου αἱ ἁμαρτίαι, since in either frame Jesus seemed to exercise the authority to forgive on God's behalf (i.e., Jesus was neither a priest nor God in the scribes' view). When it comes to the audience's cognitive process of interest in the story, since the audience's background knowledge about certain events or persons determined what is expected and unexpected in the story, tension is heightened and interest aroused through a conflict of expectations. While it made perfect sense in the JESUS frame, which involved the information regarding the one who brings the eschatological kingdom of God (Mark 1.1; 1.14),[13] Jesus' statement of forgiveness would have sounded absurd in his contemporary Jewish mental frame that the forgiveness of sins was God's prerogative or the authorized priest's right.

3. *Mounting Tension (Mark 2. 6–7)*

@@@When verse 6 begins, the audience is led to replace the HEAL-ING frame, which has operated thus far, with the LEGAL CONTROVERSY frame, primarily because of reference to the presence of the scribes (ἦσαν ... τινες τῶν γραμματέων ἐκεῖ) and their challenging questions "in their heart (ἐν ταῖς καρδίαις αὐτῶν)."[14] The HEALING frame now is backgrounded, providing the condition of the LEGAL CONTROVERSY frame. In other words, the appearance of the paralytic and, as a result, Jesus' pronouncement of forgiveness of sins serves as a reason to open the LEGAL CONTROVERSY frame by providing an issue necessary for controversy between Jesus and his opponents. In this way, once the LEGAL CONTROVERSY frame is opened as a global frame, this frame plays a dominant role in the interpretation of the whole story, including the preceding and subsequent one, and the scribes who raise a charge against Jesus for proclaiming the forgiveness of sins would fill the slot for the accuser and Jesus the slot of the defendant. This observation

---

[13] See below on Mark's Christian audience's frame related to Jesus' unique divine identity.

[14] Note the Greek article before "the hearts" ταῖς καρδίαις as a hearer-old marker, since "hearts" is a prototypical component in the frame for PERSON (also see in Mark 2.8 τῷ πνεύματι, "in the spirit" or "heart").

is congruent with Minsky's proposition, "As the story proceeds, information is transferred to superframes whenever possible, instantiating or elaborating the scenario."[15]

The appearance and accusation of the scribes are already anticipated by the preceding stage. The audience's frame based on the previous discourse which Jesus pronounced the forgiveness of sins on God's behalf also enables the audience to expect that the accusation of blasphemy against Jesus may follow next. And with the introduction of the scribes, the audience has an ideal accuser of Jesus who speaks for God since the scribes activate the frame (or social stereotype) for typical legal experts who were schooled in the written law and its oral interpretation. Regarding understanding the scribes' furious reaction, it is essential for the audience, in addition to the SCRIBE frame, to have the frame for GOD who has prerogative authority to forgive. In particular, this frame lays the groundwork for understanding the scribes' rhetorical questions ("Why does this man speak thus?" and "Who can forgive sins but God alone?"). Without such shared knowledge the accusatory intention of the rhetorical questions would not be communicated, and the scribes' furious reaction would be incomprehensible. Thus we must believe that, making use of rhetorical questions and evaluative language, the text takes for granted that the audience would share that frame knowledge with it.

4. Climax (Mark 2.8–11)

In his defence "Jesus" (ὁ Ἰησοῦς v. 8) is described as perceiving "in his spirit" (τῷ πνεύματι αὐτοῦ) even what the scribes are thinking "in their hearts" (ἐν ἑαυτοῖς) (cf., 3.2–3). Jesus' capacity to know the hidden thoughts of humans must have been understood without difficulty in light of the opening JESUS frame (a person frame), which for the early Christian audiences involved the major conviction that Jesus was a divine figure in Jewish monotheistic terms (Mark 1.2–3; 4.35–41; 6.45–51; 12.35–37, 14.62; Philippians 2.6–11; 1 Corinthians 8.6; Revelation 5.12–14).[16] Besides, for the audience Jesus' all-knowing power supports

---

[15] Minsky, "Framework," p. 236.

[16] On the fact that the early Christians believed in Jesus sharing "the unique divine identity" of God, including the Creator of and Ruler over all things, see Richard Bauckham, "The Worship of Jesus in Apocalyptic Christianity," NTS 27 (1981), pp. 322–41; idem, God Crucified: Monotheism and Christology in the New Testament (Grand Rapids, Michigan: Eerdmans, 1998), pp. 25–79. Bauckham, God Crucified, p. 27, argues, "the highest possible Christology, the inclusion of Jesus in the unique divine identity, was

his divine authority to forgive since the phrase ἐπιγνοὺς ὁ Ἰησοῦς τῷ πνεύματι αὐτοῦ ὅτι... also opens the frame for GOD, who is described in the Old Testament as having the power of discerning a person's innermost thoughts (e.g.,1 Samuel 17.28; Psalms 139.23; Proverbs 24.12).[17]

In verses 9, 11 and 12 Jesus' healing actions occur with the same expressions (bolded), with the variation of the third action:

v. 9: ἔγειρε καὶ ἆρον τὸν κράβαττον σου καὶ περιπάτει
v. 11: ἔγειρε ἆρον τὸν κράβαττον σου καὶ ὕπαγε εἰς τὸν οἶκον σου
v. 12: ἠγέρθη, ἄρας, ἐξῆλθεν

This shows that those healing actions are repetitive enough to be stereotypical in healing the paralytic. And they are an interconnected whole in terms of the paralytic's goal of being healed, thus each healing action is totally predictable in light of the paralytic's physical condition. In other words, in order to understand this type of healing, it is essential to evoke information concerning the sick person's physical condition in the PARALYTIC frame, which is also somewhat hinted at in verse 3 (αἰρόμενον ὑπὸ τεσσάρων). The word ἔγειρε can be understood against the presupposition that this man could not stand on his feet and the phrase ἆρον τὸν κράβαττον on the assumption that he could not use his hands before. In this way Jesus' healing actions foreground the paralytic's feet and hands, implying the recovery of their function. The final action of healing is ὕπαγε εἰς τὸν οἶκον σου. This may not seem a typical component in that frame in light of the modern HEALING

---

central to the faith of the early church even before any of the New Testament writings were written, since it occurs in all of them" (e.g., for passages concerning the exalted Jesus' participation in God's unique sovereignty over all things, see Matthew 22.44; 11.27; 26.64; Mark 12.36; 14.62; 16.19; Luke 10.22; 20.42–43; 22.69; John 3.35; 13.3; 16.15; Acts 2.33–35; 5.31; 7.55–56; Romans 8.34; 1 Corinthians 15. 25, 27–28; Ephesians 1.21–22; Philippians 3.21; Hebrews 1.2; 2.8 etc; and on Jesus' inclusion in the work of creation, see John 1.1–5; 1 Corinthians 8.6; Colossians 1.15–16; Hebrews 1.2–3, 19–12; Revelation 3.14). And see also Wright, *Jesus*, pp. 612–53; *idem*, "The Divinity of Jesus," in *The Meaning of Jesus: Two Visions* (ed. Marcus J. Borg; N.T. Wright; New York: Harper, SanFrancisco, 1999), pp. 157–68. Wright, "Divinity of Jesus," pp. 169–63 (the quotation from p. 162), states that the early Christians not only all regarded Jesus as accomplishing in his earthly ministry what Israel's God had promised to consummate himself (e.g., the real return from exile, the final defeat of evil, and the return of YHWH to Zion), but also believed "what had happened in Jesus was the unique and personal action of the one God of Israel." Of course Wright's point throughout his books is that this train of thought goes back to the historical Jesus himself; and see also Hurtado, *Lord Jesus Christ*, p. 650.

[17] See Robert H. Gundry, *Mark: A Commentary on His Apology for the Cross* (Grand Rapids, Michigan: Eerdmans, 1993), p. 113; and see also Marcus, *Mark 1–8*, p. 222.

frame. In ancient Jewish cultures, however, the frame for HEALING the sick person involved not only the physical but also the social aspect (Mark 1.31, 44; 4.19, 43; 8.26; 10.52); hence, Jesus' action of sending him to his household (τὸν οἶκον) may be interpreted as a demonstration of the restoration of his social role at the house, possibly as a parent and husband.[18] Note the paralytic's house has the Greek article, a hearer-old marker, though being initially mentioned. The use of the Greek article here can be interpreted in two ways: The first is that for a man to have a house is prototypical; the other is that since the house was where the paralytic being cured physically should restore meaning in life, it was already opened in the audience's mental frame for HEALING. Accordingly, it must be believed that, given the open PARALYTIC frame, this kind of healing pronouncement is not unexpected.

With respect to the resumption of the HEALING frame at this stage, however, what we should not forget is that, as discussed in the previous chapter, it is used as a subframe of the LEGAL CONTROVERSY frame. Hence, the open global LEGAL CONTROVERSY frame enables the audience to interpret Jesus' healing of the paralytic in terms of defending his authority to forgive. This argument can be apparently supported by the textual use of the purpose clause ἵνα δὲ εἰδῆτε... in verse 10, which specifies the Son of Man's intention of proving his authority to forgive sins with regard to the action of healing in the main clause.

5. Closure (Mark 2.12)

The first conflict episode ends with God's vindication of and the onlookers' doxological response to Jesus' forgiveness and healing. We have already observed that the GOD frame is implictly opened in this passage (see Chapter Five). In particular, the GOD frame involves the

---

[18] For the translation of τὸν οἶκον as "household ," see above in this chapter. It is thus important to note that, as Malina, *New Testament*, p. 91, points out, "The honourable man, the first-century male ideal, is one who knows how to live out and live up to his inherited obligations.... He works to feed and clothe his family. He fulfills his community and ceremonial obligations." Cf. Wright, *Jesus*, p. 192, also says,"... Jesus' healing miracles must be seen clearly as bestowing the gift of *shalom*, wholeness, to those who lacked it, bringing not only physical health but renewed membership in the people of YHWH"; "the effect of these cures, therefore, was not merely to bring physical healing; not merely to give humans, within a far less individualistic society than our modern western one, a renewed sense of community membership; but to reconstitute those healed as members of the people of Israel's god." [italics are the original author's]

information of a prototypical role of the ultimate Judge;[19] so the occurrence of God at the verdict stage in the LEGAL CONTROVERSY frame makes perfect sense. Likewise, because of the frame that GOD IS THE ULTIMATE JUDGE, God's favour of Jesus' defence is able to serve to resolve ultimately the tension heightened by the scribes' charge of blasphemy against Jesus. Next, the onlookers in the storyline respond in amazement (ἐξίστασθαι) and with a doxological chorus (δοξάζειν τὸν θεὸν λέγοντας ὅτι οὕτως οὐδέποτε εἴδομεν) when they see the paralytic being healed both spiritually and physically. The reference to the crowd's appearance and response at the end of story is not surprising because the text explicitly informs the audience of their presence in the story at its beginning (see πολλοὶ and τὸν ὄχλον, in vv. 2, 4); and so it is processed in the audience's mental frame that they have been present throughout the story, observing the conflict caused by Jesus' forgiveness. However, in order to be able to understand the results in the observers' amazement and doxological response (note the resultive particle ὥστε), the audience must activate extra-textual knowledge. What causes the onlookers' amazement, according to frame theory, is not just the healing processes of the paralytic (ἠγέρθη, ἄρας τὸν κράβαττον and ἐξῆλθεν ἔμπροσθεν πάντων); but the unexpected nature of the data in light of their PARALYTIC frame involving the prototypical information that the sick person perhaps has body parts which cannot move.

So the use of contraexpectation marker ἐξίστασθαι here makes perfect sense. It has already been discussed that for people to understand something is to select a relevant frame to account for it and accommodate something to the existing frame knowledge. On the contrary, something that cannot be accounted for by the existing frame leads one to amazement or incomprehension. In this regard the verb ἐξίστημι is an indication that there is something (the Paralytic's carrying of an object and walking) happening that one is not able to handle in terms of their existing frame (the PARALYTIC frame).[20] Likewise, the denial of the onlooker's expectation is also expressed in a negative statement,

---

[19] Similarly, Mark 10.2–9 shows that God's divine authority or intention of the marriage union based on Genesis 1.27 and 2.24 is used to justify Jesus' unconditional opposition to divorce.

[20] In Mark's Gospel the verb ἐξίστημι is used four times, including the passage in question (Mark 2.12; 3.21; 5.42; 6.51); except for in 3.21 in which people (probably Jesus' family members) accuse Jesus of "being beside himself" (ἐξέστη), it is used to refer to a reaction for Jesus' miracles (making Jairus' daughter alive and walking on the sea).

οὕτως οὐδέποτε εἴδομεν.²¹ People usually hunt for a relevant frame to make sense of a seemingly inexplicable event. So the crowd's subsequent response (δοξάζειν τὸν θεὸν) shows then that they opened the GOD frame to comprehend the surprising event. In other words, since for a first-century Jew God was prototypically regarded as the enabler of mighty works, or miracles, and the forgiver of sins,²² the crowd understands the paralytic's being healed and being forgiven as a result of God's power active in Jesus' word and ministry.

We have noted particularly in Chapter Five how the global LEGAL CONTROVERSY frame enables the audience to predict the development of the story by providing its prototypical event sequences. This anticipatory function of the frame is true of the subframes of the global LEGAL CONTROVERSY frame. For the audience this final stage of Confirming Healing ("he rose/was raised...went out in front of them all") in the HEALING frame has been predicted since the frame was initially opened by the paralytic's approaching Jesus in verse 3; and when they hear that the paralytic actually rose and walked out, the frame's prediction is accomplished on the part of the audience.

B. The Second Episode (Mark 2.13–17)

1. *Preparing Stage (Mark 2.13–14)*

The second episode has a relatively lengthy narrative before the main event of the conflict between Jesus and the Pharisees/scribes. This stage begins the story by encouraging the audience to open background knowledge of Jesus' actions stored in their mind. First of all, verse 13 says (the relevant linguistic item is underlined), Καὶ ἐξῆλθεν πάλιν παρὰ τὴν θάλασσαν. The word πάλιν indicates that Jesus' going beside the sea is repetitive and thus expected. Then, πάλιν intensi fies the effect of activating the information of what Jesus goes to the seashore for, what he does there, and whom he will meet there (cf., Mark 1.16–20; 4.1; 5.21). The story begins with Jesus going beside the

---

²¹ For the function of Greek negative statement as a contraexpectation marker, see Chapter Four.

²² For a similar reason, Sanders, *Jesus*, p. says, "While the miracles themselves do not dictate their own meaning, it is entirely reasonable to assume that Jesus' following, and perhaps Jesus himself, saw them as evidencing his status as true spokesman for God, since that sort of inference was common in the Mediterranean."

sea and the teaching of the crowd (v. 13). We have explored the fact that the PREACHING/TEACHING frame is made up of prototypically predetermined sequences of events (see Chapter Three and Preparing Stage of the first episode). This is true of 2.13 in which the three core actions ἐξῆλθεν, ἤρχετο, and ἐδίδασκεν are conjoined by καί.[23] Since a frame has a strong tendency to follow the norm, once the TEACHING frame is recognized, the progression of the prototypical events is readily anticipated by referring to the frame. And in this progression, the events are goal-directed in temporal sequence, so the actions of Jesus' going out and the crowd's gathering are linked to the goal of Jesus' teaching them. In story comprehension, when the audience hears the first action of Jesus' going out, the TEACHING frame enables the audience to expect that the crowd's gathering and Jesus' teaching will be mentioned explicitly or implicitly. The story of Jesus' teaching of the crowd (v. 13) is immediately followed by that of his calling of Levi (v. 14). Guelich says that since Mark 2.13 is "a general transition for what follows rather than a specific background for the calling of Levi," "that calling appears to be as abrupt as the calling of the four brothers."[24] It must be noted, however, that semantic coherence between Jesus' teaching (v. 13) and calling to discipleship (v. 14) may be made from the components in the TEACHING frame opened in 2.13. Since the TEACHING frame holds the information of a teacher and a disciple as its default value, it is prototypically predictable in light of the frame that as a public teacher Jesus not only teaches but also summons people to be his disciples.[25]

In verse 14, which has two more parallel narratives in Mark's Gospel, we can again find set expectations of prototypical events in the CALLING TO DISCIPLESHIP frame (the relevant frame components are underlined):

---

[23] For the parallel event sequence in Mark's PREACHING/TEACHING frame, see Chapter Four.

[24] Guelich, Mark 1–8.26, p. 99.

[25] Mark 3.7–19 is another example of this: Jesus' encounter and implicit teaching/ preaching the crowd (Mark 3.7–12) are immediately followed by his choosing the twelve disciples from the crowd (Mark 3.13–19). In this passage, of course, there is no direct reference to teaching or preaching, but note that it involves two core actions: A teacher's going back (ἀνεχώρησεν, v. 7) and people's coming (ἦλθον, v. 8) in the TEACHING frame.

Table 11: The CALLING TO DISCIPLESHIP Frame in Mark's Gospel

Prototypical Event Sequences	Mark 1.16–18	1.19–20	2.14
Master's Seeing	εἶδεν Σίμωνα καὶ Ἀνδρέαν	εἶδεν Ἰάκωβον…	εἶδεν Λευὶν…
Master's Calling	εἶπεν αὐτοῖς ὁ Ἰησοῦς·	ἐκάλεσεν αὐτούς…	λέγει αὐτῷ:
	δεῦτε ὀπίσω μου…		ἀκολούθει μοι
Disciples' Following	ἠκολούθησαν αὐτω	ἀπῆλθον ὀπίσω αὐτοῦ.	ἠκολούθησεν αὐτῷ

The fact that the CALLING TO DISCIPLESHIP frame is opened in these passages can also be supported by the Greek article, a hearer-old marker, before the noun τοῖς μαθηταῖς (Mark 2.15), a phrase which is the initial occurrence in Mark's Gospel. This can be best understood by presuming that the text supposes the concept of the disciples to be already opened in the audience's mind by Mark 1.16–20 and 2.14. The above figure shows that the three passages repeat in the same order the semantically same events associated with Jesus' calling of the disciples. Of course, there are lexical variations (in the second event stage δεῦτε ὀπίσω μου, ἐκάλεσεν αὐτούς, ἀκολούθει μοι and ἀπῆλθον ὀπίσω αὐτοῦ in the third stage), but no doubt they open the conceptually same frame knowledge (thus Calling in the second stage and Following in the third stage). Regarding story understanding, much information in this passage (Mark 2.14), involving other passages, would be apparently incomprehensible without having that frame. The text does not state explicitly how a total stranger can call other people to follow him or how they are able to show such an immediate response, abandoning their boat, parents, and occupation so readily. Yet since it involves its prototypical information regarding the relation between a master and a disciple, the CALLING TO DISCIPLESHIP frame enables the audience to make sense of Jesus' summons as a master's call to his disciples, and their abandonment of their former way of life and "following" as the total commitment to the master's cause (Mark 10.29–30).[26]

---

[26] As Hengel rightly points out in his book, *Charismatic Leader*, the model of Jesus' calling of his disciples fits the "charismatic leader" established by Elijah's call of Elisha (1 Kings 19.19–21) rather than the model of a rabbi and his disciples or pupil.

2. Inciting Incident (Mark 2.15)

In verse 15 the story turns from the scene of calling Levi beside the sea to the one of Jesus' table fellowship with tax collectors and sinners in a house. Concerning such a shift of spatial setting, the text leaves out information about Jesus and Levi's movement from beside the sea to the house. Despite that textual omission of the intermediate steps, the semantic coherence between 2.13–14 and 2.15 may be processed in the audience's mental frame. Since "to speak of one part of a frame is to bring to consciousness . . . its other components,"[27] the textual expression Καὶ γίνεται κατακεῖσθαι αὐτὸν ἐν τῇ οἰκίᾳ αὐτοῦ (Mark 2.15a) enables the audience to activate the missing information that 'they (Jesus and Levi) came to a house to have table fellowship.' Besides making inferences concerning the missing information, the frame helps the audience understand the correlation of two different events conjoined by the particle γάρ (an explanatory particle is bolded): πολλοὶ τελῶναι καὶ ἁμαρτωλοὶ συνανέκειντο τῷ Ἰησοῦ καὶ τοῖς μαθηταῖς αὐτοῦ· ἦσαν γὰρ πολλοὶ καὶ ἠκολούθουν αὐτῷ Given that ἠκολούθουν is used technically to refer to the disciples' following in this passage (note Jesus' calling Levi to follow [ἀκολούθει] and Levi's following [ἠκολούθησεν] in v. 14). Mark seems to attempt to explain Jesus' having table with the tax collector and sinners by adding the γάρ clauses, "many people were there and they followed him."[28]

Yet on what basis can the audience make sense of the γάρ clauses' explanation of the preceding proposition?[29] Recent research on the use of γάρ in New Testament Greek indicates that the particle γάρ serves to "signal the audience to modify the mental representations they construct of discourse: by introducing material which confirms and strengthens the preceding proposition (usually but not necessarily by giving either a reason or elaboration)."[30] If so, though the information of Jesus' table

---

[27] Fillmore, "Frame Semantics," p. 130.

[28] Many scholars take πολλοὶ as referring to Jesus' disciples excluding the tax collectors and sinners. But it is important that the toll collectors and sinners are already referred to by "many" ("many toll collectors and sinners"). Thus, as Guelich, Mark 1–8.26, p. 103, rightly says, "What would then be the significance of this comment but to indicate that Jesus had a larger number of disciples than the Twelve? Consequently, Levi's call to discipleship also fits with this larger circle of disciples for Mark."

[29] On the explanatory function of the particle γάρ, see Porter, Idioms, pp. 207–208.

[30] Black, Sentence Conjunctions, pp. 262, 265. Black's main argument is that, rather than "truth-conditional" or "logical" meaning, "procedural" meaning made in the process of discourse can do justice to the uses of γάρ-clause in Matthew's Gospel. She says:

fellowship with tax collectors and sinners is suddenly introduced into the discourse, no doubt the γὰρ clauses containing information regarding the following of Jesus by many people helps the audience to infer that such a table fellowship is part of discipleship. Yet what is more important for the present concern with the audience's mental process is the argument that such an inferential processing between the γὰρ-sentence and its preceding information is not just based on the logical content of the individual sentences, but rather on the language user's prior frame associated with the events in question.[31] In other words, the reason the explanatory γὰρ clauses can be made sense of here is because of the audience's frame knowledge that table fellowship is a typical event related to the situation of calling to discipleship (cf., Mark 1.16–20, 31; 2.18–19; 3.14; 7.2; 14.17–25).[32] Here the γὰρ clauses are used to elicit from the audience this background knowledge and relate it to the present information. Consequently, it must be said that Jesus' having a meal with the disciples is not an unexpected action in terms of the CALLING TO DISCIPLESHIP frame opened here, but rather predictable and understandable (see above).

When it comes to the interest of the story, Jesus' calling and having a meal with tax collectors and sinners would produce interest and suspense in the audience, because in light of the typical knowledge of Jewish table fellowship it was not seen as normal for a religious leader to

---

"In Matthew's narrative framework, however, the sentence appears always to follow the proposition which it strengthens."

[31] Brown and Yule, *Discourse Analysis*, pp. 31–35; Sanford and Garrod, *Understanding*, pp. 188–90. They both claim that the hearer's understanding of discourse relies not only on the formal logic between sentences but on inference based on socio-cultural knowledge or frame. And referring to Matthew's Gospel, Black, *Sentence Conjunctions*, pp. 262–72, shows how the pragmatic inference based on the audience's "off-line" knowledge may process in understanding the semantic relationship between the γὰρ clause and its preceding proposition.

[32] We need to keep in mind that one of the distinctive features that characterized the early Christians was table fellowship within the community (1 Corinthians 11.29–34; Galatians 2.11–12; Acts 2.42, 46). Beside the early Christian communities, table fellowship was a crucial social practice in various religious and social groups in the first-century Mediterranean world. For example, on the meal practices in the Qumran community as well as the Pharisaic groups, see Neusner, *Politics*, pp. 78–96; *idem*, "Two Pictures of the Pharisees: Philosophical Circle or Eating Club?," *ATR* 64 (1982), pp. 525–38; Dunn, *Partings of the Ways*, pp. 107–113 And on Greco-Roman social and religious groups' meal practices, Dennis E. Smith, "Social Obligation in the Context of Communal Meals: A Study of the Christian Meal in 1 Corinthians in Comparison with Graeco-Roman Communal Meals," Th.D Diss., Harvard Divinity School, 1980; *idem*, "Table Fellowship as a Literary Motif in the Gospel of in the Gospel of Luke," *JBL* 106 (1987), pp. 613–38 and L.E. Klosinski, "Meal in Mark," Ph.D. diss., The Claremont Graduate School, 1988.

have as meal companions those who opened the social stereotype of blatant violators of the Mosaic covenant.[33]

3. *Mounting Tension* (*Mark 2.16*)

The Pharisees' hostile question replaces the CALLING TO DISCIPLESHIP frame with the LEGAL CONTROVERSY frame; and as a result the issue of Jesus' table fellowship is processed as a condition of the LEGAL CON-TROVERSY frame in that it is a cause of controversy. In such a challenge to Jesus' behaviour the Pharisees' question is not directly addressed to Jesus but to his disciples. This was not surprising but expected in light of the CALLING TO DISCIPLESHIP frame, which included information that a master and a disciple were typically under mutual responsibility for each other's behaviour.[34] Bultmann pointed out that the introduction of the scribes/Pharisees in this situation in which Jesus had table fel-lowship with his disciples and tax collectors and sinners is an "impos-sible appearance."[35] Yet since Jesus' meal practice opened the frame or semantic information of violation of Jewish social and religious bound-aries, it would have made perfect sense in the story flow that, in order to dispute Jesus' action, the scrupulous interpreters of the laws and ritual regulations would appear, raising their accusatory question (note that this expectation of the occurrence of the Pharisees/scribes is confirmed in the use of a hearer-old marker, the Greek article before the noun οἱ γραμματεῖς τῶν Φαρισαίων). When they are referred to by the title of "the scribes of the Pharisees," the person frame leads the audience to anticipate and understand the legal teachers' typical (i.e., disputable) reaction to Jesus' practice of welcoming the tax collectors and sinners into table fellowship with himself, and this, in turn, results in the audi-ence's increased interest in the story and their sense of suspense as they anticipate a further development of conflict between Jesus and the legal interpreters.

---

[33] See Chapter Five. In addition, for the difficulty of distinguishing between the viola-tion of Mosaic laws and ritual impurity ancient Judaism, see Marcus, *Mark 1–8*, pp. 226, 239–31.

[34] Daube, "Responsibility," pp. 11–12.

[35] Bultmann, *Synoptic Tradition*, p. 18 note 3, says, "The situation is quite impossible. Whence and why do the Pharisees come? Do they arrive during the meal, or when it is over?" And see also Taylor, *Mark*, p. 203.

4. *Climax* (*Mark 2.17*)

A fuller understanding of Jesus' defence clearly requires the audience
to evoke their frame knowledge. First, whereas the Pharisees question
Jesus disregarding the Torah, and in particular the issue of ritual purity
in his public association with tax collectors and sinners, Jesus, in a very
brief statement, replies to them by appealing to the central purpose of
his ministry (οὐκ ἦλθον καλέσαι δικαίους ἀλλὰ ἁμαρτωλούς, "I did
not come to call the righteous but sinners"). In doing so Jesus unmistakably bases the justification of having a meal with wicked people on his
own authoritative mission.[36] This is a very short dispute, and also the
legal issue of purity raised by the Pharisees is left untouched by Jesus.
Mark's audience, however, is expected to understand the statements
without much clarification and probably be in favour of Jesus' position.
It is certain, thus, that, as long as Jesus is understood just as 'an ordinary Jew' by the audience, his response makes no sense at all. Yet Jesus'
answering based on his own authority must have made perfect sense
in light of Mark's Christian audience's mental frame for JESUS, which
included information that he was an eschatological Messiah (Mark 1.1;
8.29) replacing allegiance to Torah, or Jewish religious laws (Mark 1.49–
45; 2.23–28; 3.1–6; 5.25–34; 7.1–23; 10.17–22), and Temple (11.15–18,
27–33) with allegiance to himself.[37] Next, Jesus' defensive proverb is
apparently intended to evoke the HEALING frame particularly because of
the word ἰατροῦ, "physician," which is a core participant in that frame.[38]
Once the frame is recognized, thus, its default values are activated to
understand or process the information in the clause: οἱ ἰσχύοντες fills
the slot for the healthy, while οἱ κακῶς ἔχοντες fills the slot for the sick
person, and χρείαν the sick person's need of healing of illness. (Note the
Greek article, a hearer-old marker, before the noun οἱ ἰσχύοντες and οἱ
κακῶς ἔχοντες.) This indicates that the text assumes the concepts to be
already known to his audience by the open HEALING frame while by using
the article, the information accumulated by the preceding text enables
the audience metaphorically to link οἱ ἰσχύοντες to οἱ γραμματεῖς τῶν
Φαρισαίων (v. 16) and οἱ κακῶς ἔχοντες to τελῶναι καὶ ἁμαρτωλοί (vv.
15–16). Certainly, this proverb is based on the background knowledge
of the typical role of the physician, who usually does not refuse to take

---

[36] Gundry, Mark, p. 126.
[37] Wright, *the People of God*, p. 366; *idem, Jesus*, pp. 264–74; Marcus, *Mark 1–8*, pp.
231–32.
[38] As discussed, the physician can be also a frame. See Chapter Five.

care of a sick person. (Note in v. 17 ἀλλὰ, a contraexpectation marker, which is textual evidence to show that it is unexpected for the healthy to ask for the physician's help.) It is not then hard to believe that the information in the proverb and its meaning would be readily understandable, being inferred through its prototypical participants and their role in the HEALING frame.

Additionally, it is clear that the proverb is used for Jesus' specific purpose of defending his meal practice, and the open LEGAL CONTROVERSY frame essentially makes it possible to comprehend Jesus' intention of using the proverb. But the effectiveness of the proverb in such a purpose depends on the audience's ability to understand the physician proverb in reference to Jesus himself. I have already explored in Chapter Five the way in which the physician proverb and Jesus' defence of having table fellowship with sinners and tax collectors may be metaphorically linked in light of the HEALING frame, which for the ancient audience involved the information of the multi-dimensions of healing, such as curing of physical disease and healing of social and spiritual illness. Likewise, it is the knowledge of the healer's prototypical role that gives priority to the sick person that fundamentally makes it possible to understand Jesus' concluding statement in verse 17. Since it is ridiculous for a physician to refuse the sick person, as a spiritual healer Jesus' calling of sinners into a proper relationship with God must be validated. Jesus' use of the physician proverb for the purpose of defending his table fellowship with sinners and tax collectors, therefore, is highly expected and understandable in light of the background knowledge of the healer's (Jesus's) typical roles (physical, social, and spiritual healing roles, and his job priority) in the HEALING frame. All these observations show that the frame helps story comprehension by providing the culturally conditioned default values which are left out of the text.

Besides, the frame's important role in understanding the storyline of this episode can be also made obvious in the explanation that follows. The conflict between the scribes/Pharisees and Jesus takes place because they have different frames for table fellowship with tax collectors and sinners. Whereas the Pharisees/scribes evaluate Jesus' action of having table fellowship with sinners and tax collectors in light of the RITUAL PURITY frame, thus regarding that action as a violation of the frame, Jesus views the table fellowship in light of the CALLING TO DISCIPLESHIP frame, thus regarding the meal practice as acceptable. In order to understand what is said in this episode, as a result, Mark's original audience was required to activate both of these frames.

C. The Third Episode (Mark 2.18–22)

1. *Preparing Stage/Inciting Incident* (*Mark 2.18a*)

The introductory narrative information of the third episode is very brief but highly evocative of frames which play a crucial role in understanding the subsequent narrative. The expression ἦσαν οἱ μαθηταὶ ᾽Ιωάννου καὶ οἱ Φαρισαῖοι νηστεύοντες can hardly be understood without having the knowledge of who they are, what is fasting and why they are fasting. All this background knowledge is assumed by the text to be stored in the audience's mental frames. The word νηστεύοντες opened the FAST-ING frame, including its prototypical knowledge of a religious norm of pious Jews; as a result, it is very understandable that the disciples of John (the Baptist) and the Pharisees who opened the person frames for a renewal movement group and religious leaders were keeping the practice of fasting (though it is not necessary that they did so with the same purpose).[39] There is textual evidence for this frame-based information processing. This verse has two kinds of hearer-old markers: The present participle (bolded) and the Greek article (underlined): ἦσαν οἱ μαθηταὶ ᾽Ιωάννου καὶ οἱ Φαρισαῖοι νηστεύοντες. First of all, the present participle (νηστεύοντες) follows the main verb (ἦσαν). Given that the subsequent present participle represents a prototypical manner in which the main verb event takes place,[40] the implication is that the disciples of John the Baptist and the Pharisees' practice of fasting (νηστεύοντες) may be typically invoked by the groups' presence (ἦσαν). Next, though they are new information in the co-text, the nouns (οἱ μαθηταὶ ᾽Ιωάννου and οἱ μαθηταὶ τῶν Φαρισαίων) have the Greek article. A possible explanation is that John the Baptist's disciples, including the Pharisees' disciples, were already known to the audience as default participants in the open FASTING frame.

2. *Mounting Tension* (*Mark 2.18b*)

The two main verbs (λέγουσιν καὶ ἔρχονται) are conjoined by καὶ, stressing the main verb's event frame, RAISING A CRITICAL QUESTION.

---

[39] In particular, for biblical evidence of the Pharisees' fasting practice, see Luke 18.12 and for John the Baptist (and probably his disciples), see Luke 7.31–35; Matthew 11.16–19.

[40] For the participle's prototypical relationship to the main verb event and its role of hearer-old marker, see chapters four and five.

In doing so, the text situates the non-fasting of Jesus' disciples in the critics' perspective.[41] It may seem odd that the challenging question is addressed to Jesus due to his disciples' conduct. However, that a master is questioned as to his disciples' action was not unexpected, as discussed above, in light of the audience's mental frame for THE MASTER-DISCIPLE RELATIONSHIP in which the teacher was responsible for his disciples' conduct, a frame activated by the phrase σοὶ μαθηταὶ. The question itself is based on the comparison of Jesus' disciples with the disciples of John the Baptist and the disciples of the Pharisees. The question based on such a comparison can be made sense of in terms of part-whole structure in the frame. All three groups conjure up the same semantic information of a group of religious leaders (the whole); thus the specific action of one group (a part), like the non-fasting of Jesus'disciles, can be compared with that of others (a part), like the fasting of the Pharisees and John the Baptist's disciples, and evaluated in terms of fit.[42] As far as interest in the story is concerned, the reference to "why ... your disciples do not fast?" catches the audience's interest and suspense through the frame knowledge that the non-fasting of Jesus' disciples was non-standard action in the FASTING frame, and so caused conflict with other Jews (so note that the negative statement is here used as a contraexpectation marker).

3. Climax (Mark 2.19–22)

As discussed earlier, in his defence, Jesus draws on the three parables based on knowledge of how routine life works. In order to understand Jesus' parables, it is necessary to evoke the relevant world knowledge or frame and apply it to the incoming information. In verse 19a Jesus' first parable is told in the form of a rhetorical question, which certainly anticipates a negative answer (the relevant frame components are underlined):

μὴ δύνανται οἱ υἱοὶ τοῦ νυμφῶνος ἐν ᾧ ὁ νυμφίος μετ' αὐτῶν ἐστιν νηστεύειν;
ὅσον χρόνον ἔχουσιν τὸν νυμφίον μετ' αὐτῶν οὐ δύνανται νηστεύειν

---

[41] For the identification of the subject of the verbs with no specific agent as the scribes, see Chapter Five.

[42] Taylor and Crocker, "Schematic," p. 112, say: "The normative aspect of schemas also functions as a standard for explicit evaluations of the stimulus configuration."

The understanding of the rhetorical question and negative reply expressed here is possible only if and when the audience may appropriately open the WEDDING frame by means of its core participants, indicated here with a hearer-old marker, the Greek article (οἱ υἱοὶ τοῦ νυμφῶνος, ὁ νυμφίος). (The phrase οἱ υἱοὶ τοῦ νυμφῶνος refers to literally 'the children of the bridal chamber' and they may indicate either the bridegroom's attendants or the wedding guests in general in Jewish culture.)[43] This is because the frame provides two kind of information: One is that a wedding is a time of rejoicing; the other is that the wedding guest's prototypical role is to attend the bridegroom and to enjoy a time of joy and festivity with him. For this reason Jesus' answer ("as long as they have the bridegroom with them, they cannot fast") is entirely predictable and understandable. Consider that the temporal clauses led by the phrases such as ἐν ᾧ ("while") and ὅσον χρόνον ("as long as") are used to introduce the information predictable from the WEDDING frame, since the bridegroom's being with the wedding guests can be inferred from the frame knowledge. For the audience who has the relevant WEDDING frame, an unmistakable conclusion is that the wedding guests' fasting is bizarre. Given the frame's metaphorical link between Jesus and his disciples and the bridegroom and the wedding guests (see Chapter Five), the ready comprehension of this parable in terms of the WEDDING frame knowledge enhances the audience's understanding of the validation of the disciples' non-fasting.

In verse 20, however, Jesus additionally mentions the time for the wedding guests to fast. Since the fasting of the guests in the context of wedding is a non-standard event, this behaviour would be a deviation in the WEDDING frame. Such a deviation may be further apparent by other information given in verse 20. In the Jewish wedding custom, first of all, it was the bridegroom, not the guests, who left the wedding scene.[44] So Jesus' reference to the bridegroom being taken away from the guests was unexpected and must have been surprising for the audience. Next, there is textual evidence to support this deviation (the contraexpectation marker is bolded):

    v. 19b: ὅσον χρόνον ἔχουσιν τὸν νυμφίον μετ' αὐτῶν οὐ δύνανται
            νηστεύειν.
    v. 20:   ἐλεύσονται δὲ ἡμέραι ὅταν ἀπαρθῇ ἀπ' αὐτῶν ὁ νυμφίος

---

[43] See BDAG, νυμών.
[44] Nineham, *Mark*, p. 102; Guelich, *Mark 1–8.26*, p. 112.

The presence of δὲ cues the audience that there is a discontinuity of expectation between the two events mentioned: The bridegroom's being with the guests (v. 19b) and his removal from them (v. 20). This indicates that the bridegroom's elimination from the wedding scene was obviously an astonishing event and thus a violation of the event sequences in the WEDDING frame. As a result, such frame deviations give prominence in a discourse, and so a special mnemonic (emphatic) effect is put on a new situation in which the bridal friends or the disciples will fast. And the unanticipated development of the WEDDING frame in this passage must have helped Mark's Christian audience pay focal attention to the reason for the fasting of Jesus' disciples, which is different from those of the Pharisees and John the Baptist's disciples: Jesus' surprising removal indicated by the passive verb ἀπάρθη (v. 21), probably death on the cross.[45]

I have made a claim in Chapter Four that temporal clauses led by particles such as ὅταν, ὡς, ὅτε, represent hearer-old information. Verse 20 says (the temporal particle is bolded and hearer-old information is underlined): ἐλεύσονται δὲ ἡμέραι ὅταν ἀπαρθῇ ἀπ᾽ αὐτῶν ὁ νυμφίος. Indeed, this claim may seem in conflict with the argument made above that a bridegroom's being taken away from wedding guests would have been understood unusual on the part of Mark's audience in light of the WEDDING frame. Yet since the WEDDING frame and the bridegroom are, as mentioned, metaphorically used here to refer to the KINGDOM OF GOD and Jesus, if we keep in mind that Mark's Christian audiences were already familiar with Jesus' sudden removal (i.e., death on the cross), it is not impossible to believe that ὅταν clause information (the bridegroom's removal from wedding guests) may have been processed at least in a metaphorical sense as hearer-old on the part of Mark's Christian audiences. For them the unusual thing happened to Jesus, God's eschatological messiah! It must be also noted that two-level comprehension may be processed here. On the one hand, the bridegroom's sudden elimination may be perceived as a situation hard to understand, thus increasing memorability in a literal sense. On the other hand, because of their mental frame related to Jesus' earthly life, for Mark's Christian

---

[45] Taylor, *Mark*, p. 211, Cranfield, *Mark*, pp. 119–11and Guelich, *Mark 1–8.26*, p. 112 rightly point out that the verb most appropriately is used in reference to Jesus' violent death.

audiences the information must have been made perfect sense in metaphorical terms, and would in no way have seemed bizarre.

The open MENDING A GARMENT frame (note the main verb event as the frame's core action ἐπιράπτει ἐπὶ ἱμάτιον παλαιόν) and PRESERVING NEW WINE (note the frame's core action βάλλει οἶνον νέον εἰς ἀσκοὺς) frames play a key role in processing the second and third parables. The frames for MENDING A GARMENT and PRESERVING NEW WINE hold information for what are normal actions; hence it leads the audience readily and quickly to understand the action sequences as abnormal and then as normal in light of those frames:

> v. 21a: οὐδεὶς ἐπίβλημα ῥάκους ἀγνάφου ἐπιράπτει ἐπὶ ἱμάτιον
> παλαιόν;[46]
> v. 22a: οὐδεὶς βάλλει οἶνον νέον εἰς ἀσκοὺς παλαιούς
> v. 22c: οἶνον νέον εἰς ἀσκοὺς καινούς.

Likewise, provided that the frames are able to discern what is anomalous, they may use the contraexpectation marker εἰ δὲ μή (bolded) to predict what sort of information follow the marker:

> v. 21b: εἰ δὲ μή, αἴρει τὸ πλήρωμα ἀπ᾽ αὐτοῦ τὸ καινὸν τοῦ παλαιοῦ καὶ
> χεῖρον σχίσμα γίνεται
> v. 22b: εἰ δὲ μή, ῥήξει ὁ οἶνος τοὺς ἀσκοὺς καὶ ὁ οἶνος ἀπόλλυται καὶ οἱ
> ἀσκοί

The use of εἰ δὲ μή ("otherwise") here shows that if one fails to perform the standard action evoked by the frames, the patch tears away from the garment (v. 21b) and the wine bursts the skins (v. 22b).

In addition to the processing of prototypical and irregular actions, with the role of the frame in this passage two more things need to be mentioned. First, the frame cues the audience that its typical properties (or props) will be mentioned in the subsequent story, and as a result, will lead to ready memory processing of the information. Note, for instance, that in the second metaphor the nouns τὸ πλήρωμα ("the patch") and τὸ καινὸν ("the new one") are used here in reference to ἐπίβλημα ῥάκους ἀγνάφου ("a piece of unshrunk cloth"). This shows that for the audience the words πλήρωμα and τὸ καινὸν may have been substituted for ἐπίβλημα ῥάκους ἀγνάφου. It should be noted that

---

[46] It was understood among the ancients that since ῥάκους ἀγνάφου is "cloth which has not been processed by the fuller, who cleaned and combed it to remove natural oil and gum, and bleached it ready for use in making garments," that cloth was not used to mend clothing. France, *Mark*, p. 141.

this is made possible because of the audience's use of frame regarding ἐπίβλημα ῥάκους ἀγνάφου; that is, a piece of unshrunk cloth may be also called 'a new patch.' The Greek article, a hearer-old marker, before the nouns, which are new information, supports this hypothesis. The articular nominals serve to identify the referents (entities) (τὸ πλήρωμα and τὸ καινὸν) in the mental frame opened by the nominal phrases (ἐπίβλημα ῥάκους ἀγνάφου). Second, the frames help the causal connectivity between events by providing missing data. Strictly speaking, the garment stitched by the unshrunk patch does rip *after the next washing of the garment* and the wine in the old wineskin bursts *when the pressure of fermentation of the new wine makes it expand*. But this detailed information is left out of the text since the text takes for granted that the audience would infer the intervening steps, the causal connections, to make discourse coherent simply through reference to the appropriate background knowledge for frame deviations.[47] The textual expressions allow the audience to focus on only the initial indication of unexpected actions and their ultimate results.

In conclusion, when it comes to narrative processing as a whole, the deviations in the predictable actions of the two frames enhance interest in the story, giving prominence to them in the discourse. Hence the audience is led to pay special attention to the surprising or irregular actions trying to accommodate the old and the new and thus, in the frames evoked in the narrative flow, Jesus' teachings regarding the Kingdom of God and the Jewish religious traditions of his era. What the triple parables show, thus, is that the efficient understanding of Jesus' defence essentially depends on the cognitive processing of the frame knowledge opened by the linguistic input which indicates the prototypical knowledge of what are normal and abnormal actions in the frames.

D. The Fourth Episode (Mark 2.23–28)

1. *Preparing Stage (Mark 2.23a)/Inciting Incident (Mark 2.23b)*

Mark 2.23a introduces a physical setting for this episode—a grainfield Jesus was going through; and Mark 2.23b describes the disciples making

---

[47] Thus, Hooker, *Mark*, p. 100, says, "Mark perhaps envisages the garment tearing when it is washed and the unwashed cloth shrinks." Frame theory provides a theoretical foundation for this explanation.

a way, and plucking the grain. It is usually assumed that the disciples
were in the same grainfield, though this is never explicitly mentioned in
the text (note that the text says it is Jesus who walks *in the grainfield*).
Such an inference is a result of the operation of the frame on the word
τοὺς στάχυας, "ears of grain," with a hearer-old marker, the Greek article. Since the frame for GRAINFIELD opened in verse 23a held inventory
information of grain and its heads as its typical components, the audience was able to identify by means of the Greek article the ears of grain
which the disciples picked as belonging to the grainfield through which
Jesus walked. This can be supported also by the person frame for οἱ
μαθηταὶ αὐτοῦ in verse 23b, which enables the inference that disciples
typically were with their masters (cf., Mark 3.14) unless the text indicates otherwise.[48]

The text shows that the disciples made a path through the field by
cutting the grain (ὁδὸν ποιεῖν τίλλοντες τοὺς στάχυας) while Jesus
"walked through" (παραπορεύεσθαι διὰ) the field. The disciples probably made a path for Jesus. This scene leads the audience to understand
what is happening there by using the open GRAINFIELD frame knowledge. Since the frame holds the typical spatial layout of the field full of
grain, it enables the causal inference that the disciples "made a path" for
Jesus to "walk through." That this inference (the disciples' action was
done for their master, Jesus) is very natural can be supported by the
open DISCIPLES frame, which involves information that the disciples
played the stereotypical role of serving their master (cf., Mark 10.45;
John. 13.13–17).

What is interesting in these stages, however, does not arise until the
audience may appropriately open the mental frame for SABBATH in this
passage. The SABBATH frame held the prototypical information of sabbath laws that people must not do works; so it enabled the audience to
recognize that the disciples' action of making a path by plucking grain on

---

[48] Mark's Gospel shows that the disciples are with Jesus all the time (e.g., 3.7; 4.10, 35;
6.1, 7, 30; 7.2; 8.27; 10. 10, 32, 46; 11.1 and so on). In particular, in Mark 5.21–43, the story
about the healing of the woman with a hemorrhage and the raising of the dead child, at
the beginning of the story there is only reference to Jesus (bolded): διαπεράσαντος τοῦ
Ἰησοῦ [ἐν τῷ πλοίῳ] πάλιν εἰς τὸ πέραν συνήχθη ὄχλος πολὺς ἐπ᾽ αὐτόν, καὶ ἦν παρὰ
τὴν θάλασσαν (5.21). But when Jesus asked who touched his clothing on the way to the
house of the ruler of the synagogue, suddenly the disciples popped up in the story (the
relevant lexical indication is bolded): ἔλεγον αὐτῷ οἱ μαθηταὶ αὐτοῦ (5.31). The occurrence of the disciples without warning in the story is clear evidence that the text takes for
granted that information that the disciples were the ones who were with Jesus, a master,
was presupposed by knowledge in the audience's long-term memory.

the sabbath day was unexpected and surprising to their contemporary Jews.[49] The audience is led to draw his or her attention to the disciples' action through the cognitive processing of the unexpected information, on the one hand. Knowledge of the disciples' actions that deviate from the SABBATH frame, on the other hand, helps the audience predict how the story henceforth develops into a conflict between Jesus/his disciples and their contemporary Jews.

2. *Mounting Tension (Mark 2.24)*

The tension that has arisen by the cognitive processing of the disciples' action further heightens in this stage. The appearance of the Pharisees (οἱ Φαρισαῖοι ἔλεγον αὐτῷ) is primarily responsible for such an increase of tension since the person frame for THE PHARISEES enables the audience to expect that as legal experts they will be concerned with the legality of the disciples' action of making a path by plucking the grain on the sabbath day. Besides, the Pharisees' rhetorical question (ἴδε τί ποιοῦσιν τοῖς σάββασιν ὃ οὐκ ἔξεστιν;) based on shared knowledge of the sabbath laws between Jesus and the Pharisees is used here to invoke and pay attention to the fact that the disciples' action is a departure from the SABBATH frame. In particular, the negative statement ("what is not lawful") intensifies the disciples' action as a denial of expectation, an expectation that the disciples should have observed regarding the sabbath laws. Consequently, this information of conflicting expectation, by increasing suspense in the story, contributes to the enhancement of the audience's interest in how the event progresses.

Sanders argues, however, that in this conflict story the Pharisees' entrance at this point is "extraordinarily unrealistic": "Pharisees did not organize themselves into groups to spend their Sabbaths in Galilean corn-fields in the hope of catching someone transgressing."[50] But by arguing so, as Wright rightly points out, "Sanders retreats from his basic thesis, that Jesus was a prophet of restoration eschatology, into a very different

---

[49] For a similar reason, David Daube, *The New Testament and Rabbinic Judaism* (London: Athlone Press, 1956), p. 172, says: "We modern readers, when we come to an incident commencing 'At that time Jesus went on the Sabbath day through the corn, and his disciples were in hunger and began to pluck and eat', are not particularly excited: we are too habituated to such practice." With respect to the same text what makes the different response between the modern and ancient audience depends on whether one is able to open the frames which were shared between the original speaker and audience for the communication of the text.

[50] Thus Sanders, *Jesus and Judaism*, p. 265.

argument, to do with non-eschatological religion and ethics."[51] Instead, Wright states that "Jesus was not an ordinary Jew. He was a prophet, announcing that Israel's god was becoming king."[52] If so, as discussed earlier, for Mark's early Christian audiences who shared the background knowledge that Jesus was an eschatological prophet to proclaim the inauguration of God's kingdom, it was not inconceivable that the religious teachers such as the Pharisees appeared to check the kingdom-bringer and his followers' (provocative) actions out up to the standards required in relation to the observance of the Torah (so, the sabbath).

As far as text processing is concerned, since frames involve its set actions and prototypical properties, it must be said in the light of LEGAL CONTROVERSY frame that the introduction of legal experts like the Pharisees has been well prepared by the audience's cognitive processing for the surprising and disputable nature of the disciples' action, which has been activated by the SABBATH frame. The legal question about the observance of sabbath regulations is also not unanticipated because the disciples' action has already activated the semantic information of the violation of sabbath regulations.[53] In addition to the contents of the question, the addressee of the question merits consideration. Though the disciples' action is under fire, the Pharisees' question is directed to Jesus.[54] But this may have been understandable in light of the audience's mental frame that the disciples were under the master's authority and thus they typically did works with his permission. Thus verses 23 (the disciples' questionable behaviour) and 24 (the Pharisees' appearance and question addressed to Jesus) are semantically coherent (or sequential events) in light of frames for JESUS as an inaugurator of God's eschatological kingdom, LEGAL CONTROVERSY, and its subframes like SABBATH, PHARISEES and DISCIPLES.

---

[51] Wright, *Jesus*, pp. 391–93 (the quotation from p. 392).

[52] Wright, *Jesus*, p. 392.

[53] *m. Sanhedrin* 7.8 says that a warning must be given prior to prosecution for a sabbath violation: "'He that has connexion with her the first is [liable, after warning, to death by stoning] if he committed an act which renders him liable to Extirpation...'" Thus, the Pharisees' interrogation seems consistent with that warning. See Robbins, "Plucking Grain," p. 124.

[54] As one of the reasons why this conflict story should be considered "unrealitic," Sanders, *Jesus*, p. 265, points out that "it is not Jesus who is said to have been accused, but his disciples."

3. Climax (Mark 2.25–28)

As part of his reaction to the Pharisaic objection, first of all, Mark's Jesus opens the DAVID frame, a person frame (the frame is bolded and the temporal particile is underlined): οὐδέποτε ἀνέγνωτε τί ἐποίησεν Δαυὶδ <u>ὅτε</u> χρείαν ἔσχεν καὶ ἐπείνασεν…; The use of the rhetorical question and the temporal particle (ὅτε) shows that Jesus assumes the Pharisees to evoke the relevant DAVID frame and the information (being in need and being hungry) in the temporal clause from their long-term memory of the David story in the Scripture (1 Samuel 21.1–6). Since for the ancient Jews the DAVID frame held information of a prototypical character in the Jewish Scriptures, the question οὐδέποτε ἀνέγνωτε may have been understood as implying 'Have you never read the Scripture that tells what David did' (information regarding the Scriputre is implicit in this sentence). The opening of this DAVID frame (a character in the Scripture) is triggered, alongside the reference to the person's name, by the verb ἀνέγνωτε. Although the text does not explicitly refer to who David is, the verb ἀνέγνωτε enables the activation of David in the Scripture (cf., Mark 12.10, 26). This shows that Jesus' defense implicitly appeals to the authority of Scripture, which was shared by all Jews.[55]

The expression in verse 25 ὅτε χρείαν ἔσχεν καὶ ἐπείνασεν is a trigger, or "Precondition Header" (to use Schank and Abelson's term), for the MEAL frame because 'being hungry' and 'having need' are the primary condition for having a meal (ἔφαγεν in v. 26b). The trigging lexemes prepare the audience for what David will do next. However, though not inconceivable in terms of the knowledge from the Scripture (1 Samuel 21.1–6), it must have been surprising that the expression τὸν οἶκον τοῦ θεοῦ follows as a reference to a place where David and his men went to eat, given "the house of God" was not a typical place for general people to eat. The astonishing nature of David's action is also expressed in the text. Whereas ἀρχιερέως and τοὺς ἄρτους τῆς προθέσεως may have been understood readily as default values of the HOUSE OF GOD

---

[55] Indeed, Jesus' interpretation of the relevant text is quite different from the trust of the original narrative. For an example for the argument that this sort of reshaping of a biblical story is also a common feature in ancient Jews' reading of Scriptures, see Michael Fishbane, *Biblical Interpretation in Ancient Israel* (Oxford: Clarendon Press, 1985). Similarly, Daube, *New Testament*, p. 68 asserts, "It was not so much that David might conceivably have been wrong: the Rabbis no less than Jesus assumed that, for one reason or another, his action had been justified." On Jesus' peculiarity in using 1 Samuel 21.1–6, see below.

frame (thus the article noun-phrases τοὺς ἄρτους τῆς προθέσεως), David and his men's eating of the sacred food was negatively expressed, using the evaluative word (underlined): οὓς οὐκ ἔξεστιν φαγεῖν. This shows that what David and his companions did was a non-standard action in the BREAD OF PRESENCE frame, a subframe in the HOUSE OF GOD frame. Notice, as the text explicitly states, the BREAD OF PRESENCE frame held information regarding priests or high priests who had the right to eat the sacred food (v. 26). Just like the conduct of Jesus' disciples on the sabbath, thus, information that David "entered the house of God...ate the bread of Presence...and also gave it to those who were with him" is salient in the narrative discourse and provides interestedness for the audience because of its unexpected and surprising nature in light of the BREAD OF PRESENCE frame in the HOUSE OF GOD frame.[56] Consequently, the two deviated events (Jesus' disciples' making a path by plucking the grain and David and his men's eating of the sacred bread) would be better remembered by the audience

Was the example of David, however, expected in the causal flow of the present events on the audience? I have already investigated how the frames DAVID and JESUS would enable the audience to understand this example of David as part of Jesus' defense: Given Mark and his audience's mental frame for JESUS involved information regarding a Davidic Messiah or Christ surpassing it, it may have been a natural inference

---

[56] Scholars have pointed out that the account of David's case described in Mark 2.25–27 does not verbally correspond with 1 Samuel 21.1–6. For example, unlike the Markan passage, in 1 Samuel 21 there is no suggestion that David entered into "the house of God." Additionaly, the Old Testament narrative does not have a reference that David and his men were "hungry" or "in need" and "ate" the showbread. However, frames enable us to explain some of Mark's 'alterations' and 'additions.' First of all, David's coming to the priest in 1 Samuel 21.1 may have opened for the first-century audience the frame for DAVID'S VISITING OF THE HOUSE OF GOD since the priest was a default participant in the frame for THE HOUSE OF GOD. That is, because of the background knowledge that the priest belonged to the "house of God," David's visiting the priest may have been understood as David's entering the house of God. Second, though the Old Testament narrative does not include references to David and his men being hungry and eating the showbread, the MEAL frame may have enabled Mark to make the inference that David's request for food from the priest, which the Old Testament narrative includes, was a prerequisite to eating in light of the MEAL frame which had as prototypical information the scripted event sequences like having food, eating food, digesting food and so on. It was not difficult to assume by the frame that David and his men went on to the next stage, that is, eating, after receiving the food. Likewise, since the MEAL frame provided the information for motivations that people ask for food, Mark's addition of "being hungry" and "in need" can be explained by his inferential processing based on the MEAL frame.

that just as the illegal actions of David's companions were permitted under David's authority, so the disciples' action could be covered by Jesus' (Davidic) messianic authority. Thus, given such a semantic link of Jesus with David, it may not be surprising for the audience that the analogy of David is introduced as part of Jesus' defense. Yet Jesus' defense based on his authority superseding the sabbath laws reaches a climax in verse 28 in which as a Son of Man Jesus claims his authoritative role as lord of the sabbath.

The following two clauses consist of two very abbreviated statements. Hence their meaning and role in this narrative flow would remain unclear without invoking appropriate frame knowledge that makes the use of abbreviation possible.[57] First of all, verse 27 (τὸ σάββατον διὰ τὸν ἄνθρωπον ἐγένετο καὶ οὐχ ὁ ἄνθρωπος διὰ τὸ σάββατον) is clearly a thematic development expected in Jesus' defense of the disputable action of his disciples on the sabbath. We have discussed that the disciples' making a path by plucking the grain is to help Jesus' "walking through" the grainfields. Now for the justification of such action of the disciples Jesus appeals to God's original intent of establishing the sabbath, namely, the benefit of the human: Note the sabbath at creation story (Genesis 1.26–2.3), which is opened by the lexicon τὸ σάββατον, ἐγένετο ("it was made") and τὸν ἄνθρωπον, enables the audience to draw their attention to the original intention of the sabbath at creation (see Chapter Five). The implication is that the disciples' actions at the sabbath can be justified because they are made for Jesus' benefit.

Next, as a final statement verse 28 begins with the resultive conjuction ὥστε ("accordingly"): ὥστε κύριος ἐστιν ὁ υἱὸς τοῦ ἀνθρώπου τοῦ σαββάτου. It is true that the ὥστε clause has a puzzling relation to its preceding clause (how does the pronouncement that the sabbath was made for the humans result in Jesus' assertion of his lordship over the Sabbath?); however, as mentioned in the previous chapter, the ὥστε clause is best understood if we take it as a summary of the whole story (Mark 2.23–27). Of importance for such an understanding of verse 28 is the opening of the relevant frame for κύριος. The word κύριος,

---

[57] With regard to Jesus' brief saying or pronouncement, as Robbins, "Plucking Grain," p. 111, rightly points out, "Presuppositions and nuances of meaning reside in compact statements that require active involvement by the auditor to understand the implications." In other words, such abbreviated forms result from the speaker's presupposition that the original audience already has enough background knowledge i.e., frame) to understand them.

according to Louw and Nida's lexicon, is used in the New Testament documents in relation to the semantic domains such as "Lord" (i.e., a christological title; 12.9), "Owner" (57.12), "Ruler" (37.51), and "Sir" (87.53). The subject of verse 28 (ὁ υἱὸς τοῦ ἀνθρώπου) and the genitive nominal phrase (τοῦ σαββάτου) modifying κύριος are decisive in opening semantic information for κύριος. We have already pointed out that the SON OF MAN frame opens semantic information of JESUS as a Danielic figure (a son of man) who is given *divine authority*, and "the sabbath" is used in this pericope to evoke 'the sabbath laws.' Then, the expression κύριος τοῦ σαββάτου certainly evokes the frame for 'the person who is in a position of superior authority over the sabbath laws' (so "owner" or "ruler" domains, to use Louw and Nida's term).[58] And the result clause, "accordingly, the Son of Man is lord even of the sabbath," enables us to infer that Jesus claims to his '*dominion* over the sabbath laws.' In this regard, verse 28 is expected and can make perfect sense as the conclusion of Jesus' defense which has appealed to *authority* (of the Davidic Messiah and the original intent [or creation order] of the sabbath) overriding the sabbath laws.

E. THE FIFTH EPISODE (MARK 3.1–6)

1. *Preparing Stage/Inciting Incident (Mark 3.1)*

As indicated by a hearer-old marker, the Greek article before the noun τὴν συναγωγήν, it is assumed in the text that the audience shares the SYNAGOGUE frame, a place frame, which included prototypical information of the function of the place (i.e., Jewish assembly for prayer, teaching, and reading Scriptures) and who were the participants (all pious Jews, including religious teachers).[59] And the word πάλιν used in Mark 3.1a shows that information that Jesus visits the synagogue is expected. Though not recounted in the text, because of that frame knowledge

---

[58] Most scholars agree that κύριος in Mark 2.28 is not used as a 'Christological title' for Jesus. See, Taylor, *Mark*, p. 220; Cranfield, *Mark*, p. 118; Guelich, *Mark, 1–8.26*, pp. 125–27; France, *Mark*, p. 148. See the denotation of κύριος in ancient societies and the Gospels, BenWitherington III, "Lord," in *the Dictionary of Jesus and the Gospels* (Downers Grove, Illinois: IVP, 1992), pp. 484–92.

[59] Sanders, *Jesus*, pp. 35, 98–101 (the quotation from p. 35). He says that in first-century Judaism, the synagogue was a place in which "people gathered on sabbaths to study the law and pray."

for SYNAGOGUE, Mark 3.1a εἰσῆλθεν πάλιν εἰς τὴν συναγωγήν may be understood as implying that Jesus entered the synagogue for praying, teaching and reading Scriptures, with Jesus filling the slot for the teacher (Mark 1.21; 6.2).[60] Because of such a default value of participants in the SYNAGOGUE frame, it is also not surprising to hear that there were other attendants (vv. 1–2) in the synagogue where Jesus entered. Yet information that there was a man with a "withered" (ἐξηραμμένην) hand in the synagogue as Jesus went in, due to its role of opening the HEALING frame, leads the audience to wonder whether the everyday (typical) synagogue service on the sabbath, or scripted events in the SYNAGOGUE frame, will be interrupted.

2. Mounting Tension (Mark 3.2)

Tension is unmistakably indicated by information that Jesus is at the centre of the opponents' (the Pharisees's) hostile attention (the frame is bolded): παρετήρουν αὐτὸν εἰ τοῖς σάββασιν θεραπεύσει αὐτόν, ἵνα κατηγορήσωσιν αὐτου. The text does not include information regarding on what grounds Jesus' healing of the sick person on the sabbath deserves accusation. However, the audience's mental frame that Jews kept sabbath regulations enables us to fill the missing information in the clause: 'So that they might accuse him *of violation of laws which prohibit healing and work on the sabbath.*' Given that the level of interest in the story is in direct proportion to its unexpectedness, the opening of such frame knowledge of the sabbath creates interest at this stage. The SABBATH frame enables the audience to make the inferences that Jesus' action of healing on the sabbath is clearly judged as an unusual thing that deviates from the religious leaders' expectation of sabbath observance. Moreover, the SABBATH frame, including information concerning the consequence of violation of sabbath laws (i.e., the death penalty, see Exodus

---

[60] Thus, see the prototypical components like 'teaching,' 'the sabbath,' and 'the attendants' in the SYNAGOGUE (the frame title is bolded; the components are underlined):

Mark 1.21: εὐθὺς τοῖς σάββασιν εἰσελθὼν εἰς τὴν συναγωγὴν ἐδίδασκεν καὶ ἐξεπλήσσοντο ἐπὶ τῇ διδαχῇ αὐτοῦ

6.2: γενομένου σαββάτου ἤρξατο διδάσκειν ἐν τῇ συναγωγῇ, καὶ πολλοὶ ἀκούοντες ἐξεπλήσσοντο.

31.14–15; Numbers 15.32–36),[61] heightens the audience's tension around whether Jesus really will perform healing on the sabbath.

3. *Climax (Mark 3.3–5)*

This stage consists of Jesus' reactions to the situations (healing and charge) set up in the preceding ones. Jesus' first response is directed to the man with the crippled hand: ἔγειρε εἰς τὸ μέσον [of the synagogue]. The narrative, in fact, does not give information regarding the encounter of Jesus and the man with the withered hand, but verse 3 directly depicts Jesus calling the man into the middle of the synagogue. In order for the text to be semantically coherent, the missing information (Jesus' seeing before speaking to the man) should be inferred by the audience's frame for SPEAKING to someone, which prototypically includes a preceding stage of meeting or seeing another person.[62] With respect to the intention of the character's behaviour, the HEALING frame opened in verses 1–2 allows the audience to understand Jesus' calling of the crippled man into the middle as calling to healing. Yet since the HEALING frame serves as a subframe of the global LEGAL CONTROVERSY frame in this episode, that calling may also be understood as an attempt to facilitate an open conflict with the Pharisees. For this inferential understanding of Jesus' action, the SYNAGOGUE frame is important to provide knowledge of the spatial layout of this episode. The SYNAGOGUE frame, including information that it was a public place, helps the inference that whatever healing may occur on centre stage will be witnessed by all the participants. Jesus' public performance of healing was not unexpected by the open HEALING frame. Nonetheless, it was obviously a non-standard action in light of the SABBATH frame. Thus, this scene was given salience for the audience and provided them with a special mnemonic effect.

After commanding the man to stand up into the middle of the synagogue, Jesus turns his question to the accuser (v. 6): ἔξεστιν τοῖς σάββασιν ἀγαθὸν ποιῆσαι ἢ κακοποιῆσαι, ψυχὴν σῶσαι ἢ ἀποκτεῖναι; (v. 4). In several ways frames play a crucial role in understanding this

---

[61] Cf. Sanders, *Jewish Law*, pp. 16–19 says that the death penalty was usually shunned in favour of lesser penalties, such as a sin offering, in Jesus' day.

[62] For the Markan examples, where the actions of encountering (seeing, hearing, coming, calling) are mentioned before that of speaking (asking), see Mark 1.16, 20, 37, 40; 2.5, 14, 16; 3.11, 34; 5.22–23, 33, 36, 38–39; 6.2, 16; 7.2–5, 25–26; 10.14, 23, 27, 42, 47; 12.14, 18, 34, 43; 14.37, 40, 67; 15.35.

verse. First, Jesus' question to his critics seems surprising in that the Pharisees' hostile watching is unspoken and the text does not indicate Jesus' recognition of it (cf., Mark 2.17). So the semantic coherence between the Pharisees' unspoken watching, thus hidden thoughts, and Jesus' knowing of them may be established by the audience's mental frame that Jesus has divine power to know people's thoughts (see Mark 2.8).[63] Second, regarding the question itself, Jesus' reference to what is a legal action to do on the sabbath is predictable in the narrative flow because the SABBATH frame, including information about the observance of sabbath laws, has been opened explicitly since verse 2. Third, it should have caused no surprise that that kind of question is addressed to the Pharisees, since the audience's mental frame was that the Pharisees were legal experts and thus were expected to have relevant answers to that kind of question. This may be supported by the use of the evaluative language ἔξεστιν, which led Jesus' original audience to judge what is legal or not by referring to the norms in the mental frame for OBSERVING THE SABBATH LAWS.

Mark represents the Pharisees saying nothing to Jesus' question: οἱ δὲ ἐσιώπων. The silence of Jesus' critics carries a significant implication in light of the LEGAL CONTROVERSY frame. Because of the LEGAL CONTROVERSY frame, which includes the information of dispute between the accuser and defendants, the Pharisees' silence means that the accuser failed to show a relevant response to Jesus' defence, thus losing their voice in such a dispute. For the time being, Jesus is depicted as a victor over his opponents. Knowing the meaning of the Pharisees' shameful silence, however, prepares the audience for the critics' plan for the destruction of Jesus (v. 6). This is because "disputants who have lost face by being reduced to speechlessness in public are liable to become dangerous enemies."[64]

Verse 5a depicts Jesus' double emotion of anger and grief (underlined): περιβλεψάμενος αὐτοὺς μετ' ὀργῆς, συλλυπούμενος ἐπὶ τῇ πωρώσει τῆς καρδίας αὐτῶν. It is clear that the Pharisees' silence (v. 4b) and their "hardness of heart" (τῇ πωρώσει τῆς καρδίας) caused Jesus' anger and grief (note the preposition ἐπὶ used to refer to the origin of Jesus' grief). Again, this shows that the Pharisees' silence and hardness of heart were

---

[63] It may be a possible inference that Jesus' PHARISEES frame enables him to know their hidden intention of watching him in the context of healing.

[64] Marcus, *Mark 1–8*, p. 253.

originally not an expected attitude toward Jesus. I have already indicated that someone's anger and surprise is frequently related to the violation of some frame. If so, a person frame serves to explain the cause
of Jesus' anger and grief.[65] Mark's original audience had mental frames
that Jesus was an eschatological agent of God (Mark 1.1,14–15; 2.28; cf.
1.24) and that the Pharisees were the interpreters of the laws which represent God's will which is clearly opened in the co-text (see Mark 2.24;
3.2).[66] So the causal relationship left implicit between verses 4b and 5a
can be readily inferred. Though as the religious teachers the Pharisees
were expected to acknowledge that God's eschatological power works
through Jesus' sabbath healing, they refused to do so in silence and with
"hardness of heart (τῇ πωρώσει τῆς καρδίας),"[67] resulting in Jesus' anger
and grief.

The text resumes Jesus' pronouncement of healing (ἔκτεινον τὴν
χεῖρα), which has been delayed by his question of the Pharisees (v. 4)
after his command (ἔγειρε εἰς τὸ μέσον, v. 3). It must be noted that the
text does not spell out whether he came forward in obedience to Jesus'
command. Such an intermediate step missed between Jesus' command
and his pronouncement of healing may be taken in the audience's mental frame for ἔγειρε εἰς τὸ μέσον, since the event sequences in the frame
are assumed to proceed normally to its completion if the text provides
no evidence to the contrary.

---

[65] This is not a conflict of the LEGAL CONTROVERSY frame and the person frame
because, as discussed in Chapter Four, frame theory postulates that in one sentence, two
or three frames may be active at the same time so they may "compete for incoming items
of information." See Schank and Abelson, *Scripts*, p. 58.

[66] Thus, though claiming that the main issue of the conflict in Mark 2.2–3.6 is "over
behavior [Jesus and his disciples'], not christology," Dewey, *Public Debate*, p. 124, admits
that "the christological material seems to be assumed or taken for granted by the narrator [in Mark 2.1–3.6]. The treatment of the christological material would imply that the
narrator intends his writing for an audience which shares the christological assumptions
of Mark 2:1–3:6."

[67] Apparently, the speaker conceptualizes the Pharisees' silence to Jesus' question in
terms of τῇ πωρώσει τῆς καρδίας. That this onceptualization is not unfamiliar to the
audience can be supported by the fact that "hardness of heart (τῇ πωρώσει τῆς καρδίας)"
has the hearer-old markers, the Greek articles, though new information in the co-text.
That is, the Pharisees' mental state of "hardness of heart" is already opened in the audience' mental frame by the behaviour that the Pharisees shows no response to Jesus' question. For other examples of a similar conceptualization in the Gospel of Mark, see Mark
6.52 and 8.17, in both of which "the hardened heart" is used to refer to the disciples
failure to appreciate the significance of Jesus' miracles, "...their hearts were hardened
(ἦν αὐτῶν ἡ καρδία πεπωρωμένη)", 6.52; "Has your heart been hardened (πεπωρωμένην
ἔχετε τὴν καρδίαν ὑμῶν;) ? ", 8.17.

4. *Closure* (*Mark 3.5b-6*)

The tension aroused by the Pharisees' unspoken challenge of Jesus' healing on the sabbath is resolved by God's vindication of Jesus' action of healing and the Pharisees' guilty verdict.[68] Yet since the understanding of the story basically relies on causal inference for what occurs in the narrative flow, in order to know how such a verdict would make sense to the audience it is necessary to explain what causes God's vindication and the Pharisees' guilty charge of Jesus. God's eschatological power present in Jesus' healing action, first of all, seems unprepared and thus sudden in terms of the textual information. God's ultimate vindication of Jesus, nonetheless, can be made sense of by the audience's mental frame that Jesus is an eschatological agent of God who is doing his will. Next, the present stage shows that the Pharisees' guilty verdict of Jesus is directly followed by Jesus' pronouncement of healing. Here it must be noted that that healing was performed by word alone rather than by touching of the hand (cf., Mark 1.31, 41; 5.41; 7.33–34; 8.23; 9.27). In fact, since it was not a violation of sabbath observance to heal the sick person by word alone, the Pharisees' plot to kill Jesus may have been unexpected and surprising in light of the open SABBATH frame that included information that no work was allowed on the sabbath.[69] How then would the Pharisees' guilty verdict of Jesus' action of healing on the sabbath make sense? The audience here is not only led to draw focal attention to the unexpected event, but also to understand that Jesus was blameless and to see the absurdity of the Pharisees' murderous plan. I have noted that in the beginning of this episode Jesus was expected by the Pharisees to violate the scripted actions in the SABBATH frame by healing the man with the withered hand, but in the closing, the narrator shows that it is the Pharisees who violated the laws by plotting the destruction of the blameless Jesus on the sabbath.

In Mark 3.6 the Pharisees' last reaction is worth noting. The phrase ὅπως αὐτὸν ἀπολέσωσιν opens the PUTTING TO DEATH frame that prototypically holds goal-oriented sequences of events, such as plotting to kill (source, or a starting point), approaching a victim (path or an intermediate point of connecting the source and the goal) and performing murder (a goal or destination). Here the Pharisees' action of plotting against Jesus enables the audience to predict what will occur

---

[68] See Chapter Five.
[69] Flusser, *Jesus*, p. 62; Vermes, *Jesus the Jew*, p. 23.

to Jesus next, that is, violent and unlawful killing. And in the PUTTING
TO DEATH frame the Pharisees fill the slot for murderers who perform
it deliberately (at the closing of the Controversy Stories, the Pharisees'
role turns from that of accuser to that of murderer!). It is also against
this frame knowledge that the sudden introduction of τῶν Ἡρῳδιανῶν
may be understandable. What *role* the title plays in Mark 3.6 has puzzled
many scholars mainly because of the uncertain meaning of the term. It
is generally agreed that the Herodians referred to the political supporters or adherents of the dynasty founded by Herod the Great and Herod
Antipas in Galilee at this time.[70] Frame theory, as discussed in Chapter Four, claims that people draw on their person frame which includes
information regarding a person's motivations, interests, and traits to
understand and predict the behaviour and roles of others in a specific
situation. If so, it is not unlikely that the open PUTTING TO DEATH frame
helps the hearer evoke from "the Herodians" information regarding
those who had political power to inflict capital punishment under the
tetrarch Herod Antipas.[71] Note that the new information contained in
τῶν Ἡρῳδιανῶν has the Greek article, a hearer-old marker, which can
be explained by our argument that they were already known and their
role in the PUTTING TO DEATH frame would be well understood with
reference to the audience's long-term memory of the Herodians.[72] Then
the Pharisees' plot with them against Jesus enables the audience to predict that not only the religious authorities (opened by the word "the

---

[70] But the history of debate regarding the identity of the Herodians and such agreement, see John P. Meier, "The Historical Jesus and the Historical Herodians," *JBL* 119
(2000), pp. 749–46.

[71] For information about the fact that the tetrarch Herod Antipas, not Jews, had the
right to inflict capital punishment in Galilee and Perea, see Meier, "Herodians," p. 743.

[72] For another example that the HEROD frame and violent death (of John the Baptist)
are linked, see Mark 6.14–29. It must not be ignored that without the HEROD frame
opened by Ἡρῴδης (6.14), a person frame, including the information provided regarding the one who had the right to imprison and execute, the episode about the imprison-
ment and execution of John the Baptist must have been hardly understandable on the
part of Mark's original audience. Mark 12.13–17 (the episode about the coin of tribute)
is also an example where the word "the Herodians" occurs, assuming a political tone as
its background knowledge. In that story, people (presumably the chief priests, scribes
and elders of 11.27) sent the Pharisees and the Herodians to Jesus so that they may raise
a question about whether they should pay taxes to Caesar. The stereotype of "Herodians," that is, those who were involved in political issues, is a key to understanding their
appearance to ask that kind of question to Jesus in that episode. All these examples show
that the text suppose the audience shared such background knowledge or frame for THE
HERODIANS or HEROD.

Pharisees") but also political power (opened by "the Herodians") will be involved in doing away with Jesus. Then the occurrence of "the Herodians" makes perfect sense in terms of a plot to destroy Jesus.

F. Conclusion

In this chapter our concern has been to explore how frames may have contributed to the audience's ready and quick comprehension of the information in Mark 2.1–3.6. Several conclusions can be drawn here. First, the observations above show that the five stories of Mark 2.1–3.6 operate in a somewhat fixed story frame (Stage, Inciting Incident, Mounting Tension, Climax, Closure) which is based essentially on the prototypical sequence of events in the LEGAL CONTROVERSY frame. Second, since frames include background information of persons, events, things, and place, they provide basic knowledge structures which are necessary for processing narrative elements consisting of character, event, and setting in each episode. Third, frames enabled the expectation of the actions and events to happen next. Besides the global LEGAL CONTROVERSY frame, particularly, I have shown how many subframes, because of "configurations of culture-based, conventionalized knowledge," could have aided Mark's original audience to comprehend readily what is explicitly stated and predict what will follow.[73]

Fourth, frames helped the audience fill in what was left implicit or omitted in each episode since they contained conceptually or semantically interlinked elements within them. Certainly, the cultural conditions in which Mark and his audience lived and the frames' capability of causal inference must be taken into consideration when we account for the gaps left implicit by the text between sentences and in a paragraph or episode. Given that the contents of a frame are culturally conditioned, thus, if the the text and audience come from the same culture, story processing in terms of frames will produce the best results. In this respect, Mark's contemporary audience was in a better position to understand Mark 2.1–3.6 in terms of frames since the early church was an interpersonal community that held the same identity and culture. Fifth, in order for a story to be interesting, surprising events or violations of expectation

---

[73] On such a definition of frame, see Taylor, *Linguistic Categorization*, p. 89.

are necessary, so frames, by allowing the audience to determine what information was expected and unexpected, made the conflict stories in Mark 2.1–3.6 much more understandable as well as interesting and suspenseful. All these observations, therefore, lead us to the conclusion that frames played a crucial role in readily and quickly understanding Mark 2.1–3.6 in the oral and aural communicative situation.

CHAPTER SEVEN

CONCLUSION

In this monograph I have sought to present frame theory as a cognitive model that operates on Mark's oral-aural narrative, in particular the Controversy Stories (Mark 2.1–3.6). In doing so I have attempted to show how frames play a crucial role in identifying the framing structures that are present in the text itself, thus facilitating the audience's processing and understanding of the narrative. I noted in the introduction that as an oral-aural narrative, Mark's Gospel relied on human memory for its transmission and communication, and so it was constructed in such a way as to make the memory process of a listening audience easier. This recognition of the important position of human memory in the communicative environment of Mark's Gospel made it necessary to bring a cognitive model to the interpretation of Mark's oral-aural narrative, in particular the hypothesis of cognitive linguistics that language is a representation of the cognitive faculty; and so frame theory was suggested as a major tool for analyzing the cognitive processing of the Controversy Stories. Before launching my major investigation into the relationship of frame-based information processing and the Markan oral-aural narrative, I also pointed out an important assumption that this study is based on the assumption that human information processing in terms of frames is universal. Frames are language and culture specific as well, hence the study of the operation of the frames in the Markan oral-aural narrative must be conducted in consideration of the characteristics of its oral language and the early Christian audience's cultural and social experiences.

In Chapter Two, we saw that Mark's Gospel, though it is a written text, was intended to be orally performed and aurally received. This observation is not new in biblical studies, but in this study it served to open a way for frame theory as a cognitive model whereby we can come into the study of Mark's Gospel as introduced in the subsequent chapters. Chapter Three focused on frames that operate on Mark's oral-aural narrative. In doing so, two arguments were made. The first was concerned with the orally-based thoughts and expressions that may be elucidated as frame-based information processing. The second argument was that frames are capable of best illuminating the cognitive processing of the thematic and episodic structure of Mark's Gospel and the gist of a story. In Chapter Four, I introduced the properties of frame theory as it has been studied in the fields of cognitive linguistics and psychology, and Bible translation.

In Chapters Five and Six, I sought to adapt frame theory to analyzing structurally and semantically the five episodes in Mark 2.1–3.6. When it comes to episodic structure, the global LEGAL CONTROVERSY frame enabled the thematic composition of Mark 2.1–3.6 by means of its prototypical sequential events consisting of provocative event, charge, defence, and verdict. It was also claimed that frames, by providing the information of their typical event sequences, characters, and physical setting, allow the audience to process each episode in that unit as a conceptually unified story. And then I noted how frames help to describe what the gist, or summary, might be, at the level of not only sentences but also paragraphs or episodes. Finally, in Chapter Six we saw how frames, not only the LEGAL CONTROVERSY frame but also its subframes, help the audience to comprehend the narrative information, such as characters' intentions and behaviour, and conflict between Jesus and his opponents. I also noted that the frame, by making it possible to predict what would come next in the narrative flow and make inferences of missing information and causal relationships between events, helps the audience to be involved in story processing. In addition to story comprehension, frames allow the stories to be interesting and suspenseful by providing what is expected and unexpected.

I have tried so far to read Mark 2.1–3.6 in the light of frame theory. What we can say from our observations is that frame theory is the model that can best account for those cognitive processes on the part of speakers and hearers which are involved in their organizing and understanding of Mark's oral-aural narrative and its linguistic features. Of course, frame theory is a modern cognitive construct. Nonetheless, as discussed, the facts that human frame-based information processing is universal, and many characteristics of oral narrative may be explained by frame theory, strongly endorse the appropriateness of frame theory for the interpretation of Mark's Gospel. Yet this study does not pretend that frame theory can alone explain all features of Mark's oral-aural narrative. As shown in our study, rather frame theory is greatly dependent on other methodologies like socio-scientific study and form criticism, discourse analysis, and even traditional grammar. Nonetheless, in that it incorporates extra-linguistic knowledge (human cognitive processing, social and cultural information) and linguistic knowledge (lexemes, grammar, and semantics) in its methodology, frame theory lays a crucial theoretical foundation for the application of this interdisciplinary work into the study of the Gospels in an attempt to illuminate the meaning of the oral-aural texts.

GLOSSARY

Agentless verb

A reference to verbal forms which have no explicit subject. This is used in this monograph as a hearer-old marker.

Artificial intelligence

A field of research attempting to build computer systems that correspond to human cognitive processing of information.

Chunking

A term to refer to a frame's cognitive function to cluster incoming information or entities, whether in sentences or paragraphs, into a conceptually or semantically bound unit. For example, consider the following string of letters: N H L C B S I R A M T V. The 12-letters seem random and would be hardly recognizable at first glace. But if you read them carefully, "they really form four sets of abbreviations for well known entities: NFL (the National Football League), CBS (one of the three major television networks currently operating in the United States), IRA (an individual retirement account), and MTV (the rock video cable television station)."[1] If you are North American readers and have the frames for NFL, CBS, IRA, MTV, the seemingly random 12-letters may be "chunked" into four organized sets; and then by such four frames' chunking function all 12 letters may be chunked into a single unit. Cognitive model. Memory device to understand and process information (e.g., frames, scripts, schemata). It is a configuration of culture-based, conventionalized knowledge which is believed to be shared by a speech community.

---

[1] The 12-letters example and quotation is from Galotti, *Cognitive Psychology*, p. 136. Galotti uses this example to explain short-term memory's chunking capacity.

Cognitive psychology	A field of psychology which is concerned with how people perceive, understand, remember, and think about information in the real world or a narrative world.
Cognitive linguistics	A branch of linguistics which is interested in human use of language and grammar in cognitive terms.
Concept	A reference to mental representation of the meaning of linguistic units (i.e., words).
Contraexpectation marker	A term to indicate that certain expectation is violated in light of frame knowledge in Greek narrative.
Default values	The typical properties that frames represent. In frame-based information processing people expect such typical properties to occur or to be stated.
Dictation	A normal mode for the ancient to compose texts.
Discourse	Any verbal production, whether written or oral.
Discourse units	Conceptual structures in a text, such as words, phrases, clauses or sentences, paragraphs or episodes, thematic units. Viewing those conceptual structures as a speaker or writer's tools to communicate his or her message to a hearer or reader, discourse analysis is concerned with how those units function and are processed, both by the speaker or writer and by the hearer or reader.
Encyclopaedic knowledge	A term for knowledge a frame represents. People, according to cognitive linguists, call on encyclopaedic knowledge in their mental frame in order to understand a concept. For in-stance, our concept of DOG is inseparably connected with our world knowledge about dogs ("about the status of dogs as a species within the animal kingdom, about different breeds of dog, about their appearance and behaviour, their

relationship with humans, and so on").[2] This monograph argues that Mark's Gospel language is a reflection of social and cultural knowledge and thus the understanding of it is fundamentally based on the opening of such encyclopaedic knowledge or frame.

Episode or episodic structure
In this monograph this concept is used to refer to a discourse unit equal to a paragraph, which consists of the semantically coherent event as a whole. It serves in cognitive terms to unity a a series of sentences (or information) within it into a coherent unit; and for this unifying operation the episode has boundary markers. In narrative discourse the text marks the division of the text into separate chunks, that is, episodes or paragraph, so that the audience may process the information within their boundaries as an entire sequence by recognizing that a new episode begins and hence that the last episode has ended.

Evaluative language
Words which are used when specific things are evaluated against the frame for goodness of fit. This is used in this volume as a hearer-old marker.

Expectation-driven processing
A narrative processing technique which is enabled by frame-based information processing in which, once a frame is identified, the frame enables the audience to expect and predict future events and states in a story.

Frame
As defined by Minsky and Fillmore, a reference to a semantic structure of concepts interrelated with each other. In order to understand the concept of a word, according to frame theory, people need to understand the whole structure of the conepts, that is, frame of the concept. Note the example to follow: "He was on land briefly this afternoon. He was on the ground briefly this afternoon."[3] In this

---

[2] Taylor, *Linguistic Categorization*, p. 82 (the original is capitalized).
[3] For the example used here, see Fillmore, "Linguistics," pp. 15–16.

example the words "on land" and "on ground" seem to refer to the same entity of the dry surface of the earth. However one cannot understand and use the expression properly until opening their larger frames: the SEA VOYAGE frame for "on land" and the AIRPLANE TRIP frame for "on the ground." For the present study of Mark's narrative the frame is divided largely into four types: Event or script-like frame, thing (including place, object), person, and story frames.

Frame deviation A term to refer to doing or mentioning something that is different from what is perceived to be prototypical or typical in light of a frame. Human capacity to recognize something as "weird," "ridiculous" or "interesting" relies on the information processing of frames that consist of generic knowledge structures that typically occur in specific exemplars. Attention is directed to information that deviates from the frame.

Frame instantiation A process for a frame's own properties or slots to be filled by incoming information. In discourse analysis, understanding the input involves a process by which people organize and encode it into a familiar, coherent, conceptual representation that is stored in the mind.

Frame(ed) knowledge Knowledge evoked and processed by certain frames.

Frame indicator A term to refer to key information in an event frame at the sentence level. In this book the main verb's event serves as an indicator to a cluster of main verbs and participles or subordinate clauses in order to call into play in the mind of the listener as a whole the information at the level of sentence.

Frame title A term to refer to core information at the top of the hierarchy of the global frame. It includes a core event in an event frame, person name in a person frame, place name in a place and so on. All components in a certain frame can be opened just with reference to its title.

Gist memory   A term to refer to a way of understanding and remembering a story in an oral or rhetorical culture

Global frame and   A frame not only includes its components but
Subframe   also itself serves as part of another frame. Thus, one higher in hierarchy is called global frame, and those lower than the global frame are called subframes. Consider the example below:

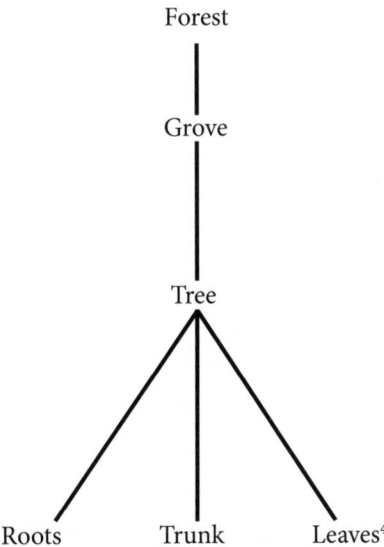

In this example, forest may be called a global frame and grove, tree, roots, trunk, leaves are its subframes. And regarding roots, trunk, and leaves, tree is a global frame and they are subframes of the TREE frame. In particular, in this study a global frame is used as conceptual knowledge dominant in the episode or paragraph and thematic unit (e.g., the LEGAL CONTROVERSY frame); and subframes are used to refer to various events, persons, places, objects occurring within such an episode.

---

[4] This example is quoted from Howard, *Schemata*, p. 33.

Greek article	A grammatical indicator for information already known to the speaker and audience.
Hearer-old marker	A term to refer to grammatical categories or expressions which are used to mark information already known to the speaker and audience, whether in the co-text or in long-term memory.
Homeostatic	A term to refer to a cognitive operation in which people in oral cultures adjust new experiences and information to their typical knowledge system.
ICM (IDEALIZED COGNITIVE MODEL)	As George Lakoff's terms for a frame, ICMs represent "idealized" models of the world knowledge or reality. According to Lakoff, people organize and understand knowledge by means of this idealized world knowledge, that is, ICM and "the meanings of lexical items are defined relative to ICMs, and that ICMs provide the motivation for the existence of the lexical item."[5] For example, a cluster of the ICMs for MOTHER includes:

BIRTH:	the person giving birth is the mother
GENETIC:	the female who contributed the genetic material is the mother
NURTURANCE:	the female adult who nurtures and raises a child is the mother of that child
MARITAL:	the wife of the father is the mother GENEALOGICAL: the closest fe-male ancestor is the mother.[6]

However, the cases that do not fit the MOTHER ICM well are usually indicated by adjective + noun expression:

a. *stepmother*: fits the NURTURANCE and Marital MODELS but none of the others
b. *foster mother*: fits the NURTURANCE model but none of the others

---

[5] George Lakoff, "Categories: An Essay in Cognitive Linguistics," in *Linguistics in the Morning Calm* (ed. The Linguistics Society of Korea; Seoul: Hansin, 1982), p. 164.
[6] Croft and Cruse, *Cognitive Linguistics*, p. 31. Originally the example of MOTHER ICM comes from Lakoff, *Women*, pp. 74–76; but Croft and Cruse slightly change the example. I quote the one provided by Croft and Cruse.

c. *birth mother*:	fits the BIRTH model but none, or not all, of the others
d. *genetic mother*:	fits the GENETIC model but not all of the others
e. *unwed mother*:	fits (probably) all but the MARITAL model [etc].[7]

Information-processing	This term is used by the cognitive scientist in an analogy between human cognition and computerized processing of information. In human information processing "cognition can be thought of as information (what we see, hear, read about, think about) about, think about) passing through a system (our minds)."[8] In this information processing, according to the cognitive scientist, "information is processed (i.e., received, stored, recoded, retrieved and transmitted) in stages and that it is stored in specific places while being processed."[9]
Instantiation	Each frame has its prototypical components and roles. When a frame is activated for use in the story, that processing is called "instantiation." So we may call frame-based story "instantiated story."
Linguistic item or a word	It is a label for a concept, not a concept in and of itself.
Long-term memory	Much of the data people acquire in our lives in the everyday world is stored into memory. There are, according to the cognitive psychologist, three models of human memory: Sensory memory based on sensory modality (e.g., visual, auditory), short-term memory (e.g., this memory operates when we look up a number in a phone book, walk to a telephone and dial the number), long-term memory.[10] In particular, it is believed that long-term memory is a place for storing large amounts of information over long periods of time, perhaps indefinitely (e.g., word meanings, people's names, faces, characteristics, birthdays, physical attributes);

[7] Croft and Cruse, *Cognitive Linguistics*, p. 31.
[8] Galotti, *Cognitive Psychology*, p. 28.
[9] Galotti, *Cognitive Psychology*, p. 28.
[10] Robert J. Sternberg, *Cognitive Psychology* (Fort Worth: Harcourt Brace College, 1996), p. 228.

GLOSSARY

and people rely heavily on their long-term memory throughout their daily activities. The interpretative processing of cognitive models, thus, frames, is fundamentally based on knowledge in long-term memory.

Main verb
A verb form (unlike participles with no person suffix) with person and number suffix, such as indicative, subjunctive, optative, imperative verb forms; in New Testament Greek discourse it marks new information or events. And at the clause or sentence level the independent main verb plays a role of a pointer (or main event) of a single frame including participial and subordinate clause information.

Memory
A cognitive mechanism referring to a range of mental representations and processes such as encoding, storing, and retrieval of information.

Oral-aural communication
A communicative way of a written text in rhetorical cultures in which a text was intended to be orally performed and aurally received.

Oral-aural narrative
A narrative whose communicative way is intended for oral performance and aural reception. In this type of communication human memory plays a crucial role in transmitting and preserving the narrative.

Participial noun phrase
A reference to participle which is used to define the referent or provides information about the referent. This usage of the participle is traditionally known as the substantive and adjectival usage of the participle. This book argues that the participle is used by the language user when its referent is hearer-old information.

Predicative participle
There are three types of uses of the Greek participle Substantive (like a noun), predicative (like a finite verb), and adjectival. In New Testament Greek discourse frame theory contributes to explaining the relationship of the predicative participle to its main verb; that is, a cluster of participle and its main verbs consists of a single frame frame chunk at the sentence level; but participial information conceptually belongs to the main verb frame, whereas the main verb's event serves as a pointer of the frame.

Prototypical	That certain information is prototypical means that it, like frames, is commonly stored through every-day experience and shared by people in a speech community.[11]
Rhetorical culture	A culture between oral culture and scribal culture in which writing and speaking is inseparably interlinked, rather than sharply distinguished as in a modern print culture.
Rhetorical question	A question to call attention to information commonly shared among the speaker and hearer, without expectation to be answered. This is used as a hearer-old marker in this study.
Scene actions	Detailed actions conceptually belonging in the scene headers.
Scene headers	Main events in a global frame by which people usually understand frame-based information.
Schema.	A term used for the first time by F.C. Bartlett and developed by D.E. Rumelhart. Schemas are used by them to refer to generic knowledge structures that enable people to interpret, inferfrom, expect, and pay attention to incoming information.
Script	A term which is used by Schank and Abelson to refer to a frame with a prototypical sequence of events supposed by a social activity.
Stereotype	A term to refer to a default value that a frame contains. Since the frame is culture specific, its knowledge structure often consists of cultural expectations about what a typical person (e.g., a policeman) is supposed to do in a certain situation and what a place (e.g., a library) looks like and is used for.
Temporal clause	A clause introduced by such particles as, ὅταν, ὡς, ὅτε. It refers to prototypical information stored in the original audience's long-term memory or entirely expected from the frame being activated in the co-text.

---

[11] Eleanor Rosch, "Principles of Categorization," in *Cognition and Categorization* (ed. Eleanor Rosch and Barbara B. Lloyd: Hillsdale, New Jersey: Erlbaum, 1978), p. 36.

| *Thematic structure* | An oral-aural narrative discourse unit consisting of a series of episodes which are dominated by the same global frame (the LC frame) and its prototypical event sequences. |
| *World knowledge* | A term to refer to knowledge about the words employed in text, such as "the things referred to, and the functional relations among them. This knowledge is derived from the understander's prior perceptual and verbal interaction with the world and it bears upon both the logical and informational relations."[12] |

---

[12] William H. Warren, David W. Nicholas, and Tom Trabasso, "Event Chains and Inferences in Understanding Narratives," in *New Directions in Discourse Processing* (ed. Roy O. Freedle; Norwood, New Jersey, Ablex, 1979), p. 26.

BIBLIOGRAPHY

Abbott, Valerie, John B. Black and Edward E. Smith, "The Representation of Scripts in Memory," *JML* 24 (1985), pp. 179–99.

Abramowski, Luise, "The 'Memoirs of the Apostle' in Justin," in *The Gospel and the Gospels* (ed. Peter Stuhlmacher; Grand Rapids, Michigan: Eerdmans, 1991), pp. 323–35.

Achtemeier, Paul J., "*Omne Verbum Sonat*: The New Testament and the Oral Environment of Late Western Antiquity," *JBL* 109 (1990), pp. 3–27.

Alba, J.W., and L. Hasher, "Is Memory Schematic," *PB* 93 (1983), pp. 203–31.

Alexander, Loveday, "The Living Voice: Scepticism towards the Written Word in Early Christian and in Graeco-Roman Texts," in *The Bible in Three Dimensions: Essays in Celebration of Forty Years of Biblical Studies in the University of Sheffield* (ed. David J.A. Clines, Stephen E. Fowl and Stanley E. Porter; JSOTSup, 87; Sheffield: JSOT Press, 1990), pp. 221–47.

——. *Gospels for All Christians: Rethinking the Gospel Audiences* (ed. Richard Bauckham; Grand Rapids, Michigan/Cambridge, U.K.: Eerdmans, 1998), pp. 71–112.

Allison, D.C., "Mountain and Wilderness," in *the Dictionary of Jesus and the Gospels* (Downers Grove, Illinois: IVP, 1992), pp. 563–66.

Andersen, Øivind, "Oral Tradition," in *Jesus and the Oral Gospel Tradition* (ed. Henry Wansbrough; JSNTSup 64; Sheffield; JSOT Press, 1991), pp. 17–58.

Arnaldo Momigliano, "The Historians of the Classical World and Their Audiences," (1977–78), pp. 193–204.

Assmann, Jan, "Form as a Mnemonic Device: Cultural Texts and Cultural Memory," in *Performing the Gospel: Orality, Memory, and Mark* (ed. Richar A. Horsley, Jonathan A. Draper, and John Miles Foley; Minneapolis: Fortress, 2006), pp. 67–82.

Aune, David E., *The New Testament in Its Literary Environment* (Philadelphia: Westminster Press, 1987).

——. "Prolegomena to the Study of Oral Tradition in the Hellenistic World," in *Jesus and the Oral Gospel Tradition* (ed. Henry Wansbrough; JSNTSup 64; Sheffield: JSOT Press, 1991), pp. 59–106.

Bacon, Benjamin W., *The Gospel of Mark: Its Composition and Date* (New Haven: Yale University Press, 1925).

Baddley, Allan, *Human Memory: Theory and Practice* (Hove and London: Lawrence Erlbaum, 1990).

Bahr, Gordon J., "Paul and Letter Writing in the First Century," *CBQ* 28 (1966), pp. 465–77.

——. "The Subscriptions in the Pauline Letters," *JBL* 87 (1968), pp. 27–41.

Bailey, Kenneth E., "Informal Controlled Oral Tradition and the Synoptic Gospels," *Themelios* 20 (1995), pp. 4–11.

Bartlett, Frederic C., *Remembering: A Study in Experimental and Social Psychology* (Cambridge: Cambridge University Press, 1932).

Barton, John, *Holy Writings Sacred Text: The Canon in Early Christianity* (WJK: Louisville, Kentucky, 1997).

Bascom, Robert, "The Role of Culture in Translation," in *Bible Translation: Frames of Reference* (ed. Timothy Wilt; Manchester: St. Jerome Publishing, 2003), pp. 81–111.

Bauckham, Richard, "The Worship of Jesus in Apocalyptic Christianity," *NTS* 27 (1981), pp. 322–41.

——. "Jesus and the Wild Animals (Mark 1:13): A Christological Image for an Ecological Age," in *Jesus of Nazareth: Lord and Christ: Essays on the Historical Jesus and New*

Testament Christology (ed. Joel B. Green and Max Turner; Grand Rapids: Eerdmans, 1994), pp. 3–21.

——. "For Whom Were Gospels Written?," in *The Gospels for All Christians: Rethinking the Gospel Audiences* (ed. Richard Bauckham; Grand Rapids, Michigan/Cambridge, U.K.: Eerdmans, 1998), pp. 9–48.

——. *God Crucified: Monotheis and Christology in the New Testament* (Grand Rapids, Michigan: Eerdmans, 1998).

——. *Jesus and the Eyewitnesses: The Gospels as Eyewitness Testimony* (Grand Rapids, Michigan/Cambridge, U.K.: Eerdmans, 2006).

Bauer, Walter, F.W. Danker, W.F. Arndt, and F.W. Gingrich, *A Greek English Lexicon of the New Testament and Other Early Christian Literature* (Chicago: The University of Chicago Press, 3rd edn, 2000).

Beekman, John and John Callow, *Translating the Word of God: with Scripture and Topical Indexes* (Grand Rapids, Michigan: Zondervan, 1974).

Bird, Michael F., "The Markan Community, Myth or Maze? Bauckham's The Gospel for All Christians Revisited," *JTS* 57 (2006), pp. 474–86.

Black, David A., "Discourse Analysis, Synoptic Criticism, and Markan Grammar: Some Methodological Considerations," in *Linguistics and New Testament Interpretation: Essays on Discourse Analysis* (ed. David A. Black, K.B. Barnwell and S. Levinsohn; Nashville, Tennessee: Broadman Press, 1992), pp. 90–98.

Black, John B and Gordon H. Bower, "Episodes as Chunks in Narrative Memory," *VLVB* 18 (1979), pp. 309–18.

——. "Story Understanding as Problem-Solving," *Poetics* 9 (1980), pp. 223–50.

Black, Stephanie L., *Sentence Conjunction in the Gospel of Matthew: καί, δέ, τότε, γάρ, οὖν and Asyndeton in Narrative Discourse* (JSNTSup 216; Sheffield: Sheffield Academic Press, 2002).

Blass, F., A. Debrunner, and Robert W. Funk, *A Greek Grammar of the New Testament and Other Early Christian Literature* (Chicago: The University of Chicago Press, 1961).

Bock, Darrell L., *Blasphemy and Exaltation in Judaism and the Final Examination of Jesus* (WUNT 106; Mohr Siebeck: Tübingen, 1998).

Boer, W. Den, *The Art of Memory and its Mnemotechnical Traditions* (Amsterdam: North Holland Publishing, 1986).

Boomershine, Thomas E., "Peter's Denial as Polemic or Confession: The Implications of Media Criticism for Biblical Hermeneutics," *Semeia* 39 (1987), pp. 47–68.

——. *Story Journey: An Invitation to the Gospel as Story telling* (Nashville: Abingdon Press, 1988).

Botha, Pieter J.J., "Mute Manuscripts: Analysing a Neglected Aspect of Ancient Communication," *TE* 23 (1990), pp. 35–47.

——. "Mark's Story as Oral Traditional Literature: Rethinking the Transmission of Some Traditions about Jesus," *HTS* 47 (1991), pp. 304–331.

——. "The Social Dynamics of the Early Transmission of the Jesus Tradition," *Neotestamentica* 29 (1993), pp. 205–31.

——. "The Historical Setting of Mark's Gospel: Problems and Possibilities," *JSNT* 51 (1993), pp. 27–55.

——. " Mark's Story of Jesus and the Search for Virtue," in *The Rhetorical Analysis of Scripture: Essays from the 1995 London Conference* (ed. Stanley E. Porter and Thomas H. Olbricht; JSNTSup 146; Sheffield: Sheffield Academic Press, 1997), pp. 157–84.

Bower, Gordon H., John B Black and Terrence I. Turner, "Scripts in Memory for Text," *CP* 11 (1979), pp. 177–220.

Bransford J.D. and M.K. Johnson, "Contextual Prerequisites for Understanding: Some Investigations of Comprehension and Recall," *JVLVB* 11 (1972), pp. 712–26.

Brown, Gillian and George Yule, *Discourse Analysis* (Cambridge: Cambridge University Press, 1983).

Bultmann, Rudolf, "The Study of the Synoptic Gospels," in *Form Criticism. A New Method of New Testament Research* (trans. Frederick C. Grant; New York: Willett, Clark and Company, 1934), pp. 7–75.
——. *The History of the Synoptic Tradition* (Oxford: Basil Blackwell, 1972).
Burridge, Richard, *What are the Gospels? A Comparison with Graeco-Roman Biography* (Grand Rapids, Michigan: Eerdmans, 2nd edn, 2004).
——. "About People, by People, for People: Gospel Genre and Audiences," in *The Gospels for All Christians: Rethinking the Gospel Audiences* (ed. Richard Bauckham; Grand Rapids, Michigan/Cambridge, U.K.: Eerdmans, 1998), pp. 113–45.
Burton, E.D. *Syntax of the Moods and Tenses in New Testament Greek* (Chicago: University of Chicago, 1943).
Byrskog, Samuel, *Story as History—History as Story: The Gospel Tradition in the Context of Ancient Oral History* (Boston: Brill Academic Press, 2002).
Callow, Kathleen, *Man and Message: A Guide to Meaning-Based Text Analysis* (Lanham: University Press of America, 1998).
Campenhausen, Hans von, *The Formation of the Christian Bible* (trans. J.A. Baker; Philadelphia: Fortress, 1972).
Caragounis, Chrys C., *The Son of Man* (WUNT 38; Tübigen: J.C.B. Mohr (Paul Siebeck), 1986).
Carruthers, Mary J., *The Book of Memory: A Study of Memory in Medieval Culture* (Cambridge: Cambridge University Press, 1990).
Carson, D.A., *Exegetical Fallacies* (Grand Rapids: Baker Book House, 1984).
Casey, M., "Culture and Historicity: The Plucking of the Grain (Mark 2.23–28)," *NTS* 34 (1988), pp. 1–23.
Chafe, Wallace, "The Flow of Thought and the Flow of Language," in *Syntax and Semantics*. Vol. 12: *Discourse and Syntax* (ed. Talmy Givón; New York: Academic Press, 1979), pp. 159–81.
——. "The Deployment of Consciousness in the Production of a Narrative," in *The Pear Stories* (ed. Wallace Chafe; Norwood, New Jersey: Ablex, 1980), pp. 9–50.
Chomsky, Noam, *Knowledge of Language: Its Nature, Origin, and Use* (New York: Praeger, 1986).
Clark, Herbert H., and Susan E. Haviland, "Comprehension and the Given-New Contract," in *Discourse Production and Comprehension* (ed. Roy O. Freedle; Norwood New Jersey: Ablex, 1977), pp. 1–40.
Clausner, Timothy C. and William Croft, "Domains and Image Schemas," *CL*10–1 (1999), pp. 1–31.
Cranfield, C.E.B., *The Gospel According to Saint Mark* (CGTC; Cambridge: Cambridge University Press, 1974).
Croft, William, "The Role of Domains in the Interpretation of Metaphors and Metonymies," *Cognitive Linguistics* 4 (1993), pp. 335–70. Revised version printed in *Metaphor and Metonymy in Comparision and Contrast* (ed. René Dirven and Ralf Pörings; Berlin: Mouton de Gruyter, 2002), pp. 161–25.
Croft, William and D. Alan Cruse, *Cognitive Linguistics* (Cambridge: Cambridge University Press, 2004).
Cuddon, J.A., *A Dictionary of Literary Terms* (London: Andre Deutsch, 1997).
Dahl, Nils A., *Jesus in the Memory of the Early Church* (Minneapolis, Minnesota: Augsburg, 1976).
Dalman, Gustaf, *Sacred Sites and Ways: Studies in the Topography of the Gospels* (trans. Paul Levertoff; London: SPCK, 1935).
Danove, Paul, *The End of Mark's Story* (Leiden: E.J. Brill, 1993).
——. *Linguistics and Exegesis in the Gospel of Mark:Applications of a Case Frame Analysis* (Sheffield: Sheffield Academic Press, 2001).
Daube, David, *The New Testament and Rabbinic Judaism* (London: Athlone Press, 1953).

——. "Responsibilities of Master and Disciples in the Gospels," *NTS* 19 (1972), pp. 1–15.

Davis, Casey W., *Oral Biblical Criticism: The Influence of the Principles of Orality on the Literary Structure of Paul's Epistle to the Philippians* (JSNTSup 172; Sheffield: Sheffield Academic Press, 1999).

Davies, W.D. and Allison, D.C., *A Critical and Exegetical Commentary on the Gospel According to Saint Matthew*. Vol. 1 (ICC; Edinburgh: T. and T. Clark, 1988).

Deissmann, Adolf, *Light from the Ancient East* (London: Hodder and Stoughton, 1927).

Dewey, Joanna, *Markan Public Debate* (SBL Dissertation Series, 48; Chico, California, Scholars Press, 1980).

——. "Oral Methods of Structuring Narrative in Mark," *Interpretation* 43 (1989), pp. 32–46.

——. "Mark as Interwoven Tapestry: Forecasts and Echoes for a Listening Audience," *CBQ* 53 (1991), pp. 221–36.

——. "The Gospel of Mark as an Oral-Aural Event: Implications for Interpretation," in *The New Literary Criticism and the New Testament* (ed. Elizabeth S. Malbon and Edgar V. McKnight; JSNTSup 109; Sheffield: Sheffield Academic Press, 1994), pp. 145–63.

——. "Textuality in an Oral Culture: A Survey of the Pauline Tradition," *Semeia* 65 (1995), pp. 37–65.

——. "The Gospel of John in Its Oral-Written Media World," in *Jesus in Johannine Tradition* (ed. Robert T. Fortna and Tom Thatcher; Louisville: Westminster John Knox Press, 2001), pp. 239–52.

Dibelius, Martin, *From Tradition to Gospel* (trans. Bertram Lee Woolf; New York: Charles Scribner's Sons, 1934).

Donahue, John and Harrington, Daniel, *The Gospel of Mark* (Collegeville, Minnesota: The Liturgical Press, 2002). Dormeyer, Detlev, *The New Testament Among the Writings of Antiquity* (trans. Rosemarie Kossov; Sheffield: Sheffield Academic Press, 1998).

Dunn, G. James, *Jesus, Paul and the Law: Studies in Mark and Galatians* (Louisville, Kentucky: WJK, 1990).

——. *The Partings of the Ways: Between Christianity and Judaism and Their Significance for the Character of Christianity* (London: SCM/Philadelphia: Trinity, p. 1991).

——. *Jesus Remembered* (Grand Rapids, Michigan: Eerdmans, 2003).

——. *Unity and Diversity in the New Testament: An Inquiry into the Character of Earliest Christianity* (London: SCM, 3rd edn, 2006).

Dwyer, Timothy, *The Motif of Wonder in the Gospel of Mark* (JSNTSup 128; Sheffield: Sheffield Academic Press, 1996).

Edwards, James. R., "Markan Sandwiches: The Significance of Interpolations in Markan Narratives," *NovT* 31 (1989), pp. 193–216.

Einstein, Gilles O., Lackey, Scott and McDaniel, Mark A., "Bizarre Imagery, Interference, and Distinctiveness," *JEP* 15 (1989), pp. 137–46.

Elliot, John E., *What is Social-Scientific Criticism?* (Philadelphia: Fortress, 1993).

——. *1 Peter* (AB, 37B; New York: Doubleday, 2000).

Emmott, Catherine, *Narrative Comprehension: A Discourse Perspective* (Oxford: Clarendon Press, 1997).

Epstein, Richard, "Roles, Frames and Definiteness," in *Discourse Studies in Cognitive Linguistics. Selected Papers from the Fifth International Cognitive Linguistics Conference Amsterdam, July 1997* (ed. Karen van Hoek, Andrej A. Kiibrik and Leo Noordman; Amsterdam, Philadelphia: John Benjamins, 1999), pp. 53–74.

Eriksson, Karl, *Das Präsens Historicum in der nachklassischen griechischen Historiographie* (Lund: Hakan Ohlsson, 1943).

Esler, Philp F., *Community and Gospel in Luke-Acts: The Social and Political Motivations of Lucan Theology* (SNTSMS 57; Cambridge: Cambridge University Press, 1987).

Evans, Craig A., *Mark 8:27–16:24* (WBC 34B; Nashville: Thomas Nelson, 2001).

Fanning, Buist M., *Verbal Aspect in New Testament Greek* (Oxford: Clarendon, 1990).

Farmer, William, *The Synoptic Problem: A Critical Analysis* (New York: Macmillan, 1964).
——. *The Gospel of Jesus: The Pastoral Relevance of the Synoptic Problem* (Louisville: WJK, 1994).
Ferguson, Everett, "Review of Geoffrey Mark Hahneman, The Muratorian Fragment and the Development of the Canon," *JTS* 44 (1994), pp. 691–97.
Fillmore, Charles J, "The Case for Case," in *Universals of Linguistic Theory* (ed. E. Bach and R.T. Harm; New York: Holt, Rinehart and Winston, 1968), pp. 1–90.
——. "An Alternative to Checklist Theories of Meaning," in *Proceedings of the First Annual Meeting of the Berkeley Linguistics Society* (ed. Cathy Cogen et al.; Berkeley: Berkeley Linguistics Society, 1975), pp. 123–31.
——. "The Need for a Frame Semantics within Linguistics," in *Statistical Methods in Linguistics* (ed. Hans Karlgren; Stockholm: Språkförlaget, 1976), pp. 5–29.
——. "Scenes-and-Frames Semantics," in *Linguistic Structures Processing* (Fundamental Studies in Computer Science, 5; ed. Antonio Zampolli; Amsterdam: North-Holland, 1977), pp. 55–81.
——. "Frame Semantics," in *Linguistics in the Morning Calm* (ed. The Linguistics Society of Korea; Seoul: Hansin, 1982), pp. 111–37.
——. "Ideal Readers and Real Readers," in *Analyzing Discourse: Text and Talk* (ed. Deborah Tannen; Washington, D.C.: Georgetown University Press, 1982), pp. 248–70.
——. "Frames and the Semantics of Understanding," *QS* 6 (1985), pp. 222–54.
——. "Linguistics as a Tool for Discourse Analysis," in *Handbook of Discourse Analysis*. Vol. 1. *Disciplines of Discourse* (ed. Teun A. van Dijk; London, San Diego: Academic Press, 1985), pp. 11–38.
——. "<<U>>-Semantics, Second Round," *QS* 7 (1986), pp. 49–58.
——. "Ideal Readers and Real Readers," in *Analyzing Discourse: Text and Talk* (ed. Deborah Tannen; Washington, D.C.: Georgetown University Press, 1982b), pp. 248–70.
——. *Form and Meaning in Language*. Vol. 1: *Papers on Semantic Roles* (Stanford, California: CSLI Publications, 2003).
Fishbane, Michael, *Biblical Interpretation in Ancient Israel* (Oxford: Clarendon Press, 1985).
Fitzmyer, Joseph A., *The Gospel According to Luke I–IX* (AB, 28; New York: Doubleday, 1981).
Flusser, David, *Jesus* (Jerusalem: Magnes Press, The Hebrew University, 1968).
Foley, John Miles, "The Traditional Oral Audience," *BS* 18 (1977), pp. 145–154.
——. *Immanent Art: From Structure to Meaning in Traditonal Oral Epic* (Bloomington and Indianapolis: Indiana University Press, 1991).
——. *The Singer of Tales in Performance* (Bloomington and Indianapolis: Indiana University Press, 1995).
Fowler, Robert M., *Loaves and Fishes: The Function of the Feeding Stories in the Gospel of Mark* (SBLDS 54; Chico, California: Scholars Press, 1981).
——. *Let the Reader Understand: Reader Response Criticism and the Gospel of Mark* (Minneapolis: Fortress Press, 1991).
France, R.T., *The Gospel of Mark: A Commentary on the Greek Text* (Grand Rapids, Michigan: Eerdmans, 2002).
Frederiksen, Carl H., "Structure and Process in Discourse Production and Comprehension," in *Cognitive Processes in Comprehension* (ed. Marcel A. Just and Patricia A. Carpenter; Erlbaum, 1977), pp. 313–22.
Galotti, Kathleen M., *Cognitive Psychology in and out of the Laboratory* (Pacific Grove, California: Brooks/Cole, 1999).
Gamble, Harry Y., *The New Testament Canon: Its Making and Meaning* (Philadelphia: Fortress, 1985).
——. *Books and Readers in the Early Church: A History of Early Christian Texts* (New Haven and London: Yale University Press, 1995).

Gavrilov, A.K., "Techniques of Reading in Classical Antiquity," *CQ* 47 (1997), pp. 56–73.

Georgakopoulou, Alexander and Dionysis Goutsos, *Discourse Analysis. An Introduction* (Edinburgh: Edinburgh University Press, 1997).

Gerhardsson, Birger, "Oral Tradition (New Testament)," in *A Dictionary of Biblical Interpretation* (ed. R.J. Coggins and J.L. Houlden; London: SCM, 1990), pp. 498–501.

——. *Memory and Manuscript: Oral Tradition and Written Transmission in Rabbinic Judaism and Early Christianity with Tradition and Transmission in Early Christianity*. Forward by Jacob Neusner (Grand Rapids, Michigan: Eerdmans, 1998).

——. *The Reliability of the Gospel Tradition* (Peabody, Massachusetts: Hendrickson, 2001).

Gibbs, Raymond W., "What's cognitive about cognitive linguistics?," in *Cognitive Linguistics in the Redwoods The Expansion of a New Paradigm in Linguistics* (ed. Eugene H.Casad; Berlin, New Yord: Mouton de Gruyter, 1996).

Gibson, Jeffrey B., "Jesus' Wilderness Temptation according to Mark, " *JSNT* 53 (1994), pp. 4–43.

Gilliard, Frank D., "More Silent Reading in Antiquity: *Non omne verbum sonat*," *JBL* 112 (1993), pp. 689–96.

Givón, T., *Syntax: An Introduction*. Vol. 1 (Amsterdam/Philadelphia: Benjamins,1984).

Glasson, T.F., "The Place of the Anecdote: A Note on Form Criticism," *JTS* 32 (1981), pp. 142–50.

Goody, Jack and Watt Ian, "The Consequences of Literacy," in *Literacy in Traditional Societies* (ed. Jack Goody; Cambridge: Cambridge University Press, 1968), pp. 27–68.

Graesser, Artheur C., *Prose Comprehension Beyond the Word* (New York: Springer-Verlag, 1981).

Graham, William A., *Beyond the Written Word. Oral Aspects of Scripture in the History of Religion* (Cambridge: Cambridge University Press, 1987).

Grimes, Joseph E., "Narrative Studies in Oral Texts," in *Current Trends in Textlinguistics* (ed. Wolfgang U. Dressler; Berlin. New York: Walter de Gruyter, 1978), pp. 123–32.

Guelich, Robert A., *Mark 1–8:26* (WBC 34A; Dallas: Word, 1989).

Gundry, Robert H., *Mark: A Commentary on His Apology for the Cross* (Grand Rapids, Michigan: Eerdmans, 1993).

Haberlandt, K., "Encoding of Story Constituents," *Poetics* 9 (1980), pp. 99–118.

Hadas, Moses, *Ancilla to Classical Reading* (New York: Columbia University Press, 1961).

Hahneman, Geoffrey M., *The Muratorian Fragment and the Development of the Canon* (Oxford: Oxford University Press, 1992).

Halbwachs, Maurice, *The Collective Memory* (trans. Francis J. Ditter Jr. And Vida Yazdi Ditter; New York: Harper and Row, 1950).

Hamilton, David L., "Cognitive Representations of Person," in *Social Cognition: The Ontario Symposium*. Vol. 1 (ed. E. Tory Higgins, C. Peter Herman, and Mark P. Zanna; Hillsdale, New Jersey: Erlbaum, 198), pp. 135–59.

Harris, William, *Ancient Literacy* (Cambridge, Massachusetts: Harvard University Press, 1989).

Harvey, John D., *Listening to The Text: Oral Patterning in Paul's Letters* (Grand Rapids: Baker Books, 1998).

Hastie, R. "Schematic Principles in Human Memory," in *Social Cognition: The Ontario Symposium* (ed. E.T. Higgins, C.D. Herman and M.P. Zanna; Hillsdale, New Jersey: Eribaum, 1981), pp. 39–88.

Havelock Eric, *Preface to Plato* (Cambridge, Massachusetts; London: The Belknap Press of Harvard University Press, 1963).

——. "The Alphabetization of Homer," in *Communication Arts in the Ancient World* (ed. Eric A. Havelock and Jackson P. Hershbell; New York: Hastings House, 1978), pp. 3–22.

——. "Oral Composition in the Oedipus Tyrannus of Sophocles," *NLH* 16 (1984), pp. 175–97.

Haviland, Susan E. and Herbert H. Clark, "What's New? Acquiring New Information as a Process in Comprehension," *JVLVB* 14 (1974), pp. 512–21.

Henaut, Barry W., *Oral Tradition and The Gospels: the Problem of Mark 4* (JSNTSup 82; Sheffield: JSOT Press, 1993).

Hendrickson, George L., "Ancient Reading," *CJ* 25 (1929–30), pp. 182–96.

Hengel, Martin, *The Charismatic Leader and His Followers* (Edinburgh: T. and T. Clark, 1981).

——. *Studies in the Gospel of Mark* (London: SCM, 1985).

——. *The Zealots: Investigations into the Jewish Freedom Movement in the Period from Herod 1 until 70 A.D.* (trans. David Smith; Edinburgh: T. and T. Clark, 1989).

Herman, David, *Narrative Theory and the Cognitive Sciences* (ed. David Herman; Standford, California: CSLI Publications, 2003).

Hidi, Suzanne and William Baird, "Interestingness—A Neglected Variable in Discourse Processing," *CS* 10 (1986), pp. 179–94.

Hildyard, Angela, and David R. Olson, "On the Comprehension and Memory of Oral vs. Written Discourse," in *Spoken and Written Language: Exploring Orality and Literacy* (ed. Deborah Tannen: Norwood, New Jersey,: Ablex, 1982), pp. 19–34.

Hill, Charles E., "The Debate over the Muratorian Fragment and the Development of the Canon," *WTJ* 57 (1995), pp. 437–52.

Honeck, Richard P., P. Reichman and Robert Hoffman, "Semantic Memory for Metaphor: The Conceptual Base Hypothesis," *Memory and Cognition* 3 (1975), pp. 409–15.

Hooker, Morna D., *The Son of Man in Mark* (Montreal: McGill University Press, 1967).

——. *The Gospel According to Saint Mark* (Peabody, Massachusetts: Hendrickson, 1991).

Horbury, William, "The Benediction of the Minim and Early Jewish Christian Controversy," *JTS* 33 (1982), pp. 19–61.

——. "The Wisdom of Solomon in the Muratorian Fragment," *JTS* 45 (1994), pp. 149–59.

Horsley, Richard A., *Hearing the Whole Story: The Politics of Plot in Mark's Gospel* (Louisville: WJK, 2001).

——. "Prominent Patterns in the Social Memory of Jesus and Friends," *Semeia* 52 (2005), pp. 57–78.

Howard, Robert W., *Concept and Schemata: An Introduction* (London: Cassell, 1987).

Howe, Nicholas, "The Cultural Construction of Reading in Anglo-Saxon England," in *The Ethnography of Reading* (ed. Jonathan Boyarin; Berkeley: University of California Press, 1992), pp. 58–79.

Hoyle, Richard A., "Scenarios, discourse and translation: The scenario theory of cognitive linguistics, its relevance for analysing New Testament Greek and modern Parkari texts, and its implications for translation theory," Ph.D. diss., The University of Surrey Roehampton, 2001.

Hultgren, Arland, *Jesus and His Adversaries* (Minneapolis: Augsburg, 1979).

Hurtado, Larry. W., "The Gospel of Mark: Evolutionary or Revolutionary Document?," in *The Synoptic Gospels* (ed. Craig A. Evans and Stanley E. Porter; Sheffield: Sheffield Academic Press, 1995), pp. 15–32.

——. *Lord Jesus Christ. Devotion to Jesus in Earliest Christianity* (Grand Rapids, Michigan/Cambridge, U.K.: Eerdmans, 2003).

Iersel, M.F. Van., *Mark: A Reader-Response Commentary* (JSNTSup 164; Sheffield: JSOT Press, 1998).

——. *Reading Mark* (Edinburgh: T. and T. Clark, 1989).

Jeremias, Joachim, *The Parables of Jesus* (New York: Charles Scribners's Sons, 1963).

——. *Eucharistic Words of Jesus* (Fortress: Philadelphia, 1966).

——. *Jerusalem in the Time of Jesus: An Investigation into Economic and Social Conditions during the Time of Jesus* (Philadelphia: Fortress 1969).

——. *New Testament Theology* (London: SCM, 1971).

Judge, E.A., *The Social Pattern of Christian Groups in the First Century* (London: Tyndale, 1960).

Just, M.A., and H.H. Brownell, "Retrieval of Concrete and Abstract Prose Descriptions from Memory," *Canadian Journal of Psychology* 64 (1974), pp. 339–50.

Kahn, Charles H., *The Art and Thought of Heraclitus: An Edition of the Fragments with Translation and Commentary* (Cambridge: Cambridge University Press, 1979).

Katz, Albert N., "On Choosing the Vehicles of Metaphors: Referential Concreteness, Semantic Distances, and Individual Differences," *JML* 28 (1989), pp. 486–99.

Keck, Leander E., "Oral Traditional Literature and the Gospels: The Seminar," in *The Relationships Among the Gospels: An Interdisciplinary Dialogue* (ed. William O. Walker, Jr.; San Antonio: Trinity University Press, 1978).

Kelber, Werner H., "Mark and Oral Tradition," *Semeia* 16 (1979), pp. 7–55.

——. *The Oral and Written Gospel: The Hermeneutics of Speaking and Writing in the Synoptic Tradition, Mark, Paul and Q* (Philadelphia: Fortress, 1983).

——. "Jesus and Tradition: Words in Time, Words in Space," *Semeia* 65 (1994), pp. 139–67.

——. "Orality, Rhetoric, and Scribality," *Semeia* 65 (1995), pp. 193–216.

——. "The Case of the Gospels: Memory's Desire and the Limits of Historical Criticism," *OT* 17 (2002) pp. 55–86.

Kenyon, Frederic G., *Books and Readers in Ancient Greece and Rome* (Oxford: Clarendon, 1951).

Kim, Seyoon, *"The 'Son of Man'" as the Son of God* (Grand Rapids, Michigan: Eerdmans, 1985).

Kirk, Alan, "Social and Cultural Memory," *Semeia* 52 (2005), pp. 1–24.

Kirk, Alan and Tom Thatcher, "Jesus Tradition as Social Memory," *Semeia* 52 (2005), pp. 25–42.

Klauck, H.J., "Die Frage der Sündenvergebung in der Perikope von der Heilung des Gelähmten (Mk 2, 1–12 parr.)," *BZ* (1981), pp. 223–48.

Klingbeil, Gerald A., "Metaphors and Pragmatics: An Introduction to the Hermeneutics of Metaphors in the Epistle to the Ephesians," *BBR* 16 (2006), pp. 273–93.

Klosinski, L.E., "Meal in Mark," Ph.D. diss., The Claremont Graduate School, 1988.

Kosmala, H. "The Time of the Cock-Crow," *ASTI* 2 (1963), pp. 46–52.

Kövecses, Zoltán, *Metaphor in Culture: Universality and Variation* (Cambridge: Cambridge University Press, 2005).

Kuhn H.W., *Ältere Sammlungen im Markusevangelium* (SUNT 8; Göttingen:Vandengoeck and Ruprecht, 1971).

Kümmel, Werner G., *Introduction to the New Testament* (trans. Howard Clark Kee; Nashville: Abingdon Press, 1973).

Labov, William, *Sociolinguistic Patterns* (Philadelphia: University of Pennsylvania Press, 1972).

Lakoff, George, "The Role of Deduction in Grammar," in *Studies in Linguistic Semantics* (ed. Charles Fillmore and D. Terence Langendoen; New York; Holt, Rinehart and Winston, 1971).

——. "Categories: An Essay in Cognitive Linguistics," in *Linguistics in the Morning Calm* (ed. The Linguistics Society of Korea; Seoul: Hansin, 1982), pp. 140–93.

——. *Women, Fire and Dangerous Things: What Categories Reveal About the Mind* (Chicago: University of Chicago Press, 1987).

Lakoff, George and Johnson, *Metaphors We Live By* (Chicago: University of Chicago Press, 1980).

Lakoff, George and Turner, Mark, *More Than Cool Reason: A Field Guide to Poetic Metaphor* (Chicago: The University of Chicago Press, 1989).

Lane, William, *The Gospel of Mark* (NICNT; Grand Rapids, Michigan: Eerdmans, 1974).

Langacker, Ronald W. *Foundations of Cognitive Grammar*. Vol. 1: *Theoretical Prerequisites* (Stanford, California: Stanford University Press, 1987).

Lehnert, W.G., "The Role of Scripts in Understanding," in *Frame Conceptions and Text Understanding* (ed. Dieter Metzing; Berlin. New York: de Gruyter, 1980), pp. 79–95.

Lemcio, Eugene L., *The Past of Jesus in the Gospels* (SNTSMS 68; Cambridge: Cambridge University Press, 1991).

Lentz, Tony M., *Orality and Literacy in Hellenic Greece* (Carbondale: Southern Illinois University Press, 1989).

Levinsohn, Stephen H., *Discourse Features of New Testament Greek* (Dallas: Summer Institute of Linguistics, 1992).

Liddell H. and R. Scott, *Greek-English Lexicon with a Supplement* (Oxford: Clarendon, 1968).

Lieberman, Saul, *Hellenism in Jewish Palestine. Studies in the Literary Transmission: Beliefs and Manners of Palestine in I Century B.C.E.–IV century C.E.* (New York: The Jewish Theological Seminary of America, 1950).

Lindars, Barnabas, *Jesus Son of Man* (Grand Rapids: Eerdmanns, 1983).

Longacre, Robert E., "The Paragraph as a Grammatical Unit," in *Syntax and Semantics 12: Discourse and Syntax* (ed. Talmy Givön; New York: Academic Press, 1979), pp.115–34.

——. "A Top-Down, Template-Driven Narrative Analysis, Illustrated by Application to Mark's Gospel," in *Discourse Analysis and NewTestament: Approaches and Results* (ed. Stanley E. Porter and Jeffrey T. Reed; JSNTSup 170; Sheffield: Sheffield Academic Press, 1999), pp. 140–67.

Longenecker, Richard. N., "Ancient Amanuenses and the Pauline Epistles," in *New Dimensions in New Testament Study* (ed. R.N. Longenecker and M.C. Tenney; Zondervan: Grand Rapids, Michigan, 1974), pp. 281–97.

Lord, Albert B., *The Singer of Tales* (Cambridge, Massachusetts: Harvard University Press, 1960).

——. "Perspectives on Recent Work on Oral Literature," in *Oral Literature* (ed. J.J. Duggan; Edinburgh: Scottish Academic Press, 1975), pp. 467–503.

——. "The Gospels as Oral Traditional Literature," in *The Relationship among the Gospels: An Interdisciplinary Dialogue* (ed. William O. Walker; San Antonio: Trinity University Press, 1978), pp. 33–91.

Louw, J.P., "Reading a Text as Discourse," in *Linguistics and New Testament Interpretation: Essays on Discourse Analysis* (ed. David Alan Black; Nashville, Tennessee, Broadman Press, 1992), pp. 17–30.

Louw, J.P.and Eugene A. Nida, *Greek-English Lexicon of the New Testament: Based on Semantic Domains* (2 vols.; New York: United Bible Societies, 1988).

——. *Lexical Semantics of the Greek New Testament* (Atlanta, Georgia: Scholars Press, 1992).

Lowy, S. "The Motivation of Fasting in Talmudic Literature," *JJS* 9 (1958), pp. 19–38.

Lyons, John, *Introduction to Theoretical Linguistics* (Cambridge: Cambridge University Press, 1969).

MacCormac, Earl R., *A Cognitive Theory of Metaphor* (Cambridge, Massachusetts; London, UK: Bradford Books, 1985).

Mack, Burton L., "Elaboration of the Chreia in the Hellenistic School," in *Patterns of Persuasion in the Gospels* (ed. Burton L. Mack and Vernon K. Robbins; FF; Sonoma, Cal.: Polebridge, 1989), pp. 31–68.

Malbon, Elizabeth S., "TÇ OIKIA AUTOU: Mark 2.15 in Context," *NTS* 31, pp. 282–92.

——. *Hearing Mark: A Listener's Guide* (Harrisburg, Penn.: Trinity Press International, 2002).

Malina, Bruce, *New Testament World: Insights from Cultural Anthropology* (Louisville, Kentucky: WJK, 2000).

Malina, Bruce and Jerome Neyrey, "Honor and Shame in Luke-Acts: Pivotal Values of the Mediterranean World," in *The Social World of Luke-Acts* (ed. Jerome Neyrey; Peabody, Massachusetts: Hendrickson, 1991), pp. 36–51.

Mandler, J.M., *Stories, Scripts and Scenes: Aspects of Schema Theory* (Hillsdale, New Jersey: Erlbaum, 1984).

Manson, T.W., *The Teaching of Jesus* (Cambridge: Cambridge University Press, 2nd edn, 1935).

Marcus, Joel, *The Way of the Lord: Christological Exegesis of the Old Testament in the Gospel of Mark* (Louisville, Kentucky: WJK, 1992).

——. *Mark 1–8: A New Translation with Introduction and Commentary* (AB, 27A; New York; Toronto: Doubleday, 2000).

Marshall, I.H., "Son of Man," in *Dictionary of Jesus and the Gospels* (ed. Joel B. Green, Scot McKnight and I. Howard Marshall; Downers Grove, Illinois: IVP, 1992), pp. 775–81.

Marshall, Sandra P., *Schemas in Problem Solving* (Cambridge: Cambridge University Press, 1995).

Marschark, Marc, and John Warner, Roxann Thompson, and Charles Huffman, "Concreteness, Imagery, and Memory for Prose," in *Mental Images in Human Cognition* (ed. Robert H. Logie and Michel Denis; North-Holland: Elsevier Science Publishers B.V., 1991), pp. 191–207.

Marrou, Henri I., *A History of Education in Antiquity* (trans. George Lamb; New York: Sheed and Ward, 1956).

Martin, Henri-Jean, *The History and Power of Writing* (trans. Lydia G. Cochrane; Chicago and London: The University of Chicago Press, 1994).

——. "Mark, John," in *The International Standard Bible Encyclopedia*. Vol. 3 (ed. Geoffrey W. Bromiley: Grand Rapids, Michigan: Eerdmans, 1986), pp. 259–60.

Martin, Ralph P., *Mark. Evangelist and Theologian* (Grand Rapids, Michigan: Zondervan, 1973).

Martin, Richard P., *The Language of Heroes: Speech and Performance in the Iliad* (Ithaca and London: Cornell University Press, 1989).

Martyn, J. Louis, *History and Theology in the Fourth Gospel*, rev.ed. (Nashville: Abingdon, 1979).

McCown, C.C., "Codex and Roll in the New Testament," *HTR* 34 (1941), pp. 219–50.

McDonald, Lee Martin and Stanley E. Porter, *Early Christianity and Its Sacred Literature* (Peabody, Massachusetts: Hendrickson, 2000).

McKnight, Edgar V., *What is Form Criticism?* (Philadelphia: Fortress Press, 1969).

Meeks, Wayne A., *The First Urban Christians: The Social World of the Apostle Paul* (New Haven and London: Yale University Press, 1983).

Meier, John. P., "The Historical Jesus and the Historical Herodians," *JBL* 119 (2000), pp. 740–46.

Metzger, Bruce M., *The Canon of the New Testament: Its Origins, Development, and Significance* (Oxford; Clarendon, 1987).

Minchin, Elizabeth, *Homer and the Resources of Memory. Some Applications of Cognitive Theory to the Iliad and the Odyssey* (Oxford: Oxford University Press, 2001).

Minsky, Marvin, "A Framework for Representing Knowledge," in *The Psychology of Computer Vision* (ed. Patrick H. Winston; New York: McGraw-Hill, 1975), pp. 211–81.

Momigliano, Arnaldo, "The Historians of the Classical World and Their Audiences," *AS* 47 (1977–78), pp. 193–204.

Moore, George F., *Judaism In the First Centuries of the Christian Era: The Age of the Tannaim*. Vols. 1 and 2 (Cambridge, Massachusetts: Harvard University Press, 1966).

Moore, Stephen D., *Literary Criticism and the Gospels: The Theoretical Challenge* (New Haven: Yale University Press, 1989).

Moule, C.F.D., *An Idiom—Book of New Testament Greek* (Cambridge: Cambridge University Press, 1971).

——. *Essays in New Testament Interpretation* (Cambridge: Cambridge University Press, 1982).

Moulton, J.H., and W.F. Howard, *A Grammar Of New Testament Greek* Vol. II (Edinburgh: T. & T. Clark, 1919).

Muddiman, John B., "Fast, Fasting," in *The Anchor Bible Dictionary*. Vol. 2 (ed. D.N. Freedman; New York: Doubleday, 1992), pp. 773–76.

Müller, Robert, "Wortfeldtheorie und Kognitive Psychologie," in *Studies in Lexical Field Theory* (ed. P.R. Lutzeier; Tübingen: Max Niemeyer Verlag, 1993), pp. 215–28.

Neirynck, Frans, *Duality in Mark: Contributions to the Study of the Markan Redaction* (BETL 31; Louvain: Louvain University Press, 1972).

Neusner, Jacob, *From Politics to Piety: The Emergence of Pharisaic Judaism* (Englewood Cliffs, New Jersey; Prentice-Hall, 1973).

——. "Two Pictures of the Pharisees: Philosophical Circle or Eating Club?," *ATR* 64 (1982), pp. 525–38.

Neyrey, Jerome, *Honor and Shame in the Gospel of Matthew* (Louisville, Kentucky: WJK, 1989).

Nineham, Dennis E., "Eye-Witness Testimony and the Gospel Tradition," *JTS* 9 (1958), pp. 13–25.

——. *Saint Mark* (Middlesex: Penguin, 1963).

Noordman, Leo, Ingrid Dassen, Marc Swerts, and Jacoues Terken, "Prosodic Markers of Text Structure," in *Discourse Studies in Cognitive Linguistics. Selected Papers from the Fifth International Cognitive Linguistics Conference Amsterdam, July 1997* (ed. Karen van Hoek, Andrej Kiibrik and Leo Noordman; Amsterdam, Philadelphia: John Benjamins, 1999), pp. 133–48.

Notopoulos, James A., "Continuity and Interconnexion in Homeric Oral Composition," *TAPA* 82 (1951), pp. 81–101.

——. "Homeric Similes in the Light of Oral Poetry," *CJ* 52 (1957), pp. 323–28.

Olbricht, Thomas H., "Delivery and Memory," in *Handbook of Classical Rhetoric in the Hellenistic Period 330 B.C.–A.D. 400* (ed. Stanley E. Porter; Leiden: Brill, 1997), pp. 159–67.

Ong, Walter J., *The Presence of the Word: Some Prolegomena for Cultural and Religious History* (New Haven and London: Yale University Press, 1967).

——. *Rhetoric, Romance, and Technology: Studies in the Interaction of Expression and Culture* (Ithaca and London: Cornell University Press, 1971).

——. *Orality and Literacy: The Technologizing of the Word* (New York: Methuen, 1982).

——. "Text as Interpretation: Mark and After," *Semeia* 39 (1987), pp. 7–26.

Parunak, H.Van Dyke, "Oral Typesetting: Some Uses of Biblical Structure," *Biblica* 62 (1981), pp. 153–68.

Pilch, John, *Healing in the New Testament: Insights from Medical and Mediterranean Anthropology* (Minneapolis: Fortress Press, 2000).

Porter, Stanley E., *Verbal Aspect in the Greek of the New Testament, with Reference to Tense and Mood* (New York: Peter Lang, 1989).

——. "Discourse Analysis and New Testament Studies: An Introductory Survey," in *Discourse Analysis and Other Topics in Biblical Greek* (ed. Stanley E. Porter and D.A. Carson; JSNTSup 113; Sheffield: Sheffield Academic Press, 1995), pp. 14–35.

——. *Idioms of the Greek New Testament* (Sheffield: JSOT Press, 1996).

——. *Studies in the Greek New Testament* (New York: Peter Lang, 1996).

——. "Greek Grammar and Syntax," in *the Fact of New Testament Studies: A Survey of Recent Research* (ed. Scot McKnight and Grant R. Osborne; Grand Rapids, Michigan: Baker Academic, 2004), pp. 76–103.

Prager, Jeffrey, *Presenting the Past: Psychoanalysis and the Sociology of Misremembering* (Cambridge: Harvard University Press, 1998).

Reed, Jeffrey T., "The Cohesiveness of Discourse: Towards a Model of Linguistic Criteria for Analyzing New Testament Discourse," in *Discourse Analysis and NewTestament: Approaches and Results* (ed. Stanley E. Porter and Jeffrey T. Reed; JSNTSup 170; Sheffield: Sheffield Academic Press, 1999), pp. 28–46.

Rhoads, David, Joanna Dewey, and Donald Michie, *Mark as Story. An Introduction to the Narrative of a Gospel* (Philadelphia: Fortress Press, 2nd edn, 1999).

Robbins, Vernon K., "Last Meal: Preparation, Betrayal, and Absence (Mark 14:12–25)," in *The Passion in Mark: Studies on Mark 14–16* (ed. Werner H. Kelber; Philadelphia: Fortress Press, 1976), pp. 97–114.

——. "Chreia and Pronouncement Story in Synoptic Studies," in *Patterns of Persuasion in the Gospels* (ed. Burton L. Mack and Vernon K. Robbins; Sonoma, California: Polebridge Press, 1989), pp. 1–30.

——. "Plucking Grain on the Sabbath," in *Patterns of Persuasion in the Gospels* (ed. Burton L. Mack and Vernon K. Robbins; Sonoma, California: Polebridge Press, 1989), pp. 107–42.

——. "Writing as a Rhetorical Act in Plutarch and the Gospels," in *Persuasive Artistry. Studies in New Testament Rhetoric in Honor of George A. Kennedy* (ed. Duane F. Watson; JSNTSup 50; Sheffield: JSOT Press, 1991), pp. 114–48.

——. *Jesus the Teacher: A Socio-Rhetorical Interpretation of Mark* (Minneapolis: Fortress Press, 1992).

——. "Oral, Rhetorical, and Literary Cultures: A Response," *Semeia* 65 (1995), pp. 75–91.

Roberts, Colin H., *Manuscript, Society and Belief in Early Christian Egypt* (London: The British Academy, 1979).

Roberts, Colins and T.C. Skeat, *The Birth of Codex* (London: The British Academy, 1983).

Robertson, A.T., *A Grammar of the Greek New Testament in the Light of Historical Research* (Nashville: Broadman Press, 4th edn, 1934).

Rosch, Eleanor, "Principles of Categorization," in *Cognition and Categorization* (ed. Eleanor Rosch and Barbara B. Lloyd; Hillsdale, New Jersey: Erlbaum, 1978), pp. 28–49.

Rosch, Eleanor E., Carolyn B. Mervis, Wayne Gray, Johnson David, and Penny Boyes-Braem, "Basic Objects in Natural Categories," *CP* 8 (1976), pp. 382–439.

Roskam, R.N., *The Purpose of the Gospel of Mark in its Historical and Social Context* (Leiden: E.J.Brill: 2004).

Ross, J. and Lawrence, K.A., "Some Observations on Memory Artifice," *PS* 13 (1968), pp. 107–108.

Rubin, David C., *Memory in Oral Traditions. The Cognitive Psychology of Epic, Ballads, and Counting-out Rhymes* (New York; Oxford: Oxford University Press, 1995).

Rudzka-Ostyn, B., *Conceptualizations and Mental Processing in Language* (Berlin; New York: Mouton de Gruyter, 1993).

Rumelhart, David E., "Notes on a Schema for Stories," in *Representation and Understanding: Studies in Cognitive Science* (ed. D.G. Bobrow, and A.M. Collins; New York: Academic Press, 1975), pp. 211–36.

——. "Schemata: The Building Blocks of Cognition," in *Theoretical Issues in Reading Comprehension: Perspectives from Cognitive Psychology,Linguistics, Artificial Intelligence and Education* (ed. Rand J. Sapiro, Bertran Bruce, and William F. Brewer; Hillsdale,New Jersey: Lawrence Erlbaum Associates, 1980), pp. 33–48.

Rumelhart, David E. and Andrew Ortony, "The Representation of Knowledge in Memory," in *Schooling and the Acquisition of Knowledge* (ed. Richard C. Anderson, Rand J. Spiro, and William E. Montague; Hillsdale, New Jersey: Lawrence Erlbaum Associates, 1977), pp. 99–135.

Rumelhart, David E., P. Smolensky, J.L. McClelland, and G.E. Hinton, "Schemata and Sequential Thought Processes in PDP Modes," in *Parallel Distributed Processing: Explorations in the Microstructure of Cognition. Vol. 2. Psychological and Biological Models* (ed. J.L. McClell and D.E. Rumelhart, and PDP Research Group; Cambridge, Massachusetts; MIT Press, 1986), pp. 7–57.

Sanders, E.P., *The Tendencies of the Synoptic Tradition* (SNTSMS 9: Cambridge: Cambridge University Press, 1969).

——. *Jesus and Judaism* (Philadelphia: Fortress, 1985).

——. *Judaism: Practice and Belief 63 B.C.E.–66 C.E.* (London: SCM; Philadelphia: Trinity International Press, 1992).

——. *The Historical Jesus* (London: Penguin, 1993).

——. *Jewish Law From Jesus to The Mishnah* (SCM: London; Philadelphia: Trinity Press International, 1990).

Sanders, E.P. and Margaret Davies, *Studying the Synoptic Gospels* (London: SCM Press; Philadelphia: Trinity Press International, 1989).

Sanford, A.J. and S.C. Garrod, *Understanding Written Language. Explorations of Comprehension Beyond the Sentence* (Chicester: John Wiley and Sons, 1981).

Schank Roger C., "The Structure of Episodes in Memory," in *Representation and Understanding: Studies in Cognitive Science* (ed. Daniel G. Borow and Allan Collins; New York: Academic Press, 1975), pp. 237–72.

——. "Predictive Understanding," in *Recent Advances in the Psychology of Language: Formal and Experimental Approaches* (ed. Robin N. Campbell and Philip T. Smith; New York and London: Plenum, 1978), pp. 91–101.

——. "Interestingness: Controlling Inferences," *AI* 12 (1979), pp. 273–97.

——. *Dynamic Memory* (Cambridge: Cambridge University Press, 1982).

Schank Roger C. and Robert P. Abelson, *Scripts, Plans, Goals and Understanding An Inquiry into Human Knowledge Structures* (Hillsdale, New Jersey: Lawrence Erlabaum Associates, 1977).

Schank, Roger, Birnbaum, Lawrence, and Mey, Jacob, "Integrating Semantics and Pragmatics," *QS* 6 (1985), pp. 313–25.

Schürer, Emil., *The History of the Jewish People in the Age of Jesus Christ (175 B.C.–A.D. 135)*. Vols. 1 and 2 (Edinburgh: T. and T. Clark, 1979).

Schwartz, Barry, "Christian Origins: Historical Truth and Social memory," *Semeia* 52 (2005), pp. 43–56.

——. "The Social Context of Commemoration: A Study in Collective Memory," *SF* 61 (1982), pp. 374–97.

Sevenster, J.N., *Do you know Greek? How much Greek could the First Jewish Christians have known* (SNT19; Leiden: E.J. Brill, 1968).

Shiner, Whitney, *Proclaiming the Gospel: First-Century Performance of Mark* (Harrisburg; London: New York: Trinity Press International, 2003).

Silva, Moses, *Biblical Words and Their Meaning: An Introduction to Lexical Semantics* (Grand Rapids: Zondervan, 1983).

Sim, D.C., "The Gospels for All Christians? A Response to Richard Bauckham," *JSNT* 84 (2001), pp. 3–27.

Smith, Dennis E., "Social Obligation in the Context of Communal Meals: A Study of the Christian Meal in 1 Corinthians in Comparison with Graeco-Roman Communal Meals," Th.D. Diss., Harvard Divinity School, 1980.

——. "Table Fellowship as a Literary Motif in the Gospel of in the Gospel of Luke," *JBL* 106 (1987), pp. 613–38.

Smyth, Herbert W., *Greek Grammar* (Cambridge, Massachusetts: Harvard University Press, 1956).

Sperber, Dan and Deirdre Wilson, *Relevance: Communication and Cognition* (Oxford: Blackwell, 2nd edn, 1995).

Stanford, W.B., *The Sound of Greek: Studies in the Greek Theory and Practice of Euphony* (Berkeley and Los Angeles: University of California Press, 1967).

Starr, Raymond J., "Circulation of Literary Texts," *CQ* 37 (1987), pp. 213–23.

Sternberg, Robert J., *Cognitive Psychology* (Fort Worth: Harcourt Brace College, 1996).

Stock, Brian, *Listening for the Text: On the Uses of the Past* (Baltimore: John Hopkins University Press, 1990).

Stockwell, Peter, *Cognitive Poetics: An Introduction* (London and New York: Routledge, 2002).

Sundbert, Albert C., "Canon Muratori: A Fourth-Century List," *HTR* 66 (1973), pp. 1–41.

Tannehill, Robert C., "The Pronouncement Story," *Semeia* 20 (1981), pp. 1–13.

——. "Varieties of Synoptic Pronouncement Stories," *Semeia* 20 (1981), pp. 82–100.

Tannen, Deborah, "What's in a Frame?: Surface Evidence for Underlying Expectations," in *New Directions in Discourse Processing* (ed. Roy O. Freedle: Norwood, New Jersey: Ablex, 1979), pp. 137–79.

Taylor, E. Shelley and Jennifer Crocker, "Schematic Bases of Social Information Processing," in *Social Cognition: The Ontario Symposium* (ed. E.T. Higgins, C.D. Herman and M.P. Zanna; Hillsdale, New Jersey: Erlbaum, 1981), pp. 89–134.

Taylor, John, *Linguistic Categorization: Prototypes in Linguistic Theory* (Oxford: Clarendon, 2nd edn, 1995).

Theissen, Gerd, *The First Followers of Jesus: A Sociological Analysis of the Earliest Christianity* (London: SCM, 1978).

——. *The Social Setting of Pauline Christianity: Essays on Corinth* (trans. John H. Schutz; Philadelphia: Fortress Press, 1983).

——. *The Gospels in Context Social and Political History in the Synoptic Tradition* (tran. Linda M. Maloney; Edinburgh: T. and T. Clark, 1992).

Theissen, Gerd and Annette Merz, *The Historical Jesus* (trans. John Bowden; London: SCM, 1998).

Thiselton, Antony C., "Semantics and New Testament Interpretation," in *New Testament Interpretation: Essays on Principles and Methods* (ed. I.H. Marshall; Grand Rapids: Eerdmans, 1977), pp. 75–104.

——. *New Horizons in Hermeneutics: The Theory and Practice of Transforming Biblical Reading* (Grand Rapids, Michigan: Zondervan, 1992).

Thomas, Rosalind, *Literacy and Orality in Ancient Greece* (Cambridge: Cambridge University Press, 1992).

Thorndyke, Perry W., "Cognitive Structures in Comprehension and Memory of Narrative Discourse," *CP* 9 (1977), pp. 77–110.

Thorndyke, Perry W., and B. Hayes-Roth, "The Use of Schemata in the Acquisition and Transfer of Knowledge," *CP* 11 (1979), pp. 82–106.

Thorndyke, Perry W. and Frank R.Yekovich, "A Critique of Schema-Based Theories of Human Story Memory," *Poetics* 9 (1980), pp. 23–49.

Tolbert, Mary A., *Perspectives on the Parables: An Approach to Multiple Interpretations* (Philadelphia: Fortress Press, 1979).

——. *Sowing the Gospel: Mark's World in Literary-Historical Perspective* (Minneapolis: Fortress Press, 1989).

Tulving, Endel, "Episodic and Semantic Memory," in *Organization of Memory* (ed. Endel Tuving, and Wayne Donaldson; New York: Academic Press, 1972), pp. 381–403.

Turner, E.G., *Greek Papyri: An Introduction* (Oxford: Clarendon Press, 1968).

van Dijk, Teun. A., *Text and Context: Explorations in the Semantics and Pragmatics of Discourse* (London and New York: Longman, 1977).

——. "Semantic Macro-Structures and Knowledge Frames in Discourse Comprehension," in *Cognitive Processes in Comprehension* (ed. M.A. Just and P.A. Carpenter; Hillsdale, New Jersey: Lawrence Erlbaum, 1977), pp. 3–32.

——. "Episodes as Units of Discourse Analysis," in *Analyzing Discourse: Text and Talk: Georgetown University Round Table on Languages and Linguistics 1981* (ed. Deborah Tannen; Washington, D.C., Georgetown University Press, 1982), pp. 177–95.

——. *Discourse and Literature* (Amsterdam: Benjamins, 1985).

——. *Discourse and Context: A Sociocognitive Approach* (Cambridge: Cambridge University Press, 2008).

van Dijk, T.A., and W. Kintsch, *Strategies of Discourse Comprehension* (New York: Academic Press, 1983).

Jan Vansina, *Oral Tradition as History* (Madison: University of Wisconsin Press, 1985).

Vermes, Geza, *Jesus the Jew: A Historian's Reading of the Gospels* (Philadelphia: Fortress, 1973).

Warren, William H., David W. Nicholas, and Tom Trabasso, "Event Chains and Inferences in Understanding Narratives," in *New Dirsctions in Discourse Processing* (ed. Roy O. Freedle: Norwood, New Jersey: Ablex, 1979), pp. 23–52.

Widengren, G., "Tradition and Literature in Early Judaism and in the Early Church," *Numen* 10 (1963), pp. 42–83.

Wilt, Timothy, "Translation and Communication," in *Bible Translation: Frames of Reference* (ed. Timothy Wilt; Manchester: St. Jerome Publishing, 2003), pp. 27–80.

Witherington III, Ben, "Lord," in *the Dictionary of Jesus and the Gospels* (Downers Grove, Illinois: IVP, 1992), pp. 484–92.

Wright, N.T., *The New Testament and the People of God* (Minneapolis: Fortress, 1992).

——. *Jesus and the Victory of God* (Minneapolis: Fortress, 1996).

——. "The Divinity of Jesus," in *The Meaning of Jesus Two Visions* (ed. Marcus J. Borg; N.T. Wright; New York: HarperSanFrancisco, 1999), pp. 157–68.

——. *The Resurrection of the Son of God* (Minneapolis: Fortress, 2003).

Yates, Frances A., *The Art of Memory* (London: Routledge and Kegan Paul, 1966).

Zerwick, M., *Biblical Greek* (Rome: Pontifical Biblical Institute, 1963).

INDEX OF MODERN AUTHORS

INDEX OF SUBJECTS

INDEX OF ANCIENT SOURCES

I. Bible

Old Testament

II. Apocrypha, Pseudepigrapha, and Qumran

Apocrypha

Pseudepigrapha

Qumran

IV. Josephus and Philo

Josephus			13.408	174
Life			18.11–25	174
196–98	175		20.97–99	207
Jewish War			20.167–72	207
2.119–68	174		20.286	207
2.258–63	207			
Jewish Antiquities			Philo	
4.202	203		*de vita Mosis*	
13.297	174		2.206	203

V. Church Fathers' Literature

1 *Clement*			Justin Martyr	
13.1–2	70		*Dialogue with Trypho*	
46.7–8	70		100.4	53
			101.3	53
Clement of Alexandria			103.6	53
Adumbrationes ad I	50		103.8	53
Petr.			104.1	53
5.13			105.1	53
Stromateis			105.5	53
6.61.2–3	68		105.6	53
To Theodore			106.3	50
1.20	53		107.1	53
			Apology	
Eusebius			1.66	53
Ecclesiastical History			1.67	53
2.15	50			
3.39.4	49		Origen	
3.39.15	50		*Commentary on Matthew*	
6.25.5	50		Homily 1	50
			Tertullian	
			Apologeticum	
			39.3	68

VI. Greco-Roman Literature

Ad Herennium			Athenaeus	
1.3	63		*Deipnosophists*	
2.30.47	64		10.432 B	56
3.10.18	64			
3.16.28–3.24.40	63		Cicero	
4.42.54	44		*De oratorie*	
			2.85.350–88	63
Apuleius			2.85.359	66, 86
Metamorphoses				
1.1	59		*Epistulae ad Atticum*	
			10.3a 1	47
			15.20.4	48

Linguistic Biblical Studies

Series Editor
Stanley E. Porter

Professor of New Testament at McMaster Divinity College
Hamilton, Ontario

1. Foley, T. *Biblical Translation in Chinese and Greek*. Verbal Aspect in Theory and Practice. 2009. ISBN 978 90 04 17865 6
2. Park, Y.-M. *Mark's Memory Resources and the Controversy Stories (Mark 2:1-3:6)*. An Application of the Frame Theory of Cognitive Science to the Markan Oral-Aural Narrative. 2010. ISBN 978 90 04 17962 2